Freedom Inside?

Freedom Inside?

Yoga and Meditation in the Carceral State

Farah Godrej

OXFORD
UNIVERSITY PRESS

Oxford University Press is a department of the University of Oxford. It furthers
the University's objective of excellence in research, scholarship, and education
by publishing worldwide. Oxford is a registered trade mark of Oxford University
Press in the UK and certain other countries.

Published in the United States of America by Oxford University Press
198 Madison Avenue, New York, NY 10016, United States of America.

Library of Congress Control Number: 2022930594
ISBN 978–0–19–007009–0 (pbk)
ISBN 978–0–19–007008–3 (hbk)

DOI: 10.1093/oso/9780190070083.001.0001

1 3 5 7 9 8 6 4 2

Paperback printed by LSC Communications, United States of America
Hardback printed by Bridgeport National Bindery, Inc., United States of America

For Miko, *in memoriam*

Contents

SECTION IV. REVOLUTIONARY EXPERIMENTS

Acknowledgments

My first debt is to the many incarcerated and formerly incarcerated people whose lives, experiences, voices, and stories have made this project possible. I dedicate this work to them, in the hope that it shines a light inside the dark, closed world that they have inhabited, reminding them that they are not forgotten.

In writing this book, I have grasped what it means to stand on the shoulders of giants. So many people have affirmed, supported, and championed what began as an ambitious, far-fetched pipe-dream—they read draft chapters, they patiently answered my many questions, and they unstintingly shared advice and insights that taught me how to navigate the closed systems I sought to study. Carol Horton read this manuscript several times, and offered essential feedback, for which I am tremendously grateful. Keramet Reiter has been an incredible font of knowledge about prisons—without her help, I doubt that some of the most important aspects of this project would have come to fruition. I am similarly indebted to Samantha Majic, Peregrine Schwartz-Shea, Dvora Yanow, and Timothy Pachirat, all of whom warmly welcomed me into the community of interpretive scholars and gave me precious advice that shaped this book in the early stages. So too with Ethel Tungohan, Sarah Wiebe, Sarah Marusek, Kimala Price, Renee Cramer, Elisabeth Jean Wood, Lisa Wedeen, Ido Oren, and Frederic Schaffer. Keramet, Peri, and Sam patiently read and provided feedback on the entire manuscript, along with Bronwyn Leebaw, Tiffany Willoughby-Herard, Mark Golub, Lisa Beard, Sokthang Yeng, Lila Kazemian, Ben Fleenor, I.E. Moos, and Nancy Deville. These friends and colleagues have immeasurably enhanced my work through their careful engagement with it. Others who have read and/or provided commentary on parts of this manuscript include Naomi Murakawa, Andrew Dilts, Lisa Miller, Sarah Pemberton, Wendy L. Wright, Thomas Dumm, Kirstine Taylor, Naveed Mansoori, Melvin Rogers, Kirstie McClure, Joshua Dienstag, David A. Green, Anthony Grasso, Charles Lee, Kevin Olson, Cristina Beltrán, Jessica Lopez, Stefan Kehlenbach, Sean Long, Serenity Jones, Sandra Brown, Chaplain Eric, and Michael Cox. Graduate students in two seminars on mass incarceration at the University of California, Riverside (in 2019 and 2021), and attendees at a 2017 political theory colloquium at the University of California, Los Angeles, also provided constructive critique. I also want to thank participants at the

Prison University Project's 2018 Corrections, Rehabilitation and Reform conference at San Quentin prison, an excellent group of interlocutors living inside one of the country's most notorious sites of incarceration.

Friends and colleagues who supported and advised me on my quest for access to prisons include Keramet Reiter, John Cioffi, Emily Thuma, Danielle Rousseau, Haider Hammoudi, Jules Lobel, David Harding, Jonathan Glater, and Alonzo Wickers. Many key parts of this manuscript became possible due to the help and insights they provided. I must also thank faculty and staff at the Institutional Review Board at the University of California, Riverside, all of whom went above and beyond. These include: Dario Kuzmanovic, Derick Fay, Lorraine Joy Castro, Monica Wicker, Yolanda R. Morris-Barnes, and Jennifer Merolla. Zara Aijaz provided essential research assistance, as did Narayani Chaurasia, Madiha Akif, and Anna Poplawski. Friends and colleagues who co-organized and participated in the Western Political Science Association miniconferences on The Politics of the Mindful Revolution were among the earliest and most enthusiastic audiences for various parts of this project: Their encouragement has meant the world to me. For this, I especially thank Shannon Mariotti and James Rowe, as well as Anita Chari, Dean Mathiowetz, Michaele Ferguson, Matthew Moore, Jasmine Syedullah, Desirée Melonas, Deva Woodly, David L. McMahan, Robin L. Turner, Peter Doran, and David Forbes. Tiffany Willoughby-Herard has been a deep source of inspiration—everyone should be lucky enough to have such a colleague and friend. Loyola Marymount University's Yoga Studies program provided a warm intellectual space for engagement and constructive critique: For this, I thank Christopher Key Chapple, Christopher Jain Miller, Maureen Shannon-Chapple, Serenity Tedesco, Taina Rodriguez-Berardi, and Amy Osborne. In my previous career as a comparative political theorist, I learned a great deal from Fred Dallmayr, Anthony Parel, Andrew March, Joseph Prabhu (in memoriam), Keally McBride, Peggy Kohn, Daniel Bell, Avner De-Shalit, Dan Rabinowitz, Mark Bevir, Dustin Howes (in memoriam), Melissa Williams, Stuart Gray, Bettina Koch, Karuna Mantena, and Jane Gordon.

In the Indian tradition, every important endeavor begins by honoring the teachers whose wisdom and grace underlie our accomplishments. Even though many years have passed since I studied with them, the influence and mentorship of Cynthia Enloe, Martha Nussbaum, R. Bruce Douglass, Gerry Mara, Mark Warren, and Lloyd and Susanne Rudolph (in memoriam) pervade my work. The University of California, Riverside, has served as my academic home for many years. I am grateful to Georgia Warnke and Katharine Henshaw at the Center for Ideas and Society, which provided research funding. I also benefited greatly from the generosity of colleagues such as Shaun Bowler, John Medearis, Chris Laursen, Jennifer Merolla, Dana Simmons, Setsu Shigematsu, Susan Laxton, Margherita Long, Amanda Lucia, Helen Regan, Jade Sasser, and Dylan Rodríguez, all of whom have given graciously of their time and energy. Words are scarcely sufficient to describe the meaning and value of Pat Morton's friendship. Bronwyn Leebaw's advice, solidarity and camaraderie have also been invaluable—if there is such a thing as an academic sibling, she is the closest thing to it.

Given the issues of confidentiality woven throughout this project, it is difficult to thoroughly acknowledge all of those who have contributed to it. In some cases, naming these individuals would put them at risk. I have therefore chosen to use pseudonyms, and even so, this remains a necessarily partial and incomplete list. I cannot fully capture the depth of my gratitude to the many people who agreed to give their time and energy to being interviewed by me, or introduced me to other contacts who in turn eased my path. These include several prison officials, employees, and volunteers, all of whom were instrumental in furthering my understanding of the prison context. Above all, Victoria, Hannah, Chaplain Eric, Venerable Tan, Sunshine, and Ariel Stein played a crucial role in my access to various prisons and their programs. I am in debt to them all.

I am fortunate to have had the unwavering support of Angela Chnapko, my extraordinary editor at Oxford University Press—her faith in this project has sustained me through some of its toughest moments. I am grateful to Tin Thang for his original artwork on the cover of this book, and to the entire production team at Oxford, including Alexcee Bechthold, Rachel Perkins, Louise Karam, Preetham Raj, and Saloni Vohra. My circle of tireless cheerleaders has included dear friends who keep me sane: Jennifer Walter, Verónica Benet-Martínez, Firouzeh Afsharnia, Sam Majic, Pat Morton, Hillary Caviness, Bronwyn Leebaw, Judy Lai-Norling, Mark Norling, Edvarda Braanaas, Katja Guenther, Tuppett Yates, Ana Paula Duarte, Sindhu Venkatanarayanan, Christine Bourgeois, Stephen Kirk, Eric Rosenblatt, Rena Haley, Liz Carr, Eyvette Jones-Johnson, Jada Byrne, Gautam Godse, Hoofrish Patel, Zafar Mawani, and Katie Telser. My family—including and especially my sister Delara—has kept me going on more than one occasion when I was ready to throw in the towel. And finally—Greg, my significant other and life-companion, whose towering intellect, discernment, incisive commentary, and deep, nurturing compassion have made this work far richer than it could ever have been. Everything I do is better because of him.

SECTION I
SETTING THE STAGE: MOTIVATION, METHODOLOGY, AND ETHICS

1

Introduction

Why Prison Yoga and Meditation?

Consider Lee and Michael: Each of them intensively studied and practiced meditation while imprisoned. Lee is in his early forties and served over 22 years. Like most others who have done time, Lee describes a difficult childhood marked by poverty, addiction, trauma, abuse, and discrimination. Isolated and outcasted, Lee joined a gang at 15, and was incarcerated by the age of 17. Lee describes his transformation in prison, attributing it to his meditation practice: "[As] I got more involved with Buddhism and meditation, I realized I created my own suffering," he says. "It's a choice I made, that led to all the suffering within myself. I was not accepting responsibility for my poor choices, I was blaming everybody for my suffering, but I had to blame myself. It all comes down to choices that *you* make in life. That's what I got out of studying Buddhist philosophy and meditation . . . the whole 22 years and 6 months, I deserve it and accept it, because I used that time wisely to better myself."[1]

Michael is in his late twenties—he also grew up severely disadvantaged in the foster care system, bouncing in and out of group homes, schools, and special education institutions. He began using drugs to cope, and eventually served five years on substance abuse–related charges. Michael offered a very different interpretation of meditation, developed both during and after his incarceration. Meditation practice, Michael says, "teaches us to see our conditioning . . . it taught me how to think and how to inquire, not just internally but also externally." As a result, his practice not only transformed him personally, but also gave him a "moral compass" to critique an unjust world: "This entire system of mass incarceration clearly causes suffering . . . why do we have such long sentences? Why don't we give more leeway to folks who come from really rough backgrounds who didn't have a fighting chance to begin with? Where did I learn that it's OK to get a ten-year sentence for having a bag of cocaine?" Michael reports that his meditation practice also inspired nonviolent resistance: "I became much less fearful, I would just tell [the officers], 'no, that's not fair, you don't have a right to [do this.]' . . . I wasn't aggressive either, I was just

Freedom Inside?. Farah Godrej, Oxford University Press. © Oxford University Press 2022.
DOI: 10.1093/oso/9780190070083.003.0001

like 'no, you're not gonna keep pushing me around' . . . the things that used to make me afraid no longer made me tremble in the same way." Michael was sent to solitary confinement multiple times, but insists, "I would rather go to the hole than compromise my beliefs."

These contrasting perspectives present us with a paradox: In one case, meditative teachings are interpreted as acceptance of one's external circumstances, while in the other, they cause the practitioner to inquire critically into the root of those circumstances. In one case, they entail the belief that one's circumstances—including one's suffering—are self-created; in the other, they inspire sharper and more critical examination of the systemic, collective causes of suffering. And, while Lee reports avoiding all forms of resistance in prison, Michael credits his meditation practice with giving him the strength to occasionally undertake nonviolent resistance.

For many years, I had struggled with precisely these contradictions. I had long been a practitioner of both yoga and meditation, contemplating the question of how—if at all—these traditions could guide us to respond to social or political injustice. I had diligently trained in the principles of nonreactivity, nonattachment, and nonjudgment: to know that life in the material world was transient and ultimately illusory; to see suffering as created by one's own mind rather than by circumstances; to work on acceptance of external circumstances as the route to releasing inner suffering. But I had always been troubled by what I saw as a political passivity or quietism that seemed to be encouraged by this training.

I first wrestled with this as a student of yogic philosophy, reading yoga's canonical text, the *Bhagavad-Gītā*. Growing up in India, exposure to yogic philosophy, practices, and values was fairly commonplace. I began studying these texts in my twenties, developing a personal yoga and meditation practice that became steadier as I pursued graduate education in the United States. I initially took from the *Gītā* the lesson most commonly taught: that of inward-oriented spiritual pursuit, doing one's duty with nonreactive acceptance, and working to detach from fluctuating worldly circumstances. Over time, my study and practice deepened beyond the yogic tradition to include Buddhism. I attended a variety of yoga and meditation centers, and found lessons of detachment and acceptance in many schools of Buddhism, similar to those found in the yogic texts. Across these traditions, I learned that the causes of suffering were internal rather than external, and that the route to happiness lay in changing one's inner state rather than focusing on external circumstances. Still, I began asking: What about collective suffering? Are we supposed to accept inequity and injustice as part of the fluctuation of life, or worse, as created by our own minds? Surely injustice—caused by powerful political structures—exists as a cause of collective suffering in the world, no matter how our minds choose to view it? What (if anything) can these traditions tell us about balancing nonreactivity and acceptance with justified opposition to social and political oppression? These questions led me inside prisons, to explore whether these practices could assist marginalized people in navigating systemic injustice.

Why prisons? By the time I began exploring these questions, I was immersed in literature demonstrating that mass incarceration in the United States is a patently unjust and unequal system. Though not everyone may consider this obvious, the evidence has long been considered incontestable by many in the legal, policy, and academic worlds. Often referred to as a "carceral state," the United States polices and cages the world's largest prison population of over 2.3 million, while an additional 8 million are on probation, parole, or facing deportation.[2] Whether in absolute numbers or in percentage terms, the United States holds more people in prisons and jails than any other country, by a long margin. More Americans are incarcerated today than have been killed in all wars in which the United States has fought in history combined.[3] One in twenty-three American adults are thought to be under some form of government control or supervision.[4]

In addition to the staggering numbers of persons incarcerated (at a rate ten times higher than comparable democracies), the majority of those confined and controlled in such institutions are "black or brown, and poor."[5] Those from low-income communities and communities of color, which often overlap, are incarcerated at disproportionately higher rates than relatively affluent, white populations, which automatically diminishes their life-chances.[6] The collateral consequences of these imbalances are endless, shaping and distorting everything from urban space and electoral maps to family structures, public health, cultural norms, and political and economic outcomes. Their ripple effects are intergenerational: 113 million Americans— or one in two adults—have had an immediate family member incarcerated,[7] and millions of children have at least one parent in detention, compounding the effects of disadvantage through the separation and further impoverishment of families. The rising incarceration rates of women, and in particular Black women, intensify these effects.

Practices such as cash bail, pretrial detention for those unable to post bail, and debtors' prison (the incarceration of those unable to pay monetary penalties)[8] ensure that poorer populations are overrepresented in prisons, often without meaningful legal representation.[9] One-quarter of incarcerated Americans have not been convicted of a crime and are being held in pretrial detention, usually due to the high cost of cash bail.[10] Unconvicted Americans alone constitute the fourth-largest incarcerated population in the world, surpassed only by the entire prison populations of Brazil, China, and the United States.[11] And, only 2 percent of those in American jails and prisons have had trials,[12] while the rest are routinely pressured into taking plea-bargains through the threat of a longer sentence by a legal apparatus that systemically disadvantages defendants. The vast network of entrenched interests that profit financially from imprisonment—police and correctional officer unions and lobby groups, private prison companies, and businesses that supply goods and services to prisons for profit—is described as the "prison-industrial complex."[13]

Meanwhile, the formerly incarcerated are relegated to second-class citizenship by legalized discrimination in everything from housing to employment and social welfare benefits. These policies have "multiplier" effects: the conditions of probation and parole—along with the lack of re-entry and employment support—tend to trap people within the system, making reintegration into society a virtually impossible task, all but guaranteeing a return to prison, often for purely "technical" violations of parole or probation (examples include failing to report for a scheduled office visit due to lack of transportation, or missing curfew).[14] Their political consequences are even more stark: many states either permanently or temporarily disenfranchise those who are currently serving time (or have previously served time) on a felony conviction. Despite recent state-led reforms that have restored voting rights, policy researchers estimate that over 5 million people—or 2.3 percent of the voting population—continue to be disenfranchised.[15] These rules fundamentally alter the shape of American democracy, by creating a permanent underclass left to a "civil death":[16] deprived of basic necessities, livelihoods, and citizenship rights, making prison time tantamount to "permanent social excommunication."[17]

To be clear, no lawyer, judge, parole officer, or prison administrator wakes up every morning and says to themselves, "I want to create more inequality today." Yet, that is precisely what happens when they conduct their daily work in a system built on incentives, rules, and norms that perpetuate inequality, "enforc[ing] laws they didn't make, in a social context they have little power to alter."[18] A combination of draconian sentencing laws, prosecutorial discretion, and the criminalization of many nonviolent offenses has resulted in a system often described as a racialized regime, in which the structural rules guarantee discriminatory results. Noted political science researchers Amy Lerman and Vesla Weaver call this the "overreaching carceral state," which "[deepens] the divide between those who are heard and those who are silenced." The result, they tell us, is second-class citizenship for millions of "disempowered and alienated people who occupy . . . [a] subordinate position in the democratic community."[19]

Casting mass incarceration as morally unjust often prompts some to object: surely not all who are incarcerated are victims of social inequity—aren't some people in prison because they have caused real harm? Michelle Alexander's now-seminal *The New Jim Crow* asserts that prisons are filled with those convicted for victimless drug-related offenses, many of whom require treatment rather than criminalization. But progressive critics must contend with data demonstrating that 50 percent (or more) of offenders may be convicted for violent crimes entailing harm to victims.[20] It may appear difficult to make the moral case against an unjust system if half of those caught up in it are ostensibly guilty of violent crimes, while many Black citizens concerned about violence seem to be campaigning for harsher laws.[21] The "personal responsibility" explanation for incarceration has remained predominant, pointing to unraveling morals, poor choices, and lack of perseverance: It appears as though "those who are trapped within [the system] could have avoided it simply by not committing crimes."[22]

Countless researchers and policymakers have warned that the narrative of individual responsibility has long been used to obscure the role of social inequity: Too much insistence on "better choices" can downplay the systemic problems that constrain choices for marginalized communities.[23] Discussions of individual responsibility, they argue, must be nested within discussions of structural violence.[24] Violent, harmful, or irresponsible actions are most often the result of ongoing structural, socioeconomic harms such as poverty, unemployment, racism, trauma, or mental illness,[25] a result of society's failure to address or meet people's needs. Many people sent to prison have been exposed to a high level of violence as victims of—and witnesses to—violence. Simply punishing these individuals and expecting them to change without changing their circumstances and constraints leaves few options for law-abiding life, while continually piling the blame on individuals, who are often members of disadvantaged communities. As we will see, many policy analysts demonstrate that the specter of violent crime is used to unnecessarily classify far too many people as violent, keeping them incarcerated for far longer than necessary. We will meet many formerly incarcerated persons whose lives were devastated by precisely this phenomenon: a man who was offered a plea deal of four consecutive life sentences and eventually served 21 years for being involved in an attempted robbery in which he neither discharged a weapon nor injured anyone; a man charged with breaking and entering for trying to retrieve some of his own property from a former rental residence and threatened with a life-sentence due to a prior record, eventually serving 9 years; a woman who served 17 years of a life-sentence on a "felony murder" charge for being in a getaway car while her abusive boyfriend—also her pimp—was involved in an attempted murder; and many others, most of whom came from poor and/or minority backgrounds.

As I became increasingly aware of this biased, unequal system, I began to notice that many organizations were offering yoga and meditation programs in prisons.[26] But how exactly, I wondered, were these practices being taught to the most vulnerable and marginalized? Based on my own years of study, I began to wonder if yogic and meditative traditions might promote political passivity, taught as a palliative tool to accept, cope, and comply with a miserably unjust existence, a recipe for the continuation of unjust power structures. These worries were magnified by the deeply apolitical versions of yoga and meditation I saw in the different communities where I pursued my practice. In the variety of Buddhist temples, yoga studios, and meditation centers I attended over the years, I found that the main message was mostly one of encouraging practitioners to focus on the internal causes of suffering, while downplaying external, collective ones. I was troubled by the repeated insistence on "self-care" and "self-help," and the message that all power and choice reside within the individual. There was rarely any discussion about inequitable social structures that constrain such choices and power. Individual self-help and transformation were construed as the only worthy goals, completely separated from political issues.

One particular event stands out as illustrative. At a screening organized by a Buddhist prison meditation group, a documentary film portrayed a young immigrant man incarcerated for a murder he did not commit. He receives a life sentence, and a Buddhist volunteer begins to visit him to teach him meditation. As a result, the protagonist transforms himself over time from an angry, suicidal, and agitated person to a peaceful and happy one who learns to calm his mind and accept his fate. I watched in disbelief as audience members and Q&A panelists applauded the protagonist's peace and acceptance. No one—including the prison meditation volunteers and the formerly incarcerated practitioners on the panel—made reference to the multiple forms of systemic injustice he had endured, or how his practice might allow him to address them. I wondered: was *this* what constituted the "social justice" that the film and its audience so enthusiastically cheered?

As a student of Gandhi, I knew that this apolitical, passive approach was incomplete. From Gandhi, I had discovered that yogic and meditative practices were routinely married to nonviolent yet disruptive social and political action.[27] For Gandhi, being a practitioner of yoga or meditation was not exclusive with critique or activism. In fact, the one required the other—activists in his movement were required to be involved in some form of yogic study or meditative practice. Conversely, spiritual pursuit, in his view, should lead to contemplation of injustice, and action to challenge it through disruptive means. For Gandhi, yoga and meditation were tools to act politically—assertively, yet nonviolently—in response to injustice. Many modern interpreters of yogic and meditative traditions have echoed these ideas, showing that acceptance need not equal passivity, and that techniques for internal calm and peace can in fact allow for productively acting on justifiable anger.[28]

As I was grappling with these issues, a series of commentaries emerged, which all pointed to a crucial flaw in how these traditions were being taught: their inward, private, individualized orientation can encourage us to see misfortune as largely of our own making, leading us to ignore or downplay the systemic causes of social and political suffering. Several leading critics asserted that meditation in the West has become a banal form of spirituality that avoids social and political transformation, and instead reinforces the status quo of oppression.[29] Corporations, governments, militaries, and other powerful institutions have co-opted it as a technique for social control and pacification. Mindfulness is taught to corporate employees for greater productivity and adaptation to stressful workplace conditions, without ever acknowledging the economic structures that create these stressful conditions in the first place.[30] It is also taught to students in public schools to make them more "calm" or "disciplined," with no critical inquiry into structures like race and class which serve as the very source of stress.[31] Similar claims have been made about yoga: Because it encourages its practitioners to see everything in terms of one's private thoughts and behaviors while tolerating discomfort in outer circumstances, its philosophy can end up supporting dominant or unjust political arrangements, even if unwittingly.[32]

These traditions and practices could thus end up in the role of apologists for "neoliberalism"—a worldview that insists on individual choice and behavior as a catch-all solution, refusing to acknowledge that some structures are so entrenched and systemic that they require collective change and action.[33] Neoliberalism takes the logic of the market and applies it to everything: If individuals behave correctly, collective issues will sort themselves out. In turn, this view gives power structures the excuse for maintaining an unequal status quo, while putting the entire burden of change on individuals.[34] (A good example is the often-repeated message that individuals should take responsibility for recycling, conserving water, and "mindful" personal consumption in order to save the environment—an argument that assigns responsibility to individuals and masks the role of governments and corporations, which use energy at exponentially higher rates than private individuals, and wield far more systemic power.[35])

While these commentaries struck a chord with me, they did not capture the entire story. From personal experience, I knew that yoga and meditation practices could be transformative in ways that did not fall prey to standard, conventional beliefs. There was no denying that my practice had empowered me personally by making me more skilled at choosing and reacting well. But it did not make me passive or accepting of the idea of "individual choice" as the panacea for all ills. On the contrary, it gave me the tools to develop my critical capacities and awareness of systemic, collective causes of suffering. It allowed me to see how structural factors—such as relative economic comfort and access to education, not to mention race, ethnicity, gender, sexuality, and ability—shape the contours of our lives, and constrain our choices. Soon, I found myself at odds with the predominant messages I heard in the yogic and meditative communities around me (eventually parting ways with almost all of them): Continuing to focus on individual self-help and self-improvement without attention to systemic factors began to seem increasingly absurd.

Through the lens of this struggle, I began to contemplate the systemic injustice of mass incarceration. I wondered how these complex forces might work when self-disciplinary practices such as yoga and meditation were taught inside an unjust system: Could they encourage incarcerated practitioners to internalize and comply with the logic that "improving oneself" was the only appropriate response to systemic injustice? Or, might they prove disruptive to mass incarceration, if incarcerated practitioners developed more nuanced forms of self-improvement that produced nonconformist, critical responses, challenging the system's own logic? And, was it obvious that one of these responses was clearly more desirable than the other? These questions motivated me to undertake this inquiry. They led me to take my own practice inside prisons,[36] to investigate how yoga or meditation were being taught to those punished, caged, and controlled by a deeply unjust system.

Between August 2016 and March 2020, I volunteered with organizations offering yoga and meditation in local prisons and jails.[37] My goal was to learn how yoga or meditation were being taught to—and received by—people incarcerated at these institutions, by doing the work myself. I strove to understand the missions and leadership of these organizations, attended their trainings, and interviewed fellow volunteers. I eventually took on leadership roles in several organizations. I learned about yoga and meditation programs at different local facilities, and their relationships to prison administration. I found myself immersed in the logistical landscapes of prison life, where I did yoga and meditated with incarcerated students, getting to know some of them well, engaging them in conversation about the meaning of their own practice, and learning how they interpreted the principles of yoga or meditation in the face of incarceration. I volunteered regularly at four facilities (and visited several others), learning about the variation in norms, protocols, and cultures at different institutions, especially as it pertained to whether those imprisoned identified as male or female. Because of my involvement with these organizations, and the connections they created, I was granted the rare opportunity to conduct officially sanctioned ethnography inside one facility. Meanwhile, my network of relationships allowed me to produce over sixty semistructured, in-depth interviews with both prison volunteers and formerly incarcerated practitioners. While much of what follows is based on the academic research I conducted, the conclusions are informed and deepened by my personal experiences of volunteer work, which allowed me to embed myself in the contexts I was studying.

For the reasons I have just described, I entered prison work with a great deal of personal ambivalence. Over almost four years of volunteering, combined with interviews, ethnography, and public discourse analysis, this project partly confirmed certain intuitions, but caused me to rethink others in ways that did not lead to any simple conclusions. I found that yoga and meditation often leaned in the direction of political passivity and acceptance, teaching people to adjust better to their disadvantage by focusing purely on improving themselves. While these narratives made me uncomfortable because they seemed to support the status quo, I also found that it was impossible to dismiss the power and resonance of self-improvement, which gave people a sense of efficacy and control over their fate, a critical component of personal happiness.[38] Simultaneously, I also found small pockets of resistance in which marginalized people developed political attunement and made meaningful choices to challenge systemic injustice, whether implicitly (through beliefs and conversations) or explicitly (through actions).

In this minority of cases, self-improvement did not mean ignoring or denying structural injustice. Even if yoga or meditation did not directly lead to political action, they were able to encourage and support a posture of ethical defiance, opposition, and refusal toward the prison system. In these cases, yoga and meditation seemed to express the potential to be subversive rather to accommodate the status quo, although the former was by far the rarer outcome.

But this binary framework did not fully capture the complexity of what I found. Across the board—and regardless of the political views they fostered—I found that practices of self-control and self-discipline could help incarcerated practitioners to develop an internal strength and sense of freedom that defied the institution's capacity to define their lived experience. Yoga and meditation could allow practitioners to *feel* humanized in the face of an institution intent on eliminating their existence,[39] creatively allowing them to assert their own agency and autonomy, whether or not they called this subversion. Even if this did not necessarily lead to outright resistance—and most often, it did not—it sometimes allowed practitioners to feel more liberated and more human, despite the indignities they suffered in a system that routinely deprived them of their humanity. In the words of the noted Black scholar Tiffany Willoughby-Herard, it gave people a new tool to survive the continuous "psychic and physical assault" on their beings, and as such, became "incredibly strong armature."[40] Or, as one interview participant put it, in the face of routine institutionalized violence, her yoga practice opened her eyes to the "super-hero inside me."

Yoga and meditation might seem apolitical and innocuous to many, but I will show here that this is far from the case, especially when taught in contexts like prisons which are so politically shaped. This book presents a contrast between two models of yoga and meditation in prisons, while also offering the caveat that this "clean" division does not explain everything. One model is based solely on individual improvement, combined with acceptance and coping; the other on a more capacious self-improvement that fosters critique of the standard narratives that perpetuate unjust systems. These two models could encourage very different stances or ways of being in the world. The first model can give disadvantaged persons the message that they must deal with their own discomfort and learn to transcend their circumstances, so that people simply get better at adjusting to and accepting them, while focusing only on improving themselves. The second model also focuses on self-improvement, but in so doing, seeks to transform people's understanding of the systemic factors that constrain or shape their lives. As a result, it can have a liberating effect on both individual and group consciousness, even if it doesn't always translate into political action or systemic change.

As we will see throughout this investigation, few people who enter prisons as volunteers (no matter how well-intentioned) seemed attuned to these issues. The predominant assumption I uncovered—through examining public discourse, undertaking ethnography, and talking to those who taught and practiced in prisons—was that yoga and meditation were always beneficial because they assisted in coping with the brutality of incarceration through stress management, or because they made the prison experience more humane, or because they are supposedly "peaceful" and "nonviolent." While all of this is at least partially true, there are good reasons to be concerned about the co-optation of yoga and meditation, to ask whether these self-care practices could contribute to or reinforce the prison's social control. Yogic, meditative practices—and their inward-oriented self-discipline and self-transformation—might support the project of population-control through mass incarceration, if they teach incarcerated individuals to focus only on the internal mental causes of suffering, to the exclusion of unjust external circumstances. Without social critique, these practices can allow people to retool their emotional-cognitive terrain to reconceive an unjust, miserable reality as personal choice,[41] to cope and function more effectively within an unjust status quo[42]—even though, as Michelle Alexander notes, who is behind bars today has far more to do with our collective choices as a society than individual ones.[43]

But these concerns were almost entirely absent among most of the people I studied, spoke to, or worked with (with a few notable exceptions). Those with whom I cautiously raised these questions in the course of my volunteer work had little interest in considering them. I discovered that many prison practitioners (whether volunteers or incarcerated) seemed to understand yoga and meditation merely as "helping people" to improve themselves, with either a marked absence of reference to structural issues, or a sense that such issues could only be met with acquiescence. They emphasized individual improvement and personal responsibility as the main purpose of yoga and meditation, fully consonant with the prison's messaging: people are largely incarcerated due to bad choices, suggesting that all incarceration must be deserved. But the research and personal narratives I offer here also point to a more promising and potentially emancipatory set of possibilities. A small minority of the people I spoke to and worked with showed how yoga and meditation can encourage the development of a consciousness more explicitly critical of the system's narratives. Designed, implemented, and co-created in these ways, yoga and meditation programs provided glimpses of moments in which they fostered more complex and subversive effects in prisons, enabling the "collective genius of rebellion [and] survival" among those who "inhabit oppressive circumstances."[44]

At stake in this inquiry, therefore, is an examination of both the promises and pitfalls of yoga and meditation, when taught in prisons in these different ways. Throughout this book, I explore how these practices could unwittingly exacerbate systemic forms of inequity and injustice, but also how they might serve as resources for challenging and resisting such injustice, whether internally (via the realm of belief) or externally (through action). I grapple continually with the complexity of what I found in my interviews and ethnographic work: Even when yoga and meditation repeat the pernicious neoliberal message that individuals alone control their destiny, they are met with unflagging enthusiasm by some of the very people who themselves appear to be victimized by systemic injustice. The message of "accept-the-situation-and-improve-yourself" can have tremendous psychological power, even if it is less politically desirable—it can be far more empowering to focus on what one *can* control (namely oneself), rather than dwelling on structural and political factors that seem overwhelmingly difficult to change. Many other practitioners, however, reject this message outright, calling it a kind of "Kool-aid"—they insist instead that yoga and meditation must draw attention to the role of oppressive structures and systemic suffering, and produce eman-cipatory effects on political consciousness. Yet, even as I present these two models, I caution against an "either/or" lens. The powerful but complicated narratives I share reveal that regardless of which posture they promote toward the prison system (acquiescent or oppositional), yoga or meditation may be a way of strengthening oneself to find freedom within—and despite—the brutal constraints of a dehumanizing system; to become internally free despite being outwardly confined, whether or not this is considered rebellion by those who teach or practice it.

Outline of the Book

In contrast to the kind of social science research that attempts to capture a single reality with precision, this book engages in interpretive analysis, which holds that reality is composed of multiple truths, co-constructed through interactions between the researcher and the researched.[45] Interpretive re-search is a context-specific way of knowing, which unearths what people themselves believe about the meaning and purpose of the actions they en-gage in, how they describe what is important to them, and how that informs their view of their place in the world—activities that scholars would describe as "meaning-making." The focus of such research is not on "getting facts right," but on describing various experiences and viewpoints in order to un-derstand their nuances more fully.[46] In interpretive ethnographic research, the researcher is deeply immersed within the community under study, en-gaging in as many of its activities as possible. This approach produces what scholars call "thick description": detailed observations of field experiences and conversations that rely on layers of contextualization. Such immersion allows the researcher to offer nuanced explanations about the relationship among different phenomena, which account for community members' varied understandings.[47] This book unearths two—often overlapping—narratives about the meaning and purpose of yogic or meditative practice. It examines the prevalence of each kind of view, what experiences might be associated with them, and what potential political stances (if any) are supported by them.

One could imagine a more quantitative approach to these questions, which would identify links among different variables. The claims in this book do not rest on making connections between variables to infer causality in the statistical tradition. My conclusions are not based on measured relationships between how these practices are taught and received, such as what fraction of people hold certain views or undertake specific political actions. We would need a different kind of research to test yoga and meditation's isolable impacts on political views or actions. Many models exist of how this might be done,[48] but that kind of research lies beyond what I offer here, which rests on more holistic premises.

Section I includes two chapters that set the stage for the entire inquiry: what motivated this project, and how I approached it. Chapter 2 describes the limitations of attempting to learn about prisons and engage with incarcerated persons as a researcher. The norms that govern prison research force researchers to defer to the punitive, restrictive, custody-and-control mission of prisons— a mission intrinsically at odds with the open inquiry needed for research.[49] This chapter brings the reader into my struggles for research access. It reveals how my volunteer role enhanced my understanding of the prison space, and led me to combine research with personal narrative throughout the book. I also reflect on the question of who I was relative to the system I was entering: how I came to be doing this work, how I navigated its multiple, often contradictory demands, and how I considered my ethical obligations to the different communities within which I was embedded.

Chapter 3 speaks to the theoretical concerns that animate this project. I address a number of debates—both historical and contemporary—that set the stage for what follows in the rest of this book. This chapter walks the reader through the broad sweep of commentaries revealing the darker, more insidious possibilities that lurk within yogic and meditative practices, particularly when they are taught to those routinely targeted by unequal or oppressive forms of power. Here, we find that the dangers of co-optation are very real; but so are the emancipatory possibilities. I point to the emergence of newer, more activist versions of yoga and meditation, which produce a kind of individual self-cultivation that is thoughtfully critical and politically challenging.

Section II, which includes Chapters 4, 5, and 6, takes us inside the world of prisons and introduces us to those who have been forced to live in them. Chapter 4 describes the "total institution" nature of prisons, mapping and visualizing them for readers. The research protocols described in Chapter 2 restrict my ability to take readers inside the prisons I volunteered in: I cannot fully elaborate on their sights, sounds, and smells; I cannot describe their spatial layouts or architectural details; I cannot recount the daily routines and practices that I witnessed. Instead, in Chapter 4, I take readers inside this world using interviews with volunteers, along with other scholarly and journalistic resources. This chapter also introduces a set of claims central to the rest of the book: making punishment more therapeutic through rehabilitative programming can seem benevolent or progressive, but in practice it can reinforce the social control function of prisons, namely, the efficient containment and corralling of minorities and poor persons.[50] Prisons and jails are replete with self-help and psychology programs (such as substance-abuse, anger-management, and parenting classes, to name just a few) which emphasize behavioral changes to "make better choices" and "inculcat[e] a sense of personal responsibility."[51] Rehabilitative programs that moralize about "improving" and "transforming" offenders are used to indoctrinate people into repeating the message that their own flawed individual choices and "lack of discipline" are responsible for their incarceration. As a result, many incarcerated persons become amenable to the prison's psychological and therapeutic interventions, adopting the prison's view of themselves as diseased or flawed, recasting their life-story in a way that "emphasizes [their] own moral blameworthiness."[52]

For this reason, scholars argue that many self-help and therapeutic programs in prisons function "to keep the already-excluded in their place":[53] treading water on the cycle of being sent to prison because they are already marginalized in the first place; then set up to fail upon release due to legalized exclusion, virtually guaranteeing a return to prison; all the while learning to parrot the message of their own flaws, forced to deny the existence of systemic oppression. The so-called self-improvement offered by the prison's rehabilitative programming celebrates "better choices," yet occurs under coercive, often violent conditions where people pay a price for refusing to repeat the party line, and the only available option is to accept a narrowly defined version of one's own life-narrative. This chapter examines both punitive and so-called rehabilitative practices, showing how they each serve as a facet of the prison's population-control project.

Chapter 5 introduces us to the two narratives about the purpose of yoga and meditation in prisons, through interviews with formerly incarcerated practitioners. One narrative is characterized by a focus on individual improvement and personal responsibility, while the other offers a version of self-improvement that includes discussions of the collective and systemic causes of suffering. These narratives often overlap, and are not mutually exclusive. But this chapter ultimately takes us beyond the binary, to an important common theme: how incarcerated persons can assert internal freedom and control in the face of routine dehumanization. These interviews show how they can preserve a more capacious, expansive sense of self, without needing to undertake explicit resistance against the system. In so doing, they reveal that "resistance" need not entail grappling publicly with social or political issues, but instead can lie in the realm of one's interior life.

Chapter 6 illustrates the predominance of the first narrative, through an ethnography of a meditation class in an incarceration facility, where I was a participant-observer. It demonstrates the power of the prison's messaging: that incarcerated individuals must take ownership of their situation, their choices, and their attitudes, retooling their reality and reframing it as more "workable" since it is a product of their own choices. It shows the resonance that this idea has for incarcerated persons, many of whom seem to endorse it despite their strong systemic critiques.

Section III includes Chapters 7 and 8, which take us inside communities of volunteer yoga and meditation teachers who offer these practices inside prisons. Chapter 7 analyzes how the world of the prison intersects with that of the volunteers: How do volunteers confront the prison system, and what do they believe, learn, or think they know about it? What conventions and protocols shape their ability to offer yoga and meditation programs in prisons? What messages do they receive from prisons, and what messages in turn do they disseminate to their members through their own organizational trainings and orientations? What are the values, goals, and commitments of these organizations; and how are these evident in the styles of teaching in each organization? I also describe how my own attempts to push for a more political stance in volunteer communities culminated largely in frustration, revealing that enthusiasm for politically oriented yoga or meditation was limited among fellow volunteers, and leaving me with few models of politically engaged volunteer work to draw on.

Chapter 8 describes how narratives about the purpose of yoga and meditation are disseminated inside prisons by volunteers and their organizations. In this chapter, I look at public discourse about the purpose of yoga and meditation in prisons, and ask what perspectives are offered by the volunteers I interview. My interview evidence shows that the majority tend to emphasize individual improvement and responsibility as the main purpose of yoga and meditation, fully consonant with the prison's messaging: People are only incarcerated due to bad choices, suggesting that all incarceration must be deserved. Strikingly, many held these views despite their awareness of systemic injustice: For them, "social justice" was interpreted to mean helping flawed or criminogenic individuals to "behave better." But a small minority of prison volunteers held a far more radical view, interpreting yoga and meditation to combine individual improvement with reference to the collective and systemic causes of suffering. These few volunteers reported some success with alternative models of teaching. Some of their experiences are tentative and experimental, and suggest that there are barriers to teaching yoga and meditation in this way, especially inside prisons.

Section IV draws our attention to the novel forms of experimentation around resistance that are possible inside prisons. Chapter 9 is a unique collaboration between myself and two formerly incarcerated coauthors who were part of a yogic philosophy study group in a women's prison. I served nominally as the volunteer facilitator of the group. In this chapter, I describe the challenges of trying to offer a more politically engaged perspective on yoga within prisons. My coauthors each describe, in different ways, how studying yoga allowed them to develop new reservoirs of self-discipline and self-awareness, but also offered resources for nonviolent resistance and subversion toward the messages they received from the prison system.

Throughout the course of this project, I have struggled with many ethical questions. Above all, I have wondered: for whom should a book like this be written? In freely interweaving academic research with personal narratives, my goal is to make this book accessible beyond a narrow circle of fellow academics. As such, I have attempted—with varying degrees of success, no doubt—to avoid academic jargon, and to write in ways that make the book's main arguments more readily available to a general audience. My hope is that the very individuals and communities that teach and practice yoga or meditation inside prisons will find something of value in this book. More specifically, I hope it can make its way to those who are currently or formerly incarcerated, perhaps inspiring them to consider the arguments I make, and discuss them in community with others. I also hope that the issues I raise will generate conversations within communities of those who volunteer inside prisons, and more broadly, among those who consider themselves advocates for social and political change. A perhaps more naïve hope is that parts of this book may resonate with policymakers—including those who work in and around the criminal punishment system—though it is far from obvious that these ideas will find a receptive audience among them.

In the end, this is not a book about whether or not yoga and meditation should be taught in prisons. Given that we are unlikely to see an overnight shrinking of the carceral state, there is no doubt about the value and importance of these practices. Rather, this is a book about *how* these practices are taught, whether they appear to support or hinder the project of mass incarceration, and to what extent that should matter. Its purpose is to think through more carefully what exactly constitutes a positive outcome when these practices are taught in prisons. One possible conclusion is that yoga and meditation's excessive emphases on personal ownership and responsibility can be politically detrimental, if self-development does not include tools that go beyond accepting, coping with, and accommodating injustice. But another set of possibilities complicates this conclusion: These practices appear tremendously meaningful and empowering, even to those who may seem to hold apolitical and acquiescent perspectives while incarcerated (and after). It allows them to transcend their hellish circumstances, to exit the mental cage of shame, self-blame, and guilt, to find some measure of freedom, agency, and control in an environment where they are entirely deprived of autonomy—ultimately, to endure an assault on their very self.

Put differently, the findings in this book rethink the concept of "resistance" in a way that considers people's interior lives as a crucial arena for such resistance. Although yoga and meditation in prisons are the case through which such resistance is studied, paying attention to its internal aspects has implications beyond yoga, meditation, and even prisons. Ultimately, what I report on is something we could call (for lack of a better term) "spiritual" resistance—an internal stance or posture that is sometimes accompanied by political resistance, but also goes well beyond it. This kind of resistance often results from a mysterious interplay between person, practice, and environment. It reveals the resilience of the human spirit, and demonstrates how valuable it can be for people—particularly those in terrible circumstances—to have resources and knowledge that connect them to their internal strength, to their intrinsic sense of value, dignity, and meaning.

2

Who Was I?

Scholarship, Personal Narrative, and the Testimony of the Unprotected

Throughout the years that I worked on this project, I struggled to find ways to gain access to an opaque, fortress-like system.[1] I quickly found that prisons are notoriously closed to scrutiny, and that incarcerated persons are given no unmediated ability to describe their lives to "outsiders." To engage directly with those who lived inside these places—and to center their experiences and testimonies—traditional scholarly approaches proved to be utterly inadequate. It became clear that there was no way to learn about how yoga and meditation were taught, practiced, and received in prisons without entering prisons and doing the work myself—that is, if I wanted to make my understanding come alive in a more than purely academic way. And so, during the years that I relentlessly knocked on doors seeking approval for research inside prisons, I also joined several volunteer organizations that offered yoga or meditation in various area prisons and jails. I found that as a volunteer, I was able to gain far more insight into the world of prisons than I would ever gain as a researcher. I interacted freely and regularly with my incarcerated students, and was able to engage more fully with, and learn more directly from, their lives and their voices.[2]

The work I have produced in this book relies partially on my scholarly research but also on the innumerable experiences and relationships inside prison communities that framed the context for my volunteer work with incarcerated students. Over the years, I inhabited these roles of scholar/researcher and activist/volunteer concurrently, and the boundaries between them were often fuzzy. My struggles for research access demonstrated the limitations of attempting to learn about prisons and engage with incarcerated persons as a researcher. Meanwhile, what I learned as a volunteer inside prisons immeasurably enhanced my ability to write about these spaces as a researcher. As a result, this book often toggles between research—which required many layers of approval mediated by both the university and the prison—and a series of personal and collaborative narratives which sometimes involve incarcerated persons as active co-participants in generating new knowledge. The

Freedom Inside?. Farah Godrej, Oxford University Press. © Oxford University Press 2022.
DOI: 10.1093/oso/9780190070083.003.0002

scholarship and research that resulted from years of negotiations with university and prison administrators is supplemented by personal narrative and autobiographical writing in which I examine my own experiences, but also think together *with* incarcerated persons[3]—jointly undertaking political conversations and contemplating forms of resistance, in ways that sought to make them co-equal partners in producing knowledge.

In this chapter, I discuss my own positionality vis-à-vis prisons and those who are made to live in them: Who was I, and how did I come to be doing the work that unfolds in the rest of this book? I describe how I navigated the multiple, often contradictory, demands of scholarship/research and volunteering/activism. I consider how the requirements of traditional scholarship and the discipline of the academy squelched certain forms of inquiry, forcing me to pursue other, less "scholarly" but ultimately far richer avenues of knowledge. I also describe how I thought through the complexity of my obligations to the different communities in which I was embedded, in order to bring this book to life.

The Research: Negotiating Access with Prisons and IRB

There are few available routes for those seeking to look inside the prison system in the United States. American prisons have become increasingly closed off to scrutiny in recent years, almost entirely impervious to oversight and accountability of any kind.[4] Access for journalists, academic researchers, or any others seeking to document the lives and worlds of incarcerated persons is exceedingly rare. Prisons and incarcerated persons are largely rendered invisible to both the public eye and the academic researcher.[5] Only a handful of academics in recent years have gained access to US prisons in ways that allow for qualitative inquiry, including direct engagement with incarcerated persons.[6] Early on, fellow researchers I contacted for advice gently warned me about the opacity of these systems. And indeed, for the most part, my requests for access were met with years of routine obstruction, stonewalling, and outright silence by prison authorities. As some scholars have dryly observed, "Without being convicted, it is not easy to learn about what occurs behind prison walls."[7] In fact, journalists who have gained rare access to US prisons in recent years have done so by going undercover as correctional officers.[8]

The very few scholars who have entered prisons in recent years have typically had connections to an insider who can advocate for them in order to grease the wheels of authorization. I learned firsthand that absent such connections, research access through "cold-calling" prison officials is virtu-ally impossible. It was only through a combination of serendipity and volun-teer work that I met such insider contacts, which in turn greased the wheels of access.[9] My ability to connect with these insiders was partly a function of my own doggedness in refusing to take "no" for an answer, and partly of being embedded in the very same system as a volunteer. The research I produced as a result was a rare exception to the norm, resulting from years of (politely) pushing uphill past the resistance of staff and administrators, combined with the sheer luck of insider support.

My attempt to undertake research inside prisons began with approaching my university's Institutional Review Board (IRB).[10] The IRB officials were helpful, but insisted that written authorization for access from prison administrators was a minimum precondition of approval. In other words, they would not approve any research project which was not already author-ized by the prison itself. From the get-go, it was made clear that the very system I sought to study—a coercive system with (at best) a dubious record on human rights—was considered the gatekeeper by university bodies that pro-vided the stamp of "ethical" approval for research. The noted prison researcher Keramet Reiter tells us that although IRBs' "human subjects protections were designed primarily to protect vulnerable research subjects from physically in-vasive medical experimentation . . . university IRBs and prison administrators alike often apply these rules to prevent almost all forms of research involving currently incarcerated people."[11] IRBs' increasingly formalized processes of bureaucratic oversight "complicate, hamper or censor" certain forms of qual-itative and critical social science research.[12] The process of triangulating be-tween prison and IRB officials revealed how the IRB-prison nexus limits the scope of what can be known and said about prisons, leading me to consider other avenues besides scholarly research.

Meanwhile, I connected with a Buddhist chaplain who offered to allow me to sit in as a participant-observer in one of the many mindfulness classes he regularly conducted inside a men's incarceration facility. For the next two years, I relentless chased down officials at this facility, seeking their ap-proval to "shadow" the Chaplain during his class, and produce research based on this participant-observation.[13] Over these years, I wrote many emails to prison officials, and left many voicemails. I received few replies, most of which bounced me from one official to another, with each one claiming the issue was in someone else's purview. I often found myself on the verge of giving up, but forged ahead, continuing to politely follow up with the next person, and then the next. Months would often pass between each set of communications, making clear that I was last on anyone's priority list. Eventually, I managed to connect with the right people, who directed my request through appropriate channels. My role as a volunteer—and eventually, a co-leader of several volunteer organizations—opened up the doors that provided these connections, as things began to move in the right direction. I still found myself wading through multiple layers of both formal and informal approval, with further delays at every point. But officials eventually agreed to consider a signed research agreement between the facility and my university, the terms of which would eventually govern the research that appears in Chapter 6.[14]

In a series of meetings to iron out the details of this agreement, officials expressed concern about any research that would negatively impact the public image of their department and its facilities. To gain access, I agreed to keep all identifying information confidential, to give no geographic information about the location of the facility (beyond the state of California), to anonymize the jurisdiction or type of facility, and to omit any details that would make the facility or its employees identifiable. This seemed satisfactory, allowing us to move on to the next and most important sticking point: officials' insistence that every participant sign their name to a consent form.

Protecting the interests of vulnerable populations requires us to ensure that they can give informed consent to participating in any research. These concerns arise from the now-infamous stories of medical experimentation conducted on prison populations without their consent, taking advantage of their captive status.[15] The long history of these coercive practices requires scholars to think very carefully about the protection of these vulnerable populations in any research endeavor. Because incarcerated persons are literally a captive population, there is always the possibility that even non-medical research—with ostensibly benign intentions—has the potential to be degrading, exploitative, or otherwise unethical.[16] I had extensively studied the ethical issues entailed in research with prison populations, thinking long and hard about whether and how consent in the prison context could be truly ethical, and whether it could be given freely. I lost much sleep thinking about the possibility that my research could—even unwittingly—end up exploiting incarcerated persons or treating them with anything less than full respect for their personhood. I soon found, however, that my own carefully considered views about what was ethical in dealing with vulnerable populations would have to be sidelined in favor of what was acceptable to prison authorities.

Scholars tell us that the most ethical approach to research in prisons is one that maintains complete anonymity of all incarcerated research participants. This requires obtaining verbal consent carefully and repeatedly, but not written consent: "eliminat[ing] the recording of names and the signing of forms by offenders minimizes the harm to the prisoner at the time of the research and forever thereafter."[17] Certainly, signed consent forms seem to provide legally defensible "proof" of informed consent. But they may also pose a threat, because they provide a record of participation in a research project, allowing documentation to later be subpoenaed and the identity of participants to be revealed. The main worry is that prisons may later retaliate against incarcerated participants if they disapprove of their revelations. This may also have a chilling effect: Incarcerated persons may be inhibited in what they can disclose, if they worry about their identities being revealed to the prison.

With mountains of this scholarship under my belt,[18] I tried during the negotiation process to explain the ethical issues with requiring signed consent. But officials were unyielding on this issue, citing potential legal liability and the threat of lawsuits. I was somewhat sympathetic to this claim: As one colleague reminded me, relations between incarcerated persons and prison staff are hostile enough—and prison conditions bad enough—that lawsuits are one of the few ways in which incarcerated persons can legitimately express their grievances.[19] Another official reassured me that it would actually empower incarcerated participants to sign a document, and would make them feel protected. Any which way we came at it, it became clear that the signed consent form was a nonnegotiable condition of the research agreement.

I found myself uncomfortable with this outcome. In conversation with the chaplain, I rehearsed the many reasons to worry about asking participants in a prison mindfulness class to sign a consent form. The mindfulness class was explicitly intended to be a refuge of nonjudgmental quiet inside the chaos of a prison, one of the few places where students could have quiet in a context where they were already being extensively policed and monitored. Producing bureaucratic forms and requiring signatures would intrude awkwardly into such a space, potentially undermining the peaceful quality of the one place where participants are not simply a number, seen as objects of legal intervention and control by the state. Introducing a researcher into a pre-existing class dynamic and having to explain the consent form was a high-impact proposition: It could present too much new information, raise too many questions, and possibly deny some students the opportunity for meditation if they were uncomfortable with being observed. This was virtually guaranteed to disrupt the meditative space, potentially defeating the very purpose of the class. Meanwhile, the drop-in format meant that up to half the participants could be new each time, forcing us to repeat the explanations of the research and the informed consent form during each session. Throwing so much information at these participants was scarcely a way to begin a class about quieting the mind. All of this ran completely contrary to the spirit of my project—doing damage to a prison community so painstakingly built by the chaplain over years was completely antithetical to my research goals.

Eventually, after many more meetings, a number of compromises were reached, which allowed the agreement to move forward. The chaplain would start a whole new mindfulness class in that same facility—separate from his other regular classes—which would have the sole purpose of allowing me to be embedded as a participant-observer. The class—and its research aspects— would be advertised in the facility. It would run for ten weeks, and anyone seeking to be part of that class would sign up in advance. The first session would be focused on issues of giving informed consent for research, and signing the consent form. The forms would each be placed by me inside a sealed and signed manila envelope. I would then drop them to an off-site ad- ministrative location, and they would be destroyed after the end of the class. This would ensure that no one—including myself—would have a written record of any participant's identifying information.

While I was conducting what seemed like endless negotiations with prison officials at every level, I was concurrently seeking approval from my university IRB, satisfying them by producing the signed research agreement to docu- ment the prison's authorization. Still, there was the matter of the informed consent form that would need to be signed by the participants. Here too, I un- derwent many rounds of IRB review, and at their insistence, inserted various legalistic clauses that made the consent form longer and more formalized. IRB insisted that the consent form fully explain to participants the potential limits to the anonymity I could guarantee them, given that some participants might be awaiting trial: "What happens if someone says something incriminating during a class, and you are later subpoenaed to testify at their trial?" asked one IRB member. I was told I would have to produce a consent form that accounted for a variety of scenarios and forms of risk. The final consent form that sat- isfied IRB looked far longer and more legalistic than anything I would ever have presented to a group of people attempting to practice mindfulness in a prison. This form (which I reproduce in Chapter 6) also relied on expectations of literacy and linguistic fluency, which, as we will see, ended up being a non- trivial barrier, given that up to 40 percent of incarcerated persons are thought to be "functionally illiterate."[20] University or prison "gatekeepers" can require forms to be more convoluted and less understandable,[21] and the chaplain too found this consent form unnecessarily mystifying and bureaucratic.[22] But, as I explained to him, there would be no moving forward without satisfying the IRB. At every stage, it became increasingly clear that research controls es- tablished ostensibly to ensure the protection of vulnerable populations were in fact having inhibiting effects on their participation. I began to see why scholars argue that incarcerated persons are often "overprotected as a subject group with the unanticipated result of actually discouraging their participation in studies that have critical implications for their welfare."[23]

About two years after I first started the process, a final research agreement was eventually signed between my university and the prison administration. This agreement satisfied a variety of stakeholders: the prison itself, my university IRB, and the chaplain who ran the classes. To be clear, I am grateful for the rare access I was given, and for the work that a multitude of people—including the chaplain, other prison staff, and my university IRB—did to make it possible. Every single prison official I interacted with was polite and respectful, and some went above and beyond in assisting me at many points. So too with IRB staff, who were supportive of my project. I was privileged to be offered a rare glimpse into the incarceration system, and the research that resulted from this opportunity has been illuminating in moving forward our understanding of meditative practices in the incarceration environment. Overall, I am hopeful that the results of this research will be beneficial for the most vulnerable among us, and for society at large.[24]

Still, I am keenly aware that the extraordinarily rare access I was granted came at a price. The compromises I made ensured that incarcerated research participants were the only group who could not speak for themselves in stating their needs and concerns regarding the research process. The institution purported to speak for incarcerated persons and decided what would constitute "protecting" them, serving as gatekeeper in the consent process. My research participants would be given one opportunity—at the start of the first class—to hear me describe my research, and to decide whether to sign the consent form I produced. My ability to obtain consent from my research participants—a process that would normally have been characterized by much give-and-take, over a longer period[25]—would become a one-shot deal in which my participants could say little besides "yes" or "no." (When the time came, I of course did my best to encourage questions and dialogue, within limitation of the one session we were given to discuss these issues). Well before I would ever set foot inside this facility, its representatives would decide the terms on which I could engage with research participants.[26]

While the prison's ostensible mandate was to "protect" the interests of incarcerated participants, in practice, institutional interests far outweighed ethical considerations. Despite well-established ethical protocols warning against the dangers of keeping written records of those who participate in prison research, incarcerated participants were required (by both the prison and the IRB) to sign consent forms.[27] This forced me to treat my incarcerated participants in ways that felt ethically counterintuitive. I was compelled to approach my research—and my participants—in a legalistic, contractual way that was potentially damaging to the very community I was hoping to learn from. In a class where the goal was to offer practices for quieting the mind, we were required to present the issue of consent in a far more bureaucratic way than we otherwise would have done. And, these legalistic interactions may have ended up reinforcing to participants their subordinate, suspect status in the eyes of law and society, rather than allowing us to meet them as co-equal partners in this project, as no different from ourselves.

There were a few issues on which I was able to assert some control, such as academic freedom and independent ownership over the research results. In the final version of the research agreement, it was determined that I would share a pre-publication draft of the research with prison officials, and that all resulting research would be my exclusive intellectual property. Prison officials did, however, insert a clause into the agreement giving them the authority to ask me to remove any information they deemed as "confidential," broadly construed. As a result, they retained some measure of control over what would eventually see the light of day, at least in theory—although they ultimately never exercised this control in practice.

I have spent much time considering the ethical implications of trade-offs made in order to gain access. Were these the correct compromises to make, and did I choose my battles wisely? Was compromising in the name of gaining access the ethical thing to do?[28] Did the access gained outweigh the costs? Had I chosen to push back against some of these conditions, I likely would not have obtained the access that I did. But that access cost me, in some ways, the ability to engage fully and equally with the people involved in my research. They would be allowed to speak to me, but only in ways—and in spaces—that were dictated by the very institution that caged them. I had little unmediated access to them, could only "observe" them and their reactions, but could not interview them or probe their views more fully. I certainly could not treat them as equal partners in learning about the prison system, and their experiences within it. They would only ever be objects of knowledge, rather than creators of it.

Scholars acknowledge that IRB approval may be "insufficiently informed by the dilemmas of prison-based research" and that "procedural ethics" does not always serve "ethics in practice."[29] But in my experience, the problem went even further: My understanding of research ethics—which hinged on the ideal of respect for incarcerated participants, through a careful understanding of their needs and concerns—was at odds with institutional priorities which, according to IRB, would trump everything else. Standard research ethics recommendations assume that consent occurs only between the researcher and the participant. But I learned that there are in fact multiple stakeholders who must be satisfied in prison research, and layers of mediation intervene between the researcher and incarcerated participants. I also learned that prioritizing the needs and concerns of prison officials might stand in tension with respect for incarcerated persons. I found that the standard recommendations gloss over the very real power relations and hierarchies entailed in prison-based research, rarely addressing the "control that correctional services can have over research agendas . . . assessing what counts as harms and benefits [and] determining to whom the researcher is accountable."[30]

My IRB's position that any researcher seeking prison approval must meet the prison's conditions meant that I had to abide by these power relations and hierarchies in all of my interactions with incarcerated participants. To many researchers—and certainly to most prison administrators—nothing may seem terribly wrong with any of this. In the rare event that researchers are given access to prisons, it requires monumental effort, and must occur under conditions fully compatible with the prison's mission of custody and control—this is perhaps not a surprising takeaway. But this official approval of prison research (either by IRB or prisons) did not, in my view, comport fully with what was ethical.[31] The constraints on my interaction with research participants may have turned me into a pseudo-authority figure who repeated the messaging and logic of the law enforcement apparatus, rather than allowing me to focus fully on their needs and concerns regarding the research process. Although I did my best to minimize this, I was haunted by the feeling that the existing system of IRB controls for research with incarcerated persons "may provide little more than ideological legitimation" for the perspective of the criminal-legal system.[32]

Writing Personal Narrative as an Activist/Volunteer

As the limitations of doing research inside prisons became increasingly clear, I realized that research could only take me so far in being able to fully hear—and learn from—the voices of incarcerated persons. The channels available to me as a researcher posed substantial limits. In contrast, in my volunteer work, I found that I was able to interact with incarcerated persons much more freely, and with little mediation by the prison. Volunteering in prisons allowed me to build rapport with people who lived and volunteered in these places, to observe and experience (to a limited extent) what they did. My immersion in the prison world was hardly unfettered—I was not entirely free to explore and interact with people in different parts of the facility as I saw fit. As an out-sider, I could "feel the prison's draining force" and its "existential chill," but would never experience the "real soul-sapping tendencies of serving time."[33] Volunteers were subject to varying levels of surveillance and restricted move-ment inside prisons. In some facilities, we had to be escorted by staff; in others, volunteers had some autonomy to move about unescorted, but it was typically limited to a small segment of an otherwise massive institution—wandering too far afield would immediately be noticed, and pointedly redirected. Nor could I participate fully in the different "life-worlds" inside prisons.[34] Some facilities allowed volunteers to attend a few cultural or religious events with incarcerated persons, but for the most part, the everyday world of prison life—work, education, communal eating, and so on—remained opaque to me.[35] But—as my struggles with undertaking research inside prisons had taught me—I would never be allowed such unfettered access as a researcher either. Within the limits of the prison's control and surveillance mechanisms, this volunteer immersion was an invaluable means of learning.

As part of my volunteer work, I was occasionally able to nourish and ac-company my students in thinking through political questions via the lens of yogic or meditative practice. As a result, my work as an activist—in a realm where I could pursue personal relationships relatively unfettered by institu-tional interests and procedural requirements—yielded a kind of knowledge that treated my conversation partners not only as subjects whose "voices must be heard" but also as collaborators who were able to teach me, and to disci-pline my thinking to a certain extent. This form of knowledge is described in a coauthored personal narrative in Chapter 9, showing how my incarcer-ated conversation partners were able to shape the very contours of my under-standing—I was able to learn what *they* found to be important.

Scholars distinguish between simply expanding opportunities for incar-cerated persons "to be heard" and incorporating their voice into the actual decision-making process about what even constitutes relevant knowledge.[36] It is certainly important to have research that illuminates the voices of incar-cerated persons—the work I present in Chapters 5 and 6 achieves this to some extent, albeit constrained in a variety of ways.[37] But here I have aspired to a more rare narrative form, one goes beyond simply "including the voices" of incarcerated persons, and allows them to actively shape the process of thinking and writing about the very issues that involve them and their lives.[38] Byrne calls this the "full and respectful continuing participation" of vulner-able populations, in which incarcerated persons are "seen as leaders within their own . . . community and so [can] speak knowledgeably about their own perspective."[39] Without incorporating incarcerated persons into the decision-making process about what constitutes important knowledge, their voices may be neutralized at best, or marginalized at worst.[40]

The distinction between the collaborative relationships I established as an activist/volunteer and the stilted, carefully controlled scholar/researcher role I was allowed to inhabit could not have been more stark. In the coauthored narratives in Chapter 9, incarcerated persons were agents and not simply objects of knowledge, as we did political thinking together. I hesitate to call this political education, because I scarcely saw myself as "educating" anyone, given that I likely learned more from them than they from me. Rather, to me, it was the work of doing resistance together, of sharing stories and personal narratives, of bearing witness, engaging in solidarity, and learning from one another, through exchanging worldviews and perspectives.

None of this could have happened in the kind of research I described in the previous section. The coauthored work we produced went far beyond these parameters, allowing incarcerated persons to go beyond simply "speaking" to me, to shaping my work in fundamental ways. Accounts of the system by those who have been caught within it and lived it experientially are a precious, fundamental resource: The knowledge they produce "sets the compass."[41] Recuperating their narratives—in their own words, on their terms, as far as possible—is a way of centering the experiences of those who have been discarded by our society.[42] The noted prison scholar Mary Bosworth discusses the importance of working directly *with* incarcerated persons and forming coalitions with them through writing, instead of simply writing *about* them, especially given that much prison-related writing still tends to be in an academic voice, for an audience made up of academics or penal administrators.[43] Others note that "[t]he cumulative wealth of prisoners' writing . . . constitutes a firmly established and highly influential body of work within western literary and intellectual traditions."[44] Yet, their important contributions are often overlooked, marginalized, and ignored in both academic and literary spheres.[45] The written collaboration in this book offers a platform to disseminate the written work of incarcerated thinkers that is not sanctioned by prison officials, precisely in order to limit the influence that prison gatekeepers have on the content of these writings.[46] Such collaboration is contrary to the prison's interest in controlling and shaping all information pertaining to the institution, making it all the more crucial to maintain independence from the administrative and control mechanisms of prison staff. In undertaking written collaboration with incarcerated persons, I followed the lead of those who suggest that scholars act as facilitators for the contributions of incarcerated persons, by "creating venues for their written works, providing resources to deepen their analyses, and offering support to help them overcome barriers they face" in producing and publishing their writings.[47]

One might wonder whether the same textured understandings gleaned through this collaborative work could also have been obtained by interviewing formerly incarcerated research participants (which I did, and on which I report in Chapter 5). But, as I show in the next section, traditional models of research—which governed my interviews with formerly incarcerated participants—still center the perspective of the researcher and the university model of knowledge, in which the academic researcher decides what is important to know, and research participants are "objects" of knowledge. Prison scholars have called for "destabiliz[ing] the primacy usually given to the aims and objectives of the researcher,"[48] displacing the academic as a privileged knower, while acknowledging more directly the standpoint, knowledge, and contributions of incarcerated persons.[49] In contrast to academic conventions that objectify incarcerated research participants,[50] the collaborative, participatory approach in Chapter 9 highlights how vulnerable persons—particularly women—can become, literally, authors of their own experiences. They can tell their stories on their own terms, rather than on the terms set by the researcher, university regulatory bodies, and the prison itself.

In doing the volunteer work that resulted in Chapter 9, I took my cues from many researchers who combine research with activism and solidarity work, for whom the questions and analyses driving research came from those encountered in everyday activism.[51] To be clear: not all volunteers inside prisons considered themselves activists (as I was to learn). Many were quite neutral regarding the prison system, and reserved judgment about matters of justice or injustice. Some explicitly claimed that one must not have a political agenda when volunteering in prisons; others were wary of losing access if they were too explicitly activist. But my work in prisons was scarcely neutral or "objective"—it was rooted in the critique of an unjust system.[52] Of course, I did not always wear this commitment on my sleeve.[53] As we will see throughout this book, political action in prisons tends to be the exception rather than norm: It is discouraged and even punished, and volunteers who express any political commitments inside prisons do so with great caution.

I was under no illusion that generating these personal narratives with my incarcerated students would be without risk. Perhaps the most important risk was that of retaliation by the institution. Prisons and jails often engage in recriminatory treatment when incarcerated persons report on the conditions of confinement.[54] This includes the possibility of "denial of parole, loss of 'good-time' credits, physical threats from staff or inmates, frequent cell searches, confiscation of manuscripts, trips to 'the hole,' [solitary confinement] and disciplinary transfers to other prisons."[55] Incarcerated scholars have described how routinely and effectively solitary confinement is used to censor writing by incarcerated persons, separating them from their writing tools, as well as their friends and colleagues inside the prison.[56] Keenly attentive to this risk, I consulted a variety of people in the attempt to ethically "audit" my own project. In addition to wide-ranging conversations with many colleagues, press editors, lawyers, and others who had experience working with prisons or other marginalized populations, I also consulted several trusted formerly incarcerated interviewees. I described our project at length, and asked them to list their concerns.

Overwhelmingly, I was advised that the main goal would be to minimize— preferably to zero—the likelihood of any retaliation against my coauthors while incarcerated. Of course, anonymizing the names of the facility and my coauthors was a given. But more importantly, my formerly incarcerated consultants insisted that incarcerated persons should be allowed to assess risk for themselves when engaging in political work of any kind. Michael, whom I cited at the beginning of this book, told the story of his activist work after his release from prison. His activist group collaborated with incarcerated persons who wanted to speak publicly about their experiences:

> A gentleman was helping us expose extreme [conditions] inside state facilities, [he was] writing essays and speeches. We would write [them] as he dictated, and we would read them off at protests. We took directions from him, we let him have his own autonomy, and we would follow [his] lead. He insisted on having his name used. I felt paternalistic because I didn't want him to take that risk, and I wanted to substitute my judgment for his. Eventually, he was placed in solitary confinement for 3 weeks [as retaliation for this activism]. But he said "*I knew what the risk was, you guys were able to help me fulfill my dream of standing against the system.*" It broke my paternalistic view. I think it sucks what happened to him, but what's more beautiful is that this man was able to take political action with the help of folks on the outside. He has done everything on his own, was fully aware of consequences and repercussions, and he had his autonomy.

Separately, I connected with Sandra, a Black woman who was serving two decades on a murder charge for defending herself during an assault. Sandra insisted on giving incarcerated persons autonomy for risk assessment and decision-making power. Speaking as an incarcerated person, she noted, "I've been submerged in this [prison] culture for 20 years, I've assessed my risks, I know what they are. . . . To cower to the institution in fear of what institutions may do is empowering or fueling the cycle of oppression. How will knowledge progress if the oppressed cannot speak? The transformative power of speaking out outweighs the transient consequences." Sandra echoed the words of Jon Marc Taylor, an incarcerated scholar who likewise believes that the pursuit and dissemination of knowledge is justified despite the potential for retribution: "I invested the effort and gambled the potential ramifications of my critical discourse to stand up for my fellow prisoners . . . to carry the lamp illuminating . . . the largest penal system in the history of the world."[57] All of my consultants agreed with Michael, who asserted that empowerment for incarcerated persons could be "life-changing: once you find your voice, you think, *where and how else can I use this?*" They all argued it was respectful to leave decisions about risk to my incarcerated collaborators. "You have to remember," said Chloe, "considering and giving value to something we feel or think [is] not something that incarcerated individuals have experienced."

These consultations confirmed for me that the principle of respect required me to let my incarcerated coauthors take the lead in conversations about risk-assessment. We had repeated discussions on the topic, and I listened carefully as they made arguments about how they wanted to move forward. In the end, both my coauthors were released from prison well before the project came to completion, ensuring that the risk to them was nonexistent. But the ongoing conversations we had on these issues—both during their incarceration and after their release—were eye-opening to me. They convinced me that opportunities for self-expression were few and far between for people in their position, and that being denied such opportunities —not to mention the ability to make decisions about *how* to engage in such expression—was a form of disregard. While I worried endlessly—and perhaps paternalistically— about "protecting" them (even if these worries were ultimately rendered moot), I also came to see Michael, Sandra, and Jon Marc Taylor's arguments that the benefits of such meaningful self-expression could outweigh the suffering inflicted by institutional retaliation. It led me to believe that we may not always "protect" a vulnerable group by refusing to give them avenues for self-expression and the ability to decide the terms of expression. It also led me to the hope that society as a whole would benefit[58] from increased opportunities for such expression by incarcerated persons.

Who *Was* I? Navigating a Fraught Web of Power, Position, and Privilege

Worrying about collaborating with prisons or anticipating recrimination against my incarcerated coauthors were by no means the only fraught aspects of this project. Writing this book induced many different forms of anxiety, causing me to grapple with what one colleague perceptively called "big feelings." Most of these had to do with my sense of my "place" and "position" in the prison, and vis-à-vis incarcerated persons. Every aspect of my identity felt charged, and different aspects of it became salient at different times and in different ways. In addition to being a researcher, I was also a volunteer, an activist, a female Indian-American academic, and a scholar and practitioner of both yoga and meditation. I wore my researcher hat at some points, and my volunteer-activist hat at others.[59] I navigated a complex web of power relations, feeling subordinate and abject in some circumstances (for instance, while negotiating with prisons and IRB), but accorded a great deal of deference in others (often by incarcerated persons, and by fellow volunteers, as I became increasingly experienced in their ranks). My status as a professional academic bought me entrée into both the volunteer world and the world of prisons, while my gender identity allowed for forms of solidarity with incarcerated women in particular. And my Indian identity, as I will show, came into play frequently.[60]

Entrée into the Volunteer World

My foray into the world of prison volunteers began in 2016, and was surprisingly smooth. As in all other things, the internet proved to be the first line of inquiry. A quick online search revealed the contact information of the main individuals and organizations offering yoga or meditation programs within prisons and jails in the local area of my interest. In some cases, these organizations represented informal, loosely affiliated networks of a few individuals; in other cases, they had wider membership and more formalized nonprofit structures. Finding these and contacting them via email proved to be relatively easy. I received almost-immediate responses, and everyone I contacted agreed to meet with me.

I began by scheduling relatively informal meetings and "pilot" interviews with these contacts in coffee shops and restaurants where, over a meal or a beverage, we could chat about their organizations and its values, commitments, and approaches to teaching in prisons. In these initial meetings, the volunteer leaders I met were welcoming and receptive. In addition to learning about their approaches, I tried to indicate something about my own interests and my research. I explained that my goal was to understand the world of prison yoga and meditation by becoming an insider as a volunteer-participant, while also writing about whichever aspects I could, as a researcher. To that end, these initial interviews served to establish rapport and credibility, soon allowing me to join the organizations.

Things moved fairly quickly once I had been vetted and deemed acceptable. I was invited to take a "toe-in-the-water" first step with several organizations, to observe a prison yoga or meditation session through a one-day visitor's pass. Leaders in each organization were willing to facilitate the paperwork with administrators, and these initial visits superficially informed my early understanding of the prison landscape. They also seemed to serve as something of an "audition" or screening-process for me, I later realized—they allowed the group leaders to get a sense for whether I would be an appropriate addition to their group. I seemed to have passed muster, since I was invited to join three such organizations as a regular volunteer with full security clearance.[61]

In reflecting on why my entrée into these organizations was so smooth, I found that several factors seemed to pave my way. My identity as South Asian and my status as an academic—along with my long-term immersion in these traditions—seemed, in different ways, to confer legitimacy and credibility. I am a light-skinned South Asian woman with the vestiges of an Indian accent, usually dressed in something just south of "business casual," neither too overdressed nor too scruffy, and usually wear glasses. In initial meetings at coffee shops or restaurants, I would explain the contours of my research interests, and refer to my scholarship on South Asian political and philosophical traditions. For some yogis who had themselves studied—and to a great extent identified with—these traditions, my personal background, combined with my academic interests, appeared to resonate greatly.

For instance, Rachel had founded a yoga program in a women's prison almost ten years ago. She is deeply devoted to Iyengar yoga, a school shaped by the teachings of B.K.S. Iyengar of Pune, India. All the volunteers she recruits for her prison program must be trained in the Iyengar method. I have some experience with Iyengar yoga, though I am not trained specifically in its approach. I mentioned to Rachel that I had grown up in Pune and done my early yoga studies with direct disciples of Iyengar. This seemed to strike a chord with her, and she later enthusiastically introduced me to the group over email as "Professor Farah Godrej, formerly of Pune, India." This enthusiasm rubbed off on others and became a recurring theme—in introducing me to prison staff and to incarcerated students, volunteers from this group would invoke both my South Asian heritage and my academic identity. "She's from India," some would say, "and she's also a professor who teaches about yoga."

My own racial identity as a South Asian *and* a scholar of South Asian thought surely enabled my access—it made some more willing to embrace me, because of their assumptions about my knowledge base (which I admittedly did not hesitate to emphasize). Scholars remind us that race and ethnicity are deeply relevant to the research enterprise,[62] but in my case, these issues seemed to carry particular weight. The yoga world is already rife with debates about authenticity, legitimacy, and cultural appropriation. Many South Asians claim cultural ownership of yoga, and many Western practitioners either denounce the cultural appropriation of yoga or authenticate their own practice by "studying at the source" in India, often within a Guru lineage. Rigorous knowledge of Sanskrit and of key texts such as the *Yoga-Sūtras* become markers of legitimate knowledge. I was careful never to assume the air of an authority figure, or to appear intimidating—instead, I tried to emphasize how much I had to learn. Yet, in some spaces, given the weight of concerns about cultural competency, I was quickly perceived as an expert because of my "heritage" ties and credentials.

But not all volunteers were as preoccupied with "authenticity" or my South Asianness. Lena, who had also founded a prison yoga organization several years ago, showed less interest in my cultural fluency with yoga's Indian roots, or with Sanskrit. She seemed to care more about my academic credentials, occasionally mentioning how honored she was to have someone so "accomplished" express interest in her group. I got the sense that these were small, relatively underrecognized communities of people working against large obstacles, eager to speak to anyone who showed any interest in the topic. Meanwhile, volunteers who taught Buddhist-inspired meditation seemed less interested in my racial identity. But here, another kind of cultural competency seemed to matter more: my identity as a practitioner who shared a common knowledge of the basic Buddhist conceptual toolkit, and the different schools of Buddhist thought and practice. When volunteers would reveal that they were trained in specific schools of Buddhism—for example, the *vipassana* or Shambhala traditions—I was able to speak knowledgeably about my own experiences with these practices, or to ask well-informed questions about how these practices worked in the prison context. In a variety of ways, my prior academic knowledge, my South Asian identity and my own personal practice all seemed to serve as the pathway to cultivate rapport with contacts.

Whatever the case, I found that everyone seemed to respond to me well, at least as far as I could tell. All of my initial conversations were characterized by a warm welcome and an eagerness to speak—most people were so enthusiastic and had so much to say that none of my initial meetings went much under two hours. This is not to say, by any means, that the relationships I developed over time were entirely devoid of tension: Eventually, my critical, activist leanings occasionally left me at odds with fellow volunteers, causing me to question key assumptions and practices, sometimes leaving me feeling like the proverbial sore thumb. But at the outset, I was integrated into this world relatively easily.

Positionality, Gender, Race, and Place

As I became increasingly embedded in this world of prison volunteers, I struggled with the question of who I was relative to the system I was entering, and the people I was encountering. Who *was* I, to be doing this kind of work in prisons, whether research, activism, or volunteer work? I felt dogged by the sense that there was something presumptuous and intrusive about my being in those spaces, and working with those who endured them. Who exactly did I think I was, to try and understand their worlds, to probe their consciousness, or try to articulate this in writing—how could I ever know what any of it was like, much less represent it appropriately? I struggled with the fact that my background conferred a position and a set of privileges far removed from the world that my interlocutors lived in. As a South Asian immigrant who had spent decades in the United States before finally obtaining citizenship, I certainly had enough experience of the "not-whiteness" that translates into vulnerability for so many incarcerated persons. But what I had in common with them was far outstripped by what I did not share: I had lived a relatively comfortable, middle-class existence for most of my life (despite the tenuous years of being a struggling student). I had little experience of the race- and class-based indignities that most of them had lived. I had never been incarcerated, nor had I met anyone who was incarcerated until I began this work. My encounters with police had been limited to a handful of polite, routine traffic stops. I had never seen the inside of a jail or prison, nor visited anyone in such a facility. My knowledge of prisons was limited to popular media, and later, to academic accounts. I moved in a bubble of well-meaning progressives (many of whom were fellow academics) who approached the world through the lens of fairness and social justice. But our middle-class lives intersected not at all with the lives of the people I met in prisons, or those who were formerly incarcerated. Given both my class privilege and my cultural background, I had no experience of what one colleague called "the police stops and daily insults and aggravations and humiliations and injuries and criminalization of everyday activities, let alone survival activities"[63] that these communities had endured. So who was *I*, to make sense of their lives and worlds?

I did my best to counter this by taking to heart the recommendation to educate myself about the context and communities I was working in. I tried to talk little, and did as much listening and learning as I could. Even so, I continually felt like an interloper. As a researcher, I worried that my motivations were trite,[64] especially as I considered the often exploitative nature of most research with human subjects. I fretted about turning prisons and incarcerated persons into a means for my own professional advancement, trading on their suffering and humiliation in prurient, voyeuristic ways. As Lee Ann Fujii noted, "being granted time by participants . . . [and being allowed into their worlds] is a privilege, not a right."[65] These worries applied most urgently to my research with formerly incarcerated persons. While interviewing formerly incarcerated participants, I became keenly aware of their extremely limited time, energy, and resources, and worried that the measly stipend I offered could never compensate them for the time they took out of their difficult lives for me. The push to "find more research participants" felt like a violation. Here are my field notes from this period:

> I become keenly aware that asking literally anything of formerly incarcerated people who are trying to get back on their feet is an intrusion, a nontrivial "ask," a favor that they have no reason to grant me. Not to mention asking them to enter into the emotional territory of reliving their incarceration. Assuming that the simple monetary exchange mitigates that discomfort is so mercantile . . . I worry about the reduction of [their] lives to observable, reportable "data," the idea that the exchange of money reduces them and their lives to something that I now have the presumptive authority to speak about, to report on, to make known. By what authority do I presume to speak for them, to take the context of their entire lives, and reduce it to the "data" I need? (Field notes)

Moreover, what good would any of this *do*? Even research like my own, which I considered progressive and justice-oriented, "is often of limited utility in improving the lives of incarcerated people in any real way."[66] Like most researchers who spend time contemplating these issues, I attempted to build relationships of trust and reciprocity with my research participants. I kept in regular touch with them. I helped some find housing or employment, wrote support letters for pardon applications for others, helped to crowd-source funding for yoga teacher-training courses, and even occasionally sent money privately when some found themselves broke. I sent all of them draft chapters to read and encouraged them to offer correctives (although few of them actually did read or provide feedback). I constantly found myself wondering whether I was doing enough to mitigate the imposition on their time and energy, to build equitable research practices that treated them as more than simply a source of information to be extracted.

As a volunteer and an activist developing personal relationships with people inside prisons through yoga, meditation, and political work, I had an overlapping but slightly different set of concerns. I worried about hierarchy, and the deference with which some incarcerated students seemed to treat me, either because I was a professor, or a long-term South Asian practitioner steeped in yogic traditions, or both. I did everything I could to decenter these hierarchies: I dressed as casually as possible (usually in some version of loose-fitting yoga pants and T-shirt), tried to behave as informally as possible, was generally self-deprecating, and always introduced myself by first name only. In group discussion settings, I encouraged students to set the agenda and lead their own discussions. I stayed as silent as I could, learning and listening, offering commentary only when asked. I tried to act like any other member of the group, rather than a leader. I encouraged interjection whenever I or another volunteer were speaking, and tried to foster an atmosphere of collaboration, telling my students that I wanted to learn from them.

Over time, some of my volunteer work turned more explicitly political and critical. I began to experiment with raising political questions and introducing themes of justice and injustice. I even cautiously engaged incarcerated students in conversations around modes of resistance, both internal and external. But I also wondered: who was I to politicize anyone, or raise their consciousness, especially if they wanted to keep their head down and do their time? What if these structural issues were too overwhelming to think about, or their magnitude induced hopelessness and despair, as some students later suggested? Most of all, I worried that perhaps these modes of resistance needed to stay under the radar, rather than be blown open by my writing about them. Would prison administrators clamp down on yoga or meditation programs if I—and other volunteers as described in Chapter 8—openly acknowledged that such practices could foster political education and consciousness-raising?

Joshua Price, an activist researcher who interviewed incarcerated persons, acknowledges that since the days of slavery, "creative tactics of everyday survival in the face of massive state violence" have involved dissembling through half-truths and omissions, which are "understandable responses to hostile treatment and oppressive conditions."[67] The fear, disgrace, and stigma of incarceration make silence or evasion a reasonable response by those who have been subjected consistently to oppression. In the face of a hostile and menacing society that dehumanizes them, many vulnerable populations have "[hidden] the truth of their inner lives and selves from their oppressors," using a culture of secrecy to protect the sanctity of their inner lives.[68] In fact, as one colleague rightly reminded me, this secrecy may produce an outward sheen of conformity and compliance,[69] even apparent obedience or submission.

Resistance, meanwhile, may occur under the radar, in creative, imaginative, and often interiorized ways, not amenable to the disclosure I sought.

Black writers such as Toni Morrison and Alice Walker have suggested that when dealing with oppressed populations, the insistence on "knowing everything," and the attempt to reconstruct their interior life in service of revelation, may be an arrogant or otherwise suspect desire.[70] The transparency I was pursuing through written collaboration with my students did not always sit well with the possibility that incarcerated persons might prefer to keep their inner lives and resistance strategies intentionally obscured to the prying eyes of outsiders. Like Price, I grappled with whether "retaining a certain distance"—as Morrison or Walker recommend—rather trying to "plumb the inner depths," would have been the more respectful option.[71] Yet, incarcerated and formerly incarcerated colleagues eventually persuaded me of the value of revelation: Being silenced, forgotten, and rendered invisible, they reminded me, are also important forms of suffering and disrespect.

Most striking to me was how quickly, in both my research and my volunteer work, incarcerated persons seemed to want to share life-stories and narratives that were unimaginably devastating. I would like to believe—although perhaps I delude myself—that I adequately developed the bonds of mutual trust required to earn the confidence of those who shared these horrifying tales.[72] The stories kept coming: stories of homelessness and addiction and police brutality and poverty and being prostituted by family members; of being forced to carry pregnancies to term in prison, of being shackled while giving birth, of being separated from children, of not being allowed to hold or breastfeed one's newborn after giving birth; of having parental rights terminated due to incarceration and involuntarily losing children to adoption; of being repeatedly raped and assaulted, yet given a two-decade prison sentence for killing one's assailant in the course of self-defense; of being cavity-searched after visiting with families; of gross medical negligence in prison; and much, much more.[73]

It was no coincidence that the most vivid and detailed stories were those of gendered shame, stigma, and devastation shared by incarcerated women.[74] Although I regularly volunteered in men's prisons, I spent the most time with incarcerated women, and became closest to them. Here, my gender identity became relevant in a particular way. I was never uncomfortable around my male-identifying students, but the intimacy and familiarity we created as women doing yoga, meditation, and political work together was of a different order altogether. We got to know each other well, and the fact that we were all women, sharing gendered experiences and life-stories, added an extra layer of solidarity. Yet, the bonds I forged also left me keenly aware that I was afforded the rare privilege of intimacy with my incarcerated students, despite the fact that I felt like an interloper in their world, having not walked the paths they had walked. Whether teaching yoga or meditation, or doing activist political work, I had the privilege of nurturing and accompanying them, a privilege denied to many of their own family members and loved ones.

In the end, Joshua Price says: "I left the people at the jail . . . in their despair and their suffering, and traveled by car . . . to the university campus, its academic chitchat in the halls, cappuccinos and graduate students, classes and department meetings, undergraduates and email. The experience was one of crossing back and forth across seemingly incommensurable worlds."[75] Like Price, I underwent this dissonance multiple times a week, "seeing massive social suffering up close," yet returning back to everyday middle-class life, where the chaos, violence, and terror of incarceration were mostly abstract. I bore witness to unbearable suffering, yet walked away every day, leaving my students behind. I felt helpless, inadequate, and complicit, as I carried the weight of their suffering home with me, aware of how insulated I would remain, of the cliché that my privilege would likely continue to protect me from a similar fate.[76]

To be clear, I also spent a great deal of time contemplating my obligations to another less vulnerable set of collaborators and research participants: my fellow volunteers. Here too, the lines were blurry: My fellow volunteers were at times research subjects (e.g., when I interviewed them), at other times collaborators (when I worked with them as a fellow volunteer and organizational leader). This group was for the most part far more privileged than my incarcerated collaborators and my formerly incarcerated interviewees. Its members were overwhelmingly white, and economically relatively secure. I describe at length my interactions with them in Chapters 7 and 8. Leaders of these volunteer groups had welcomed me into their communities, entrusted me with a great deal of insider information, and, in some cases, asked me to take on leadership roles. As I hope will be clear, I was never anything less than impressed by their singular dedication to serving the individuals we encountered inside prisons. Yet, I was not always convinced that they viewed the political dimensions of incarceration through quite the same critical lens that I did. More importantly, few seemed to be attuned to the danger that yoga or meditation could be employed to produce docility or compliance in a violent, abusive, and (in my view) unjust system, a concern I grappled with continually. Even as I realized I was not obligated to produce portrayals that were necessarily sympathetic, I worried about the fluid boundaries when these relationships turn, as they inevitably do, into something resembling friendships. The warmth and rapport entailed in such relationships can sometimes imply an obligation to avoid any analysis that is unflattering: Writing critically about what one has observed as an "insider" can seem like a betrayal.[77] Taking part in and studying these communities raised a somewhat different set of concerns, which I considered carefully and discuss at length in the Methodological Appendix.

Conclusion

Scholars tell us that the question of research ethics has often been used to protect correctional institutions from scrutiny.[78] The research in this book, which provides an "officially approved" glimpse inside a prison has been crucially shaped by my university IRB's insistence on ceding all authority to the very institution being studied. The IRB's elevation of the prison as the arbiter of ethical research effectively ensures either that prisons remain opaque and inaccessible to researchers (because of the low likelihood of obtaining access without insider contacts), or that the resulting research is shaped by compromise with institutions that have vested interests in resisting scrutiny.

Giving the prison ultimate authority to approve what could and could not be seen, said, done, or observed has shaped parts of this project in crucial ways. It has allowed prisons (at least in theory) to excise or modify what could be published, and has constrained my ability to report on my interactions within prisons, and with incarcerated persons. To conduct research inside prisons is to accede to the prison's version of hierarchy over incarcerated persons, to follow the prison's rules, to regard incarcerated persons as inherently dangerous, avoiding any interactions beyond the bare minimum required.

Had I remained restricted to my researcher role, the scope of what I ended up learning about prisons would have been extremely limited. Only because I had connected with volunteer organizations and built relationships inside prisons could I go beyond the confines of this highly restricted role. As a result, I have been able to offer descriptions of prison life and engagements with incarcerated persons that are richer and more revelatory than might otherwise have been possible. These descriptions emerged because I eventually complemented my scholarship with the perspective of a volunteer-activist, seeking to engage fully with incarcerated persons, to not only "hear" directly from them, but to collaborate and think *with* them.

Above all, writing this book has taught me that the notion of a perfectly ethical project is a fantasy.[79] A colleague and I once mournfully joked that there was no way to do research or volunteer work in prisons without "feeling like a bad person": that is, continually complicit in the power structure of the prison, forced to abide by the terms set by the prison itself, but also in danger of instrumentalizing our incarcerated fellow-citizens. Even in those moments when I found myself outside the bounds of the prison's authority, or rejecting its gatekeeping—whether through activist collaboration with incarcerated students, or while interviewing formerly incarcerated persons—I never felt free of the burdens of guilt. I worried about the vulnerability of my incarcerated and formerly incarcerated conversation partners, about adequately respectful and reciprocal relations, about how I was wielding my limited set of privileges and whether it was for the benefit of the most vulnerable among us, and in the end, whether I had any right to share the things I do in this book. At every turn, I have wrestled with difficult decisions about what to say and not say; what to reveal and what to keep concealed; how to write about things I'd seen and people I'd developed relationships with; whether to cave to the power structures that limit our access to prisons and to incarcerated persons' lives and worlds. Most importantly, even when it was clear that prisons have a vested interest in denying us this transparency, I questioned whether any of us has the moral authority to reveal what remains hidden or silenced inside these worlds. No matter which way I turned, I was confronted with the unending dance of weighing the risks and benefits of every decision. No choice I ended up making ever felt entirely fair, appropriate, ethical, or respectful to all concerned; yet the responsibility for each of these decisions ultimately lay with me alone.

3

Yoga and Meditation

Historical and Contemporary Debates

In the spring of 2020, public opinion regarding law enforcement in the United States underwent something of a shift. The immediate catalyst for these events was the murder of George Floyd, a Black man who begged for his life, pleading that he couldn't breathe, while a white police officer knelt calmly on his neck for almost nine minutes, asphyxiating him. The video of Floyd's murder—along with the police murders of many other Black men and women around the same time—prompted huge crowds of protestors to gather in many cities, expressing vocal public anger at the systemic devaluing of Black life by law enforcement. Meanwhile, public opinion shifted largely in favor of the protestors, as polls increasingly showed a majority of Americans to be concerned about unequal treatment by law enforcement. Politicians across the spectrum took note. "Systemic racism" became a buzzword, and everyone from Nike to McDonald's and Netflix immediately jumped on the bandwagon, issuing heartfelt statements of support and "ally-ship" on their websites. The idea of defunding police departments began to gain currency in mainstream political debates, with some city councils and local government bodies pledging to defund, and in some cases, dismantle their police departments.

Suddenly, yoga studios and meditation centers across the country which had long remained silent on political issues began sending missives to their listservs, making statements of solidarity regarding social and racial justice, hosting events on these issues, and pledging to "do better" by changing their organizational structures. Virtually overnight, the national conversation shifted dramatically: These groups appeared to have no choice but to position themselves as deeply concerned about social inequities—particularly as pertaining to race. Statements were written, training programs were implemented, and webinars were being advertised left and right. Suddenly, no matter which way one turned, the yoga or meditation world seemed ablaze with people wanting to discuss how concerned they were about systemic racism and injustice. It was unclear, however, to what extent these conversations would go beyond the conformist sloganeering of simply "recognizing" injustice. What remained to

Freedom Inside?. Farah Godrej, Oxford University Press. © Oxford University Press 2022.
DOI: 10.1093/oso/9780190070083.003.0003

be seen was what exactly could—or would—be done about systemic injustice by those who practiced yoga and meditation. Did these traditions have any history of speaking to political concerns about equity or justice? And, were those who practiced in the West equipped to confront such issues?

I was one of the practitioners who had been grappling with these questions long before the events of 2020. (Admittedly, I found myself skeptical about whether all the earnestness we were suddenly seeing among yogis and meditators was much more than a performance, or at best, an oversimplification of the issues at stake.) Both as a scholar and a practitioner, I had long been wondering what, if anything, yoga and meditation practitioners could (and should) say or do about political injustice. After years of personal practice, the benefits of individual transformation and personal cultivation through yoga and meditation could not have been more evident to me. But even as my own personal practice flourished, I became increasingly concerned about whether and how these traditions and practices could help us to confront or oppose oppressive power structures, especially in their North American version.

I had been reading literature that suggested the opposite: These practices could make people overly focused on their own self-development, causing them to prioritize turning inward in order to address their own suffering, as a substitute for organizing with others to resist the systems that gave rise to collective stress and suffering. I worried, along with many others, that the messaging from these traditions could downplay the need to engage with— or even analyze and criticize—the social or political world. As a result of this inward withdrawal, people could become more inclined to accept the very power structures that caused stress, rather than focus on the role of their underlying causes. I wondered if these practices could lead, unwittingly perhaps, to the support of an unjust or inequitable status quo, if practitioners tended to "tune out, turn inward, and drop out of everything that feels difficult."[1]

Meanwhile, in American public discourse, an excessive focus on the internal, individual causes of suffering seemed to be accompanied by a neglect of its external, social and political causes. At-risk youth in public schools were being taught how to be more "mindful" and "disciplined," but this seemed to serve as a substitute for confronting the deep social and political inequities at the root of their trauma and stress. So too with the corporate world: Employees were being given meditation exercises for "stress-reduction" and greater "productivity," with no discussion of the deeply inequitable economic system that caused so much anguish. More "self-care" by individuals seemed to be touted as the solution to all woes, without connecting this to the fundamental, systemic causes of those woes. Scholars and practitioners had begun to warn that without social critique, these practices could lead to uncritical acceptance, in which individuals simply became more efficient at coping and complying with injustice all around, "justify[ing] and stabiliz[ing] the status quo."[2] They publicly worried that practitioners were emphasizing those aspects that "[induce] inner calm, equanimity, and acceptance" of the present structures of society, "[enabling] people to function more effectively and peacefully within it," rather than engaging in critique.[3]

In this chapter I address a number of debates—both historical and contemporary—that set the stage for what follows in the rest of this book. This chapter shows us why we should care about yoga and meditation in prisons. It walks the reader through the broad sweep of commentaries that point to darker and more insidious possibilities lurking within these practices, particularly when they are taught to those routinely targeted by unequal or oppressive forms of power. Here, I think through how these traditions have historically spoken about injustice, both in their Asian contexts, and more recently, in their contemporary Western contexts. I also look at both historical and newer movements of yoga and meditation which reject the purely inward-oriented focus of practice, and insist on cultivating skillful ways to acknowledge—even oppose—social and political suffering. For these movements and practitioners, addressing systemic change is not an *optional* feature of yogic or meditative practice; rather, personal practice is necessarily intertwined with a critique of social structures, and in some cases, action toward social justice. Certainly, not all practitioners are quick to subscribe to this newer, more activist version of yoga and meditation. All the recent hubbub around systemic racism notwithstanding, many remain wedded to a vision of yoga or meditation as mainly something that individuals do for their own self-improvement. But despite the ongoing reticence of many yogis and meditators to get involved in political questions (and the concern that when they do so, it is mere posturing) new developments do point to a promising possibility: that the ethical virtues and other capacities prized by the yogic and meditative tradition can be put to work for social justice ends, rather than for conservative ones. In this chapter we will see that the dangers of reproducing the conservative elements of these traditions are very real; but so are the emancipatory possibilities contained within their more radical interpretations.

Summarizing the Debates

In contemplating these questions, I first came at them through my scholarly work, and my immersion in academic debates. To begin with, what exactly did we mean by referring to "yogic and meditative" traditions? Clearly, they could not be characterized in any simple or monolithic way, and we needed to pay attention to their diversity. What had these traditions historically said about political engagement? Were they inherently conservative? And, what happened when they traveled to new contexts and evolved to address new kinds of social issues and preoccupations? Addressing all of these issues in depth could in itself be a book-length project. Indeed, many scholars have written books of precisely this nature, in far greater depth and with far more expertise than I could possibly replicate. So I restrict myself here to summarizing the debates around these questions, and thinking through why they matter for the question of yoga and meditation in prisons.

What do we mean when we say "yoga" or "meditation"? In this book, I refer to practices that emerge from the spiritual and philosophical traditions of South Asia—mainly Hindu or Buddhist—which offer "a way of self-cultivation or self-transformation."⁴ This self-cultivation involves a variety of physical and mental practices of discipline and training. Again, we can hardly treat yogic and meditative traditions as a single category. Hinduism and Buddhism each contain many different schools of thought, a great deal of internal debate, and millennia-old movements of commentary and reinterpretation. The Buddha's teachings have spawned an array of schools, including Mahāyāna, Theravāda, Vajrayāna, and Zen, as well as Ambedkarite Buddhism of India. Buddhism's spread across different Asian cultures has led to its Tibetan, Sri Lankan, Burmese, Thai, and Japanese variants, not to mention the newer Western forms. Beyond this, there is even more fragmentation that has produced differences in textual emphases and forms of practice in each national context.

So too with yoga: Yogic philosophy emerged as part of the classical Hindu canon, with the *Bhagavad-Gītā* and Patañjali's *Yoga-Sūtras* often assumed to be its key texts. But what has gone on to be systematized across time was in fact a hotch-potch: it absorbed influences from later Advaita and Tantric schools, producing different versions of both postural (*haṭha-yoga*) and meditative (*rāja-, jnāna-, bhakti-,* and *karma-yoga*) practice.⁵ Modern forms taught by iconic teachers such as Vivekananda, Krishnamacharya, Iyengar, Jois, and Sivananda are fragmented enough, to say nothing of the development of Western forms such as Anusara, Bikram, Forrest, and so on. The question of to what extent yoga is a "Hindu" practice is complex and controversial. While the origins of the yoga tradition certainly lie in the Hindu philosophical canon, the contemporary global yoga tradition has developed independently of what is now called "Hinduism" or "Buddhism," but has also merged with both. (In fact, whether or not yoga is characterized as Hindu or not is a political question in and of itself.[6])

Despite the diversity we see across these traditions, certain ideas and practices are common across them, reappearing in their Western variants: the idea of the material world as fluctuation and change; the notion of detaching from—and eventually transcending—one's emotions, feelings, and thoughts, learning to watch them as they come and go; the idea of external circumstances as fleeting and illusory; the nondual idea that judgments of "good" and "bad" must be transcended; the notion that the world around us, indeed our very selfhood, is not only unstable and impermanent but rather is a construction of the mind. In some cases, these traditions also teach that self-cultivation must be geared toward transcending ordinary consciousness, toward a deeper and more mystical state. But not everyone who undertakes these practices—particularly in the West—aspires to the more transcendent goals. Most often, the practices often are oriented toward secular, worldly goals of "stress management" through states of peace, calm, and focus informed by nonjudgment and nonreactivity.[7]

Because the traditions I am describing are so complex, my intention is not to reduce them to these few principles, but to point out themes that are most often emphasized. Particularly important is the idea that suffering is the result of one's own mind and one's reactions to external circumstances, rather than the circumstances *per se*—therefore, one is better off dealing with one's own mind, rather than trying to change the world to be more in keeping with one's desires. It is not external objects, people or conditions that cause our suffering, but our attachment to them—thus, we create our own suffering. The purpose of training and self-discipline is a mind that rests in ease despite unstable external conditions, cultivating acceptance for, rather than judging or struggling against, these conditions. The more we watch the mind's constructs arise and pass away, the more we realize that what we view as "problems" are a result of our mind, which tends to fabricate ideas, opinions, and views. Steady, dispassionate observation of the mind is the most important purpose of meditative practice, along with the ability to release its fabrications without striving, grasping, or judgment.

In order to achieve these states of nonreactive calm or peace, these traditions offer a variety of practices that bring about a more heightened awareness of thought patterns, through inward attention. Focusing on the breath, while watching thoughts as they arise and dissolve, is perhaps the most common practice, although there are countless others. One scholar divides all meditative practices into three types: "concentrative," "integrative," and "contemplative."[8] Concentrative practices involve concentrating the mind on a particular object, such as the breath, a repetitive phrase, an image, or even parts of one's own body, so that the mind is trained to hold its focus. Integrative practices allow one to tune in to several aspects of one's inner experience—whether emotions, thoughts, or bodily sensations—without judging them, giving us a greater capacity to tolerate the discomfort that may arise. Contemplative practices cultivate specific states of feeling, such as lov-ingkindness or gratitude or peace, as an antidote to negative mind-states. The yogic tradition involves the practice of physical postures (or *āsanas*) to achieve beneficial mind-states. Although the physical practice is thought to increase strength, flexibility, breath control, toleration of discomfort, and other physical benefits, its ultimate aim is the same as meditative practices: to still the fluctuations of the mind, and enter a transcendent state beyond ordi-nary worldly preoccupations.[9]

Do These Traditions Promote Individual Spiritual Pursuit over Political Engagement?

One common thread across these traditions is precisely the idea that practitioners must transcend the ordinary, material world of everyday life, which is considered less important relative to the pursuit of spiritual goals. In Hinduism, ascetic discipline—controlling the mind through conquering sensual desires—is arguably the route to spiritual transcendence.[10] Buddhism (which also originated in India, but emerged from a critique of Hinduism) tells us that the human condition is inherently one of *dukkha* or suffering: Because of our tendency to crave impermanent things or conditions, we create much of our own suffering. Buddhism, it is said, calls for us to develop detachment from—and eventually transcend—the material world through contentment and acceptance, or a liberation from worldly preoccupations and desires.[11] As a result, scholars have suggested that both Hinduism and Buddhism call for a kind of self-cultivation that requires individuals "going within" to address the internal source of their suffering and their problems, while neglecting or downplaying the need for addressing external circumstances.

Social and political issues—which are part of these external circumstances—can thereby seem less significant in these traditions, rela-tive to individual spiritual progress. They could also be seen as igniting our passions, destroying the contentment we are trying to achieve. Meanwhile the emphasis on confronting the fluctuation of one's own mind can suggest that all problems arise ultimately from our mind-states, rather than from external circumstances. Instead of trying to control outer circumstances, practitioners should focus on cultivating acceptance of constant change. This can lead to political apathy or passivity: Why bother acting in the political world, if it is all impermanent and ephemeral anyway? And, isn't it more important to focus on training the mind to remain nonreactive to external circumstances, regardless of what they bring?

Are These Traditions Inherently Conservative?

As a result, some scholars have charged the yogic and meditative traditions with an inherent conservatism: The focus on individual spiritual pursuit at the expense of social and political change means that the status quo typically ends up staying intact, because there is little incentive for social or political action. But even at the level of philosophy, there is disagreement about this: First, it is not as though these traditions were purely ascetic and entirely unconcerned with issues of material well-being. Second, in both Hinduism and Buddhism, there is emphasis on the need for ethical action to change the world, rather than simply accepting it as it is. Hinduism contains a vast body of reflection on issues such as ethical conduct, social norms, and economic policies, which call for secular involvement with the social world—personal spiritual progress toward liberation was not the only priority.[12] Similarly, Buddhism has always recommended that "choices be made between what to cultivate and what to avoid,"[13] with clear guidance for the states of mind, modes of living, and ethical outcomes that are most valuable and beneficial.[14] Both traditions have reflected extensively (if in different ways) on the ethical value of qualities such as truthfulness, nonviolence, self-discipline, contentment, love and service toward all other beings, and so on.[15]

But just because Hinduism and Buddhism insist on ethical action within the world, that doesn't tell us what *kinds* of political outcomes those ethics result in. Do they simply end up maintaining the status quo, supporting existing rulers and hierarchies? Or do they lead to social or political change, transforming oppressive systems, critiquing hierarchies, or empowering marginalized groups? When we look at the historical record within the countries where these traditions have flourished, we find a mixed bag. In their South, Southeast, and East Asian contexts, these traditions were not always progressive, egalitarian, or social justice–oriented: in many instances, they were patriarchal, classist, and casteist. Until relatively recently, the study of yoga in India was the exclusive privilege of elites, typically upper-caste, ascetic, Brahminical males.[16] More recently, scholars show that yoga in contemporary India is being employed as a weapon of Hindu right-wing nationalism: Practitioners, whether they choose to or not, may end up in a "naive and unwitting support of a Hindu supremacist ideology."[17]

Similar tensions arise within Buddhism. One prevailing view is that the Buddha was an egalitarian social reformer who rejected prevailing power structures such as caste, and insisted on making the teachings democratically accessible to all. On this view, Buddhism was, from its inception, a countercultural and anti-mainstream force.[18] Other scholars argue that while the Buddha may have taken an anti-caste stance at times, he was not opposed to the caste system as a social institution.[19] But regardless of how radical the Buddha himself may have been, as Buddhism spread to other parts of Asia and became the dominant cultural and religious force, it often ended up serving as a handmaiden to the political status quo. It "[formed] unholy alliances with the wealthy and powerful," supporting conformity and unquestioning obedience to social norms.[20] Buddhism played an important role in supporting the violence and militarism of the Japanese empire, embracing the worst aspects of Japanese imperialism. The Zen Master Yasutani Roshi preached a jingoistic nationalism and filial obedience to the emperor, defending killing to "assist good and punish evil."[21] Meanwhile, caste, gender, and class inequities have been sustained by Buddhism in many different Asian contexts, from using caste as a determining factor in monastic orders,[22] to denying monastic pursuits to women in certain contexts.[23]

But we also find that things have changed in the recent past. In the modern era, some activists in South or Southeast Asian cultures have insisted that political subversion and critique *necessarily* go along with yogic or meditative commitments. Perhaps no one exemplifies this as well as M. K. Gandhi, who was fiercely committed to yogic, meditative practice, and drew inspiration from these traditions for the revolutionary goals of resisting British colonial rule as well as opposing India's caste hierarchy. For him, the *Bhagavad-Gītā* was a call to sociopolitical activism. Moreover, there was no compliance, passivity, or quietism entailed in this; rather, he used active, provocative methods—including civil disobedience campaigns—to pose aggressive challenges to unjust power structures.[24] So too for Southeast Asians like Thich Nhat Hanh and Sulak Sivaraksa (a Thai prodemocracy activist), who insist that Buddhism must be directed toward social justice and critique.[25] These modern Asian practitioners all used spiritual self-cultivation to strengthen minds and bodies for disciplined, nonviolent resistance to oppression. And, they all insist that acting to fight injustice is not *optional* for the committed practitioner: it is the correct way to interpret and live by these traditions. For them, inward spiritual work must be married with outer work to actively challenge injustice.

The short answer, then, is that there is no fixed or necessary relationship between these traditions and political action, and nothing in these traditions leads inherently to any particular political outcome.[26] Some aspects of these traditions may lead to private spiritual pursuit, political passivity, or apathy regarding the public good, while others may lead to a progressive political engagement. Historically, yogic, meditative traditions have served hierarchical, unjust, or conservative political regimes in some times and places, while in others, they have criticized and challenged unjust power structures. They seem to have supported a variety of political ends across time, depending on how they are interpreted, and by whom.[27]

What Happens When Yoga and Meditation Travel to the West and Evolve?

For precisely this reason, scholars and practitioners are becoming increasingly concerned as these traditions have been "imported" to the West. Although they seemed countercultural in the early days of their arrival in the West, in their more recent iterations, they have become relatively mainstream and increasingly commercialized. The most heated debates revolve around what happens when these traditions evolve to accommodate Western preoccupations. Many scholars and practitioners celebrate the growth of these traditions in the West. They argue that new, secular variants are a natural evolution as the traditions travel to new times and places, and are available to become whatever the practitioner chooses to make of them. For some Westerners, Buddhism is a religion or a spiritual teaching; but for many others, it remains a secular, rationalist philosophy compatible with self-help, psychotherapy, and Western medicine. Similarly, modern Western yoga is countercultural enough to appeal to Westerners in search of "alternative" spirituality, but also able to speak to Western preoccupations with body image and consumerism.[28] It has spawned a variety of unapologetically Western forms such as "stand-up paddleboard" yoga and "yogalates," yet retains the use of Sanskrit and the occasional invocation of Hindu deities and prayers. It walks a tightrope between being "too secularized" and "too Hindu": It is routinely cited by the Western medical establishment for its physical and mental benefits, but conservative Christians simultaneously claim that yoga is too Hindu to be taught in public schools.[29] Many Western yoga practitioners want a more "authentic" practice clearly linked to Hinduism, but many others only want a version of yoga that is secularized enough to be palatable—nothing too foreign that requires a belief in "woo-woo" things like Hindu deities and chanting.

Commentators applaud the development of these new, hybrid forms of yogic and meditative practice, and the variety of options—spiritual and secular—that they provide. For many Westerners, it seems appropriate to reframe these contemplative practices as secular, precisely so that they can function freely in state-supported Western institutions where they cannot have any religious attachments.[30] This also has democratizing benefits: What were once esoteric practices only available to monks and other spiritual elites are now widely available to many, including women, who were notably excluded in earlier periods. As patterns of authority have shifted, yogic and meditative practices and communities have become more egalitarian, accessible, and democratic.[31] In fact, it is precisely this "paring down" of both yoga and Buddhism to their nonsectarian, universal components that allowed them both to gain such traction in the West.[32]

But vocal critics insist that there are clear losses entailed in excessive westernizing and secularizing. Over time, as these practices have traveled to the West, they have done so in a kind of vacuum—the set of values and social commitments that they were once attached to did not always follow them.[33] Detached from ethical content and severed from their roots in philosophical systems,[34] they have been distorted and misappropriated. These critics insist that the traditions were not simply taught as ways for us to "feel better about ourselves" in dealing with our worldly stress. They had higher aims that were ethical and spiritual in nature. To reduce them to the pursuit of ordinary stress relief, physical flexibility, or mental focus without greater ethical purpose is, they argue, a disrespectful violation. It turns these practices into consumer commodities, instruments for commonplace preoccupations that are quite mundane in comparison to the highest search for meaning taught by these traditions.[35]

For instance, what the Buddha taught was not just relief from everyday stress.[36] It was far more transcendent: to detach from the very idea of a separate, identifiable self that suffers. For this, practitioners were required to be immersed in a whole worldview, including philosophical and ethical training.[37] None of this is apparent in most Western forms of practice, which conveniently skip to the stress-relief without addressing the worldview, preferring "Buddhist meditation without the Buddhism."[38] Similarly, some yogis argue that yoga was never meant to be for the shallow, commercial purpose of fitness so predominant in North America. The goals of āsana (postural practice) were always attached to the transcendent goals of stilling the mind (*citta-vṛtti nirodha*), uniting with the divine, and attaining mōksha, liberation from the human attachment to desire,[39] which required philosophical and moral training—what the *Yoga-Sūtras* refer to as *yamas* (moral restraints) and *niyamas* (ethical observances). But many Western practitioners may prefer their yoga minus the awkward spiritual bits, simply seeking bodily improvement and mental peace without these higher purposes.[40]

Of course, many Western commentators counter that there is nothing wrong with encouraging individuals to improve their minds or bodies, to deal with stress, to become more resilient, flexible, and peaceful. They reject the notion that these are mundane, trivial, or meaningless goals.[41] They argue that secular, Western problems of stress-relief should not be considered less important than so-called higher spiritual pursuits. In fact, many Westerners may be resistant to the spiritual aspects of these traditions, given that they are quite alien to Judeo-Christian principles.[42] There is no need, therefore, to adopt the whole-hog of spiritual transcendence—why not just take the pieces that make us fitter, stronger, calmer, and more resilient, and leave it at that?

"Sit Down and Shut Up"? Neoliberalism, McMindfulness, and McYoga

The most compelling response is that applying these traditions in a purely secular way—without critical inquiry into ethics and value systems—allows them to passively support dominant, oppressive sociocultural structures.[43] Critics are particularly concerned about how easily these practices have accommodated the consumerist capitalism, militarism, surveillance, social control, and inequity seen in Western societies, particularly in North America.[44] The most popular focus of such concerns is "mindfulness," a secularized adaptation of Buddhist meditation for self-help. Mindfulness is a broad tent, but its best-known version is "mindfulness-based stress reduction" (MBSR), pioneered by Jon Kabat-Zinn. Zinn has defined MBSR as "paying attention, on purpose, in the present moment, nonjudgmentally," through the cultivation of a "nonreactive mind," the orientation of nonstriving and "letting go [of] expectations, goals, and aspirations."[45] Its use for pain and stress reduction has been adopted in hospitals, prisons, schools, corporate offices, and other settings. The clinical application of MBSR has spread to psychotherapy for the treatment of conditions such as depression and anxiety, and has become the object of much scientific research.

In what one author calls the "mindfulness wars,"[46] Kabat-Zinn and others have come in for bashing by those who are concerned with the commodification and Western appropriation of meditative traditions.[47] They argue that these new modes of practice lead to overemphasizing individualism through withdrawal into an inner realm, reinforcing political passivity and discouraging social engagement. Instead of encouraging social action, the emphasis on acceptance and nonjudgment leads to excessive focus on the personal causes of suffering, rather than on its social and systemic causes. These practices purport to "set practitioners free," but only do so by helping them adjust to the social and structural conditions that cause much suffering.[48] Psychologized or medicalized versions of practice come under particular fire for refashioning meditation into a banal self-help technique that assumes that individuals are "responsible for their own healing,"[49] suggesting that suffering and healing are located inside one's head.

Along with this medicalization, particularly problematic is the scientific narrative of the "fight/flight" response often invoked by mindfulness teachers and communities, as though the stress response were simply a "biological flaw . . . inherited from our caveman ancestors."[50] How could one possibly reject the appeal to science or medicine, we might wonder? But the issue here is not the invocation of science, but rather, doing so in detachment from broader economic and political conditions. Citing scientific evidence in this narrow, decontextualized way conveniently implies that the human brain should simply learn to compensate for these biological instincts, without ever examining the political and structural conditions that cause collective stress.[51] In turn, this "covertly depoliticize[s] socio-economic problems," locating all distress within the individual without ever acknowledging that the "difficult life" is a result of society.[52] Such critiques apply to yoga too. North American yoga culture is charged with becoming consumerist, competitive, and hyper-individualistic in its pursuit of personal enhancement: "the best way to better the world is to focus intensively and . . . exclusively . . . on one's self."[53] Practitioners become flexible and manageable, tolerating discomfort while working against the strains of an inequitable society they rarely pause to question.[54] The onus is "on individuals to be more resilient," to keep functioning well within a dysfunctional system, to "sit down and shut up" instead of attending to the root causes of the dysfunction.[55]

The most urgent concern is that yoga and meditation have been appropriated by "neoliberalism," a worldview which holds that individuals alone determine the outcomes of their own choices, without regard for any social or structural constraints. Neoliberalism tells us that each private person should meet their own needs and take responsibility for their own personal wellbeing: We can simply choose happiness over misery by constantly improving ourselves through self-help and self-discipline. No matter how bad things get, we alone are both the source of any unhappiness and the solution, responsible for overcoming presumed deficits rather than looking to analyze and change difficult social conditions.[56] Failures are attributed to a lack of resilience, discipline, or self-improvement, outcomes of bad choice or pathology: "It can't be the system, it must be me."[57] Neoliberalism relies on a "cultural tendency to focus on private wellbeing rather than collective wellbeing," a tendency that is often exacerbated in those with privilege.[58] It individualizes oppression by claiming, "It is always your problem, deal with yourself," continually reasserting the "freedom" to create our own reality. As a result, practices of self-care can turn into internalized social control,[59] as people become more resilient, adaptable, governable, and accommodating toward the often unjust forces that structure their lives. This mode of control is not a coercive or sinister form of brainwashing. It is much more sophisticated, relying on people's internalization of the concepts of "freedom" and "choice" in order to shape them through self-discipline.[60] And, there is no one identifiable source of power behind neoliberalism, no "they" who are controlling "us": Rather, it is a set of assumptions that we all internalize.

The health and wellness industries are deeply implicated in this neoliberal appropriation: they "fetishize fulfillment and well-being," and despite the absence of basic social goods like job security and healthcare, often direct blame at those who "[fail] to think positively enough."[61] The worry, then, is that yogic, meditative techniques may encourage us to retool our emotional-cognitive terrain to accept an unjust, miserable reality reconceived as personal choice. We can accept the present moment and quiet our mind, which is telling us to want more than this grueling life that will keep us mired in poverty or oppression.[62] Some call this a political "sedative"[63] that simply helps us cope with structural difficulties rather than critique or change them, thus ensuring that we remain apolitical.[64]

Yogic and meditative traditions can seem particularly vulnerable to these interpretations, because of their history of preference for inner spiritual progress over outer political change, or apolitical "nondoing" over action.[65] Many argue that this can lead Western practitioners to "spiritual bypassing": invoking notions like "karma" or "impermanence" as a way of normalizing injustice, or as an excuse for inaction through "checking out."[66] Nondual philosophies sometimes discourage right-versus-wrong analyses, showing that such feelings are illusory.[67] As a result, several popular Western teachers end up dismissing political beliefs about injustice or inequity as irrelevant to spiritual practice.[68] If the posture of acceptance, nonjudgment or detachment seems to call for neutrality on political issues, many remain unwilling to get involved in criticizing the status quo: this seems too concrete, practical or partisan for the utopian other-worldliness they are pursuing.[69]

Many rebuttals are offered to these critiques: some call them "evidence-free fear-mongering," others insist that such critiques would prevent these practices from reaching populations that have a right to benefit from them.[70] The more persuasive refutation, however, comes from the increasing willingness of contemporary practitioners to "call out" mainstream yoga and meditation for their complicity with powerful institutions. The yoga world has seen an explosion of self-critique about yoga's "whiteness," its inaccessibility to poorer communities and communities of color, its leaning toward markers of privilege such as ableism, sexism, and heteronormative beauty-standards.[71] So too with American Buddhists who have started to look askance at largely white, middle-class *sanghas*, demanding that silences around difficult issues of systemic inequity be addressed.[72] The Black feminist scholar (and self-identified Buddhist) bell hooks bluntly states that "the politics of race and class exclusion permeates the dissemination of Buddhist thought in West."[73] Perhaps most telling is a public dialogue in which the Black feminist abolitionist Angela Davis presses Jon Kabat-Zinn to acknowledge the gap between the deeply personalized practices he promotes and the lack of attention to structural injustice. Kabat-Zinn's attempts to respond are embarrassingly awkward, flailing, and inadequate. He laughs nervously, and eventually sheepishly acknowledges that he has no real response: "That may be my white privilege? I don't know."[74] As this exchange demonstrates, a powerful movement has recently emerged, in which politically attuned practitioners have begun to hold communities accountable for the dangers of neoliberal appropriation.

The New Yoga and Meditation: Socially Engaged Service and Revolution

In recent years, some practitioners have taken inspiration from a movement dubbed "socially engaged" Buddhism, which "engages actively yet nonviolently with the economic, political, social, and ecological problems of society."[75] For socially engaged Buddhists, "authentic Buddhism" necessitates "attempts to change the nature of society,"[76] addressing the social and systemic causes of suffering—such as militarism, racism, inequality, poverty, and environmental degradation—in addition to the personal ones. Socially engaged Buddhism is thought to have originated in social justice movements in Asian countries. Famous examples include Thich Nhat Hanh's nonviolent opposition to the Vietnam war, Sulak Sivaraksa's prodemocracy movement in Thailand, and the Sarvodaya Shramadana movement in Sri Lanka.[77] Sivaraksa, for instance, is emphatic that Buddhism is not concerned merely with "private destiny," but rather with the "lives and consciousness of all beings." Any attempt to understand it apart from its social dimension is, he claims, "fundamentally a mistake."[78] Buddhists inspired by this movement insist, therefore, that mindful practices must go far beyond personal well-being, to be "inclusive of social, economic, and environmental concerns . . . this includes the reality of unhealthy working conditions, low wages, and environmental destruction."[79]

Many contemporary Western practitioners call themselves "socially engaged," but their efforts often fall into the realm of service, educational, and humanitarian work, without taking any firm political stand on the sources of suffering in those realms. Many who identify as "engaged" Buddhists or yogis are involved in ameliorative work: addressing suffering through social service and welfare projects, or ministering to socially disadvantaged groups. This includes a wide variety of service projects such as soup kitchens, food pantries, homelessness services, environmental work, educational work, and health and wellness services. Many of these projects are ethically motivated: They entail assisting the oppressed, and thus addressing racial and economic inequities.

But as noble and necessary as such work is, it seeks to improve the lives of individuals, or the relationships of groups to one another, without challenging the underlying, established power structures that allow injustice to continue. Making the world more "humane" or "peaceful"—important as it is—does not necessarily address the causes of structural injustice. Reducing suffering is deeply worthy and humanitarian work, but is not always revolutionary or politically activist—it may be service-oriented, but it can leave intact the political structures that cause suffering. Scholar-activists like Bhikkhu Bodhi and Sivaraksa insist that meditative practices alone are not sufficient to bring about social or political transformation; the vow to liberate fellow beings from suffering must go beyond training the individual mind, to transforming oppressive social systems.[80] In other words, ethical motivation alone does not seem to guarantee a revolutionary politics. To be truly revolutionary, social justice work would have to take on aspects of society and politics that systematically produce inequities. Absent an ability to address these systemic issues, many forms of "socially engaged" yoga or meditation are ameliorative, but not transformative: They can serve as band-aids or tools for "improvement," but do not revolutionize anything through political critique or challenge.

I make this distinction between ameliorative and transformative work[81] not in order to dismiss the importance of ameliorative work—there should be no doubt that it is highly valuable. But newer versions of activist yoga and meditation have emerged, which address suffering in truly revolutionary and transformative ways. These movements not only seek to serve marginalized populations but also insist on political challenge, critique, and resistance. They oppose structures that perpetuate inequity in all forms, including racism, patriarchy, ableism, homophobia, mass incarceration, consumer capitalism, food inequity, and environmental degradation, to name just a few. They do not simply offer yoga and meditation as tools for people to adjust better to an unjust world; rather, they offer them as ways to both cope with and eventually transform that world, to make it more just and equitable.

Take, for instance, the case of newer yoga movements. Until recently, yoga has not been particularly socially engaged or progressive, either in its Indian context, or in the West.[82] But the North American yoga world has recently seen the emergence of politically progressive groups that address questions of justice. An excellent example is the organization "Off the Mat into the World," which conducts trainings to use yoga as a vehicle to challenge and dismantle systems of power, through the study of "prejudice, oppression, and privilege."[83] Systemic patterns of trauma are investigated with an eye toward their linkage with marginalization and oppression, so that poverty, racism, ableism, [and] homophobia are studied as factors in (re)producing trauma.[84] Such organizations are still in the minority, but are steadily growing.

Racial oppression and class inequity are also being confronted by practitioners of meditation, particularly Black feminists and other Buddhists of color.[85] The Black Buddhist teacher angel Kyodo Williams challenges the idea that meditators must remain neutral on difficult political issues. Only the privileged, she points out, can afford the luxury of "not taking sides": oppressed persons cannot afford *not* to take sides, since their very survival may be at stake.[86] For these activists, reducing suffering requires taking a stand on these issues, rather than relegating them to the realm of "karma" or "worldly impermanence," or remaining content with "awareness" and "acceptance." Mindful, compassionate exploration must be accompanied by critical inquiry into one's experiences, beliefs, and value systems[87] as well as action. These practitioners are encouraged not just to "sit with" the discomfort of oppression and privilege through meditative praxis, but also to envision and enact resistance. In fact, the American monk Bhikkhu Bodhi bluntly states, "If, from fear of upsetting others, [Buddhist] teachers shy away from addressing these critical matters, their silence could even be considered an abdication of their responsibility."[88] Political disputes about power, privilege, and oppression are "burning ethical issues" on which practitioners, Bodhi says, "should take a stand."[89] Anne Gleig writes about several Buddhist-inspired communities in North America doing exactly this: the Insight Meditation Community of Washington (IMCW), the East Bay Meditation Center (EBMC) in Oakland, and the Buddhist Peace Fellowship (BPF). These organizations clearly center issues such as racial injustice, oppression, and inequity in their mission statements, sometimes meeting resistance from their own members. As a result, some members walk out of dharma talks, insisting that they "[did] not come to hear about politics," while others question why such divisive issues that "cause anger" should be emphasized in meditative settings.[90] Despite these challenges, leadership by members of minority groups is encouraged and fostered, as is addressing structural injustice and oppression within the community setting. Meanwhile, members of privileged groups—such as white practitioners—attend trainings in which they examine their own racial conditioning and biases.[91] One of these organizations leads a year-long training program for transformative social action, in which meditative practices assist activists in bringing about sociopolitical and systemic change.[92] Another group sees direct nonviolent action and civil disobedience as a necessary extension of spiritual practice, staging sit-ins and blockades to protest issues such as racialized police violence, and conducting civil disobedience trainings for practitioners to negotiate "righteous anger" with skillful political action.[93]

Besides race, economic inequity is another important focal point: American Buddhists have not only actively supported the Occupy movement, they have also been heavily involved in offshoot movements focused on fair wages and tax policies, supporting labor unions, limiting the power of corporations, and buying defaulted debt.[94] The Buddhist Peace Fellowship, meanwhile, insists that "urgent social problems like poverty, climate change and racism will not be resolved unless we challenge and transform the oppressive and exploitative social structures which are key contributors to these problems."[95] To this end, the organization has taken a strong stand against policing and prisons: It exhorts its members to "stop calling the police when it is clearly unnecessary," to educate themselves about alternatives to police and prisons, to attend local protests against policing whenever possible, and to "radically rethink what community safety means," building communities based on repair and restoration, rather than punishment and incarceration.[96] Each of these communities displays an exemplary "shift from the individual to the collective," confronting collective social and political issues head-on, while rejecting the idea that personal spiritual progress alone is adequate for this.[97]

As a result, yogic and meditative practices have gone beyond being part of a personal self-care and wellness regimen, to becoming a political resource, because they "[put] practitioners in a more powerful place from which to address" injustice.[98] Here, self-care is not presented as the coddling of a luxurious lifestyle involving spas, massages, and other self-nurturing activities pitched to those with disposable income. This version turns self-care into a commodity, assigning responsibility for wellness to individuals, or turning self-care into a sedative for coping, while ignoring systemic inequities.[99] Instead, a new generation of activists see self-care not as a luxury but as a political act,[100] designed to provide them with the physical and mental sustenance to struggle against oppressive systems. Caring for oneself, Audre Lorde insisted, is not an act of indulgence, but rather "an act of warfare," particularly for those who have spent generations in servitude while their own bodies were deemed expendable.[101] Yogic and meditative practices have become central resources in this activist tool-kit of "self-care as warfare." For instance, daily meditations and yoga classes were woven throughout the Occupy movements of 2011, offered to facilitate communication among organizers, especially as the challenges of democratic decision-making intensified.[102] The EBMC leader Mushim Patricia Ikeda requires her students to commit to a vow of self-care while working to create a more just world, guarding against exhaustion and burnout.[103] These examples are only the tip of the iceberg: In many activist movements, yoga and meditation are now taught as means for individuals to maintain their own physical, emotional, and spiritual health, precisely so that they can work against oppressive power structures.

Self-Cultivation without Co-Optation

The new, revolutionary yoga and meditation show us that accepting injustice or becoming submissive is not the only outcome of these practices: Powerful institutions may structure our choices, but we do have choices to both see and act differently.[104] We need not throw out the "baby" of self-cultivation with the neoliberal "bathwater" of docility or compliance. Capacities like acceptance, choice, and responsibility for self-cultivation can be combined with ethical virtues prized by yogic and meditative traditions, so that they can be employed for social justice rather than appropriated by conservative forces. How precisely might this work?

One important ability fostered by these practices is that of "seeing differently," unsettling or unwinding our "default modes of perception."[105] Powerful structures rely on conventional narratives and ways of seeing, which need to be disrupted in order for existing arrangements to be challenged. Often, scholars point out, meditative and yogic practices can create a new kind of attentiveness to ourselves and the world around us, allowing us to stand apart from our own thoughts, without becoming so enmeshed within them.[106] This "witness-consciousness," as some call it, can have ripple effects outward. It can allow us to observe how the world operates without reacting habitually, seeing it more clearly and critically. In turn, this can give us insight into the nature of established institutions that control narratives about the world, rather than being mindlessly driven by circumstance or previous history or beliefs.

Self-cultivation through such expansive awareness can become a force for critique, when directed by either yogic or Buddhist virtues. Take, for instance, Patañjali's yogic virtues such as *satya* or truth, *brahmachārya* or self-control, and *aparigraha* or renunciation of possessions. These values can lead us to critically examine and reject the focus on consumerism and purely physical self-improvement often promoted by yoga in North America. Directed by these values, self-discipline might lead to a truthful inward gaze reflecting on how consumer desires are shaped by powerful forces in society, perhaps contemplating how to detach from such desires as the route to fulfillment. These values are also central to the engaged Buddhist toolkit: Bhikkhu Bodhi calls for increased scrutiny of our quest to satisfy desires, and the constant stimulation of craving. This can allow us to become more aware of the consumerist economic order upheld by powerful structures that exploit both people and natural resources, seeing them as nothing more than sources of financial profit, to be discarded when they are no longer useful or valuable.[107]

Another important capacity fostered by these practices is that of skillful action. Activist practitioners insist that the equanimity, radical acceptance, and nonjudgment promoted by yogic and Buddhist traditions are by no means excuses for inaction. Rather, they become the foundation for the virtue of skillful action. The scholar of race Rhonda Magee notes that nonjudgment must be distinguished from discernment: the considered, deliberative evaluation of any situation that is necessary in order to alleviate suffering.[108] The yogic tradition refers to this discernment as *viveka*, and along with radical acceptance, this discernment leads to skillful action. Before one can act in a skillful way, they should have a clear and accurate idea of what they are up against. The cultivation of skillful means (*upāya*) allows us to respond appropriately, expressing righteous convictions with compassion and without alienating others, while also maintaining equanimity in the face of opposition.[109] The Buddhist feminist Rita Gross points out that skillfully responding to sexism required her to change not her opposition to it, but the aversion and attachment with which she had typically responded: through meditative practice, anger eventually transmuted into the clarity of critical intelligence required for skillful response.[110] The *Bhagavad-Gītā* refers to *karma-yōga*: selfless, disciplined action according to ethical duty on behalf of the common good. One interpreter tells us that this "involves mustering our best selves to meet the overwhelming challenges of our times."[111] In other words, it requires skillful choices in a world of difficulty and uncertainty, for collective welfare.

Finally, yogic and meditative practices can be combined with—and put in service of—nonviolent political action. The virtue of *ahimsā* (nonviolence) is paramount in both yogic and Buddhist teachings. Although classically it was interpreted to mean noninjury or nonharming, it was radicalized by modern spiritual activists such as Gandhi (and many others) into civil disobedience and other forms of direct protest against injustice. Contemporary social movements based on nonviolence—such as the Occupy movement—have also employed yogic and meditative practices to cement movement discipline. These practices attune activists to emotions like fear and anger as they arise, creating a mental space between emotion and action, and allowing for appropriate—rather than purely instinctive—responses.[112] Meanwhile, Gandhi noted that strong bodies and strong minds, cultivated through relentless yogic discipline, were better able to withstand the retaliations and sacrifices that inevitably accompanied nonviolent resistance.[113]

Yogic and meditative practices can promote a kind of self-development or self-cultivation that fosters a critical perspective on the world, rather than an inclination to simply accept conventional ways of seeing. This self-development can in turn allow us to make meaningful choices, rather than simply being propelled by our conditioning, or by the cultural messaging we are prone to. Instead of withdrawing into an inward-oriented bubble and accepting patterns of oppression, exclusion, and injustice as an excuse for inaction—or as part of some "higher" meaning or purpose that we must surrender to— these practices can foster thoughtful, skillful awareness, and possibly even action. Meanwhile, the capacities and actions these practices foster can be liberating, in keeping with democratic values: It can be empowering for individuals to understand their social environment more accurately, and feel empowered to think into it critically, possibly even devising skillful action (within the constraints they face).

Conclusion

Many commentators have claimed that practices such as yoga and meditation will *automatically* induce people to act more ethically, because compassion, empathy, reduced aggression and prosocial conduct are already implied in these practices.[114] This leads to the fantasy that mindful (or yogic) individuals will automatically create a more mindful (or yogic) world. One critic calls this "laissez-faire" mindfulness, and points out that the emphasis on practices like "nonjudgmental awareness," can "just as easily disable one's moral intelligence"[115] when not accompanied by moral inquiry, ethical commitments, and visions of the social good.

Teaching people to detach themselves from the flow of their thoughts and judgments is just as likely to bring about acceptance of the world as it is, causing people to remain "neutral" on political questions and allowing powerful interests and institutions to continue their dominance. Alternatively, it can suggest that "working on oneself" is the main goal, allowing people to cultivate more wellness and resilience in order to function better within deeply inequitable systems. These practices are often invoked to suggest that if we are "mindful, calm, hardworking, and disciplined" enough, we can "be happy regardless of . . . the reality of suffering and oppression."[116] These warnings suggest that the social and political force of these practices cannot be left to "automatic" development; they must be married to activist commitments—along with serious social and political education[117]—in a deliberate way.

We should care about how yoga and meditation are taught in prisons precisely because of the possibilities outlined in the chapter, which show how these practices can be co-opted, particularly when they are taught to the most vulnerable and marginalized among us. Yoga and meditation are thought to encourage a vaguely countercultural outlook among their practitioners in the West: In the popular imagination, they are associated with less individualistic cultures of Asia, which are supposedly more "peaceful" and "nonviolent" compared to the West. For this reason, it may seem like a no-brainer to bring these practices into prisons. But these stereotypes ignore the very real danger that these practices can also foster docility and compliance, teaching people to accept an unjust or miserable reality by seeing it largely as the result of their own individual pathologies, rather than of broader structural oppression.

Scholars remind us that these contemplative practices do not operate in a vacuum; instead, they absorb culturally available ideas and values, which direct them toward certain goals and give them certain meanings.[118] The way these practices "work," especially on an everyday level, depends on the norms that are predominant within the cultures they operate in.[119] If they are imported into cultural contexts where neoliberal logic predominates, the goals and purposes of these practices may shift to bend toward that logic.[120] So too with the authoritarian contexts of total control, such as prisons: The goals of these practices may shift to accommodate the prison's logic. Those practicing yoga and meditation in prisons in the United States in the twenty-first century may be taught to easily adjust to the goals of the prison system: compliant toward the logic that they must improve themselves because their incarceration is always their own responsibility, and thus better-adjusted to their miserable fates as likely targets of an oppressive carceral regime.

Some readers might find these dangers of co-optation to be overstated, excessively polemical or one-dimensional.[121] Indeed, scholars do suggest that we need more understanding of the lived experiences of actual practitioners. This book undertakes precisely such an investigation through interviews and ethnography: Once we speak to those who actually teach and learn these practices inside prisons, do we find that the dangers of co-optation are borne out in their lived experience? Like so many other forms of service work, yoga and meditation in prisons may see itself as "socially engaged." But is it truly revolutionary if it *only* helps people cope better—and comply—with an unjust system, without providing resources for acknowledging (and perhaps even addressing) this injustice?

What follows in this book gives us cause for some concern, but also some cautious optimism. In the interviews, ethnography, and personal experiences that follow, I detail the patterns of both co-optation and resistance that I have discussed in this chapter. In many instances, I found that yoga and meditation were being taught to incarcerated persons—often unwittingly—in a way that promoted compliance toward the prison's logic, namely, that their own individual defects caused their own suffering. I found many incarcerated persons wholeheartedly embracing that logic, without going any further. But I also found small pockets of resistance where yoga and meditation were being offered—and received—as ways to critically analyze the root causes of the suffering caused by unjust structures. Self-cultivation was certainly being practiced, but with a very specific emphasis: acceptance, equanimity, and nonjudgment went along with awareness of the social, political, and structural causes of incarceration, and of the unjust nature of the law enforcement and prison systems. In fact, yogic and meditative practice sometimes entailed skillful discernment of the patterns at work in these systems, without getting caught up in habitual reactivity.

Occasionally, through writing and discussion, I saw incarcerated persons develop new forms of awareness and new kinds of attentiveness to the world around them, that went far beyond their default modes of perception. Even if this did not necessarily lead to outright political resistance and action—and most often, it did not—it allowed practitioners to *feel* more free, more liberated, and more human, despite being caged and controlled by a system that consistently undermined their humanity. I saw and heard from incarcerated practitioners who began to develop keener awareness of how oppression worked both inside prison walls and beyond it, paying attention consciously to these painful experiences and memories, instead of denying or repressing them. I heard from people who used these practices to illuminate their previous conditioning and negative self-beliefs, grappling with the knowledge that their incarceration was not simply a result of their own defective actions. I heard and learned from incarcerated people who reported feeling genuinely empowered, not simply because they were taking individual responsibility for self-improvement, but because they were able to articulate the ways in which social, political, and legal arrangements constrained their ability to "simply choose not to commit crimes."[122]

The lessons of tolerating physical discomfort during the practice of yoga postures were sometimes geared toward building strength to face challenge, rather than simply being passive or docile. Not all of this translated to actual political activism, whether during or after incarceration (in fact, we will soon learn more regarding the dangers of activism in prison). But I did learn about—and even witness—shifts in consciousness that resulted in a more resistant mindset. Much of the service work I saw happening in prisons was largely ameliorative—it served incarcerated persons, but often by giving them "self-help" tools to cope and comply with the regime that governed them. Yet, I also saw glimmers of hope that were transformative, when yogic and meditative practices became resources to better understand, navigate—and occasionally work toward changing—a world that seemed stacked against them.

SECTION II
GOING INSIDE: THE WORLD
OF PRISONS

4

The Total Institution

The World of Mass Incarceration, Prisons, and Population Control

Before we consider how yoga and meditation are taught or received in prisons, it is important to understand the terrain of the prison itself: how exactly are prisons organized? What do they look, sound, and feel like? How does the space work, and what practices are used, to control and corral both bodies and minds? In this chapter, I describe what scholars have called the "total institution" nature of prisons, mapping and visualizing them for readers. I take readers inside this world using interview data, as well as scholarly and journalistic resources. I examine both punitive and so-called rehabilitative practices in prisons, showing how they each serve as a facet of its population-control project. In particular, I consider the commonly held view that what happens in prisons must be necessary, and therefore legitimate or justifiable. I offer a more nuanced understanding of who ends up in prisons, and how violence is produced by prisons themselves, in order to re-examine these conventional views. Finally, I argue that the problem with prisons is not simply that they are violent and dehumanizing (although this is certainly a crucial problem). Most people—including those who volunteer in prisons with the intention of "helping"—continue to believe that reforming prisons means making them more humane, by offering therapeutic tools to transform individuals. But here I show that even so-called humane and therapeutic practices, such as rehabilitative programs, despite seeming "kinder and gentler," can serve as a breeding ground for deep alienation, humiliation, subordination, and inequity.

Rehabilitative programming in prisons can serve an educational function, disseminating messages that accentuate the marginalization of people from poor and/or minority communities, reiterating their second-class status, and encouraging their compliance toward the system. As such, they are part and parcel of the population-control project, a fact that remains largely obscured from view. Yet, I end by suggesting that this need not be the only option. Volunteers who enter prisons can subvert the prison's logic, when they are self-conscious in thinking critically about how to engage with incarcerated persons, and offering programming that counteracts the prison's narratives.

Freedom Inside?. Farah Godrej, Oxford University Press. © Oxford University Press 2022.
DOI: 10.1093/oso/9780190070083.003.0004

All of this forms the context into which prison yoga and meditation programs enter. Rather than assuming, therefore, that yoga and meditation are always unequivocally beneficial in the prison context, we might pay closer attention to the specific *type* of rehabilitative program and *how* it is disseminated. This complex terrain must be fully considered and navigated by those who purport to bring healing, therapeutic programs such as yoga and meditation to incarcerated persons.

Mass Incarceration: The World of Prisons and "Population Control"

Many scholars now use the term "carceral state" to describe the United States, referring to its apparatus of law enforcement and criminal punishment, along with its ever-growing network of parole, probation, community sanctions, drug courts, and detention institutions that police, cage, and control more than 8 million people through a variety of supervisory mechanisms. This network of facilities is often called the "carceral continuum" or "carceral archipelago," as the carceral state "metastasizes"[1] and extends its supervisory reach far beyond jails or prisons.[2]

There is general consensus that the current system disproportionately incarcerates members of marginalized communities. Beyond that, however, there is debate about whether race, class, or other factors are determinative in expanding the prison population. Many follow Michelle Alexander's now-seminal *The New Jim Crow*, which argues that the criminal-legal system functions as a system of racial control, replacing slavery and Jim Crow–era laws, fueled by the War on Drugs that targeted Black men and destroyed Black communities.[3] But others argue that while racial animus and white supremacy were clearly key factors in the development of the system, its policies and practices have "migrated to other dispossessed groups."[4] James Forman Jr. argues that because 60% of prisoners are not Black and a third are in fact white, we must pay attention to factors beyond race, such as class.[5] The criminalization of poverty is a compelling explanation for Loïc Wacquant, who argues that mass incarceration is a punitive strategy for containment and disciplining of the poor, the "management of dispossessed populations" uprooted when low-wage manufacturing jobs migrated overseas and unskilled labor became redundant, leaving large swaths of the population unemployed.[6] In a capitalist society, prison "functions as a reservoir for the underemployed, unemployed," and others at the bottom of the socioeconomic order.[7] The geographer Ruth Wilson Gilmore argues that entire regions became economically dependent on prisons to absorb the surplus land and labor displaced by economic restructuring.[8] Many of these facts were reflected in my own work in and around prisons: The overwhelming majority of the incarcerated and formerly incarcerated people I met came from disadvantaged communities, whether by virtue of race or poverty. And, although I did not spend as much time with correctional officers, my occasional conversations confirmed that many came from the same socioeconomic categories as people who were imprisoned: largely working-class Black, Latinx, or other immigrant communities, in which a unionized prison job was one of the few decent options for those with a high-school diploma.[9] Prisons, it seems, are spaces to funnel society's undesirables from two different ends: a way to control and contain them, but also to appoint many of their fellow community members to undertake the work of controlling and caging.

Other important explanations for mass incarceration are rooted in legal structures. Alexandra Natapoff argues that misdemeanor policing and arrests constitute a tool of social control that exacerbates racial inequities in law enforcement, convicting thousands of people (often wrongfully) through laws that criminalize minor offenses such as loitering, jaywalking, open containers, or disorderly conduct.[10] John Pfaff argues we must look primarily at the role of prosecutors, who receive political incentives for overcharging and oversentencing. They are given virtually limitless powers known as "prosecutorial discretion," including pressuring (sometimes coercing) defendants into plea-bargains, which account for resolution in 95% of criminal cases.[11] One standard narrative suggests that public defenders are overwhelmed enough to encourage these plea-bargains. But this minimizes the systemic disadvantaging of defendants in the legal system: Many factors, including the rules of evidence, are weighted so far against the defendant and defender such that going to trial typically makes the defendant worse off.[12] Those who invoke the right to trial and lose face exponentially higher sentences than ones offered in plea deals, making plea agreements an offer many defendants cannot "afford to refuse."[13] Again, this ensures that those without resources routinely plead guilty and are incarcerated at vastly disproportionate rates. In the next chapters, readers will meet people whose life-stories illustrate the devastation these patterns wrought—people like Danny, who was threatened with multiple life sentences for a crime that involved no injury to any victims; Alex, who was targeted by prosecutorial discretion and overcharging, threatened with a life-sentence for an attempt to recover his own property from a former rental residence; and Lucas, who was pressured into a plea-bargain through the threat of charges in cases he had no involvement in, as prosecutors started "stacking charges, trying to find something that would stick."[14]

The sociologist Erving Goffman argued that prisons are "total institutions": they have all-encompassing tendencies and are separated off from the rest of society. They are closed social systems that require permission to both enter and leave, and they exist to resocialize people into changed identities or roles.[15] They are places of surveillance and control, where the movements of those incarcerated are highly restrained and monitored, and where resistance, dissent, or challenge of any kind—physical, verbal, or otherwise—is immediately suppressed, often with violence. Marie Gottschalk refers to US prisons as authoritarian or semiauthoritarian, comparing them most closely to the mode of governing in China after the Cultural Revolution.[16] Incarcerated persons have described them as containing multiple forms of tyranny,[17] and many describe a phenomenon called "institutionalization" which results from years of incarceration: becoming so thoroughly identified with being controlled by the institution that one internalizes its perspective, unable to think for oneself, make decisions, or act without permission.[18] "You get so used to being governed," says Danny, who served twenty-one years. "You've been told 24/7 what to do. I'm at loss sometimes. . . . Even when I go to a restaurant, I find myself just waiting for instructions, or I'll still ask people if I can use the restroom [laughs]."[19]

Much scholarship shows us how prisons do the work of "disappearing abnormal outsiders":[20] In this category, immigrants and mentally ill persons are subjected to increasing levels of criminalization and incarceration. "Crimmigration" refers to the blurring of criminal laws with immigrations laws, as harsher sanctions are imposed on non-US citizens for various civil infractions.[21] The US Border Patrol is the nation's second-largest police force, and immigrant detention—the process of forcibly confining immigrants during deportation proceedings—is now the largest system of caging operated by the US government.[22] Meanwhile, up to half of the people in US prisons are thought to suffer from mental illness.[23] Those with mental illness may remain incarcerated for four to eight times longer than others—as a result, urban jail systems in major cities are now the largest psychiatric care providers in the nation.[24] Jails and prisons are now said to serve as warehouses for the mentally ill; yet incarceration "routinely makes mentally ill people worse . . . [and] renders stable people psychiatrically unwell."[25] There are harrowing accounts of the ways in which policing and imprisonment compound the effects of mental illness, and of the medieval conditions that await mentally ill persons in US prisons. Patrice Cullors, cofounder of Black Lives Matter, details the intersection of poverty, race, and disability that resulted in her mentally ill brother emerging from encounters with police and jails "a brutalized man":[26] stripped, beaten, starved, tased, kicked, and humiliated for reactions triggered by his schizophrenia, deprived of dignity and repeatedly forced back into a system that kept multiplying the seriousness of charges resulting from each episode of mental breakdown.[27]

In his extensive interviews with incarcerated persons, Joshua Price reveals that incarceration is characterized by three basic qualities: generalized humiliation, institutionalized violence, and isolation and severance from families and communities of support, which recalls the forced separation of slavery.[28] Poor healthcare—or withholding of adequate healthcare—is rampant, routine, and institutionalized, while incarcerated persons are treated with indifference and sometimes antipathy: ignored, shunted aside, and "treated as garbage," according to one.[29] Prison violence is not limited to intentional physical abuse by correctional officers or other incarcerated persons: It includes "institutionalized forms of mistreatment" such as pat-downs, cavity searches, and shackling, among others.[30] Keramet Reiter demonstrates how the "total institution" nature of prisons is exacerbated by administrators' lack of accountability to the public, courts, and legislators. Prisons, she notes, resist admitting researchers, journalists, and any others who might investigate prison conditions and provide for public oversight.[31] American prisons also lack legal accountability: once-robust court oversight is now highly limited by both judicial precedent and federal legislation. This includes laws that actively discourage prisoners from bringing lawsuits to challenge their conditions of confinement.[32]

Mapping and Visualizing Prisons

What exactly are contemporary prisons and jails like? How are they laid out, how does the space work to control and manage people, and what do these spaces look, smell, sound, and feel like? Academic research on US prisons has become increasingly rare over the past few decades: Prisons are structurally and bureaucratically closed off, resistant to academic investigation, and as a result, rendered largely invisible to the public eye.[33] Direct accounts of conditions in US prisons come from a variety of sources: essays and memoirs by those who have been incarcerated,[34] along with the journalistic and academic accounts discussed in Chapter 2. As we have seen, there is a vibrant intellectual tradition of writing by incarcerated persons, although it is largely marginalized and ignored by the wider academic and literary worlds. Even though these writings tell us much about the life and thought of incarcerated persons, there are still precious few sources that take us inside contemporary prisons, giving us a sense of their architecture, rules, sights, sounds, smells, norms, and cultures. Of course, popular culture gives us many standard accounts of what it feels like to enter a prison—steel doors clanging shut behind you, bodies locked in cells behind bars—but in "real" life, prisons are far less uniform. Some facilities are located in windowless high-rise buildings in the middle of cities, with people packed into floors full of housing units stacked atop one other; others are spread out across open land in rural or suburban areas, containing courtyards dotted with a mishmash of trailers and low-rise brick or cinderblock buildings which serve as housing units and administrative offices.[35] Almost all accounts note that prisons are loud places where doors constantly slam and shouts echo throughout, and the surroundings are almost uniformly drab, gloomy, and run-down: peeling, chipped paint, water stains, scuffed concrete or linoleum floors, barbed-wire fencing, and little natural light indoors. These spaces are almost always byzantine by design, full of mazes difficult to navigate, and virtually impossible to remember at first glance without a map. And, incarcerated persons universally describe the food served to them as SOS or "shit on a shingle": gloppy, brown, food items made from industrial ingredients designed to feed large masses of people cheaply, on average for less than $3 per person per day. One report calls this the "hidden punishment" of food, which gets relatively little attention: bologna sandwiches, mystery meats slathered on white bread, soy filler masquerading as chicken, and many other items, which instill a "nearly universal sense of disgust."[36]

I learned about this range and variety of institutional settings from personal experience, as well as from interviews with fellow prison volunteers (described in further detail in Chapters 7 and 8). Some of my interviewees had experiences with both jails and prisons, while others had only taught in one or the other. Having volunteered in both, the differences between the two eventually became clearer to me. Jails are county-level facilities run by local sheriff's departments and located in areas adjacent to courthouses. They typically house those who are awaiting trial, sentencing, pretrial bail hearings, or other forms of administrative processing, as well as those serving shorter sentences. Prisons, in contrast, are state-run facilities, typically located outside urban areas, and providing long-term housing for those who are convicted and sentenced.[37] Prisons, one volunteer notes, are more horizontal, while jails are vertical. Prisons tend to be spread out over relatively open space, with low-rise buildings: "There's grounds, there's a rec area, there's a picnic area, there's a basketball court, there's grass," she says. Another describes a women's prison in this way: "it's bungalows in a circle around a big grassy yard, and the women would be walking in groups of two's or three's or five's, or they'd be sitting on the grass talking. It's like a campus.

Other than they're all wearing the same ugly outfits, you might think it's a school."[38] Meanwhile jails, due to their urban nature, tend to be located in denser buildings with little access to light or outdoor space: "they don't ever get outdoors so they have vitamin D deficiency," says one volunteer. For this reason, she reports hearing that incarcerated people much prefer to be sent to prisons to serve their sentence rather than spend time in county jails: "they say 'county time is hard time.'"

Beyond these simple distinctions, though, my respondents reported volunteering in a variety of settings, with many different types of popu- lations: juvenile hall facilities for children, including special units for populations such as pregnant teenagers or victims of sex-trafficking and prostitution (commercially sexually exploited children or CSEC); special units for populations such as sex offenders; those with "high medical needs"; those with mental illness; segregated LGBTQ populations; those over sixty; those in drug or alcohol rehabilitation units. In prisons and jails, classifica- tion is everything: How one is classified dictates what unit or section of the facility they end up in, and this in turn can have widely divergent impacts on the incarceration experience. For instance, the LGBTQ unit of the Men's Central Jail in Los Angeles County is known to be gang-free and much safer than other units—prison officials have had to screen out straight men who claim LGBTQ identity to keep away from gangs,[39] making the work of clas- sification more fraught.

Maximum- and medium-security prisons (or units) typically place a heavier emphasis on security and control, compared with the lower-level facilities. Many facilities house a variety of populations at different levels of security classification, in different units. Higher levels of security classifica- tion usually denote more violent offenders, incarcerated for the most violent crimes. Security classifications vary by facility: some use levels one to four, others use one to ten, and so on. As a rule, the higher number indicates a higher-risk population, although as we will see, the legal system allows many more people to be classified as "violent" than necessary. People are routinely reclassified for good behavior—California prisons, for instance, use a points system, and a drop in points due to consistently good behavior can lead even the most high-security offender (such as a "lifer") to be reclassified as lower- risk, and moved to a different unit or even a different prison. In fact, of all the formerly incarcerated persons I interview in Chapter 5, the vast ma- jority report serving their time in multiple prisons, and being moved around repeatedly.[40]

Several of the volunteers I interviewed taught yoga or meditation in high- security units, although the precise nature of these settings varied greatly.

One volunteer described teaching yoga to four select high-security offenders in freestanding cages in a maximum-security unit at her local jail:

> Four guys would be selected and brought out from their housing unit in hand-cuffs to a "rec room" that had four cages, each set up in advance with a yoga mat and blocks inside. This rec room had really dirty concrete floors, and maybe a few slivers of light coming in through small windows at the top of the wall. Each guy would be locked into one cage, then he would hold his hands out through the slot to be uncuffed. Then they would get on their mats, and I would roll out my mat on the floor outside the cages, and lead them in a yoga practice.

Other descriptions of high-security units are far less dramatic—one volunteer regularly teaches meditation in a variety of men's prisons divided by "yards": large open spaces segregated from one another by fences, and classified as levels one through four. He notes that he can "feel the tension in the air" and "the stress on the inmates' faces" when he is in the level-four yard. Most volunteers I spoke to, however, routinely taught in a variety of security levels, including the highest ones, without incident, and described these experiences positively.

Others taught in settings they described as less like prisons than "alternative schools." Jessica, a white woman in her forties who founded a yoga organization, describes her work teaching in an "an early-intervention program for young girls." Some facilities in this program are county-run detention centers, which end up funneling the girls into community-based treatment centers run by nonprofits upon release. She says some are "euphemistically called ranches or camps," describing them as "progressive, gender-responsive, homelike beautiful place[s]" or "therapeutic alternative day schools" where young teens are given help with substance abuse, through a "victim-centered, collaborative" approach in which staff are trained to be sensitized to the needs of the youth they work with. However, this positive report of a seemingly progressive incarceration experience was the exception in my interviews. Other volunteers who taught in youth facilities were far less impressed: Jade, a Black woman who taught in a youth facility for over a decade, reported that abusive behavior toward youth by facility staff was the norm, asking rhetorically: "Why do we [even] have 13-year old children locked up??" Another volunteer taught in a halfway house, a transitional facility where those who leave prison are required by courts to spend time in drug or alcohol programs before re-entering society. Here too, reports of the facility were largely positive: a homelike facility with lots of light, high ceilings, relatively nice décor, and food. Yet, this volunteer acknowledges that the facility is "in appearance not like a jail, but in reality, it is a jail"—the men are not allowed to leave the facility, and are monitored 24/7 through electronic ankle bracelets. This large variation in facilities underscores the fact that population control happens in a variety of settings that go far beyond what the traditional prison looks like, as the carceral state expands its reach well beyond prisons.[41]

Despite some commonalities, prisons in the United States—whether federal (Bureau of Prisons), state-, county-, or privately run—are characterized by a high degree of institutional variation. Correctional institutions are "categorized and run very differently on the basis of their security or custody levels, but even among prisons at the same level of custody, conditions of confinement can vary widely,"[42] making facilities fundamentally different from one another in crucial ways: physical layout, staffing levels, resources, correctional philosophy, and administrative leadership. The variety of administrative norms, techniques, rules, and regulation across jails and prisons is dizzying: Even within the same facility, what incarcerated persons can and cannot do, where they can and cannot move freely, can vary by unit, cell-block, or yard, to say nothing of the rules governing the movement and behavior of staff, volunteers, and other visitors.

I have volunteered in a variety of facilities, have visited several others, and experienced a wide range of settings and institutional cultures. I have walked through prison yards centered around massive lawns with trees, grass and even flower-beds, with incarcerated persons walking around relatively freely and waving to me, calling out hellos, sometimes chatting with heavily armed COs. I have taught yoga and meditation to people in large, well-ventilated rooms with a decent amount of natural light. I have also taught in facilities that were dank, dark, and claustrophobia-inducing, where my breath caught in my throat and my stomach clenched, as I fought the urge to gag at the rotting air that smelled of terrible food, sickness, and bodies in close confinement. I have taught male, female, and LGBTQ populations, and have volunteered in contexts where female volunteers have taught incarcerated men and vice-versa.[43] For the most part, however, my experience in prisons has been confined to what we might term "general population" areas—I have not been privy to the more intense control units such as maximum security or solitary-confinement areas.

Conditions in US Prisons: "Necessary" Violence for "Criminals"?

Arguably the most unique feature of US prisons is the rise of higher-security or "supermax" facilities and special housing units (SHUs—pronounced "shoe") in the last few decades. These special units, where people are segregated either due to their level of security classification or due to special needs,[44] are far more tightly monitored and controlled than general-population units, where people are not personally restrained and move about relatively freely (to jobs, educational and rehabilitative programs, religious worship, and other activities). Special areas for confinement and segregation are not new, but in recent years these special units have increasingly been used to "tighten up" through forms of severe exclusion and containment that go well beyond ordinary prison discipline.[45] Variously referred to as maximum security units, supermaximum prisons, special housing units, or control units, they are built to house and contain the so-called worst of the worst, described as "prisons within prisons" or a "black box within a black box," controlled environments that typically keep people in their cells twenty-three or more hours a day.[46] The conditions in these units may seem drastic, but as we will soon see, punitive and degrading treatment in US prisons is hardly confined to those deemed "the worst of the worst."

Scholars like Lorna Rhodes and Keramet Reiter give us a window into the conditions of confinement in this murky underbelly of the prison. They describe rows of bare, windowless, concrete-walled, 8' × 10' cells surveilled from a control booth, containing fluorescent lighting, concrete ledges with thin mattresses that serve as a bed, steel sink/toilet fixtures, and cement slabs for a desk/chair combination.[47] Inhabitants of these units spend at least 22 hours each day in these cells, where written materials and television access can be rare, and almost everything else is forbidden, including clocks. Rhodes describes the psychiatric control unit of a maximum-security prison thus: Each cell has a clear, thick plastic window and a solid steel door with a cuffport through which inmates must back their hands, in order to be cuffed (for exit) and uncuffed (for entry back into their cell). Looking inside the cells, she reports: "Most of the prisoners wear only their underwear. Some sleep on their concrete beds, or simply lie on them staring into space; others pace restlessly back and forth. Some gaze at us silently, others yell up and down the tiers to one another. Echoing in the hard-edged interior, their shouts are a blur of rage-saturated sound."[48] Incarcerated persons suggest that in order to fully understand their experience in these units, one should lock oneself into a small bathroom—or better yet a closet—and imagine the passage of hours, then days, then years, while communicating only with strangers in nearby closets by shouting out the door.[49] "It's pretty much like not living," reports one resident of a maximum-security unit, "[they] turn this into hell . . . make you go crazy . . . it's part of their psychological war that they inflict upon us."[50]

In her study of solitary confinement at California's Pelican Bay, Reiter tells us that some people can spend a decade or more in solitary confinement, without the simplest forms of contact such as a handshake or a hug—they "touch no grass, see no sunlight, and have no regular access to activities."[51] Not one of the five hundred people held in solitary at Pelican Bay for over a decade were held for specific crimes: Rather, officials alleged they were all dangerous gang affiliates, based on books, letters, tattoos, or drawings.[52] Academics who volunteer in prison education programs similarly report that some of their best students suddenly disappear into solitary confinement, often for violations as mundane as unauthorized piercings or smoking a joint.[53] Reiter notes that the decisions to place or to keep people in solitary confinement are not subject to review by judges, juries, or public officials. Although the worst forms of abuse seen in the early days—scalding, caging, beating, and shooting prisoners—have been replaced by more sanitized and rational means of control, prison officials continue to justify and make routine a practice that has been condemned as a form of torture by international human rights bodies including the United Nations.[54]

It is tempting to imagine that the harshest treatment in these supermax units is unusual or extraordinary, reserved only for the worst offenders. But I learned from interviewing both prison volunteers and formerly incarcerated persons—as well as through reading accounts of prison life—that abusive, degrading treatment and violations of basic rights and dignities are not restricted to supermax units: they appear to be the norm, no matter the type of prison or the offense for which one is incarcerated. As scholars have repeatedly argued, routine dehumanization and violence cannot be separated from punishment, as though they are somehow an anomaly or an aberration—rather, they are the very essence of punitive regimes. Many of the volunteers I interviewed used words such as "flawed," "corrupt," "barbaric" "degrading" and "abusive" to describe the ordinary units they volunteered in, describing the conditions as "inhumane." Reports ran the gamut from horrifying conditions, to demeaning treatment, to physical and mental abuse. Many referred to the system as "closed" and deeply resistant to transparency. The most common complaints were passed on by students about the conditions of confinement: overcrowding, filth, unhygienic conditions such as overflowing toilets, terrible food, and the absence of basic needs such as medical care; loud, chaotic living quarters where lights were left on through the night and disrupted sleep or insomnia were rampant; mattresses so thin and food so terrible that incarcerated students developed aches, pains, and other physical ailments; natural light deprivation and lack of access to the outdoors; degrading treatment (or worse, abuse) by correctional officers. Much of this is legally permissible (and even mandated), although there are also of course many forms of deprivation and abuse that are illegal, such as sexual assault by prison staff, which several research participants reported as a regular event. In addition to learning from research participants, I learned from many other sources about routine, legally permissible violations: I read about incarcerated women being forced to give birth while incarcerated, and being denied access to reproductive rights and healthcare.[55] Those who give birth while incarcerated almost immediately have newborns ripped from their arms, and are not allowed to hold or breastfeed them.[56] The trauma of separation from family is magnified by laws that allow for the termination of the parental rights of incarcerated persons—most often women—and the involuntary loss of children to adoption: Susan Burton refers to this nexus of prisons and child-welfare agencies as the "child-industrial complex."[57]

In particular, Joshua Price notes, "humiliation in prison is not merely pervasive: it is organized, institutionalized, routine, and largely legal."[58] Forms of routine sexualized humiliation such as public strip-searches and cavity searches are well documented and legally justified in the name of security.[59] In Chapter 9, one of my interview participants describes in detail the vaginal cavity-search all women were forced to undergo after visiting with their families.[60] Another participant, a prison volunteer, tells me her students describe to her a particularly humiliating aspect of the forced cavity-search: "[If] they have their period, they have to take their tampax out and stand there and be searched with blood coming down their legs."[61] Added to these are the compounded humiliation of being gawked at or ridiculed by staff and others during these moments. On top of these are layered everyday, routine forms of disrespect that incarcerated persons can face from staff, who sometimes refer to them in demeaning, derogatory terms such as "assholes," "dick-heads," and "criminals,"[62] "addicts," "crack-whores," and "liars."[63] Volunteers also describe students telling them about unfair treatment in matters such as employment. Morgan taught yoga in a unit where incarcerated women were "employed" to clean the floors, make food, and serve the lunches in the officers' cafeteria. However, she found out from her students that in lieu of actual wages, they were given two days off their sentence for every hour they worked. "I didn't even know that was legal," she said, in disbelief. The catch though, was this: "One misstep gets you kicked out . . . [and] if you got booted out you lost all that time, all of your service and all of that time spent working," essentially providing an endless supply of unpaid labor that kept the institution functioning.

Particularly egregious were reports of violations in the form of denial of basic medical care, and gross medical negligence. Courtney was an interview participant who, prior to serving as a meditation volunteer, had worked in the same jails with the ACLU as a licensed clinical social worker, tasked with assessing and making recommendations for people who complained they did not get access to adequate mental health treatment. Courtney found that denial of medical and psychiatric treatment was overwhelmingly the norm. She eventually became so appalled and frustrated that she reluctantly stopped doing this work: "I would meet someone, they would pour their heart out to me thinking that I would be able to help them, I would make a report, and in 9 out of 10 cases, nothing happened. [The jail staff] would say *'we don't have it in our records that this person has a mental illness, so they don't, as far as we're concerned.'*" As a clinical social worker, Courtney observed that her clients usually came out of jail in a "much worse state than they had entered in, many of them didn't receive their psych meds, they were traumatized in one way or another . . . there was basically no help while they were inside, they just lost ground on so many levels."[64]

Several volunteers reported that their students were sent to solitary confinement for no reason other than not being compliant enough toward correctional officers: "If you roll your eyes at [an officer] you can be sent to the hole and spend like a month there," says Courtney. "It's disciplinary, it's for [people] that are being asked to do something, and they might say *'fuck you, I'm not doing it.'*" Courtney describes the diet of "jute balls" given to some of her meditation students sent to solitary: "they're some kind of unidentifiable food that are rolled into these hard balls, they don't give them a lot of water while they're on this diet. . . . [One] woman told me that [those] on the diet were bleeding from their anuses because it was so hard and they weren't given liquids, so their systems couldn't digest the stuff." Like Courtney, a few volunteers I interviewed expressed frustration at being unable to help when their students complained to them of such treatment.

Prison administrators justify the use of harsh conditions—particularly in special facilities such as supermax and solitary confinement units—as necessary for security. They use the rhetoric of the "worst of worst," reinforcing the public perception that those incarcerated in American prisons require these forms of restraint, segregation, routinized humiliation, and invasive control, for the security of those who live and work inside prisons. Prisons are thought to house "violent psychopaths who plot constantly to subvert the rules of the institution"[65]—an argument made by prison staff and administrators, and repeated by media or policymakers. As a result, every person—including myself—who has contemplated volunteering inside prisons has initially grappled with some fear: Are prisons really full of wild-eyed criminals waiting for a chance to attack us? Will I be safe? But through my volunteer work and interviews, I quickly learned what many policy analysts have now established: that far too many people are unnecessarily and ineffectively incarcerated in the name of reducing violent crime, and that many of those incarcerated for ostensibly violent crimes can likely be released without threat to public safety.[66]

One report estimates that releasing the unnecessarily incarcerated (those held without a justifiable public-safety rationale), rethinking the length of sentences for violent offenders, and disaggregating what counts as violent crime would reduce the prison population by 39 percent.[67] The "unnecessarily incarcerated" include those held for crimes such as minor larceny, minor property crimes, minor fraud and forgery, simple assault, minor trafficking, minor burglary, and minor drug offenses. Violent crime also includes victims of domestic violence who kill abusers in self-defense,[68] and others whose crimes are context-based and thus unlikely to be repeated. Policy analysts also argue that lengthy sentences do not reduce violent crimes: Most violent offenders will typically "age out" of the propensity to commit crimes typical of young adults, as brain development, impulse control, and risk-management kick in.[69] Research shows that people convicted of violent acts have the lowest recidivism rate—the vast majority are not "inherently" violent or dangerous, and can be released far earlier than their sentences require.[70] I learned this firsthand when I got to know several yoga students who had served decades of a life-sentence for murders committed in their youth; they were among the most gentle and spiritually disciplined individuals I met. Other students (and, occasionally prison staff) informed me of their reputations for kindness and compassion, particularly through their mentoring of younger arrivals, and their involvement in other forms of service within the prison community.

Another issue is that the line between violent and nonviolent offenses is much harder to draw than we might think. Violent crime is often aggregated to lump together serious crimes such as rape or murder with lesser (sometimes victimless) offenses such as illegal gun possession, breaking and entering, purse snatching, or embezzlement.[71] The best illustration is provided by the felony murder law: Many states allow conviction for felony murder, for having been present during a homicide, "even if you never touched a weapon, let alone actually killed someone."[72] Chapter 5 will introduce us to Elizabeth, who served seventeen years of a life-sentence on a felony murder charge for being in a getaway car while her abusive boyfriend—also her pimp—was involved in an attempted murder. Like her, tens of thousands of people are thought to be serving life sentences without ever having committed a violent act. Meanwhile, a wide array of infractions are classified as "sex offenses"— everything from making obscene phone calls to urinating in public to consensual sex between teenagers is often treated in the same category as the rape of a child.[73] Threats to public safety are routinely cited as the rationale for incarceration, but there is plenty of evidence that the carceral state casts its net far wider than is required, unnecessarily classifying too many as violent, and keeping them incarcerated for far longer than necessary. Moreover, the evidence as to whether incarceration and prison-backed policing "meaningfully make us more secure" is "mixed at best, at least when the broader harmful effects of incarceration are accounted for."[74] As Allegra McLeod reminds us, the opportunity costs of achieving order maintenance through prison-backed criminal law enforcement and incarceration—that is, the costs of investing more resources in a dehumanizing and degrading punishment regime, at the expense of other methods not organized around punishment and prisons—are immense.[75]

This is particularly true, given that studies of violence in prison have found that it is the prison itself—rather than its inhabitants—which most often produces and exacerbates violence. Many of those construed as dangerous or "the worst of the worst" were none of those things when they first entered the system. Some were barely out of their teens when first imprisoned on lesser charges, eventually ending up in solitary or maximum-security units years later. Rhodes interviews one man in the psychiatric control unit who had a life-sentence, having come to prison at twenty after his third "strike." His worst offense was an assault during a robbery in which no one was killed. George Jackson was famously arrested at fifteen for petty theft, and incarcerated a few years later for stealing $70 from a gas station, a crime for which he received "one year to life" and spent the rest of his life incarcerated, repeatedly denied parole until his violent death at San Quentin a decade later. The legal scholar Sharon Dolovich studied different units inside a men's jail, demonstrating that in a rare unit where staff treated people with respect and decency and guaranteed their safety, violent behavior by incarcerated persons was rare. Meanwhile, in the same jail, units where guards were disrespectful, abusive, and refused to guarantee people's safety were characterized by far higher levels of violence. Like many scholars, Dolovich posits that prisons and jails are not violent because the people the state incarcerates are "naturally monstrous." Rather, prisons cultivate a "gladiator environment" in which a combination of fear, trauma, abuse, and official disregard—combined with lack of interest or ability in guaranteeing safety—compels incarcerated persons to resort to violence for the sake of security.[76] Prisons, she asserts, make prisoners and not the other way around.[77] Far from being "monsters who deserve what they get," people we incarcerate are "victims of a system that refuses to recognize those in custody as fellow human-beings."[78] As incarcerated persons remind us, "if you take a dog and put him in a corner . . . sooner or later this dog is going to come out biting, snapping"[79] . . . "You can't strip us of our humanity and then turn us loose."[80] These stories and studies underscore the fact that in many cases, the law and its institutions, such as prisons, produce the very "criminals" whom they purport to manage and contain,[81] often through widely documented abuse. For this reason, many criminologists assert that prisons are not effective at reducing criminal offending—on the contrary, they may promote offending behavior by damaging the psychological and emotional well-being of those they incarcerate.[82] On this topic, the noted prison researcher Mary Bosworth is blunt: "Administrators may sugarcoat it, but when all is said and done, prisons, as they currently operate, make people convicted of doing bad things worse."[83]

For some, this failure of the prison to contain violence is in fact part and parcel of its very functioning: the US criminal "justice" system makes the most sense if we understand it not as an apparatus to eliminate crime but rather designed to "project to the American public a visible image of the threat of crime."[84] The failure of the prison is a self-perpetuating cycle in which prisons produce criminals by violating and dehumanizing those who are incarcerated, while legal systems make their reentry into society increasingly difficult—all of which provides increased justification for more criminalizing, monitoring, and surveilling, both inside and outside prisons.[85]

In my years of regularly visiting prisons as a volunteer, I never once felt threatened by an incarcerated person, or worried about my own safety.[86] Even when I walked along cell-blocks or taught in areas classified as "high-security," all the incarcerated persons I encountered were quiet, respectful, and compliant. The catcalling, flashing of anatomy, waste-flinging, and other violent behaviors I was warned about never occurred. I saw many quiet, sad, or depressed people who looked lost or desperate, sometimes anxious or paranoid, but never hostile or threatening. If anything, I was occasionally forced to witness their humiliation—many recreational rooms, for instance, have open toilets which incarcerated persons are forced to use in full view if they need to go mid-class—leaving me saddened and embarrassed. Overwhelmingly, I was treated with respect and met with tremendous gratitude: Both men and women often called me "ma'am," shook my hand, and thanked me repeatedly for coming.

Yet, like several researcher-volunteers, I have "repeatedly confronted the dissonance between the [students] I came to know through my classes and the dangerous characters whom society imagines."[87] I have struggled to reconcile the injustice of mass incarceration with the question of whether some of my students (particularly the "lifers") have caused severe harm to others.[88] I have read both scholarly and journalistic accounts of prisons and jails as places of extreme violence and sexual abuse, where incarcerated persons perpetrate horrifically abusive acts on each other, including gang-rape and murder.[89] And, I have met many prison officials who have appeared considerate and caring rather than hostile or indifferent toward their charges—as well as the occasional prison employee who appeared to hold relatively critical views about the system. Incarcerated persons who privately report establishing friendly bonds with some staff confirm that many correctional workers are decent people doing difficult work which takes a harsh psychological toll.[90]

While I volunteered in prisons, I read work by anthropologists and ethnographers who warned of the need to remain "neutral" in prisons, avoiding the tendency to "take sides" or to overromanticize incarcerated persons.[91] Even the prison abolitionist Ruth Wilson Gilmore is clear that radical critics should not be so starry-eyed as to believe that no incarcerated person has ever caused harm.[92] I grappled incessantly with all of these issues, but continued to wonder about the usefulness of the "violent/nonviolent" distinction. It allows us to imagine that we can identify the "relatively innocent," those "deserving" of society's compassion and mercy—the "nonviolent" offenders, the addicts, the falsely accused[93]—while continuing to inflict "deserved" punishment on the rest, forgetting that many of them were unnecessarily marked as "violent" to begin with. It also obscures the complex nature of violence in disadvantaged communities, where people cycle through the roles of victim, witness, and offender, both suffering and perpetrating harm, often in order to survive.[94] This distinction does important work in justifying the continued existence of a system in which so many resources are invested in identifying, classifying, and containing—but ultimately also producing—those among us deemed the "worst of the worst."

Rehabilitation: A "Kinder, Gentler" Incarceration?

The more we recognize the violent nature of the prison itself, the more public discourse turns inevitably to the possibility of changes "that will produce a *better* prison system."[95] This too is a tempting move: to imagine that the problem with prisons is mainly that they are too violent and punitive, and that they must therefore be made kinder, gentler, and more humane via rehabilitation. Two kinds of arguments reveal how problematic this temptation is.

First, scholars have argued that "kinder, gentler" imprisonment is a contradiction in terms. The "routinized dehumanization" of imprisonment—which includes violent and violating practices such as lock-ups, body searches, and physical restraints—causes "more psychological damage than any in-prison therapy can ever cure."[96] Therapeutic attempts to reduce the pain and suffering of imprisonment are inevitably undermined by the punishing context itself. In other words, the suffering imposed by imprisonment is not an incidental or accidental aspect of the prison—it is in fact the very essence of prison-backed punishment.[97] Of course, less violence in prisons would undoubtedly render them more "habitable." But, as Allegra McLeod notes, the degradation associated with incarceration in the United States is at the heart of the structure of imprisonment.[98] One cannot expect therapeutic "rehabilitation" in a punitive institution where subhuman treatment is inherent to the experience of being incarcerated. Can providing for substance abuse programs, counseling, anger management, or yoga programs really make prisons more "humane" if the people attending these programs are also forced to submit to legally mandated shackling, invasive cavity-searches, and the many other violations described earlier? As one incarcerated person noted: "There ain't no way to think a man's rehabilitated if all that's being poured on him is more hate, more inequities."[99] In fact, a few of the prison volunteers I interviewed honed in on this right away: Even while expressing horror at what they heard or witnessed, they were at pains to point out that these horrors should not be seen as unfortunate side-effects. Rather, they were a product of the system's very design, which perverted any good intentions on the part of correctional staff: "there's a lot of rules and regulations that have to be followed," said one interviewee, "and the people who work in the prisons will be the first to tell you that many of them are ineffective. And yet they still have to jump through hoops . . . they abide by the rules and guidelines to get their paycheck . . . their job is to manage the population."

This leads us to the second and more crucial objection: What gets labeled as "rehabilitation" in prisons, while certainly humane in the sense of being nonviolent, is thought by many scholars to be a veiled population-control strategy.[100] Many incarcerated and formerly incarcerated scholars echo prison researchers who argue that so-called rehabilitative programming is part and parcel of a strategy for managing and controlling "undesirable" populations— such as persons of color and poor persons—under the guise of seeming more benevolent and therapeutic.[101] Rehabilitation is thought to have declined in prisons in the 1970s and 1980s, as "tough-on-crime" policies emphasized greater punitiveness and humane incapacitation. Although some have argued that rehabilitation has fallen out of favor in prisons in recent years—replaced with new technologies of surveillance, restraint, and population-management known as "warehousing"—others say that rehabilitation, far from disappearing, is alive and well, and has simply been reconfigured as a tool of social engineering in prisons,[102] to "hammer, bend, fold, [and] shape" the inhabitant of the prison.[103] As one incarcerated scholar writes: The goals of the "prison machine [are] limited to ensuring obedience and conformity."[104] Rehabilitative programs are "systems of knowledge and technologies that attempt to shape . . . modes of thinking and ways of being," determining "institutionally approved" behavior.[105]

Through indoctrination and moralizing, rehabilitative programming in prisons is geared toward creating a population that is more docile and governable, a population taught to accept their incarceration as an appropriate response to their "bad choices" and internalize the prison's governance techniques.[106] Despite well-documented disparities due to race or socioeconomic status, the criminal justice system teaches the principles of individual agency: "that one should take ownership of . . . one's crimes [and] that one is being punished for individual (not societal) mistakes."[107] Imprisoned people learn it is "in their interest to be law-abiding and obedient,"[108] to remain silent on the multiple forms of victimization that have contributed to their incarceration. When they attempt to demonstrate how they were forced into making compromised choices because of structural inequities, they are told they are "pathologically deficient."[109] They are told they must learn to somehow avert these supposedly foreseeable risks—such as poverty, racism, trauma, unemployment, or mental illness—by being enterprising and self-governing, leaving intact the presumption that crime is the outcome of poor choices.[110] Those who accept this logic, and demonstrate that they have disciplined, improved, and governed themselves are rewarded by parole or early release. Those who do not are further punished or stigmatized. Rehabilitation in prisons, incarcerated scholars write, is "another technology in the social control toolbox that serves to victim-blame and shame the criminalized, while evading any discussion of the structural inequalities connected to criminalization."[111]

The "treatment" and "self-improvement" offered by prisons is paternalistic and punitive, despite being pitched as therapeutic and caring. It teaches that all choices are "freely made," but ensures that there are negative consequences for those who refuse to swallow the officially sanctioned versions of "individual change" or "development." Many scholars point out the absurdity of this contradiction: The prison wields ultimate control over a person's life, and is able to punish and discipline them, yet they are expected to think of themselves as "free," rational beings with the power to "make their own choices" and thus "fully responsible for their actions."[112] Meanwhile, it is not as though incarcerated persons are able to determine their own self-improvement needs: The available "choices" are predetermined and deemed "responsible" (or not) by prison staff, judges, parole boards, or correctional officers.[113] Some scholars call this "therapunitive" incarceration:[114] Those who refuse to buy into therapeutic messaging are punished, so that treatment is always backed up by exercises of punitive power.[115] As the prison researcher Ben Crewe notes: "The might of the stick and the appeal of the carrots [are] almost inseparable."[116]

Jill McCorkel offers a dramatic example of such "therapunitive" rehabilitation, through participant-observation in a confrontational form of group therapy in a women's prison. Women in this program were encouraged to publicly denounce their former selves as "liars, thieves, and manipulators," accepting prison staff's labeling of them as "codependent," "addictive personalities," and "criminal thinkers," attesting to the changes and transformation they had undergone.[117] They were expected to take ownership of their problems even when the situations they found themselves in were not outcomes of choice. The program required surrender to intrusive and coercive psychological strategies by staff. Women were pressured to disavow their choices to take drugs, steal, or engage in sex work, in a group setting characterized by yelling, loud confrontations, and public humiliation. Every participant understood that the point of the program was to change their identities and their self-understanding, accepting that their incarceration was a result of their flawed selves and choices rather than of any structural disadvantages. Some surrendered by learning to repeat the "correct" narratives, but those who refused to accept the program's claims were subject to further humiliation and punishment: limiting of privileges such as phone calls, new rules that further restricted privacy, or surveillance by fellow prisoners.

Victor Hassine, an incarcerated intellectual whose writings are widely read in academic settings, wrote that what goes by the name "rehabilitation" in prisons is in fact a program of "behavioral modification" designed to condition people into conformity. The "end product" envisioned by "prison managers," he noted, was to create "prisoners who have suffered punishment and become obedient under supervision, and are [required] to do nothing more than obey all of the volume of rules."[118] Little Rock Reed, an indigenous incarcerated scholar-activist gives the example of AA and NA programs. Some incarcerated persons describe the near-universal implementation of substance abuse programs in prisons as "social control mechanisms . . . through which the ruling class effectively subdues the discontent of the lower classes by having their attention diverted from the true sources of their problems."[119] In most states and in the federal Bureau of Prisons (BOP), AA and NA programs are mandatory for virtually all incarcerated persons—including, sometimes, those with no history of drug or alcohol abuse. Participants become eligible for a reduction in time required for parole eligibility or release dates (also known as "good-time credits"), and/or are given special privileges or lower security status for their participation in these programs.[120] Conversely, failure to participate in AA or NA is often taken as evidence of being unco-operative or incorrigible. In describing AA and NA programs in prisons, Reed points out how their quasi-religious foundations pressure participants into the Judeo-Christian perspective of the penitent sinner submitting to a "higher power." Yet, the cultural presumptions of these programs are deeply individualistic, teaching participants that "[their] troubles are basically of [their] own making,"—a teaching utterly inconsistent with dependence on a higher power. Has it ever occurred to the founders and proponents of AA, Reed asks, that the source of someone's substance abuse problem might be the desire to numb the pain caused by being "politically, socially, culturally and economically oppressed"?[121] Meanwhile, any expression of anger, opposition, criticism, or resentment toward these teachings is "considered evidence of selfishness or dishonesty."[122]

In other words, all your troubles are of your own making, yet you must submit to a higher power, and never criticize or argue, no matter the condi-tions of injustice or mistreatment in prison (and by extension, in society). As a result, some incarcerated persons openly refer to these programs as a "complete farce," yet dutifully attend them to obtain good-time credits.[123] Although Reed does acknowledge that many do agree with AA's precepts and derive great value from them, his argument is that these programs are not nearly as universally "therapeutic" as they are made out to be. In fact, their presumptions make some people uncomfortable, and violate the cultural and religious beliefs of others, such as Native Americans. Other scholars point out how AA and NA programs compel incarcerated persons to "consider their lives through the narrow and distorting lens of addiction ideology," reducing their identities to one or two disreputable categories.[124] Incarcerated scholars testify that state-controlled prison rehabilitation programs, including so-called therapeutic ones, "continue to ensnare marginalized populations in a net of social control": framing them as being "disordered" or "pathological" for existing outside dominant social, cultural, or gendered ways of being.[125] This penal-therapeutic regime, they argue, constitutes a form of "psychological domination," in which behavioral therapists and other "psy-" professionals cast "criminals" as "guardians of their own destiny simply in need of a psycho-logical toolkit that emphasizes 'healthy choices.'"[126]

Reforms designed to make prisons more "therapeutic," as many scholars show, fail to bypass the violence or injustice of the penal system—instead, they lead to increased surveillance and monitoring,[127] through new methods that may seem more "humane" but are in the end no less a form of control. The target of these so-called therapeutic interventions is the mind: "forc[ing] the prisoner to . . . view herself from the perspective of the institution . . . [as] the institution is quite literally inserted into the minds of prisoners."[128] The goal of these programs is to make prisoners accept and "support the same value system as . . . administrators,"[129] to learn to "frame their lives according to the prison's narrative structure."[130] Some incarcerated persons ask if these programs are a form of "brainwashing, designed to make them into something they were not sure they wanted to be . . . 'they're in your head, they break you down.'"[131] Others insist that the prison is trying to "re-arrange our mind . . . [to] become society's version of a so-called model person."[132] McCorkel calls this the "institutional takeover of the self," designed to convince incarcerated persons that they are the "source of disorder."[133]

System-impacted persons also point to the contradiction entailed in claiming that prisons "rehabilitate" people, yet simultaneously releasing them into a world where social and economic support for reentry into productive life are virtually nonexistent. In their research with those who have had criminal justice contact, Lerman and Weaver show how keen the awareness of this cyclical disadvantage was. Many believed the cycle of "joblessness and criminal justice involvement" was purposeful,[134] as legalized discrimination severely limited their opportunities for decent employment, and attempts to apply for jobs were "wrought with shame and embarrassment": "Even though I paid my debt to society . . . did what they told me I had to do. It just never goes away,"[135] said one woman. Or, as another man bluntly put it: "When you have no jobs and things like that, people are going to embrace the one thing [crime] . . . who wants to starve?"[136]

Despite these extensive reports, criminological literature is also replete with research demonstrating that many incarcerated persons do derive meaning and value from the therapeutic and rehabilitative programming they encounter in prisons, experiencing positive outcomes of growth, self-improvement, and self-transformation.[137] Incarcerated persons scarcely speak with one voice on these issues: "because the direct experiences [they] have had with criminal justice systems are so diverse, their perspectives inevitably vary. Opinions are not uniform and there are many debates."[138] One formerly incarcerated scholar reminds us that there is no "single, authentic truth to incarceration."[139] In fact, there is much to suggest, as the criminologist Yvonne Jewkes notes, that there are "pockets of good practice" in prisons.[140] Though prisons are clearly places of terror, harm, injustice, and oppression, there is no denying that they are also multidimensional and complex places where humor, friendship, educational enlightenment, successful therapeutic intervention, and transformative achievement can thrive, to some extent.[141] As a volunteer, I witnessed several prison programs run by civilian employees who forged strong bonds with incarcerated persons, offering programs that were replete with decency, humanity, and life-affirming relationships and values. We will see in the following chapters that prison volunteers are kind, compassionate, and caring, focused on the genuine well-being of incarcerated persons (rather than solely on the prison's requirements and mandates). Yet, we will also see that the successes arising from these efforts often occur *despite* the obstacles presented by the prison environment, rather than *because* of the inherently "rehabilitative" nature of the prison. And, we will find that even the best-intentioned volunteers and prison employees—as caring and compassionate as they may be—can unwittingly reproduce the prison's narrative structure. As one critic notes, control in any guise is still control: Even with a kinder or gentler edge, it gives authorities the power to monitor behaviors, reward or punish appropriately,[142] and cement the legitimacy of the current system.

As an alternative, I suggest we consider a different model of success in the so-called rehabilitative endeavor, one in which volunteers explicitly work to offer a counternarrative to the system and its logic. In contrast to prison employees such as custodial and civilian staff—including "psy-" staff and other administrators—volunteers can occupy a "third party" category. Although not all of them do so, many communicate a stance making clear that they do not represent the prison system, and are not beholden to its logic.[143] As such, they can offer alternative narratives and ways of being that encourage incarcerated persons to critically examine and reject the logic of the system, whether overtly or subtly. A prime example is provided by certain educational programs in prisons, which can be emancipatory: They can be taught in ways that counteract the system's messaging, and that encourage "critical assessments of power," through the practices of free thinking and learning, galvanizing forms of independent thought that refuse the prison's narratives and allowing incarcerated persons to recognize their own worth as free and equal beings, despite their confinement.[144] The extensive literature on critical prison education[145] shows us that volunteers who enter the prison system can serve in an educational capacity that is rehabilitative yet subversive, offering a kind of self-improvement that does not require a regurgitation of the prison's logic, and counteracting the compliance-inducing curriculum of the prison. However, given everything we know about the predominant "therapeutic" model inside prisons, this requires volunteers to be thoughtful and reflective about the presumptions, attitudes, and approaches they bring to their engagements with incarcerated persons.

Conclusions

It is impossible to grapple with the problem of prisons in our society without knowing exactly what goes on behind their opaque walls, what things are silenced, and what is made invisible. Yet, as Rachel Kushner notes, "in the United States, it's difficult for people to talk about prison without assuming there is a population that must stay there."[146] Popular discourse understands the total institution as "necessary" to contain violence and safety threats to the public. But these assumptions are based on little actual transparency about who ends up in prison and why, the routine violence and dehumanization that characterize punishment, and the ways in which prisons justify these practices as necessary, while producing and exacerbating the very violence they claim to contain. In this chapter, I attempt to take readers inside the "total institution" nature of prisons, mapping and visualizing them (to the degree possible), but also asking us to contemplate whether their routinized violence and dehumanization is as necessary or legitimate as we are taught to believe. Of course, it is entirely possible, as Joshua Price argues, that making visible the suffering of prison conditions will not have the effect we think: Many people, Price points out, believe that the suffering people undergo inside prisons is well deserved.[147] One of my interviewees bluntly pointed out, for instance, that "[correctional staff] are really just executing a mandate that we have given them . . . this is how we want to run our prisons."[148]

At the same time, however, I also cast critical doubt on the idea that the problem with prisons is simply that they are too violent or too inhumane. Not only should we be questioning what happens inside prisons, our questioning should not stop at the boundaries of what appears to be violent or dehumanizing. Rather, I ask us to think critically about more nonviolent and supposedly "therapeutic" forms of punishment. The argument that prisons must simply be reformed obscures the fact that they are not just harsh, authoritarian spaces—they are also about social control, often disguised as treatment and therapy. Custody/control and rehabilitation/treatment have always been contradictory, and many who have been in prison are keenly attuned to this fact. These programs are part and parcel of what Michelle Alexander has identified as the "genius of the current caste system": incarceration appears avoidable through better choices and behaviors, and therefore voluntary. The system "depends for its legitimacy on the widespread belief that all those who appear trapped at the bottom actually chose their fate."[149] The idea of individual responsibility is used by prisons to obscure the role of social inequity, even as the system plainly reveals the results of such inequity, and exacerbates it.[150]

Little wonder, then, that Lerman and Weaver describe system-impacted persons as developing the sense of being "democratic pariahs": nagged by the feeling that they are simply objects of discipline by the carceral state, which engages with them through control, hierarchy, and arbitrary power. They experience feelings of powerlessness and diminishment, seeing government as a repressive force, a "semiauthoritarian" and all-powerful body that "exerts near total control over them," with "excessive power to control their lives and limit their choices," on which they can make few claims and exert little influence.[151] As a result, many system-impacted people feel politically alienated, marginalized, disempowered, and subordinated. To obtain a glimpse inside prisons, and to learn about both their overtly violent/violating practices, as well as their so-called humane, therapeutic practices of control, is to gain some understanding of why this might be so.

Well, what then, we might ask? Surely we are not arguing *against* reforming prisons? The point of this chapter is not to reject efforts to reform violent or inhumane prison practices. Ultimately, we do have options for dealing with harm that go beyond the prison, that do not rely on captivity, caging, and control (about which I will say more in the concluding chapter). In the interim, while large swaths of our population continue to be incarcerated, even the harshest critics of prisons acknowledge that attempts must be made to make life behind bars more tolerable. And, criticizing rehabilitation as a control strategy does not amount to suggesting that no one behind bars has ever caused harm, or that they would not benefit from treatment or therapy as tools for personal growth. As I have said, we must be clear-eyed about the fact that harm does happen. Nor am I suggesting that personal growth in prison cannot be meaningful, uncoerced, or beneficial—in fact, we will soon see many such examples. But we can ask why someone should have to be imprisoned in a punitive institution that deprives them of dignity in order to avail of tools for healing and self-transformation. Are healing and self-improvement not compromised when they occur under coercive conditions where the only available options are to accept a narrowly defined version of one's life-narrative, or pay a price for refusing to repeat the party line?[152] While many incarcerated persons do experience personal transformation while imprisoned, we will see in the following chapter that many of them point out it is largely *despite* rather than *because of* imprisonment, given the ways in which prisons inhibit free choice and agency.

In what follows, we will meet many volunteers who end up reproducing the system's messaging—often unwittingly—even when they consider themselves to be acting against it. But we will also find volunteers more attuned to political realities, who offer models of therapeutic healing that allow for personal growth, while subverting the prison's logic. Models of critical prison education demonstrate how volunteers might provide oases of freedom, equality, and independent thinking inside spaces that are otherwise rife with powerlessness, subordination, and total control. Later in this book—particularly in Chapters 8 and 9—we will learn how yoga and meditation can similarly offer therapeutic, healing opportunities that do not involve having to replicate the prison's own messaging.

5

"Rescued by Prison" or "Drinking the Kool-Aid?"

Practicing While Incarcerated

Jarvis Jay Masters is known as the "Buddhist on death row." A student of the famous Buddhist nun Pema Chödrön, Masters has been sentenced to death for a crime he claims he did not commit: the murder of a corrections officer while incarcerated at San Quentin prison. Masters has become something of a celebrity—his approved list of visitors is said to be the longest of any on death row.[1] Like others on death row, Masters is the object of a "Free Jarvis" campaign for his exoneration. Masters identifies as a Buddhist, and credits his long-standing Buddhist practice with his personal growth and transformation.

In his autobiography, Masters describes the unremitting physical and mental abuse that he endured as a child, both at the hands of his own parents as well as later, at a series of foster homes and state institutions. Like millions of others with similar histories of severe racial and economic disadvantage, Masters found himself with few options besides a criminal path, eventually landing in prison for a series of robberies. His entry into the system at age nineteen was the logical culmination of years of pain and suffering, compounded by the violence he endured in state institutions. Violence, he says, "was our culture and our currency."[2]

In the preface to his autobiography, pre-Buddhism Jarvis is characterized, as "angry, defensive and mean."[3] Jarvis's life "only turned around after his conviction," when he used his sentence to learn to meditate and "look at himself honestly," undergoing a deep transformation.[4] Masters describes himself as "having gone through life making one wrong choice after another"—his Buddhist practice "was to take complete responsibility for [his] actions" and "redeem" himself.[5] After several years of practicing in prison, Masters was eventually proclaimed a *bodhisattva* by his Tibetan spiritual teacher: one who works to end suffering. He is known to be a force of good in San Quentin: counseling and mentoring fellow prisoners, teaching meditation, responding with compassion to the suffering of others, often averting

Freedom Inside?. Farah Godrej, Oxford University Press. © Oxford University Press 2022.
DOI: 10.1093/oso/9780190070083.003.0005

disaster by intervening in disputes, convincing people to opt for nonviolent resolutions to prison conflicts. Supporters describe him as an "enlightened Buddhist practitioner who changed and saved lives," while "Buddhists and non-Buddhists alike [write] to commiserate, applaud his resilience, and acknowledge his transformation."[6]

In a variety of memoirs written by incarcerated yogis and meditators, these narratives of accepting personal responsibility for individual choices—and transforming oneself accordingly—reappear with regularity.[7] Like Masters, many of these currently and formerly incarcerated writers acknowledge the structural injustice that accounts for deep disparities in law enforcement and incarceration. They describe cycles of violence and abuse, stemming from poverty, racism, unemployment, homelessness, and other forms of marginalization. We learn about how state systems and institutions both failed to prevent such violence and perpetuated it, leaving their paths to prison largely overdetermined. Yet, like Fleet Maull, a formerly incarcerated white Buddhist who now leads mindfulness programs inside prisons, these authors believe "in the power of meditation to change [our] prisons from the inside out"— that is, structural change results from incarcerated individuals changing themselves.[8] Calvine Malone, a Black incarcerated practitioner of Buddhism writes that "a Buddhist in prison can develop a solid practice only by changing his thinking or perspective"—changing, he asserts, requires admitting to "a lifetime of reacting out of anger and fear."[9] For Masters and Maull, the path of meditation in prison entails accountability for one's life and one's actions, an approach that "encourages, [and] empowers, prisoners to take responsibility for what they've done, to make amends, to change themselves."[10]

For these writers, Buddhist and yogic practices teach that misery and suffering are "self-manufactured"—Masters was taught by his Buddhist teachers that his path would allow him to "break free of lifelong patterns . . . that cause our suffering."[11] Despite keen attention to the severe disadvantage that overdetermined his route to prison—and despite denying involvement in many of the crimes for which he has been imprisoned—Masters describes his Buddhist practice as deeply individual. That is, layers of structural oppression may have determined his path, but Buddhism "shows us how we cause so much of our own suffering."[12] Masters' practice encouraged him to see his misfortune as solely of his own making, a result of his choices. We have seen how the relentless beating of the "personal responsibility" drum—in prisons, in legal discourse, and in society at large—produces the "omnipresent message" that these individuals alone were "responsible for their outcomes in life, including the mistakes that led to their confinement."[13] Despite keen attention to multiple forms of systemic oppression, these incarcerated writers echo the logic of the prison, in which incarceration is largely a result of individual flaws and defects.

These writers also strongly advocate for remaining nonreactive to and accepting of injustice while incarcerated, by reframing these challenges as opportunities for growth and learning. Both Maull and Masters express gratitude for the obstacles of prison life, which "become . . . the fuel for transformation."[14] Masters credits the death sentence he received—for a crime he insists he did not commit—with "saving his life," while he was left waiting on death row for over 30 years, much of it in solitary confinement.

> If I wasn't in that monk's cell all those years, I would have been on that same path . . . I'd have been killed or [have] killed someone . . . I never would have meditated. Never would have learned about Buddhism. . . . In that way the death penalty saved my life.[15]

For Maull, being upset about being in prison was a "mental construct": "this prison journey was workable if I just trained in calming my own mind and stabilizing meditative awareness under any circumstances."[16] Michael Huggins, a white man who served nine months in a federal prison on a corporate malfeasance misdemeanor, similarly calls yoga a means for incarcerated persons to "find comfort in the discomfort."[17] Maull calls on prison practitioners of meditation to "rise above" and transcend the "shame-based dehumanization" perpetrated by the system.[18] Despite the layers of injustice that characterize the system, these writers ultimately seem to echo its messaging: Incarcerated persons can develop the tranquility and resilience to "bootstrap" their way out of the many forms of disadvantage that confront them. Huggins, for instance, details his "profound disappointment" in the "injustice of the justice system."[19] He describes his shock at learning the numerous forms of systemic discrimination facing system-impacted individuals, the absence of useful reentry programs while incarcerated, and the barriers to legal employment that make illegal activity the only plausible option for so many.[20] Yet, he ends his book by asserting that "yoga and other beneficial programs can reduce recidivism," by providing tools for those in need to "better deal with the stressors in their lives."[21]

Strikingly, this group of writers seem to consider contemplative or yogic practices as antithetical to fighting injustice. Maull notes that rather than reveling in "self-destructive . . . blame, justification, and resentment"[22] or "fighting back against the many injustices of the system," incarcerated persons should acknowledge their part in causing "chaos and pain."[23] Huggins provides readers an in-depth look at the abusive and inhumane conditions that incarcerated persons are subjected to; yet, he ends by recommending that they "make peace with [their] surroundings and not fight every indignity or injustice."[24] Masters offers the most striking version of this: he describes his brief flirtation with political education and radicalization earlier in his prison term. He learned about historical oppression, and was educated in the writings of Angela Davis and George Jackson, as well as the Black Panthers. He describes a Black revolutionary organization that served as his community in prison, educating its members in Black nationalism and class struggle, training them in mental and physical discipline. But in his telling, the years of political indoctrination served no constructive purpose: "He'd been hard, but it made him harder."[25] In Masters's story, his peaceful, non-violent Buddhist practice and his commitment to reducing suffering appear to have no connection to the analysis of political and class oppression that his Black nationalist comrades taught. Masters considers his Buddhist practice "an utterly different type of mental training"[26] from his earlier political radicalization.

These writings by Masters, Malone, Huggins, and Maull stand in stark contrast to another genre of prison writings, in which authors respond quite differently to incarceration, expressing a far more critical and resistant perspective toward the system. In the tradition of imprisoned activists and intellectuals such as George Jackson, many incarcerated people write "from the inside," fiercely critiquing the system and rejecting the logic of individual defects taught by the prison.[27] Political resistance by imprisoned persons calls to mind the writings—and activism—of celebrated figures like Assata Shakur, George Jackson, Mumia Abu-Jamal, Angela Davis, and many others.[28] Through their writings and activism, these figures expressed revolutionary consciousness, by reinterpreting the social world and offering alternative ways of imagining it. Many of them engaged in civil disobedience while incarcerated, taking part in a long history of prison resistance.[29] Crucially, they reject the idea that prisons exist to control crime or inflict well-deserved punishment. Rather, they write, in different ways, about prisons as a form of social control, about social issues such as poverty, unemployment, hunger, and homelessness, which "force people to seek illegitimate means to eke out an existence"[30] in response to increasingly precarious economic conditions, rejecting the prison's logic of "personal shortcomings." They write of their dissidence, of their "willed resistance," in Mumia Abu-Jamal's words, "to a system that is killing us."[31] They describe the political reading groups and other education circles formed by incarcerated persons outside the sanction of the prison,[32] and of the political consciousness developed by imprisoned persons, who were routinely retaliated against for their activism.

Of course, resistance in prisons is not restricted to these celebrated activists: it happens in a million ordinary ways every day. Scholars have shown that despite the restricted choices and opportunities that characterize all penal institutions, many incarcerated persons are able to resist and defy the effects of punishment, through everyday, "micro" resistance, as well as more "consciously disruptive, intentionally political" acts.[33] The most intentional and overt forms of resistance include actions such as noncompliance, the filing of grievances or writing letters or articles to document the system's injustices, verbal and physical challenges to prison staff, as well as more dramatic political challenges such as hunger strikes and even riots.[34] Resistance can also be more subtle, pertaining to "individual, uncoordinated acts of avoidance and defiance" that creatively express one's agency and influence without confronting authorities directly.[35] Incarcerated persons can use practices of food, education, dress, self-presentation, and religion to resist the uniformity of prison.[36] Although the power of the total institution appears absolute, in practice, there are plenty of cracks in its façade: Incarcerated persons "take liberties, construct free areas, find and explore secret means of escape, and creatively and productively put up resistance to, through and against the everyday routine forms of power in the prison . . . refusing and looking past the given, finding and exploring opportunities, and mastering a situation."[37]

Crucially, such resistance can be internal rather than external: It has to do with how incarcerated persons navigate their own identity and sense of self. Many of them undertake what the political scientist James Scott has called a "prosaic but constant struggle,"[38] "maintain[ing] their own self-respect," or "defy[ing] their own image as weak or defeated."[39] Some refuse to accept prison programs' claims about their flawed selves requiring intervention or rehabilitation.[40] Others insist on the role of race or poverty to explain their reduced life-chances, or refuse to accept that responsibility for incarceration is theirs alone.[41] Still others cast themselves as moral and upstanding, despite the system's labeling of them as "criminals."[42] Across the board, we see evidence of incarcerated people whose "sense of self transgresses the prison walls, and enables them to resist much of the daily exigencies of prison life,"[43] as they "renegotiat[e] and reconstruc[t] [their] own identity within the framework of the institution."[44] The Norwegian prison researcher Thomas Ugelvik calls this a hybrid and creative form of protest, a disidentification and escape from one's "status as a prisoner."[45]

Michael Hames-Garcia refers to "the resistant practices of the oppressed," naming these writings and practices as "fugitive thought."[46] Many formerly incarcerated writers also develop this perspective after their incarceration. Susan Burton, a Black feminist anti-prison activist, writes about how, like so many others, she cycled in and out of prison for much of her life, tormented by the violence and abuse she endured growing up in a poor Black community in South Los Angeles. While Burton acknowledges the harmful impact of her actions on herself and her loved ones, her memoir emphasizes that "helping [individuals] wasn't going to fix the broken and discriminatory system."[47] She describes how the system repeatedly fails, undermines and criminalizes people from communities like her own, "bulldozing . . . dominating and exploiting and locking up everyone in sight."[48] With examples from her own life-narrative, she demonstrates how systemic barriers to the advancement of incarcerated people operate by design.[49] Like many other incarcerated activists and intellectuals, Burton rejects the logic of "bootstrapping," arguing that individual change alone cannot be held responsible for systemic change:

> All the years I pointed a finger at my own weakness, believing that I had innate flaws and couldn't get my life together . . . the system was broken, and it had set me up to fail. . . . All this time I'd lived with great sadness and disappointment over what I'd thought was my own inability to pull myself up. Only now did I see all the ways these barriers had affected me, pushing me back into the prison system. . . . The more my understanding of these social and political structures deepened, the more I was able to release myself.[50]

These two genres of prison writing seem to present us with a binary between two types of responses to imprisonment: those who seek to face their prison experience through inward-oriented self-improvement, accepting the prison's logic of personal defects and personal responsibility; and those who point to structural injustice, through political education, activism, and resistance (both subtle and internal, as well as overt and external). In this chapter, I show that this binary is, to some extent, useful in helping us understand the perspectives of incarcerated and formerly incarcerated persons—yet, it does not capture the entire story. In what follows, I further explore different types of responses to being imprisoned, asking what role yoga and meditation might play in producing such responses. In what ways might yoga or meditation foster acceptance or compliance toward the prison's logic of personal responsibility? Alternatively, in what ways might they provide tools to challenge or resist the system's logic? To answer these questions, I interviewed twenty-five formerly incarcerated practitioners of yoga and meditation (Table 5.1). In these interviews, I was less interested in establishing a clear causal relationship between yoga and meditation on the one hand and a compliant or resistant attitude on the other. Rather, my hope was to find out something about how these individuals interpreted the meaning or purpose of their practice, as they grappled with their own incarceration. Did they interpret the practices as tools for compliance and acceptance of their situations, or for a more resistant and oppositional understanding of their condition? What aspects of the practices seem to encourage them to accept an unjust or miserable reality by reconceiving of it as a personal choice, and complying with its conditions? Alternatively, were they able to develop any internal resources for challenging the logic that they alone bore responsibility for their fate, and should simply be tasked with changing themselves? Did the practices allow them to develop—or maintain or deepen—any awareness of systemic injustice? More broadly, I wanted to know what capacities or states of consciousness the practices made available to them.

In some ways, my interviews led to the binary understanding that I described earlier; one that posits a choice between acceptance of personal responsibility or critique of structural injustice. To some extent, I did find that my respondents' views could be categorized in two ways, represented (roughly) by the two genres of writing I described. The majority of my respondents (15 of 25) cohered around one narrative fully accepting personal responsibility for their own incarceration, and seeing prison as a time for their own individual self-transformation. Their stories converged largely around themes of personal defects and poor decision-making, having only themselves to blame, and thus to improve. Yoga and meditation seemed to solidify this perspective, often used to reflect on bad choices, to hold oneself accountable, or take responsibility for changing. This was most evident among those who felt that their actions were serious enough that their prison time was warranted. But even those who insisted that their actions were not criminal—or that their incarceration was not fully warranted or legitimate—enthusiastically endorsed the idea of transforming themselves through yoga or meditation.[51]

The second group of respondents were a minority of ten, whose views cohered around a more oppositional narrative. They either outright rejected the language of individual responsibility and rehabilitation, or made clear that these ideas were to be used for the purpose of challenging the system. They refused to see their yogic or meditative practice simply as "making better choices," "learning from mistakes," or "flawed individuals needing self-improvement." Instead, they used the practices to better themselves in ways that retained awareness of injustice, rather than accepting the idea that individuals made choices that caused them to be in prison. Many conceived of responsibility or choice in far more robust ways, making sure to include the story of larger structural constraints that limited choices, whether race or socioeconomic status or lack of opportunity or legalized discrimination.

Some research suggests that contact with the criminal punishment system tends to have a depoliticizing effect—system-impacted people seemed closed off to politics and disinclined toward any action to achieve collective goals.[52] But other scholars suggest that rather than withdrawing from political engagement, individuals impacted by an unjust law enforcement apparatus can be galvanized toward political action.[53] Among my respondents, I found both patterns: All of my respondents from the first group were disinclined to engage in political action, despite offering standard critiques of mass incarceration. In contrast, my respondents in the second group not only had strong political views, at least a few of them were engaged in activist projects. In at least one case, this oppositional political consciousness seemed directly attributed to meditative teachings and practices, while in several other cases, a more indirect link was suggested between the practices and political views.

But in other ways, my interviews defied these clean, binary categories, revealing layers of complication.[54] This complexity is evident when we consider the overlap between the writers and thinkers in the two genres I described earlier. Despite the obvious differences in their perspectives, both sets of authors were concerned with an internal freedom that defies the institution's capacity to control and define their lived experience, a freedom achieved through practices of self-control and self-discipline. For instance, George Jackson was focused on cultivating a "black revolutionary mentality" in prison, and believed this required a physical, intellectual, and emotional discipline that allowed the individual to *feel* free. "Locked in jail, within a jail . . . my mind is still free."[55] Jarvis Jay Masters seems like the antithesis of Jackson: he rejects Black revolutionary training in favor of the calm, nonreactive detachment of Buddhism, seeing these two perspectives as opposed to one another. But ultimately, Masters too asserts that "when his mind was free, he was free . . . prison walls disappeared . . . [he] could find freedom no matter where [he] dwelled."[56] Maull, Huggins, and Malone, who wrote in the same genre as Masters, may all have renounced acts of resistance to the prison, but the disciplined states of mind they cultivated through yoga or meditation seemed like forms of internal resistance quite akin to the psychic freedom that Jackson and others describe. Practices such as yoga and meditation allowed these writers to feel humanized in the face of an institution intent on eliminating their existence and humanity, creatively allowing them to assert their own agency and autonomy, despite the many barriers. These practices constitute acts of resistance, even if practitioners disavow the language of resistance to injustice. They offer us a new and more complex way to understand resistance, elaborating on the many forms that prison scholars have already explored, to include the subtler and more internal—even "spiritual"—dimensions of resistance. They point to the possibility of what one scholar has called "liberty projects": creating "alternative realities," with "opportunities for turning yourself into something other, or more, than just 'a prisoner.'"[57]

In the same way, the two narratives I found among my interview respondents were not completely opposed to one other. Common to both was the possibility of a state of mind that allowed for an internal locus of freedom and control, whether or not it was *called* subversion by those who practiced it. What distinguished the two groups of respondents was the specific meaning they gave to self-improvement through yoga or meditation. (Of course, these groups were also not entirely mutually exclusive: While most respondents clearly emphasized one kind of narrative over another, a few offered both at different times in the conversation.[58]) For the first group, improvement was an internal and inward-looking project, while for the second, it had some connection to larger social or political issues. Accordingly, the second group seemed more likely to have developed what some scholars call an "oppositional" political consciousness, focused on resistance toward the prison and its logic.

Despite these differences, there was important overlap across the board: All my interview participants were able, in different ways, to feel internally free and in control, despite the indignities they suffered or witnessed. In many cases, this did not require traditional political action or even critique. Many respondents were able to turn the inner workings of their minds into a space free of the prison's messaging—their minds became a refuge where they could humanize themselves, without needing external structures and circumstances to be in their favor. These responses deepen and further develop the literature on resistance in prisons, mapping new and complex ways for incarcerated persons to "put [their] stamp on a situation, to create a feeling of autonomy and authority," to face the prison's control "by making it more liveable and . . . making [oneself] more than someone who is being controlled."[59]

Table 5.1 Basic Demographics of Interviewees

Age	
20–29	4
30–39	3
40–49	15
50–59	3
Gender Identity	
Male	15
Female	10
Race/Ethnicity	
Caucasian	13
Black	8
East or Southeast Asian	2
Latinx	2

Common Themes—Coping and Survival: "It Helped Me to Endure What I Didn't Feel Like I Could Endure"

All of my respondents used yogic or meditative practices as a tool for coping with and surviving the harshness, chaos, and emotional difficulties of the prison environment.[60] Every person I spoke to attributed some therapeutic purpose to yoga or meditation in prison. Several reported using yoga as a means to cope with a major illness or mobility issue, and many made reference to rejuvenating the body, while relieving physical tension and gaining strength through the connection between emotions and bodily reactions. As one woman noted, "It was a grounding experience in the turmoil . . . it made me aware of my body, each muscle or tendon."

Assistance with sleep was another common theme: Many described the calming effects of these practices, particularly given the lack of control in the prison environment, which often led to negative thoughts such as fear, anxiety, or helplessness. "From one moment to the next, you don't know what's happening, you don't have any autonomy, any control over anything," says one woman. It "really helped me calm my thoughts" was a common refrain, as was the ability to tame the "monkey-mind." "It gave you a safe space to go, you could have a retreat, [and] step away from the chaos going on around you," said one man. Regaining a measure of mental clarity and focus was another common theme. Many who were in jail awaiting trial reported being able to focus on their case better, while those in prison reported heightened abilities to memorize or concentrate while studying for classes.

Anger emerged as an emotion of particular significance in prison. Many reported being able to see their suppressed anger more clearly, to learn to observe it calmly, and eventually, react more productively. Other respondents spoke more directly of coping with the pain, isolation, or brutality of being incarcerated. "I was deeply lonely, I didn't have a lot of support while in prison," another man says, "so I think meditation helped me build the strength and resilience to navigate that." Many spoke of feeling dehumanized in prison and attempting to regain their sanity through yoga or meditation. One man offers this explanation: "[Meditation] gave me control of the levers of my sanity, because I knew the environment was robbing me of my humanity.... I was on the cusp of becoming the individual I never wanted to be." Another woman says: "I witnessed a lot of poor treatment... a complete disregard for the humanity in us. [I knew] it's an injustice, it's demeaning, [but] instead of getting frustrated, I would do some breathing, some meditation, and it definitely provided some relief." One woman reports feeling "like a human being again" in her yoga classes: "[being] human enough and valued enough to be offered [this] experience."

Many described the practices allowing them to mentally escape the reality of their brutal environment: "I needed to be able to go someplace else than inside my head," said one person. Another common theme was the ability to navigate and survive the violence of incarceration. One man offers a vivid account of this: "[It] was an environment where real monsters were out. I really believed I was gonna die in prison, my objective was survival. They had gangs, I had a target on my back.... I had to deal with the anguish on my own every day, not being able to turn to the cops.... I felt hopeless and helpless." In this volatile environment, where "lives were at stake," another man says, "[you have to] conduct yourself in a way that you're not making enemies. When you're angry or fearful, you tend to do stuff that can really get you hurt." This point of view was echoed by many others, like one respondent who noted, "I could feel myself getting angry, and I could either walk away, or I found myself being able to pause, and speak more mindfully, which I think saved me in a lot of situations." All of my respondents made reference, in some way, to a kind of "slowing down" and quieting the mind that allowed for new forms of self-awareness to emerge through introspection: in one respondent's words, "to sit with the reality of who they are." Others described this as "processing [the reality of] what I went through in a healthy way"; "more deeply connecting with ourselves," or "looking at the whole view." One called it "see[ing] more clearly, and then admit[ting] to myself: '*I feel angry because I was rejected by a society that I wanted to be part of.*'" It was clear that every respondent found these practices to be a crucial means of survival—and in some cases, even healing—within a brutal and degrading environment. Perhaps no respondent summarized as clearly the coping skills to be gained from yoga or meditation as this woman, who simply said, "It helped me to endure what I didn't feel like I was going to endure."

Narrative 1: Yoga and Meditation as Tools for Accepting Personal Responsibility through Rehabilitation

Despite this common emphasis on therapeutic and coping benefits, I found two distinct kinds of narratives emerging from these interviews. Narrative 1 characterizes the majority of my respondents (15 of 25), who emphasized the concepts of individual choice and accepting responsibility. For these respondents, yoga and meditation seemed to be tools to improve themselves in keeping with the prison's narrative of personal defects, in which they had only themselves to blame. The respondents in this group further subdivided into two categories: those who felt that their incarceration was fully warranted, or came to accept its legitimacy over time; and those who felt that their incarceration was unjust all along. With only one exception, every respondent, in describing their life prior to incarceration, described some form of social or economic disadvantage—whether based in race or poverty—resulting in trauma, abuse, addiction, mental illness, and other forms of ill-health and psychological difficulty. And, almost every respondent also held critical views regarding the structural inequities that functioned as a "pipeline" to the overrepresentation of minorities, immigrants, and poor people in the incarceration system. Despite these critical views, a few in this group insisted that their own incarceration was largely justifiable given the nature of their actions. But even the rest—most of whom felt that their own incarceration was unjustified—reported an emphasis on individual choice and personal change, despite the socioeconomic disadvantages they had suffered, and their critiques of mass incarceration as structurally unjust. Yoga and meditation were seen as tools to accept their incarceration and "get over" their own anger; or alternatively, to recast prison time as a "blessing" or a "growth opportunity" for personal transformation.

Narrative 1. "It All Comes Down to the Choices That You Make In Life"

Like Lee who was quoted at the beginning of this book, Matt, Javier, and Anna represent most vividly the perspectives of respondents who adopted this narrative. They all came from backgrounds of extreme socioeconomic disadvantage characterized by early childhood abuse, and in Anna's case, sexual trauma and assault. Yet, each of them spoke emphatically of the need for accepting full responsibility for the choices *they* had made that landed them in prison. Matt and Javier are Latino, while Anna is white. Matt is in his fifties, and has served over thirty years in prison for being part of a "robbery that went wrong." He offers trenchant critiques of the incarceration system, and of the pathways—from an abusive, alcoholic father to a racist school environment, to foster care—that led him to the prison system at a young age. Despite a history of political radicalization in prison through exposure to the writings of Malcolm X, Che Guevara, and Noam Chomsky, Matt insists that "you can't really blame society"—he sees his sentence as legitimate. "Buddhism allowed me to face the man in the mirror," Matt says. "I was coming to terms with who I was and how I became that person." For this, Matt credits his Buddhist practice: "[It] taught me I had to look inward, because something was wrong with me. That's the way the Buddhists see it, you activated this negative seed, and at some point you have to become responsible and accountable." Matt offers strong critiques of systemic and structural injustice during our conversation. Yet, he interprets Buddhist philosophy as a means for individuals to look inside themselves and their own defects for the source of suffering.

So too with Javier, who describes a childhood rife with trauma and abuse, much of it due to repeated contact with the carceral system at a young age. Now in his late thirties, Javier served almost twenty-two years of a fifteen-to-life sentence as an adult, despite having been incarcerated as a juvenile. He describes his early contact with juvenile facilities as "trauma piled on top of more trauma," noting, "I don't think it's a place for any child." Despite these systemic critiques, Javier sees his commitment to Buddhist meditation as the key to taking responsibility for the actions that landed him there. "Through meditation and watching my actions, seeing their karmic effect, I realized how deeply wrong [I was], how much damage I had caused in society, and in the community. . . . We have to show to [society] that we are rehabilitated and changed."

Anna is in her late twenties, and spent several years incarcerated on drug, alcohol, and other substance-abuse related charges. Her path to prison was deeply determined by poverty, sexual trauma, violence and abuse, including gang-rape. "I was told that I was a whore and it was my problem," she says. These experiences eventually led to her addiction. For her, the rehabilitative experiences of yoga and meditation in prison were crucial to healing. "[These practices] helped me because I felt like it was building new tools, it was changing my thought process. I had lost all control of my life. I had no direction, I came to that animalistic state, trying to get the next fix for survival. I needed to learn how to live life again, I needed to learn how to be a person, how to treat others, treat myself." She reports repeatedly receiving the message from prison staff: "*I don't know why you guys try, you'll just be back here . . . you did this to yourself.*" I ask how she reacted to such messages. "I would feel guilt [and] shame [at] being powerless . . . [but] now I see that message as a motivator to do better," Anna insists. The message of "having only herself to blame" was motivation to transform herself through practices such as yoga and meditation.

Danny and Elisa represent those who initially saw their own incarceration as procedurally unjust or excessive, but came to terms with the need for personal responsibility. Yoga and meditation formed one element in a panoply of rehabilitative practices that allowed them to reframe their incarceration as more legitimate or justifiable than they had initially thought. Danny, like Lee, is an Asian-American man in his early forties who describes a difficult life of poverty, racial disadvantage, and refugee status. Danny served twenty-one years for being involved in an attempted robbery, in which he neither discharged a weapon nor injured anyone. Offered a plea deal of four consecutive life sentences, Danny and his co-defendants chose to go to trial. He describes a trial process riddled with procedural irregularities, conflicts of interest, and allegations of misconduct that caused him to feel initially that his sentence was deeply unjust. Despite filing several motions and requests for changes of venue based on these procedural irregularities, Danny was convicted and given fourteen years-to-life, plus an additional life sentence. Not long after his release twenty-one years later, Danny was detained by US Immigration Customs Enforcement (ICE), and spent another eight months subject to deportation in an immigration detention facility, due to his lack of US citizenship.[61]

Danny describes the resentment and frustration with which he began his prison term, soon dissolving into acceptance. At first, he notes, he was riddled with "self-pity," trying to "justify the unfairness" of his situation. But "I've come to accept my time," he says, "I deserve [it] . . . your own action causes your karmic situation . . . it was more like, accepting the law. . . . I did the crime, so I'm responsible for any consequences." Danny identifies his meditation practice as a major factor in his change of perspective: "Instead of trying to blame everything on the outside situation, I internalized it more. Like, if someone is angry at me, well, '*What did I do to make him angry?*' That's really the teaching of Buddha, right? Your mind is the creation of events or situations, whether good or bad. When I internalize things and see things in an objective manner, I'd be more understanding of [certain] situations." Danny interprets Buddhist teaching as an injunction to accept the law, no matter how it is enforced, and to find the cause for one's own suffering in internal rather than external circumstances—to see all suffering as ultimately of one's own making.

Elisa is a white woman in her thirties, one of the few respondents who does not report any racial or socioeconomic disadvantage. She is the daughter of a police officer, raised in relative middle-class comfort, with a strong education and close family ties. She served six years as a sex-offender for being in a consensual relationship with a "mature teenager," while she was in her early twenties. Elisa, like Danny, was initially confused by the length of her sentence. "I knew what happened was inappropriate," she says. "But the enormity of the illegalness of it . . . I didn't prey on her. It was a relationship, it was totally mutual. So I'm confused, like *'Why am I going to go to prison for that??'"* Elisa reports being told even by prison staff that she had been "heavily over sentenced." But over time, Elisa came to accept her sentence as legitimate. "Now I feel, if that's what my victim felt like I deserved, then she's entitled to that. . . . It was definitely wrong." Still, Elisa, insists: "I don't like to look at myself as a criminal. I'm somebody who just made a really bad judgment, and had to own up to it. . . . I guess it's just the way the law's written."

Elisa claims that she developed insight and came to terms with her crime through Buddhist practice in prison: "You can look deeper into yourself and really start identifying behavior patterns, and figuring out: *'Why did I do what I did?'"* She also gravitated toward like-minded others while incarcerated: "The people that I became close with [in prison], almost all of them accepted their crime, and their time." Elisa is bitter about the requirement of lifetime sex-offender registry, which she knows will have an extremely severe, if not devastating, impact on her housing and employment prospects for the rest of her life. Despite her strong critiques of these laws, Elisa interprets Buddhism as a way to accept her fate, to inquire into her own deficiencies as the source, and to come to terms with the "criminal" nature of something she did not consider criminal to begin with.

Narrative 1. Choices, Decisions, Consequences: "CDC"

More strikingly, even those who did not accept responsibility for their incarceration—or found their own incarceration to be unjust or unfair in some way—used the language of personal choice, responsibility, or self-improvement. For these respondents, yoga and meditation became tools to make the best of a bad situation, to accept it without anger or reactivity, to make better choices while incarcerated, or to see the situation as a blessing in disguise, turning a negative into an "opportunity." Benjamin, a Black man in his fifties, was extremely detailed in describing the injustice of his incarceration. Despite early run-ins with the system, Benjamin eventually settled down into a middle-class life with a home, a family, and steady employment. Benjamin is emphatic that he was set up by the police, and that his incarceration for illegal gun possession entailed severe police misconduct. Despite this, Benjamin insists on the importance of personal transformation while incarcerated: "If people would just look within instead of outwardly . . . I never thought the answer was within me. And now, [after studying Buddhism], I know it is. I know what I've been doing for so many years was the wrong direction I was taking. [Buddhism] has transformed me. From before I went to prison to where I'm at today, it's night and day." Of all my respondents, Benjamin offers perhaps the most extensive critique of the injustice of his own incarceration. Yet, Buddhist meditation was a way for him to transform himself from the "wrong direction" he was taking.

Like Elisa, Lucas served eight years of a ten-year term for a sexual offense with a minor, committed when he was 18. Although he is white, Lucas came from a relatively disadvantaged background, and fell into the system early. He insists that while he did make some mistakes, he did not do everything he was charged with. "I was young . . . [The prosecutor's office] just started stacking charges, trying to find something that would stick. That's when I took a deal." Lucas describes being threatened with charges in unsolved cases, even though there was no evidence to tie him to them. Despite being targeted by prosecutorial discretion and overcharging, Lucas insists on self-improvement through meditation: "We could improve on ourselves in any aspects. And I think mindfulness or [Buddhist] meditation does that. It leads to self-rehabilitation, with the ego, and selfishness. If you put that effort in, I think there's a lot of potential for change."

Alex provides perhaps the most striking example of adopting personal responsibility language despite insisting that he was unfairly charged and sentenced. Alex is a white man in his forties from an underprivileged background. He describes being incarcerated for what was essentially a misunderstanding: While trying to retrieve some of his own property from a former rental residence, he was charged with breaking and entering. Due to a prior conviction on his record, Alex was also intimidated by prosecutors threatening him with a life-sentence, and decided not to fight the charge: "I didn't even take it to court and say, 'Well, I used to rent a room there. I'll explain all this.' They threatened me. 'Well, you want to do life? Because you're a second-termer, we can strike you out on this.' . . . At first, I'd say, 'well, they can't do that!' And then I had to remember, 'wait a second, they can do this, what legal rights do I have?'"

"I got unjustly charged and sentenced," Alex says emphatically. Yet, in the same conversation, he adheres strongly to the ideas of personal responsibility and accepting consequences for one's bad choices. He tells a story about being influenced by a presentation given in prison: "This guy says '*well, you got choices, decisions and consequences . . . it's a real simple rule to live by in life.*' And then he says '*oh, by the way, what does that stand for if you put it into an acronym? That's right, gentlemen, CDC, California Department of Corrections.*'" I ask Alex if he found this compelling. "Of course!" he responds emphatically. "What he said was very profound and truthful." Throughout our conversation, Alex harks back to the mantra of "CDC," and the Buddhist practice that allowed him to change himself: "This is one of my character defects and I have to change things. And that's one thing Buddhism and meditation did for me. . . . No matter what you do, it took a decision, and everything has a consequence. I manned up to it, and accepted responsibility for my actions."

Narrative 1. Accepting Prison as a Growth Opportunity or Blessing

Many of the respondents in the first group reported using meditation or yoga to deal with their anger about incarceration through cultivating acceptance. Certainly, among those who felt their incarceration to be largely warranted, this was unsurprising. For instance, Matt noted that he was at peace with himself having realized: "*It's ok, I created my karma. . . .* I could accept things as they were, and work on trying to change my perspective on life." But the language of acceptance was more remarkable among those who found their incarceration to be unjust. Both Benjamin and Lucas described tremendous anger at the events leading to their incarceration, including police and/or prosecutorial misconduct. Benjamin insists, "I'm in there for no reason. You just disrupted and took away my beautiful life for nothing. . . . I was angry when I first went in there. But I come out totally different. So [meditation] will help you if you allow it to." Lucas says, "It might have been through meditation that I was able to accept [my sentence] enough that it didn't bother me so much." Alex talks about those he admired most in prison: "Even though they had [a life term] to shoulder, I'd say '*how could these people be happy?*' 'Coz they said, '*we accept things the way they are, and we're going to make the best of it.*' . . . that's one thing meditation did for me. It enabled me to accept things the way they are."

Most of my respondents also reported using their yoga or meditation practice to remain nonreactive to the conditions of confinement, including unfair or inhumane treatment. Almost every respondent reported being witness to—or subject to—abusive treatment while incarcerated. These reports ran the gamut: everything from extreme medical neglect to aggressive or violent behavior by correctional officers, inconsistent application or outright flouting of prison policies by officers, retaliation for filing grievances, instigation of fights or riots by officers, unwarranted cell-searches, sexual assault or abuse, and beatings of handcuffed persons, among many other things. Danny's remarks are representative of most of the respondents in this group: almost laughing, he acknowledges being subject to violation and abuse the "majority of the time" during his incarceration, and reports dealing with this frustration by seeing it through a Buddhist lens, as a "mental attachment [that] causes us to suffer. . . . I just kinda learn how to do my time and ignore all those situations."

Another version of this acceptance emerged when some respondents chose to "reframe" their prison time as a growth opportunity or a blessing despite—and sometimes because of—the hardship it entailed. Again, respondents like Matt who found their incarceration to be legitimate were most enthusiastic. Matt muses, "I think if I had to do it all over again, I would do it all over again. The environment didn't make it easy, [but] that was the crucible for the changes that I need to make. I don't regret it, it's made me who I am today." Matt even insists that he is "grateful" at having been denied parole the first time: "I felt [they] blessed me." Lee admits that we might "think it's crazy," and says, "I don't wish it on anyone, but I'm glad I was incarcerated . . . it might have been the best thing that happened to me." He calls his twenty-two-year sentence a "timeout" to reflect on his behavior, educate himself, learn coping skills, and deal with his issues. Madeleine, a white woman in her forties, who spent six years incarcerated on substance-abuse charges, says she used her meditation practice to "reframe and shift" her perspective: " 'everything is happening for us, not to us.' That to me feels like the most powerful way to look at it." Describing the violence and abusive behavior she encountered by staff in prison, Madeleine insists, "we attract what we need for our spiritual evolution, for the evolution of our soul . . . everything happens for a reason." Elisa, like several others, casts prison time as a spiritual experience, as an "ashram or retreat," a time to read Buddhist books and reflect on herself: "I would say I probably came out a better person, even though I wasn't really broken before . . . I honestly can't say, 'I wish I could not have been in prison for six years.' Each step in that journey taught me something. There's nothing I would change." Elisa's remarks are notable, precisely because she continues to insist that she was never "broken" or "criminal" to begin with.

This perspective was also adopted by respondents who considered their incarceration unwarranted. Their incarceration may have been unjust, but their time in prison was one of spiritual growth and personal change through yogic or meditative practices, a blessing or a growth opportunity. Adam, a white man in his forties who served nine months on a misdemeanor charge for corporate misconduct, uses the language of ancient spiritual retreat: "In the old days, people went into caves to get away from things and try to figure out themselves and meditate. To some extent, the same is happening in the prison. There's less distraction from the outside world. You do have a lot of time to think about philosophy and what it all means." Adrian is a Black man in his forties who was charged and wrongly incarcerated in a case of mistaken identity. "I like to say, '*I wasn't arrested, I was rescued,*'" he notes. "I needed to be off the streets, I was running rampant. I see it as a blessing, I learned how to meditate, I learned how to fast, I got closer to God, I got some spiritual foundations." As much criminological research shows, many incarcerated individuals cope by developing a positive narrative of their predicament.[62] For my respondents, yoga or meditation were crucial coping strategies for reframing or accepting their fate.

Narrative 1. Political Views and Actions: "It's All up to the Individual"

I also explored each interviewee's political views on mass incarceration: whether they had any views on this issue, and whether they engaged in any collective political discussions or actions while incarcerated. Regardless of how they felt about the legitimacy of their sentence, every single respondent in this group was critical of mass incarceration (though to varying degrees), and produced strong critiques when invited to comment on the topic. Many described how the boom in mass imprisonment had affected their own experience through phenomena such as overcrowding, cost-savings on food, and overworked staff. Most saw the system as unjust and inequitable, and criticized the specific conditions of incarceration, including the violence and abuse they witnessed.[63] However, only three from this first group mentioned any political action while incarcerated, either through hunger strikes or other forms of protest. And, such actions were largely one-off instances rather than sustained activism. The rest all largely stayed away from any political action, mostly because such action or resistance brought inevitable consequences for release or parole. As Benjamin notes, "I was trying to get up out of there as quick as possible. I'm not trying to draw no attention." Danny elaborates that political resistance affects one's chances of being found suitable for parole, while a record of attending prison programs improves these chances. "Ultimately I wanna have a shot at going home," he says, "I have to do what's best for me and my family, so . . . I'm just gonna focus on trying to get my-self out." Some stayed away from political discussions, because they found such topics too "gloomy" or "negative." Madeleine called such discussions a "complaining-fest," where there were "never any solutions:" "I [wanted to] discuss things that had the potential for solution," she insists. Javier reports searching for "something positive" instead of the "negative things" they could not "manage and control: That's the path we chose to focus on."

Despite a strong understanding of systemic or structural issues, everyone in this group stuck to an individualized framework for making sense of their own situation, as well as of mass incarceration in general. Personal solutions were offered to problems that were admittedly structural, with the phrase "it's all up to the individual" occurring many times. This should not be surprising among those who accepted full responsibility and emphasized individual actions as the main causal factor for incarceration. As Lee says, "I would say society has some part of why I became what I became . . . but it all comes down to individual choices, to what that person chooses to do." But even among those who considered themselves unjustly incarcerated, the language of in-dividual choice and rehabilitation continued to predominate as an explana-tion for—and sometimes a response to—mass incarceration, despite systemic critiques. "Rehabilitation has to be a personal choice," insists Marshawn, a Black man in his thirties who served several decades in prison:[64] "It's on the individual." Even those who critiqued the system for being unjust—and saw their own experience as a manifestation of this—saw yogic or meditative prac-tice as an individualized solution to a systemic problem. Alex, for instance, offers a fierce, detailed critique of the "evil machine" of mass incarceration (including the financial incentives and bond issuances for prison-building, as well as the power of lobbyists and unions). Yet, he almost immediately reverts to discussing the "rehabilitation factor" as the solution to mass incarcera-tion: "[It's] up to the individual. . . . They got three meals, they got a roof . . . [they can] read books. The rehabilitation factor starts with [these] choices . . . this is where yoga and meditation come into play . . . what can we do as indi-viduals, to make a difference?"

In sum, the fifteen (of twenty-five) respondents who expressed Narrative 1 all advocated for the "rehabilitative" benefits of yoga or meditation, using it to accept their fate and overcome their anger either at the conditions of in-carceration, or the very legitimacy of their incarceration; or to see their time in prison as a growth opportunity or blessing. This was true whether they felt their incarceration was legitimate or not. And it was also true despite the fact that almost all of them produced strong critiques of the systems and structures of incarceration, as well as the conditions of incarceration. Despite these critiques, all adhered to the view that the solution to systemic or structural injustice lay on the level of personal change by individuals. These respondents were also largely apolitical while incarcerated—they may have participated in conversations about structural injustice, but did not take any political action.

Narrative 1. Freedom Inside

Despite their rejection of political action—at least traditionally understood—the respondents in this group did express a form of internal freedom and autonomy that allowed them to feel more in control of their lives and self-understandings, in ways that resisted the prison's attempts to control and label their experiences. They may not have called this "resistance," but yogic or meditative practices allowed them to assert and recreate agency in ways that went beyond traditional forms of activism. "[Through] meditation," says Alex, "I learned how to justly treat myself. So it doesn't matter what the world does. . . . Believe it or not, I had freedom inside. I refused to just exist. I'm going to make a life in here, I'm going to be happy—probably as happy as you could be inside prison." Like Madeleine, several respondents cast their spiritual growth as a form of freedom: "freedom from the attachment, from needing things to go your way." "I let go of all my attachments," she says. "I could have been really miserable inside, being annoyed by roommates, or the violence or being locked down for a couple weeks, not being able to use the phone, [it's a] really tight and awful way to live. I got to really use this practice, I didn't have to participate in the suffering of that. It can be really helpful to find joy through the suffering."

Many of the respondents in this group told stories similar to those told by Jay Jarvis Masters, the Buddhist on death row referenced earlier. Masters describes his Buddhist training as an invaluable resource, allowing him to cope not only with the unimaginable suffering of awaiting execution on death row but also with the abuse he witnesses and endures. Faced with horrific conditions, and often confronted with sadistic staff, Masters learns to remain detached and nonreactive, capable of seeing their suffering and silently offering them compassion. In one memorable story, officers who—despite his protestations of innocence—believe Masters to be responsible for the murder of their colleague, commemorated the anniversary of the murder in a particularly abusive way. Hoping to provoke Masters into a reaction that might invite and justify further abuse, they intentionally moved him into a cell left full of sewage and garbage by its previous inhabitants, forcing him to clean it in order to make it habitable. "My new home," he acknowledged, "was the worst hellhole in San Quentin."[65] But Masters quietly cleaned the filth, tying a gag around his nose and mouth to prevent himself from vomiting, all the while contemplating the anger and suffering that drove the officers to such behavior. When the cell was immaculate, he meditated for an hour. When a friend expressed rage on his behalf at the sickness and injustice—the "evil assholes who controlled every aspect of their lives"—Masters remained cheery and nonreactive, refusing to express anger or partake of his friend's rant. Echoing this notion of a freedom achieved through intense practices of compassion and nonreactivity, Madeleine describes (sometimes through tears) a similar spiritual freedom that allowed her to transcend her circumstances, without falling into anger or despair:

> This peace came over me, there was a hole in the eye of the storm . . . it gave me freedom, it was a very powerful experience for me . . . it brought me joy no matter where I was . . . through the suffering, through the pain. . . . Meditation was a way of just letting it go through me . . . [to] be present and have joy in this moment.

Many of my respondents point to the fact that accepting one's situation and coping with it is often the only option while incarcerated. In fact, nothing characterizes prison life more accurately than being forced to accept things out of one's control. Struggling against a situation without any hope of change can be unhealthy and dangerous. Danny describes the repeated frustration he experienced when officers would "toss" cells during searches: "They would just leave everything a mess. And I would get angry about that. You know, your clothes are on the floor. . . . It's like they don't care . . . it's your living quarters." But Danny points out that "the situation already happened, so getting angry at the officer doesn't do any good . . . [meditation] lessens the frustration, irritation, and anger, and allows for ease." Adrian rightly points out that there is no safe alternative to acceptance in such situations: "This is the only reality I can live in," he asserts. But he found that yogic and meditative practices taught him how to "act and not react:" "sometimes the best action is *no* action . . . you gotta redirect your energy, you gotta collect your bearings, you can't do anything enraged. You can screw up a lot of stuff acting out of anger and fear . . . [yoga or meditation] allows me to step back and choose my battle in the long haul."

Alex admitted he still found himself "getting upset about '*they can't do that!*' or '*they can't do this!*' And then you have to settle down and say, '*wait a second, who has the key to the door . . . them or me?*'" In describing himself as possessing "the key to the door," Alex echoes a principle that Masters learned from his Buddhist teachers: "We all live in a prison, and we all hold the key." At first,

Masters had been "cynical, even angry" on hearing this: "More patronizing bullshit.... You do not live in prison.... The keys to my cell are hanging off my jailers' belts."[66] But eventually, Masters came to believe that he did in fact "hold the key" to his own freedom: By controlling his mind, he felt a sense of release, while his hatred and seething rage slowly morphed into tenderness and compassion over the years. In much the same way, many of my respondents in this group, despite being largely apolitical, described a freedom that did not rely on the changing of their situation in order to feel more humanized, more in control of their inner worlds and their destiny. Instead, they created for themselves an internal refuge of freedom, without necessarily engaging in overt political action to demand structural change. This internal refuge exemplifies what Thomas Ugelvik calls "an escape from being a prisoner, a form of resistance against the objectification and 'othering' that the status of prisoner entails."[67]

Narrative 2: Resistance Rather Than Acceptance of Individual Responsibility

The second group of respondents were a minority of ten women and men who held extremely resistant views both regarding mass incarceration and their own incarceration. These respondents offered keen structural analyses of both their own situations, as well as of mass incarceration in general. Most of them also reported coming from backgrounds of racial or socio-economic disadvantage, although notably, three of them—all white women—came from relative privilege, by their own admission. The respondents in this group refused to accept the prison's narrative that they alone were responsible for their incarceration, and instead pointed to flaws in social and political arrangements.

Sean, a Black man in his fifties who spent almost 33 years incarcerated, exemplified the keener political analyses among this group of respondents: "how can the system not be held responsible for creating an environment that makes it almost implausible for an individual not to have contact with law enforcement and statistically wind up in jail or prison, if you come from socially-economically depressed communities, and you're a person of color?...I got caught in a mouse trap, it was set up to be like this." Their understanding of issues like choice and responsibility was robust, accounting for structural inequities that constrained choices. Sandra is a Black woman who details a life of poverty, homelessness, racism, and abuse (physical, sexual and emotional).[68] She served over two decades for accidentally killing her assailant while defending herself during an assault. She says: "I definitely want to be accountable, but [is the law] telling me I should not have fought back? Should I have taken the bullet so that I'd be more believable? Where was the law when I was getting beat, having cigarette burns on me, when I was raped, when I filed multiple re-straining orders? And the one time I fight back, it's my fault? It just seems like more victim-blaming."

These respondents also rejected the prison's judgmental, diagnostic notion of "rehabilitation" which told them they "deserved" their incarceration, and instead used yoga or meditation to focus on a version of self-improvement that would allow them to challenge the prison's narratives. Notably, four of them pointed to their yoga or meditation practice as the very thing that polit-icized them, and offered examples of political resistance that were inspired by these teachings. Five were engaged in activism, either during incarceration or after release, and at least one traced the roots of this activism to the meditative teachings learned in prison. Two respondents had already considered the pos-sibility of yoga or meditation producing docility among incarcerated individ-uals, and reflected on ways to use these teachings against the system instead.

Narrative 2. Resisting the Prison's "Kool-Aid"

Many of these respondents were deeply critical of the so-called rehabilita-tive goals of incarceration. These critiques fell into several different catego-ries. One strand of critique came from those who resisted the judgmental, diagnostic quality of rehabilitative language. Elizabeth, a white woman in her forties, notes, "When you're talking about '*rehabilitating*' people, what are you saying? That there's something wrong with them, and you're going to make that person into what you think they should be? . . . The system is still harming you. They're telling you '*you're a piece of crap, you're no good.*'"

A second kind of critique insisted that the prison's therapeutic or behavioral mandates were not only unhelpful, but also punitive and trauma-inducing. Respondents rejected the prison's claims of a correlation between therapeutic programs and recidivism. Grace is a white woman in her forties who served one year on a sex-offense charge which she notes would not have been a crime in many other states. Like many others, Grace insists that "therapeutic" in-carceration is a myth. "Give me a break, you're not rehabilitating anyone," she practically spits out. "It's a bunch of crap. You can't take people, pluck them out of their lives, treat them like animals, all but brand them, then say you're gonna make them better . . . [as though] that's actually gonna give people self-worth, dignity, and value." Grace notes that most prison programming follows the recovery model of substance-abuse programs such as Alcoholics

Anonymous (AA) and Narcotics Anonymous (NA). She objects to the claim that "a mandated 3-hour-a-week" program can "fix" anyone: "You treat us like we're infantile and expect us to respond to this behavior-modification. We're not fourth-graders, we don't want a sticker, we don't want a piece of candy." Evelyn is a white woman in her twenties who served several years in prison on a DUI charge involving the accidental death of a friend. She also expresses anger at therapeutic mandates, which did not resonate or help her: "I definitely resent the 'treatment' and mental health that they offered, it does not work! I am not grateful for it. It's 100% because of the justice system that I am suicidal."

Here, Evelyn notes that the prison's mandated therapeutic programs compounded her trauma, rather than relieving it. Grace takes this critique further, insisting that the so-called correlation between prison time and lowered recidivism is "bullshit." She also notes that the ongoing therapeutic mandates during her parole process have been farcical: "[This] therapy that's supposed to be 'fixing' me so I won't go out and reoffend, [this] 'containment' model is meant to make me better? It doesn't. It angers me, it embitters me, it inhibits me from living my best life. Because the assumption that if I wasn't taking their test and peeing in a cup, I would be out there looking for my next 'victim,' is absolutely ridiculous."

A third kind of critique was more political, asserting that prison programming is intended to control, neutralize, and pacify marginalized populations in a variety of ways. Some called this "brainwashing" through the idea of just deserts, and of flawed individuals requiring rehabilitation. Michael Cox, who also wanted his real name used, is a white man in his twenties who served five years on substance abuse-related charges. Michael sums up this brainwashing as the "Kool-aid" of law-and-order: "In prison that is the language that you're taught to use. I was drinking the Kool-aid, that indoctrination we all got. My inquiry didn't extend any further to: Why do we have such long sentences? Why don't we give more leeway to folks who come from really rough backgrounds and didn't have a fighting chance? You can begin to internalize [the idea that] *These programs are here to rehabilitate you—it's all your own fault if you're having a tough time.* When you try to tell people, they're like, *'no my life's fine, I deserve what I got.'*" Evelyn is even more blunt, asserting, "I [was] one of the 'brainwashed' . . . I only asked myself these [critical] questions recently, [you] can't ask too many questions in prison, they don't want you to incite a riot." In fact, Sandra shows us how prisons use the logic of rehabilitation to whitewash and side-step questions of systemic injustice: "If I am indeed in need of rehabilitation, how did I become broken if my environment was so perfect? . . . I've brought [that] up and do you know what I get? That

I'm assuming the 'poor-me,' victim mentality, blaming everybody else except myself. If you're persistent [in these critiques], it shows in your master file that you were uncooperative in the program."

Emile De Weaver, another respondent who insisted on having his real name used, is a Black man in in his forties who has been incarcerated for over half his life, and, until his release, had spent every birthday since his thirteenth in prison. Emile practiced both yoga and meditation while incarcerated. He is a writer and an activist, perhaps the most politically active respondent I spoke to, offering some of the most incisive critiques of the system. Emile asserts that the pacification of incarcerated persons is in the very nature of prison programming: "The structures of those programs are not invested in incarcerated people's success; they are invested in neutralizing incarcerated persons as a threat. Once we feel this person is no longer a threat, he doesn't matter any more, we can give them yoga so they can deal with their anger problems, but don't give him a job when he gets out." Sean likewise insists: "Prison programs don't teach you how to be free, they teach you how to do time. . . . If you're not free internally, you can accept being held prisoner." In different ways, these respondents all echoed the view we examined in the previous chapter: that prison programs served as a tool of social control through indoctrination, often in ways that were punitive and painful, despite their ostensibly "therapeutic" nature.

Narrative 2. "Prison Didn't Rehabilitate Me—I Did!"

It is worth noting that every one of the respondents in this group spoke of their yoga or meditation practice as something apart from the prison's mandated rehabilitative or therapeutic requirements.[69] Even as they resisted the prison's behavioral modification, they undertook their own version of self-transformation, which they insisted was entirely their own effort, quite apart from the prison's mandates.[70] Both Evelyn and Grace insisted that the prison's rehabilitation stood in stark contrast to what they described as "true self-improvement" through yoga and meditation. As Grace noted, "How can I improve myself, feel more connected to the 'me' I want to be, rather than the 'me' everybody else is telling me I have to be? You're just working on yourself, not you the prisoner or the addict— just *you*. . . . You don't have to accept the prison system . . . [or that it's] right."

Like Grace and Evelyn, several respondents in this group claimed that the prison had nothing to do with their self-transformation, that it was the fruit of their own hard work and their own relationship to themselves. Grace asserts: "If anybody is rehabilitated, it's not because of any program. . . . The women are doing their own work. Not '*here's this way that you can fix me,*' but rather '*I want to be a better me, not because I screwed over society and need to be fixed.*'" Monique, a Black woman in her twenties who served two years, is also most emphatic on this point: "No, no. Prison did not change me," she insists. "*I changed me. I* did that work. Unfortunately, I was in prison before I did the work. But if I had had access to this information, then maybe I wouldn't have to end up in prison to do the work." These remarks echo Sean, who asserts, "You can only be rehabilitated if you take the reins and take control." Like Sean, many insisted that positive self-transformation occurred *despite* rather than because of the prison, which is invested in perpetuating its own existence: "Once you put me in prison . . . it's like a petri dish, I can't do anything but become worse. And [the system] *knows* this and *allows* this, because it's [their] intention to criminalize and penalize individuals like me who come from these environments." Like participants in other prison studies, these respondents did report positive self-transformation while incarcerated, but credited themselves for such efforts.[71]

Narrative 2. "If I Created This Life, I Can Create Something Else"

For many of the respondents in this group, relearning choice or responsibility through yoga or meditation was empowering. For them, "choosing differently," did not mean accepting the systemic messages they received about individualized responsibility for their fate. Emile offered a robust version of this argument: "I cannot deny the power of what accountability has done for me. . . . I don't care what anybody else did to contribute to my life," he admits. "'*What are the things I did? How can I shift this situation with my own power? If I created this life, I can create something else.*'" Yet, Emile insists that "individuals transforming themselves" or "choosing differently" cannot serve as a response to systemic problems: "This idea of accountability is not a solution to mass incarceration. There are a hundred more twenty-year-olds who just went to prison for life. The cycle simply continues."

Hakeem is a Black man in his forties who came from a background of poverty, abuse, and trauma. He served twenty-four years of a life sentence. He accepts that his behavior led to his predicament, but insists, "I can also understand and remove myself from this predicament." I ask him to elaborate. "We always talk about how unjust the system is, which is the truth," he says. "At the same time, I'm trying to figure out . . . how did I end up here, with these people lording it over me? . . . When I see the problem within myself, I can fix it: That's where the meditation and yoga play a part." Hakeem's perspective was echoed by several others: If they had made choices that placed them in the grip of an oppressive system, they could also make choices to exit and resist such a system, using tools such as yoga or meditation. This view fully acknowledges systemic injustice, but sees self-improvement through these practices as a form of resistance. Sean, who earlier spoke about "taking the reins" of one's own rehabilitation, expressed the same idea: "[I decided] I'm never gonna accept this [injustice] or get comfortable with it. I'm gonna become a bigger and better person, not let this smother my spirit and soul. . . . I'm going to show the system they should never let me out, because I'm gonna be the best example of what freedom is supposed to look like."

For Elizabeth, a white woman in her forties, the choices learned from yoga and meditation were empowering in two senses: First, they taught her that she could choose how to respond to negative thoughts. Second, she also learned that her previous choices were "not her," and that she could choose to resist systemic messages about her flaws and lack of worth. Elizabeth came from a background of poverty and abuse, hitting rock-bottom while engaging in sex work to fuel her addictions. She served seventeen years of a life-sentence on a felony murder charge for being in a getaway car while her abusive boyfriend— also her pimp—was involved in an attempted murder. "My entire incarceration I felt like I was never good enough," Elizabeth says. "I belonged in prison because I deserved it, because I was a scumbag. When I started meditating . . . I saw that I had a choice to respond to [my thoughts] instead of reeling from them." These choices to think differently about herself allowed Elizabeth to stop "listening to society, to the life sentence. . . . [I was] not carrying that shame and guilt any more, being able to forgive myself for choices I made in the past, and recognize that is not me. I believe I am good, I never believed that before, I guess."

Some respondents spoke about purely pragmatic reasons to adopt the language of responsibility, while maintaining one's understanding of structural injustice. Emile says, "Systemically, this society was designed to push me into a life of crime, to arrest me, and incarcerate me. Those things aren't gonna change if I sit on my hands and say, *I'm not the problem, so I'm not gonna do anything.*' I'm not living in a position of power that allows me to do that. So from a practical standpoint, accountability allowed me to navigate a system that is designed for me to fail. This isn't ethical, but it's how people of color have to navigate white supremacist structures." But he also points out that this *must* be purely pragmatic, because personal responsibility and accountability do not constitute a solution to mass incarceration: "It's a trap, if you buy into the myth [of] legitimating the system that you have to navigate." Unlike the respondents in the previous group who insisted that individual self-improvement was the appropriate solution to mass incarceration, Emile represents the far more political view that systemic problems cannot rely on individual solutions, but require collective political action.

Narrative 2. Do Yoga and Meditation Produce Compliance, or Resistant Consciousness?

While many respondents in this group noted that prison logic worked to make them passive and accepting, a few did worry that yoga or meditation could reinforce that passivity. Emile admits to having been pacified at the beginning of his yoga and meditation practice in prison: "[Initially] it really resonated with me, [this idea of] '*I put myself here . . . I deserve this, we're coming to fix you, there's something wrong with you*' . . . the docility it can create is rather sad and tragic." Chloe, a white woman in her forties, also worried about this: "The basic premises of acceptance of the moment, and of your lot in life, and everything being transient: [all this] does seem to reinforce the concept that we should just accept [incarceration]." Michael, who earlier talked about drinking "Kool-aid" was the most emphatic on this issue. He points out that "injustice is often not taught in Buddhism . . . there's [sometimes] a lot of Confucianism involved, it teaches subservience. There's an aspect of Buddhism that's very pacifying, maybe that's why it's promoted in prison. Prison administrators are worrying about how they could control the inmate population more easily, so it's not about healing or personal growth, [just] about control of law and order." I ask Michael to elaborate on how this showed up in his own prison experience. "I rationalized [my time] as being the karmic fruit of my actions. My thinking around this would evolve later, but initially I was like '*Ok, this is your karma, you own this*.' A concept like karma is reinforcing this fucked-up society, to normalize it."

   Michael also went on to critique Buddhism's tendency toward being apolitical and ignoring issues of justice. "There's definitely something missing with our people in the Buddhist world. [Political protest] is too messy for Buddhists. [This is] the dark side of right speech, not saying what needs to be said, spiritual bypassing, '*I'm not gonna acknowledge it, just be silent*.'" Michael is adamant that this silence and bypassing is an incorrect interpretation of Buddhism: "Wake up, what's wrong with you? The Buddha was like '*fuck the caste system, what is this shit?*' We have a responsibility to use our moral authority to advocate for change in this world."

But despite such worries, these respondents also expressed optimism for the political potentials of yogic and meditative practice. For some, these practices allowed them to see structural injustice more clearly. Here again is Emile, describing the effects of his meditation practice: "It made me see more clearly, understanding the complexity . . . [and] seeing [incarceration] as a systemic problem. [Realizing that] the system is messed up. [All the] programs encourage you to ignore the systemic level, and think '*it's all my fault.*' [Instead, my meditations] just shifted my viewpoint, they helped me understand what had happened to me, because I had enough distance and could detach from the immediate feelings.'" For Hakeem, yoga and meditation allowed him to develop a "warrior spirit" that channeled his righteous anger "into something positive, [to] bring an innovative approach and resolve a problem." Using the "self-discipline and self-control" he learned through these practices, Hakeem learned how to navigate the system: "I see how they play the game, so now I know. We playin' in their backyard, it's their authority, their monopoly, so we need to navigate through that, to end up with a better hand. That's where the yoga and meditation come in."

This echoes Michael's remarks—he reported that his Buddhist practice inspired both critical inquiry into the nature of unjust systems, and nonviolent resistance. Michael clarifies that this resistance was accompanied by skillful interactions with prison staff, representing the best aspects of his meditation practice: "In some ways I was more harmonious, but in other ways I really stood in my truth, stood my ground." He notes that as he developed his practice, he began to interact with prison staff more skillfully: "I would try to engage them as a person, see them not just as my oppressors, [and that] impacted the response that I got from them." Yet, this had a "flip side," he notes: When aggressive or violent officers treated him unfairly, Michael credited his meditation practice with giving him the strength to stand his ground nonviolently, even when it entailed the threat of solitary confinement, a punishment he endured more than once as a result.

Michael notes that his thinking has now "sharpened [and] become more critical," in keeping with his understanding of Buddhism, which has led him naturally to his activism on prison abolition. "When I was introduced to abolition I was resistant at first," he admits, "but then I saw how consistent it was with Buddhist principles." In describing the evolution of his political views, Michael notes, "[It] started with Buddhism, like *does this cause suffering or does it alleviate it*? I started to critique the world around me. You could see that this system of mass incarceration clearly causes additional suffering. So I [started to think about] the causes and conditions that give rise to the need for prisons. We have behaviors, but we also have societal conditions, [like] poverty and racism. We're going for liberation of the mind in Buddhism, in abolition we're also going for liberation of our people and bodies."

Narrative 2. Volunteer Work in Prisons: Compliant or Resistant Consciousness?

Perhaps the most notable difference among the two groups was the suggestion that prison volunteers might play a role in encouraging compliance or resistance toward the prison's narratives. These respondents identified two main pitfalls, both having to do with the attitudes of volunteers. First, they emphasized that volunteers should be aware of the tendency to repeat the judgmental, diagnostic quality of the prison's discourse and its notion of flawed individuals needing "fixing." Second, they insisted on critical inquiry about social justice by volunteers, so that volunteer work could encourage an oppositional consciousness among incarcerated students.

Emile, Monique, and Sandra discussed the first issue, pointing to volunteers who uncritically reproduced the prison's story of flawed individuals needing rehabilitation. "Out here on the streets, no one is telling you in a yoga class, *'there's something wrong with you, we're gonna help you fix it,'* " says Emile. "But when you put [yoga or meditation] in a prison setting, [it becomes] *'something's wrong with you, yoga's gonna help you fix it.'* . . . There's this misguided idea [among volunteers], that *'if I equip them with emotional intelligence, that's better for society'* . . . You're failing to realize no one was born wanting to punch people in the face!" Monique points to the often-racialized dimensions of this phenomenon: "These little white women . . . there's this 'savior complex' that comes with it. Even though [their] intentions are very good, [they] are talking down to [prisoners] all the time. I don't need somebody else coming in here and telling me what's wrong with me and how to fix it. Don't come in here and assume that because you see me [here], you know who I am. . . . Just stop diagnosing, stop saying, *'This is what you deserve.'* "

Emile speaks at length about the second issue: that of yoga or meditation taught in prisons by—mainly white—volunteers without any reference to social or political or systemic issues. "Your idea [as a volunteer]—that you can bring healing without acknowledging and healing the *political* damage that has been done to [incarcerated] people—is doing more damage," he notes. "You're not seeing them. That's a form of erasure when you say *'I'm just coming in to heal.'* It's selfish, you get to feel good." Sandra offers another incisive critique of the damage done by yoga or meditation volunteers who press incarcerated persons to "take responsibility" without accounting for the structural disadvantages they suffered:

> There is power in accountability [and] so many of us are willing to accept responsibility. But we are saying that it took society, the totality of circumstances, both in and out of my control, to get me where I am. [But] none of that matters . . . my being conditioned to fight, the abuse I suffered at home [and] in relationships, the two sexual assaults by strange men at gunpoint, none of those mattered. [The law says] '*So what if that happened to you? You are a criminal now, you must take responsibility for those things.*' And then we get in here, we're trying to heal, to put the pieces of our life together, and in the one place where I would like to think our stories would be validated, we get into these meditative classes where the facilitators say, '*we're gonna do the same thing that the rest of society has done to you . . . tell you essentially it's your fault. The sooner you accept it, the better life will be*' . . . As well-meaning as the facilitators may be, when [the practice] is focused solely on personal responsibility and accountability, it can be very disempowering. Especially in a demographic of women who, at least 90% of us have been sexually assaulted, mentally abused, physically abused, we've been shown and told over and over again how powerless we are, and then to turn around and say, '*you have the power, it's your fault,*' it's hard to reconcile those.

For precisely this reason, Emile says, yoga or meditation volunteers who claim to be "apolitical" when entering prisons are invoking a form of privilege: "They are exercising the privilege [of saying '*I'm not political*'] within a white supremacy structure that gives them that privilege."

Like Emile, several others insisted that volunteers needed to provide a social justice perspective critical of the prison system. Ideally, Chloe says, volunteers should be able to "manage both [yoga or] meditation, and promoting social change . . . embody those concepts of acceptance, nonviolence, and yet, hold on to the reality of injustice [and] be the motivation for change." Sean suggests yoga and meditation must be taught as an avenue for awareness and education about inequity: "about the institutions that are really responsible for you being here: to understand that you're probably here because you never got a real chance, that the system isn't meant to uplift people from certain economic situations, ethnic or racial situations." Emile is particularly vocal, insisting that "we are in need of political education among incarcerated people," and suggesting that yoga and meditation can become a platform for such radical action and education. He offers suggestions for the content of yoga or meditation classes in prisons: yoga and meditation be taught as "an expedient" means to incarcerated persons, to "survive a system that is unjust, [to] have tools to thrive, [to] start working to move this reality closer to how it should be.'" Michael also emphasizes that yoga and meditation in prisons must be taught in ways that can "critique societies," "promote inquiry, and challenge preconceptions."

This is the closest any of my respondents came to identifying a relationship between volunteers' perspectives and the political consciousness of incarcerated people. It is worth noting that none of them seem to have experienced an encounter with politicized volunteers in prison. In fact, a few admitted that they were taught yoga or meditation in prison in ways that converged with the narratives of personal responsibility. Despite the fact that they did not see volunteers challenging this perspective, several of them developed their own political consciousness. They seemed to become politicized through other channels, and eventually came to a more resistant understanding of their own practice. Yet, they seemed to have strong views about the potential connections between a volunteer's critical perspective and the emergence of oppositional perspectives among incarcerated persons, expressing hopes and recommendations that volunteers would teach politically attuned versions of yoga and meditation. Emile provided the most succinct hope that such politically attuned teachings by volunteers would have direct political effects, and I quote him at length:

> Incarcerated people are going to be best-equipped as untapped resources to organize and mobilize, they're a huge block of power. . . . It boggles my mind that there are 2.3 million motherfuckers in prison that you can organize toward stopping the white supremacist agenda . . . [and] let's give them each five family members, so that's like 10 million people who historically have had nothing to do with politics. They're tired, but you can organize them as a power base. If an incarcerated person gets out with a political education to organize a community, everybody in that person's family who saw them as throwaway is gonna look at them as a model. That's what's gonna galvanize them and their communities [to] organize and effectively mobilize power.

Discussion

The patterns that emerged from these conversations do not leave us with simple conclusions about how yoga and meditation work in prisons. Yogic or meditative practices clearly allowed my respondents, across both groups, to transcend their hellish circumstances, and to find a measure of freedom while incarcerated. Participants in both groups were able to experience self-love and self-compassion despite the messages received about their blameworthiness. Many were able to exit the mental prisons of shame, self-blame, and guilt perpetuated by the system that imprisoned them. Their practices allowed them to discern the complex webs of cause-and-effect that shaped their lives, and as a result, choose more meaningfully and mindfully among actions, instead of being unconsciously propelled by historical patterns of reaction. This provided many of them a measure of control in an environment where they were almost entirely deprived of any autonomy. In this way, they were able to cultivate an inner realm of freedom that did not rely on external change in order to feel more in control of their lives. The spiritual growth many experienced in the midst of suffering served as a testament to their resilience in the face of a brutal system of control. There seems to be no doubt that as long as mass incarceration exists in its current form, prisons must continue offering these practices, if only to assist in enduring what is clearly an assault on the self.

Yet for some, these practices seemed to reinforce the prison's logic of flawed individuals, while for others, they seemed to present a more explicit form of opposition to the prison and its narratives. This opposition was mostly internal—that is, pertaining to how individuals saw themselves—though in a few cases, it was external, allowing individuals to act in resistant ways. A majority of my respondents showed how yogic and meditative practices could reinforce the idea that incarcerated individuals must simply own their fate and take responsibility for the choices that put them there, with systemic factors being minimized. The solution to the systemic issue of mass incarceration was presented as individuals bettering themselves: "It's all on the individual," they would insist, despite having adopted a standard understanding of mass incarceration as systemically unjust. These respondents seemed largely disinterested in pursuing any political awareness or resistant action. Rather, many withdrew into an overall acceptance of their fate, and focused on improving themselves as the solution to this fate. As with the system-impacted individuals interviewed by other scholars, stories of structural inequality or systemic disadvantage were often followed by a vigorous commitment to ideas of personal uplift.[72] Interviewees spoke of injustices visited on the poor, the homeless, and minorities, yet adopted narratives of their own intrinsic failings, echoing the messages of penal institutions to "make better choices."[73]

The second group of respondents exemplified the idea that self-improvement entails a keen awareness of structural factors. In contrast to their counterparts in the first group, they accounted for structural obstacles that shaped their circumstances, rejecting the logic that they alone were at fault. Self-improvement became an act of defiance toward an oppressive system. This meant that many of them understood more fully the reality of unjust circumstances, without ever excusing or accepting them permanently. For some, withdrawing into the inner world of yoga or meditation was not an escape from or rejection of political action, but rather a preparatory step to strengthen oneself for future resistance. Respondents across both groups offered systemic critiques of mass incarceration. Despite this, I would argue that those in the second group were distinguished by a more oppositional, defiant or resistant consciousness. Those in the first group held a position that the prison scholar Ben Crewe describes as "committed compliance" toward the prison's goals and values: Despite their critiques of the system, they directed their agency and autonomy in ways consistent with the institution's objectives and goals.[74]

I offer this analysis with caution, noting that in some ways, there is not a hard binary between the two narratives. The only two options for incarcerated persons are not accepting full responsibility or engaging in full-throated political resistance and activism. James Scott reminds us of the "immense political terrain that lies between quiescence and revolt."[75] Prison researchers note that the everyday realities of prison life take place in the "extensive space between open rebellion and absolute consent."[76] My respondents shed light on a relatively underexplored space along this continuum, an internal space in which yogic and meditative practices can become a refuge where people are able to feel free and in control, no matter their external circumstances. Like Alex, who insisted that he and not the prison guards held "the key to the door," and like Masters—the Buddhist on death row—who remained nonreactive to horrific abuse, my respondents all used these practices to gain a form of inner strength that did not require external circumstances to be in their favor. An anonymous participant in a prison meditation retreat offers this evocative example:

> Focusing on the breath, I felt my lungs opening and closing. I watched how I kept myself alive. As I stayed with my breath, I then began to scan the various parts of my body, seeing how tense and knotted up I had become. As I focused on one spot and then the next, I was able to release so much tension; softening with the in-breath, and releasing with the out. Now there was peaceful, quiet space in which my awareness could rest. However, just as I was beginning to get really settled in the space, there came forth an eruption of thought fabrications. All these thoughts turned into stories, which suffocated my mind, clouding my awareness. Then, I was able to remember that these stories were just that, stories. There was no need to hang on to them, to entertain and build upon them. These stories were *dukkha* [suffering]. They were just like the razor-wire fences that surround this prison—only, these razor-wire fences surrounded my mind. With this perception

I let go, and for another moment, I was able to return to the space, the silence, the freedom.[77]

Like this retreat participant, my respondents resisted the prison's attempts to dehumanize them, instead humanizing themselves and asserting their own freedom. Not all of my respondents may have *called* this a form of resistance, but their stories ask us to consider it as such. Making claims on freedom without having to wait for an unjust system to be fixed—even while confined in an institution set on eliminating one's freedom and diminishing one's humanity—can be an act of subversion. These respondents allow us to amplify our understanding of the many "creative forms of agency, resistance, and influence"[78] that allow incarcerated persons to establish "free spaces within the institution's walls."[79] Through yogic or meditative practices, many were able to "tackle everyday prison life," without letting themselves be broken by the regime's demand for submission,"[80] while redefining themselves and their own identities, often through reclaiming the belief in an essentially good "core" self, regardless of past actions.[81] These narratives deepen and complicate our understandings of resistance in prisons, allowing us to recognize that "resistance should not be simply equated with . . . political action,"[82] and offering possibilities beyond "public defiance and rebellion" as indicators of resistance.[83]

One colleague has described these yogic and meditative forms of resistance as "stealing back one's inner life."[84] The time and space for inward-looking projects are denied to many people in this society, but most especially to those who come from communities targeted for incarceration. One's inner life is often captured by the demands of a patently unequal social and economic system which subjects these communities to institutionalized violence at disproportionately higher rates. Yogic and meditative practices can allow for both creating space and slowing down, in order to a create a critical mental distance from the institutions purporting to teach incarcerated persons that they "deserve" the suffering they endure. Without needing to undertake explicit resistance against this system, some of my respondents were able to preserve a more capacious and more expansive sense of self amid the brutality. Serenity was one of my respondents from the second group who best articulated this capacious sense of self: "If you can't control all the stuff that's happening around you, at least you can control yourself [and] find strength. I can control whether I allow this to break me, steal my joy, contentment, and hope. . . . I don't have the power of the government [to] not treat people the way they do, [but] I do have power over myself." Sandra, also from the second group, similarly asserts, "Are not yoga and meditation exercises designed to give us personal power, which is inner power? . . . Healing and wholeness is a way to resist the oppression, it's a form of resistance."

Certainly, the absence of visible, overt resistance (traditionally understood) need not automatically translate to acceptance or going along with the prison's program. Most options for resistance while imprisoned may be dangerous or impossible. At the very least, they can lead to the lengthening of one's sentence, and at worst, to harsh sanctions like solitary confinement, or even physical violence and death.[85] For this reason, many who undertake this kind of political action in prison are often lifers without parole, or others who have no hope of seeing freedom.[86] Those who have shorter sentences often avoid making waves, given that infractions as minor as rolling up the pants of one's prison-issued uniform on a hot day can result in a write-up that adds to one's sentence. Here again is Serenity:

> Unless you're someone who is a long-termer and don't see any hope of getting out soon, or don't have children waiting for you . . . you don't want to do anything to cause your sentence to be longer. I could have done some [political action], and I could be in there for five years [instead of] three . . . [But] I knew I was getting out. I was a mid-termer, I had young children . . . if I had had support on the outside, money, or an attorney, I didn't have anything like that . . . you just keep your head down.[87]

While celebrating the forms of internal, spiritual resistance we see among these respondents, we must also contend with the strong support for the prison's narratives and logics among the first group of respondents (despite their many critiques of the system). We should not assume that all of those who reproduce the narrative of individual responsibility are dupes. The growth or spiritual freedom found in the midst of suffering was deeply meaningful to many in this group, and cannot be dismissed as "false consciousness." Much research shows that acceptance of one's fate is an essential coping and survival strategy for incarcerated persons.[88] Learning to come to terms with one's offense and take responsibility for it are often related to the desire to make prison time constructive through self-work, including spirituality. Finding a purpose for incarceration through self-improvement rituals or "conversion narratives" predicated on self-reflection are important ways of endowing imprisonment with meaning, rather than seeing it as an empty or meaningless loss of years of one's life.[89] As other scholars have shown, many system-impacted individuals respond to severe constraints and limited prospects by turning inward and putting even more stock in control over their choices and their lives, adopting the belief that they are authors of their destinies.[90]

Meanwhile, a "public transcript" of acquiescence can often mask a more complex reality, It may make sense for those in subordinate groups to navigate the world using the terms of dominant discourse—but this does not mean that they have "internalized hegemonic norms."[91] Under conditions of domination, dissent and resistance may remain concealed under an often "calm surface" of apparent consent that does not always translate to ideological submission.[92] If we start from the presumption that most incarcerated persons are already undervalued, dehumanized, and undefended in society at large, well before they arrive in prison, it is easy to see how this can compel a deep distrust of the system and its ideologies. This distrust in turn can produce a sheen of conformity based on the real threat of punishment.[93] Many may learn early in life that performing acceptance and accommodation of the system's narratives is likely to save them from further state violence. And, this performance of acceptance can become habitual for those who spend years living in constant fear, or becoming dependent on an institution for their existence. Many people from marginalized communities may cultivate a set of gestures, moods, and sentiments in which they must become practiced, in order to be able to move through a world that continually heaps shame, stigma, humiliation, and violence on them. These gestures and sentiments may become important strategies for survival in a world intent on erasing one's humanity.

Speaking with a researcher under conditions of complete anonymity offers the opportunity to discard any "public masks" of compliance which may need to be worn while imprisoned, to share "backstage" or "off-stage" views.[94] Still, like other researchers who speak with system-impacted persons, I found that the commitment to ideas of personal responsibility among many respondents appeared genuine and enthusiastic. Of course, it is scarcely my place as an outsider, someone who has only the faintest idea of what these lives entail, to label such views as overly docile or somehow mistaken. Indeed, Lerman and Weaver show that for system-impacted communities, avoidance techniques such as remaining invisible, staying "under the radar," accepting one's fate, or withdrawing from engagement with politics are perfectly sensible strategies of adaptation and survival, given the totalizing experiences of shame, stigma, humiliation, and retribution that characterize their interactions with government.

To what extent, if any, can yoga or meditation cause one to adopt (or further entrench) the perspective of accommodation or defiance? Many intervening variables may have allowed one group to adopt one set of narratives, while allowing the other group to adopt a very different one. My work here does not seek to isolate the effects of other factors, although we can certainly consider several possibilities. Most of my respondents attended other prison programs besides yoga and meditation and some engaged in self-study, all of which had some additional influence on their perspectives. Factors like race and gender are also worth considering. The first group of respondents comprised four Black men, two Asian men, three white women, four white men, and two Latino men, while the second comprised five white women, two Black women, two Black men, and one white man. The second group had a higher proportion of women and socioeconomically privileged individuals, while both groups were relatively evenly split among white respondents and respondents of color (with the first group having a slightly higher proportion of respondents of color, though not by much). At least on the face of it, both groups were diverse, though in different ways. Further empirical research might explore how factors like race, gender or socioeconomic privilege could mediate a respondent's views on yoga or meditation.[95]

The effects of variable institutional culture could also be significant, as could length of sentence: My respondents served their time in a variety of prisons (some of them did several stints, and even within the same stint were often moved around), and reported differences in the cultures of different facilities. Some prison administrations are known to take a tolerant attitude toward political organizing (some, like San Quentin, even allow volunteer programs specifically focused on political issues), while others are far less tolerant. Meanwhile, as we saw, at least a few of my respondents suggested that the specific attitude and approach of volunteers in disseminating these teachings might play a role. Volunteer perspectives may interact in complex ways with other variables such as prison messaging, institutional culture, other programming, demographic factors, prior views, or self-study.

As I have repeatedly noted, nothing in this book should be taken to mean that anyone who has been to prison should *not* adopt the tools of self-reflection or should not seek self-improvement; this would be absurd. Even scholars who are deeply critical of mass incarceration have noted that we cannot rob marginalized individuals of agency by suggesting that the capacities for responsibility, growth, uplift, or behavioral change do not apply to them. But, my respondents show that individual self-improvement need not preclude the development of political consciousness around systemic issues—in fact, many used the tools of growth and self-reflection to develop what we have called "oppositional" consciousness. Elizabeth was heavily involved in political advocacy while incarcerated, encouraging friends and family to vote for certain forms of legislation. Emile was also highly politically active during his prison terms, while Michael and Sean have both become involved with activist causes after their release. Michael is now the executive director of Black and Pink, a volunteer-fueled abolitionist organization. Sean works for an organization that encourages voter registration in marginalized, system-impacted communities, and engages in public advocacy regarding the effects of mass incarceration. Grace is contemplating applying for admission to PhD programs in critical criminology. Yoga and meditation may have been presented or viewed by the prison as standard tools of self-improvement, but a few of my respondents were able to use these tools to refuse the prison's logic, and instead developed views—and in some cases participated in actions—that opposed the system. Of course, given everything we have learned about the function of prisons and their rehabilitative programs, it would be naïve to imagine that the prison apparatus would value or support such an outcome. Yet, despite the relentless "personal responsibility" messaging of the system, some of my respondents were able to use the tools of the system against the system itself. As prison researchers show, "social subordinates" such as incarcerated persons can "turn their weakness back against the powerful,"[96] resisting by "using the very ideas that are used to restrain them."[97]

6

Mindfulness Meditation in a Men's Detention Facility

Several years ago, after almost two years of negotiation with authorities governing an incarceration facility,[1] I received approval for participant-observation in a ten-week mindfulness course titled "Mindfulness-Based Transformation Skills," to be designed and conducted by one of the Buddhist chaplains.[2] A memorandum of understanding (MOU) was signed between my university and the authorities governing Detention Facility for Men (DFM), a local incarceration facility. The chaplain and I were instructed to work with custodial staff at DFM in order to find a time and a room for the class—subject to staffing, room availability, and hours of operation of the facility's education program, which would host the class. In what follows, I describe my experiences during these ten weeks, as I participated in all practices and exercises taught by the chaplain, observing the concepts he emphasized, the reactions of the students to the teachings, and their interactions with the chaplain and with one another.

DFM's education program contracts with approved adult educational schools to provide courses at county facilities. This includes preparation for GED and high school diplomas, vocational programs, and court-mandated courses in subjects such as parenting, safe sexuality, harm reduction, drug and alcohol abuse, and so forth. Many classes qualify incarcerated persons for "good conduct" credits earned in rehabilitative and educational programs, which advance one's release date. But because the chaplain's mindfulness course did not qualify for such credits, it competed with accredited opportunities, making it a lower priority for staffing and room availability.[3] After weeks of additional negotiations with custodial staff, a room was made available for two ninety-minute classes per week, and recruitment of participants began.

Participant eligibility, we soon discovered, would be dictated by the location of the available classroom. Classes at DFM are held during specified hours, and because our classroom was available only at certain days and times, the categories of eligible participants were those housed in units (or "dorms") located on the same floor as the classroom, along with those not enrolled in any other classes during those times. This narrowed the pool of potential

Freedom Inside?. Farah Godrej, Oxford University Press. © Oxford University Press 2022.
DOI: 10.1093/oso/9780190070083.003.0006

participants even further. There are also complex regulations about different categories of incarcerated persons who must remain segregated from one another; some must be escorted by custodial staff to and from activities, while others are often seen walking unescorted around the facility.[4] Based on all of these factors, the two eligible pools of participants were identified as the gay, bisexual, and transgender population, as well as the nonviolent sex offenders. In order to recruit participants from these housing units, the following materials were posted in their dorms by the staff: a brief flyer explaining the purpose and goals of the class (provided by the chaplain), along with a consent form outlining the research aspect of the class (provided by myself), and a sign-up sheet. Enrollment—up to the class cap of fifteen—was completely voluntary. After several weeks of posting sign-up sheets and finalizing the roster, the class began.

Setting the Scene: Describing the Site

DFM has several entrances, one of which is used by the visiting public (including attorneys), while others are only accessible to employees and volunteers.[5] The main visitors' entrance takes one into a lobby with linoleum floors, light pouring in through large glass doors, and benches for waiting visitors. Here, the visitor might not yet realize that they have entered an incarceration facility, if not for the "trustees" (low-security inmates entrusted with performing various tasks under minimal supervision) sweeping the street outside the entrance, cleaning the floors of the lobby or the glass doors, or moving supplies around on large carts, clad in the uniform of poplin pants and T-shirt. Most days as I walk in, I encounter these trustees engaged in their tasks, studiously avoiding eye contact with passersby, under the sometimes watchful (but often bored) gaze of an officer. Some days, I see them sweeping the streets or blowing leaves a good block or two away from the entrance, almost on the main road. I wonder about the strange limbo this particular task must place them in: engaging and witnessing street life even while incarcerated, with more access to light and fresh air than any of their peers.

Once I enter the lobby, I greet the officers manning a long reception desk, framed by a large government seal on the wall behind them, as well as a clock and an American flag. They are always polite and friendly when buzzing me in through a side door that leads down a series of subterranean hallways, eventually bringing me to the secure custodial area. What hits me as soon as I am buzzed in is the smell: a particular musty odor combining the dankness of enclosed space with that of industrial cleaning products and food being cooked from the adjoining Officer's Dining Room (referred to as "ODR," the irony of this moniker lost on no one). I walk down a long, brightly lit (albeit fluorescent) hallway lined with trophies, commemoration plaques, workplace notices, and announcements. Here too, despite the sudden disappearance of natural light and the heavily fluorescent ambience, the general brightness of the space, combined with the notices posted in glass-enclosed bulletin boards, might make it seem like any other workplace.[6]

Having walked down the long hallway, I turn a corner and arrive at the "sally port," a controlled entryway enclosed by heavy sliding steel bars that lead to the secure custodial area. I wait while the first set of bars slides open, taking me to a control booth manned by two officers who are barely visible behind darkened glass. It is virtually impossible to see without squinting, and one often has the feel of speaking to a disembodied voice. Once I give them my driver's license and phone number, I am checked in, and a second set of sliding steel bars opens into the bowels of the facility. I am rarely the only person waiting to enter at any given time; typically, the control booth officers check in groups of people, as we all wait together for the slow steel bars to move. I speak through a small slot in the window where I hand my license to the officers, letting them know I am on the list of personnel who do not re-quire an escort.[7] I am handed a visitor's tag to be worn around my neck.

As soon as the second set of steel bars slowly clang shut behind us, there is no doubt that we are locked inside a secure incarceration facility. The lighting is suddenly extremely dim, the ceilings are low, and there is no semblance of windows or natural light. The floors are a scuffed, stained concrete, and loud sounds echo everywhere. The dank, funky smells get stronger, in this central clearing-ground area, with hallways leading every which way. A sign in one direction points to the room for attorney visits, another to the medical clinic. Hallways in other directions lead to escalators, up to the housing units on var-ious floors, or to the ODR. On days that I wait for the chaplain in this area, I encounter uniformed officers who greet me politely with "good morning ma'am." Over time, as I become more familiar, the greetings are increasingly friendly, and I make sure to reciprocate with "Morning, sir" or "Hi Ma'am, how are you?"

Equally often, I encounter incarcerated persons in various colored clothing walking in careful single-file, to and from various classes and programs, some-times escorted by an officer. Parallel lines of various colors along the concrete floors indicate the route that individuals of each category must take when they walk the halls. They are required to walk only along the colored lines, and always in single file. Some eagerly make eye contact with me as they pass by, calling out, "Hello there" or "How you doin' ma'am?" Others stare at me with undisguised curiosity, even though a female civilian in this men's facility is not an uncommon sight (I see several female officers among the custodial staff; as well as female medical personnel and other volunteers). These encounters are more confusing to me: Should I be polite and acknowledge these greetings, just as I did with the staff? Having volunteered in prisons for over two years at this point, I feel perfectly comfortable interacting with incarcerated persons. But still I waver: Should I smile, or remain expressionless, as most officers seem to do in their interactions with incarcerated persons? Isn't it rude not to reciprocate these greetings? Or is it bad form to seem "overfriendly" in clear view of custodial staff? I am a light-brown-skinned South Asian woman in my forties, of average height and build. I usually wear glasses and dress relatively professionally, in what might be described as business casual: a button-down shirt and dress pants, with a jacket of some sort. The potential for inadvertently inviting unwanted male attention is never very far from my mind, although over time I find that this ends up being a non-issue. In any event, as I wait for the chaplain in this public area during those first few weeks, I find myself grappling with these questions, never quite finding a satisfactory resolution.

Chaplain Eric is a tall white man in his sixties, and has been volunteering at this facility for over five years, conducting mindfulness meditation classes with many different groups. Prior to this collaboration, I have interviewed him for my research, and accompanied him on several visits to unofficially observe his meditation classes. Typically, we meet either at the sally port or just inside the entrance to the secure area, shaking hands and exchanging greetings. As we turn a corner and walk together down another long hallway to class, we often encounter single-file rows of incarcerated men walking past us in the opposite direction. Some of them know the chaplain well, and call out greetings to him by name, which he reciprocates. Sometimes, we see lone individuals or groups of two or three walking unescorted, producing paperwork if they are stopped by custodial staff, for an authorized visit to the attorney visiting room, the medical clinic, or some other legitimate purpose. As Chaplain Eric and I walk down the long hallway, we typically make small talk, exchanging details about our lives, or discussing logistical details for the day's class plan.

The Buddhist Chaplain at DFM

I first met Chaplain Eric more than two years prior to the start of this class, when I interviewed him in a coffee shop just down the road from DFM.

We spent several hours talking in a concrete-floored café with large windows overlooking the parking lot, sipping our caffeinated beverages while surrounded by hipsters and loud music. We had a wide-ranging conversation of over two hours, in which we discussed his background, his views on prisons, and his motivations for prison work. We stayed in touch for several years after this conversation, as I became embedded in local communities of prison yoga and meditation volunteers, and learned more about the landscape. Eventually, Chaplain Eric offered his support for my research at DFM, and attended multiple meetings with prison staff in order to advocate for our collaboration.

Over seven years, Chaplain Eric has spent at least one entire day (and sometimes more) per week in the facility, which includes commuting a long distance of over an hour each way by either train or car at personal expense. He does all of this on a volunteer basis, with no compensation, offering different forms of meditation instruction to different groups of people within the facility over the course of a single day.[8] His initial entrée into to this role came when a friend who was a prison volunteer described her work. "I was really intrigued and fascinated," he says. He then went to meet the Buddhist chaplain at the time, "hit it off," and decided to "give it a shot": "the way one gets involved with this on a personal level is, you make a connection with someone, you go in and spend a few hours, you make an application with [the facility] which can take three months of background checks, fingerprinting, and after that you're put on the list, and you can go in with an escort. You spend twelve months with an escort, someone who is teaching, like an internship or apprenticeship . . . just tag[ging] along." Eventually, when prior volunteers retired or shifted out of the role, he took over as chaplain.

I ask Chaplain Eric about his long-standing Buddhist practice. It becomes clear that he is highly conversant with various scriptural and textual foundations of Buddhism. He describes himself as a Shambhala Buddhist: He is trained as a meditation teacher in the lineage of Chögyam Trungpa Rinpoche, but also widely read and trained in other Buddhist traditions. In recent years, however, his approach has become "more and more secular": "I've been doing a lot of study in secular mindfulness [which] has introduced me to a number of different teachers, people who are engaged in many different aspects of social services, and people who are working with addiction, abuse, homelessness. I've been introduced through my studies to all these different styles and approaches, and the idea of doing trauma-informed meditation has been really useful to my work in [prisons and jails]."

Chaplain Eric is deeply influenced by the trauma-informed paradigm in working with under-resourced populations: "What I have been learning is that basically trauma comes when people are in a situation where they are overpowered, a situation they would like to change, and do not have the power to change. They're not able to emotionally find equilibrium, because of verbal, physical, sexual, drug abuse . . . being in jail is itself a trauma, never mind what brought you there. . . . When you have people come in to a meditation center, they are seeking, they have the means to get there, they're not on a subsistence level. But in here [at DFM], I'm offering it to people who aren't asking, [and] in general, [are] suffering from any number of levels of trauma, and being under-resourced, from the get-go."

Chaplain Eric describes his motivation for bringing meditative practices to incarcerated persons in this way: "I really see this practice as . . . these guys are horribly shamed, being blamed, our entire society is telling them they're bad, we're going to put you in this horrible hell-hole. I don't think they're bad, they're not broken. We can embrace and befriend all of who we are in totality, and from there, accept ourselves, not beat ourselves up, not be our own worst critic. That's why I call it a human practice. . . . My longing is to offer people tools to become empowered on their own." He pauses and chokes up a little at this point, apologizing: "Sorry, this makes me a bit emotional."

Chaplain Eric then describes the "two main ways" that he reaches different populations in this facility:

> One is called "walking rows," which is an old jail set up in linear fashion. I walk down the rows and encounter people in their cells, either 1, 2, 4, or 6 people, depending on where I am. I just say hello, some of them ask what I'm doing, I have a badge that says chaplain, sometimes they think I'm a lawyer, some think I'm a Christian chaplain, they ask me for Bibles. . . . If I say, "*how are you holding up?*" all of a sudden their face changes, they become serious and say, "*I'm having trouble.*" Then we just engage in conversation, I tell them I'm a Buddhist chaplain, I've been doing meditation, it's been helpful to me, and I'm happy to provide them some books. . . . I spend half my time doing that, sometimes I provide standing meditation instruction directly through the bars, for about 10–15 mins. I've done some where there are 4 guys to a cell, and we're all standing there doing mindfulness meditation.

In addition to walking rows, Chaplain Eric also offers structured classes in different wings of the facility, to populations at different levels of security and classification—the low-risk general population who are allowed to move freely from their housing units to a classroom; a population in the hospital ward of the facility; the segregated mentally-ill population in a different wing; and various categories of high-security offenders, some of whom he teaches through the bars of their cells, while others are required to be handcuffed to metal chairs for the duration of his class. These classes are typically set up in complex negotiations with prison staff: Many are in drop-in format, and some occur in spaces resembling regular classrooms. In these classes, he teaches "low-level offenders, generally people who are out of the dorm many hours a day, doing GED, anger management classes, etc." From the first time we meet, Chaplain Eric always pulls behind him a rolling briefcase of a sort—a milk crate on wheels—filled with folders containing detailed notes on the people he visits or who have requested to see him; books on Buddhism or meditation to hand out to his students; class materials such as handouts, a meditation bowl and gong, and various other necessities. Incarcerated persons can submit a form requesting to see a chaplain of any denomination, and Chaplain Eric keeps close track of these requests for repeat visits, which often require him to navigate the intricate maze of the facility's different floors and housing units in order to retrace his steps, rolling crate in tow—no mean feat, as I will soon learn. He typically eats his lunch on a quick break in-between classes in the ODR, the facility's basement cafeteria staffed by incarcerated cooks and busboys, serving standard fare such as salads, burritos, burgers, and fries.

The most substantive part of the chaplain's training comes from one of the leading national organizations I will further describe in Chapter 8. He speaks enthusiastically about the training program he attended: "It's this brilliant program, it's a training for facilitators and for incarcerated people. It's an emotional intelligence program [of] self-reflection and self-understanding, self-regulation, and self-management. Sometimes you have to look inside before you realize, 'maybe there is something I want to change.' [It's premised on] the concept of basic goodness, how to become aware of yourself, how to manage your triggers and emotions, how to transform our emotional state, social awareness, relationship management. But our first relationship is with ourselves, being able to manage ourselves." As we will soon see, Chaplain Eric's teaching at DFM is deeply influenced by the training and principles of this organization.

Arriving at the Class Space

Returning now to our class at DFM: Once the Chaplain and I meet past the sally port, we navigate a labyrinthine maze of hallways on our walk up to the classroom. It takes me several visits to orient myself. I pay careful attention, so that I can eventually find my own way. We walk down long hallways, make sharp turns, and ride up escalators to reach our destination floor. There are two sets of escalators: one for visitors and staff, and another set for incarcerated persons and their staff escorts. At each floor landing, there is a darkened control booth and a heavy metal sliding door (known colloquially as "slider") leading into the housing units on that floor. When we arrive at our destination floor, we loudly but politely call out "slider please," and an officer in the control booth slides the door open for us. We walk through a metal detector, nod or wave our thanks to the officer, and take a sharp right, proceeding down another long hallway to the educational office, where our class will be held. Before we turn, however, the first sight that greets us is a clear view of one of the housing units with a semi-open grilled window facing us. On my first few visits, I instinctively find myself avoiding the urge to look directly at the fleeting glimpses of dorm life offered through this opening, feeling it rude to stare at caged humans as though they were a curiosity for my interest or edification. Later, the chaplain and I make several stops at that window in an attempt to communicate with class participants, and I am given a more detailed look into dorm life.

Most often, we walk past the dorm window down another hallway, passing a classroom on our right where classes are often in session, the entrance to the rooftop on our left (where the legally mandated weekly outdoor hour happens), and eventually stop at the educational office, which also doubles as a classroom. Half the room serves as an office with desks, computers, filing cabinets, and cubicles for the custodial staff. The other half serves as a relatively cozy library-cum-classroom: The walls are lined with books (and signage strictly warning against taking books without permission); there are tables, chairs, a TV, and a DVD player. On several occasions, we see a class being held in this half of the room, and on one occasion, the chaplain and I are given this space to use for our class. But for most of the ten weeks of our curriculum, we are given a classroom across the hall for our own use.

Officers Gomez and Romero are the two custody assistants who manage the educational office, and are charged with handling logistics for our class. We typically greet them on arrival, shaking hands and exchanging pleasantries. Officer Gomez is friendly, smiles a lot, and easily engages in personal conversation from the very beginning. He opens the door to our classroom with an almost comically gigantic key that recalls something from the medieval era. The classroom we are given is long and rectangular, with unused desks and office cubicles on one end, and a long empty area on the other end with stacks of plastic chairs. Our plan is to unstack and restack the chairs on the empty end of the room, setting them up in a circular formation for our class. Officer Gomez often asks two trustees who work in the educational office to assist with the unstacking and placement of the chairs. We see these two young men (who look scarcely older than teenagers) every week, either doing clerical work for the educational office on a computer, or assisting with tasks like the setup of classrooms.

Our classroom is, for most of the ten weeks, almost always freezing. The chaplain and I get in the habit of keeping all our outer layers on, including our coats (although our students, we soon see, can wear only their poplin shirts and pants, with a thin T-shirt underneath, often shivering throughout the class). We are oriented to the staff bathroom, which is surprisingly cheery. Chaplain Eric is given a makeshift whiteboard consisting of a large pad of blank white paper that can be hooked onto the wall. The flooring of the classroom is somewhat uneven, and a long metal strip of tracking runs the length of the room, leading us to speculate that the room was once used for a filing system tracked along the floor. The room is carpeted, with cinderblock white walls and bright, fluorescent lighting. Officer Gomez asks the young trustees to pick up a long table and place it lengthwise to form a preventative barrier across half the room, so that the class participants are contained to one end of the room and are not tempted to wander over to the other side (later, I see that this is completely unnecessary since our participants turn out to be extremely focused on their practices, rather uninterested in trying to explore the room). Once we arrive and settle in, Officer Gomez goes down the hallway to the housing unit to bring our participants to the classroom.

The Opening Sessions: Setting Purpose and Intention, Obtaining Consent

Our class consists of two separate ninety-minute sessions during the week: class A meets on a Monday and consists of the nonviolent sex offender[9] participants, while class B meets on a Friday and consists of the self-identified LGBTQ participants. As the class begins, we soon discover that participation is rather unpredictable, due to the transitory nature of the population. During our first meeting of class A, three participants show up. Despite high levels of enthusiasm and engagement, one participant was already anticipating a release date within a week or two. A second anticipated being released within four to five weeks, and by the second half of the ten weeks, class A had dwindled down to a single regular participant (two other participants try the class once or twice, but never return). Similarly, class B begins with fifteen participants signing up in advance, and ten showing up to the first few classes. Over the course of the ten weeks, however, due to a combination of release dates and disciplinary actions stemming from a fight in the dorm, class B dwindles down to four regular participants, of whom only two remain till the very end. (Later, I will address this attrition in more detail.)

Themes of Self-Care and Self-Acceptance

Although seven participants signed up for class A, only three participants show up on day one. All are in dark blue uniforms, with wristbands that indicate their nonviolent sex offender status. All three politely shake our hands as soon as they arrive and take their seats, some of them smiling and muttering, "Hello ma'am," to me. All seem quiet and respectful yet engaged as we greet each other, settling into our circle of chairs. Chaplain Eric begins by asking what the participants have heard about this class. "Basically, nothing," they all say. "We don't get any programming in the unit, except for church and Sexual Offenders Anonymous, because we're considered weirdos," one participant offers.

Chaplain Eric calls for us to go around the room and introduce ourselves. Mark is a balding white man with thick glasses, a marked complexion, and a scruffy beard; J. D. is a heavyset, redheaded white man in his thirties; and Peter is a young Latino man with longish hair in his twenties. Following these introductions, the Chaplain offers some introductory remarks about the class. "This is a ten-week class called Mindfulness-Based Transformation Skills. We're going to learn techniques to help us manage our stress, balance our psychological and emotional states, and develop resiliency. We'll have a few different themes, we'll do some practices, and we'll debrief after. There will be handouts, and the encouragement is to establish your own daily practice. It doesn't have to be long, it could be 5, 10, 20 minutes." All the participants listen keenly, and nod along.

"So does anyone have any ideas about what mindfulness is?" Chaplain Eric asks. All three seem keen to engage in discussion. "Does it mean knowing what's on your mind"? Mark offers. "Having open opinions?" J. D. asks. "Well," says Chaplain Eric, "there's awareness of our external environment, and our internal environment—being present, thoughtful, and open to everything around us and inside us. It's really a way of getting to know ourselves, how our minds work." In this first session, as he explains the purpose of the class, Chaplain Eric says, "There are three important things: The first is attention regulation. When we notice the mind wandering away from the object of focus, we gently bring it back. The second is intention: What's the point of this? It's to be of benefit to ourselves, we develop a better relationship with ourselves, we develop self-care, wellness, and resiliency. And finally, what are the qualities of this effort? Acceptance and nonjudgment. We're so good at '*I'm bad*,' we need to develop gentleness, kindness, caring, deep self-acceptance."

From the outset, Chaplain Eric offers here an understanding of mindfulness that is opposed to self-criticism and self-judgment, instead emphasizing kindness and acceptance toward the self. "We have really good training in criticizing ourselves," he notes. "It starts when we're young. We get told '*bad, bad, don't do that!*' So we need to step out of shame and blame. And in doing that, we work with what we've got: the body, the mind and the senses." This understanding of mindfulness as noncritical, nonjudgmental self-acceptance constitutes one of the most important themes of the class, and occurs repeatedly throughout the ten weeks.

In class B, we get ten participants on day one. These students wear lighter, powder-blue uniforms, with wristbands that mark them as LGBTQ. This group is somewhat more vocal and enthusiastic, which is evident as soon as they enter the room and greet us. Demographically, class B is more diverse than class A, in terms of both race/ethnicity and gender/sexual orientation. The majority are Black or Latinx. Here too, the chaplain offers similar introductory remarks about the goals of the class, emphasizing the learning of skill sets, developing "our natural intrinsic qualities of human being," and cultivating "resiliency, strength of mind, inner peace, and tranquility."

As we go around the room and introduce ourselves, the chaplain seems to have noticed that there is at least one transgender person in the room, and asks us to use our preferred pronoun when we say our name. Although only one participant, Tanisha, asks for the pronoun "she," several others say they appreciate this effort to be attentive to pronouns. This group too is respectful, if a bit more high-spirited. When asked about their familiarity with mindfulness, several participants report attending another meditation class with a different chaplain in the same facility. Others enthusiastically report having practiced in the past, either in meditation centers, or from online resources like YouTube, and prior prison stints. Jay, a young Black man says: "I served about twelve years in a federal prison, and I learnt Buddhism there, from some guys on the yard. When I practiced, my awareness was just off the charts, it was really amazing . . . my comprehension for simple things became so clear."

"No One Here Is Broken:" The Emphasis on Loving-Kindness Toward Self

At almost every session during these opening weeks, whether during a guided meditation practice or during informal remarks, Chaplain Eric notes, "No one here is broken, and no one needs to be fixed. We are all welcome to be who we are, and as we are. We're all just here to develop our own innate human capacities." On one occasion, he asks rhetorically, "Who here has judged or criticized themselves?" Everyone, including the chaplain and myself, raises a hand. "So we have lots of training in that," he notes, "and we're going to develop training in the opposite: kindness to ourselves." Prefacing almost every practice session in this way, Chaplain Eric insists: "You can't really do this practice wrong. You might think, '*Oh I'm not doing it right, I'm not trying hard enough*,' but really, that's just judging yourself." Chaplain Eric's encouragement is always to "just do the best you can." "It's perfectly natural and normal for the mind to wander away . . . there's no need to beat ourselves up if we notice more mental activity."

On another occasion, Chaplain Eric says, "We're all taking up just the right amount of space—there's no need for embarrassment, we are who we are." Within a few weeks of our course beginning, the holidays approach, bringing about an extra emphasis on self-care and loving-kindness toward self. "I meet an incredible level of humanity here," the chaplain tells the participants during one such class. In a rare acknowledgment of the specific challenges of incarceration, he notes, "There are physical challenges, threats, violence, all that—and you guys take care of each other. There could be riots here daily, but there aren't. Generally I meet people with high levels of intellect and insight. . . . This is a challenging place, and I just want to say you guys are doing a great job."

In one early session of class A, when the Chaplain repeats, "Nothing is wrong, no one is broken, and no one needs fixing," Mark, one of our more vocal participants, responds: "Well . . . we're *all* broken, aren't we? I mean, we're here . . . ." trailing off with a bitter laugh. Although Chaplain Eric offers no response to this comment, Mark has hit on a pattern that continues throughout the ten weeks of the course: The class is called Mindfulness-Based *Transformation* Skills, which entails a consistent emphasis on participants being able to make "different choices." On the one hand, the chaplain gives the message that no one is broken or requires fixing, but on the other hand, there is a repeated emphasis on self-transformation, and choosing differently. As the flyer advertising the course suggests: "Men . . . who are motivated to *shift the course of their life* are welcome to attend. . . . Participants will develop the strength and confidence . . . [to] support positive personal *growth* and *healthy life choices* over the long term [emphasis added]." (See Figure 6.1) As we will soon see, Mark's response to the chaplain's insistence that no one needs "fixing" turns out to be prophetic. As the class progresses, two quite different ideas emerge. An early emphasis on self-love, self-acceptance, and nonjudgment is combined with a later emphasis on learning to make different choices, take ownership of one's own contribution to one's situation, and transform one's approaches to life-situations or events.

Figure 6.1 Advertising Flyer

Mindfulness Based Transformational Skills™ training • Teacher: Chaplain Eric
in collaboration with the University of California Riverside

Ten Week Mindfulness Meditation Program & Research Project

DFM students are invited to engage in a 10 week, 1 session per week, intensive secular (non-religious) Mindfulness-Based self-awareness and self-care program. Men of any race, culture, creed, spiritual tradition and background who are motivated to shift the course of their life are welcome to attend. A Certificate of Completion will be awarded at the end of the program.

This Mindfulness Based Transformational Skills™ training will also be the subject of a unique research project led by a faculty member at the University of California, Riverside. Our researcher will be a "participant- observer" during each class. Any published research will be entirely anonymous, with no listing of names of participants, teacher, facility or staff. More information can be found below and on the consent form posted in your dorm.

The purpose of this program is to offer Mindfulness and Meditation techniques with practice opportunities that help develop each individual's self-awareness, self-acceptance, self-care, self-regulation, wisdom, resilience, kindness, compassion and self-worth. Current neuroscience research indicates observable positive changes in brain health, physical health and general positive well-being attributes for people who engage in and complete as short as an 8-week mindfulness based program. We will hold the highest ethical standards, while creating a safe and confidential environment where participants can realize their own truths in their own time.

The intended outcomes are to help participants recognize and regulate long held patterns, and to nurture unconditional, innate, positive qualities. Participants will develop the strength and confidence to make wise choices in their lives. Even though these choices may be difficult, they can serve and support positive personal growth and healthy life choices over the long term.

Class size is limited. Maximum 15 participants per-class.
Each participant is required to commit to the entire 10-week program.
Each participant will be included in the Research Project and will need to sign a consent form. The first class is an orientation where any questions about the research or the class will be answered and the consent forms will be signed and sealed.

Additional information about the Research Project:
The researcher will be a member of the class (and will therefore do all the mindfulness exercises with the participants), but will also be taking research notes. The researcher will not use any real names, including the name of this facility. Neither the instructor, nor the researcher, nor any of the DFM staff will have access to signed consent forms: they will be placed in an envelope, security-sealed across the back, and then stored off-site and destroyed after the class ends, protecting the confidentiality of the participants. Participating in this course will give students at DFM an opportunity to participate in important academic research that explores how these meditative practices and traditions are being interpreted in prisons.

Guided Practices: Invitational, Nonjudgmental, Noncommanding Language

Each class session entails at least one formal sitting practice session (sometimes more), guided by the chaplain. These sessions last no more a few minutes to begin with, although as the class progresses, they last closer to five or even ten minutes. Even with two (and sometimes three) such practice sessions within a ninety-minute period, this leaves the bulk of each session for teaching and discussion. The chaplain usually introduces a daily theme, offers some ideas around that theme, and invites participants to discuss and dialogue in response. Although the specific practices offered vary greatly, the format of the class is relatively consistent: We arrive and settle in to the classroom each time, waiting for the officers to escort the participants in. We greet the students when they arrive, and they greet us in turn, seating themselves in the circle we have created. Chaplain Eric usually opens the class by jumping into a brief, breath-centered practice (described at length below), followed by a "check-in" process, where each participant is invited to say how they are doing: how their week has been, how the practice is working in their lives, or anything else significant. The chaplain also encourages participants to listen respectfully to one another during the check-in process: "Everyone deserves respect and deserves to be heard, and part of that is being brief, so that everyone gets a chance to talk." Typically, we go around the room and each say a few sentences in response to the check-in invitation. Some students ramble on at length, while others are more laconic. Then, the chaplain launches into one of the teachings based on the day's theme, introducing one or two practices that complement the theme. Following each practice, he asks participants to comment on how it felt to them, or to offer what he calls "statements of learning, appreciation, and insight."

As he leads us into guided meditations, the chaplain uses gentle, invitational language, repeatedly reassuring us that there is no "right" or "wrong" way to undertake this practice. There are no commands about what participants must or must not do, and many options are given for how to proceed. Participants are reassured that all reactions and thoughts that may arise are perfectly fine, perfectly normal, and perfectly human. The tone of the guidance is encouraging and suggestive, rather than directive.

Typically, a practice session begins with instructions on posture: "Let's begin by finding a posture that feels upright, alert, and awake," the chaplain might say, or "We can bring a sense of personal dignity and stability, alignment, balance to this posture. . . . Our hands can swing at our sides and then come to rest on the lap." There are also instructions about eye gaze, with the option to keep eyes closed or to drop the gaze downward toward the ground, lowering the eyeline to four or six feet in front of us. From here, the chaplain typically uses "invitational" language: "The invitation is to tune into physical sensations." He draws our attention the surface of our skin, the temperature in various parts of our body, such as the hands and the feet, sensations such as warmth or cold, sweat or dryness, and so on. He also invites us to notice points of pressure in the body, as well as the weight of fabric and clothing on the body. Repeatedly, we are assured, "Whatever is arising for you is perfectly fine. . . . We're not trying to generate or create any feelings, just noticing our experience." The chaplain also repeats often, "There's no right or wrong way to do this. The encouragement is just to honor your experience, to have curiosity to tune into physical sensations." He reassures us at this point that the mind will naturally wander and move, and that's "no problem." The invitation is to "gently, with light effort, bring it back to physical sensations." We bring ourselves back to the breath, and try to notice the ribcage, the air filling the lungs and the diaphragm, and going through the throat, nose, and lips, as we breathe in and out. "You might notice happy or sad thoughts, loving, angry, hateful, lustful, boring thoughts," the chaplain notes. "All these thoughts are natural, part of our shared humanity." Each time we notice the mind wandering away, he encourages us to bring our mind back to the breath.

Toward the end of the session, he gives us two minutes to practice in silence. "I'll ring the bell at the beginning, and then again at the end," he typically says. He rings the bell once, and we sit in silence for two minutes. Almost all the participants have their eyes closed, and are sitting in complete stillness. A few fidget or shift around, but mostly the room is still. The two minutes pass quickly, with noise from the hallways interrupting us throughout: people shouting or talking to one another with voices echoing in the concrete hallways, supply carts being dragged around, loudspeaker announcements. At the end of the two minutes, the bell rings twice to signal the end of the session.

Here, we can see that in keeping with newer methods of "trauma-informed" yoga and meditation, the language of guidance leans toward "we can," rather than "you must." No distinction is made between the teacher and the students, indicating an absence of hierarchy. The use of "we" suggests that everyone in the group is making the same effort, rather than a single authority figure directing commands toward incarcerated participants. We are all invited and encouraged rather than told what to do, reassured that no matter what, all of our reactions are fine. The chaplain also makes sure to offer the participants many choices, from eye gaze to hand placement, and so on.

In these first few weeks, there is an excitement in the air after practice sessions end, and many participants want to share their experience. Some report feeling relaxed and calmer, yet also more awake and alert. "It helped me dismiss all the clutter in my mind," one participant notes. Daniel, a young Black man says, "I really felt the temperature of the air." Many participants nod and murmur assent at this remark. "I could feel my own heartbeat," another says. Thomas, a Black man with dreadlocks says, "I experienced things right now, in this moment, and kept coming back to that." Another person says, "I felt my brain traveling off a lot, but every time you said, '*bring it back*,' I really felt all those sensations." "I normally don't notice sounds so much," says Ed, a bald, heavily tattooed white man in the LGBTQ group, "but I noticed them a lot more this time, and I found myself getting irritated with the cops." Chaplain Eric responds that one's sense perceptions can indeed become sharper and more refined. Josh, a tall, burly, tattooed white man in his mid-forties (who goes on to become one of our most vocal participants), offers the following: "I don't know if epiphany is the right word for what happened to me today. I've been doing these practices for years, and I've always understood them intellectually, but I never fully internalized them until this moment. I really felt my thoughts gently going away today." As class wraps up and the officers arrive to escort them back to their dorm, several participants express appreciation to us on their way out, shaking our hands and saying "This is a great opportunity, thank you guys for coming here."

In introducing the purpose of the class in the first few sessions, Chaplain Eric is also at pains to specify that while he himself is a Buddhist, this is not a Buddhist class. Instead, he notes, "these are human practices, and have existed in many traditions. I've taught Catholics, Protestants, Muslims, Jews, agnostics, Wiccans, and many others. I really want to invite and include all people." (Josh jokes in response that he considers himself a "Jew-Bu," a colloquial term for the growing community of secular Jews who practice Buddhism). "These practices have now been stripped of their religious dogma," Chaplain Eric says, "and they've become part of mainstream society. NBA and NFL teams are doing them, Phil Jackson considers himself a Zen Buddhist, he's taught Kobe and those guys to meditate, it's happening in businesses, schools, K-12 students are doing it." Even while casting these practices as secular and nonreligious, Chaplain Eric also notes that "there's nothing magical or mysterious" about them: "It's accessible to anyone, and it's all part of our common humanity."

Consent

Along with these introductory themes, an essential task in the opening sessions is to explain the research project to the participants, and to obtain signatures on the informed consent form. This was a nonnegotiable requirement of both my university IRB and the DFM authorities. The explanation of the form requires several repetitions for the benefit of new arrivals each time. This is much to the chagrin of other participants, some of whom seem frustrated at having to sit through the explanation more than once. During these first few sessions, Chaplain Eric turns the floor over to me. I reintroduce myself, and offer as simple an explanation of my research as possible. I then walk the class through the consent form, which was heavily influenced and edited by my university IRB (see Figure 6.2). I explain that such forms are standard protocol, and explain the importance of protecting the rights of human subjects. Most participants nod along or remain passive, with little reaction.

The difficulty arises when we begin discussing the clause on anonymity and confidentiality, which was inserted at the insistence of my IRB. IRB officials held that that we could not over-promise confidentiality to incarcerated research participants, some of whom were awaiting trial. Such participants, I was told, needed to be cautioned against saying anything in our class that could later hurt them in a court of law, if I were subpoenaed (the chaplain would presumably be exempt from such a subpoena). The section of the consent form which stated "All identifying information will be confidential, unless required by law," was followed by a footnote warning participants that I, the researcher, may be forced in a trial to reveal information I may have seen or heard in class. "Therefore," the footnote ends by exhorting, "please be judicious about the information you share publicly in the course of this class."

Chaplain Eric and I were uncomfortable with this addition to the consent form. We both felt it inappropriate to begin a class with such language, reminding participants of their suspect status in the eyes of law and society. Now, in the opening sessions, I attempt to explain the purpose of this awkward, legalistic clause. In a context where average levels of education are relatively low, I can immediately see that this does not land with all the participants, no matter how much I try to simplify it. Eyes glaze over, gazes start to wander, and people shift in their seats, although a few participants are nodding to indicate they understand. Chaplain Eric interjects in an attempt to clarify: "It's really about taking care of ourselves. . . . We want people to feel comfortable sharing, and we want to build trust. But try not to say anything that could hurt you in a court of law." One participant, Benjamin, summarizes: "Basically, don't rat yourself out, right?" I say "yes, exactly," relieved that at least one person seems to have grasped the purpose of this awkwardness which has taken up so much of our precious time. I reassure every potential participant that they can absolutely refuse to sign, but that remaining in the class does require signing a consent form. Keenly aware that coercion is the rule rather than the exception in this space, I repeatedly insist, "There is absolutely no pressure, and this is all totally voluntary." Chaplain Eric asks if people are ready to sign, and most nod or say "yes." As they sign, some of our participants make remarks like, "This is a really great opportunity," "I feel special," or "I feel like I'm a part of something important," sentiments we continue to hear throughout the ten weeks. With one notable exception, every single person signs, and I get all my consent forms back.[10] It is hard to know, of course, whether the language in the form ended up being prohibitive for some participants, and whether it had something to do with the tremendous attrition rate we later experienced.

As the class moves into the next few weeks, I now turn to describing the themes that accompany the various practices Chaplain Eric offers. As we will soon see, the initial emphasis on gentle, loving, acceptance of—and kindness toward—the self is soon combined with an emphasis on self-regulation, individual choice, ownership of, and responsibility for, one's circumstances. It may be that no one is broken or in need of fixing, but as the class progresses, it becomes clear that everyone appears to be in need of taking personal ownership over their situation, and transforming themselves accordingly.

Figure 6.2 Consent Form

Consent Form for Participation in Research Study on Prison Meditation

You are being invited to take part in a research study on prison meditation programs. This is important research which will help us to better understand the way in which the yogic and meditative traditions are being interpreted.

Please read this form carefully and ask any questions you may have before agreeing to take part in the study.

What the study is about: The purpose of this study is to learn how the yogic and meditative traditions are being interpreted in the United States, specifically in prisons and jails.

What I will ask you to do: If you agree to be in this study, I will participate in the ten-week mindfulness class, led by the Senior Buddhist Chaplain. Each class session will be ninety minutes long. I will be a participant-observer in the class, which means that I will participate in all mindfulness exercises and discussion with you, while observing both the teaching of mindfulness, and your responses to the teachings. I will not record anything on electronic devices, and will only take handwritten notes in order to record my observations.

The concepts/topics being observed during this class include (but are not limited to) the following: the teaching of different breathing techniques, self-regulation, lovingkindness meditation, body scan, dealing with discomfort, mindful communication, self-acceptance, mindful leadership. I would like to report on what the mindfulness exercises mean to you, and what role they play in your life while incarcerated. Examples of observational notes would be as follows: "In our post-meditation discussion, Jose [name changed], a young Latino inmate who looked to be in his 20's, reported feeling more relaxed and less anxious after our meditation. 'I feel like I can breathe more easily, and it really helps me deal with challenging situations in here.'" OR "Andre [name changed], an older African-American man, states: 'I need something to help me deal with the noise. It's so loud in here, I can barely hear myself think. These meditation exercises just help me to go inside, to block out the noise and just focus on my breath.'"

Inclusion/Exclusion criteria:
All participants in this study will be incarcerated persons participating in the ten-week mindfulness course at DFM. All participants will be males over the age of 18, able to communicate in English, and not requiring any physical restraints.

Figure 6.2 Continued

Risks and benefits:
I do not anticipate any risks to you participating in this study other than those encountered in day-to-day life within the facility. It is possible that you may derive several benefits from participating in this research. Your ability to demonstrate to a researcher the value of your mindfulness practices could boost your personal development and/or your commitment to your meditation practice.

All identifying information will be confidential, unless required by law. The records of this study will be kept private. Any information that is obtained in connection with this study and that can be identified with you will remain confidential. Research records will be stored securely on a password-protected and encrypted computer hard drive by the researcher; and no one other than the researcher will have access to these records.[1]

At no point will you, your mindfulness instructor, the facility you are incarcerated in, or the staff from that facility, be identified by name in any published work. All names of instructors, attendees, facilities and staff will remain confidential, and will be anonymized in any published research.

Taking part is voluntary: Taking part in this study is completely voluntary. However, you may only enroll in the ten-week mindfulness course if you agree to take part in this study. If you decide not to participate, it will not affect your ability to participate in any other programming at the facility. However, in your own best interest, we ask that you remain in the class for the duration of the introductory session even if you decide not to participate in the rest of the class, so that those who decide not to participate will not be immediately identifiable to custody staff.

If you decide to take part, but later decide that you are not comfortable with being included in the study, you may ask me to delete any data pertaining to you from my research notes, and I will be happy to do so. There will be no penalty or negative consequences if you ask for your data to be deleted, and you may continue participating in the course.

Reporting Requirements: The researcher is required to report any incidents or injuries that occur during this class to the facility's Watch Commander and to the Inmate Services Bureau Unit Commander.

---

[1] The only exception would be the unlikely scenario in which the researcher may be subpoenaed or otherwise required by law to reveal information that she has heard or seen in the class, only if it pertains to an ongoing trial. Therefore, please be judicious about the information you share publicly in the course of this class. However, this would not affect published research results, which will always remain anonymized.

Figure 6.2 Continued

Compensation: There will be no compensation for participation in this study.

Research results: If you would like to see a summary of research results after publication, they will be made available to you upon request. Please contact staff at DFM if you would like to ask for any published research results.

If you have questions: The researcher conducting this study works at the University of California, Riverside. Please ask any questions you have now. If you have questions later, you may contact the staff at DFM.

If you have any questions, concerns or complaints regarding your rights as a subject in this study, you may contact the chairperson of the Institutional Review Board (IRB) at the University of California, Riverside, at the following mailing address or phone number:

Office of Research Integrity
211 University Office Bldg.
Riverside, CA 92521-0217
(951) 827-4811

In some instances, a representative of Office of Research Integrity (ORI) may review research-related records for quality assurance in order to ensure that relevant laws and guidelines are followed. All information accessed by ORI will be held to the same level of confidentiality stated here.

Your signature indicates that you have read and understood the information provided above, that you willingly agree to participate, that you may withdraw your consent at any time and discontinue participation without penalty. Please check the following box if you agree.

This information has been read to me and/or provided to me by the researcher, and I understand all of the above.

Your Signature _____ Date _____

Your Name (printed)

_____

Signature of person obtaining consent _____ Date _____

Printed name of person obtaining consent _____

Date _____

Neuroscience, Agency, Self-Regulation, and Choice: Shifting Our Brain Function and "Straw Breathing"

From the very beginning, scientific research plays a prominent role in the chaplain's explanations for practicing mindfulness. The flyer advertising the class states: "Neuroscience research indicates positive changes in brain health, physical health and general positive well-being . . . for people who . . . complete as short as an eight-week mindfulness based program." On the first day of class A, Chaplain Eric notes, "There's a tremendous amount of research showing that mindfulness has a healthy effect on the brain, on well-being and resiliency. So it's about taking care of ourselves." In these and other remarks, resiliency is repeatedly equated with self-care and well-being: To take care of oneself is often interpreted as learning to cope well with one's situation. The chaplain cites fMRI scans that show changes in brain function after practicing meditation: "The parts of the brain associated with positive feelings tend to thicken, while the parts associated with the 'fight or flight' response tend to get thinner." At least one session (and in some cases more than one) is spent on describing the functioning of the nervous system. A handout is distributed (see Figure 6.3), describing the autonomic versus the conscious nervous systems, and the reptilian "stress response" in the amygdala in contrast to the "relaxation response" or "rational response" in the neocortex.

Chaplain Eric spends much time describing the triggering of the "fight or flight" response during moments of negative challenge—the heart rate, adrenaline, and cortisol all go up, while the digestive system shuts down, leading to tunnel vision. "Does this sound familiar to anyone?" he asks, eliciting some nods and quiet murmurs of assent. He describes the sympathetic nervous system, which "up-regulates us and brings us energy," a stress response to perceived threats as we go into survival mode. "The neocortex, which does all our reasoning and rational thinking, goes offline," he says. But the parasympathetic nervous system "down-regulates" us, bringing our heart rate, cortisol and adrenaline down, as we breathe deeper and slower. Our goal, he notes, is to engage the relaxation response, "the executive functioning of the brain, our ability to think abstractly and navigate relationships, which went offline in the fight-or-flight response."

Figure 6.3 Autonomic Nervous System Handout

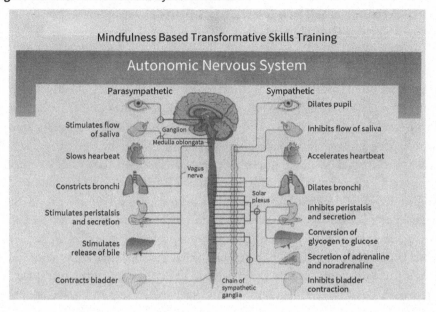

This summary of the nervous system is connected almost immediately to making good choices: When our neocortex shuts down, Chaplain Eric says, "we don't make good decisions and we're not able to see the consequences. . . . Instead, we want to bring it back online, so we can make better choices." He connects this to the idea of "neuroplasticity"—the notion that the brain can rewire itself by creating new neural pathways and habits, "through our own agency and choice." The good news, he says, is that "when we're in charge, we can have agency and control over our own development."

This theme of agency, choice, and control is accompanied by a teaching on self-regulation: "Through self-regulation, we can choose to keep our attention where we want it to be. We develop self-awareness through practice, which then gives us the choice to self-manage. . . . Things are shifting and changing in life, so can I change something in my practice that would help me deal with that?" This choice to self-manage is presented as empowering: "We want to empower everyone to find out for themselves what's meaningful or healthy for them." Chaplain Eric also presents neurological self-regulation as a way to control one's own life in the midst of difficult circumstances. "There are lots of things we cannot control, you guys are prime examples of this," he acknowledges. "You get told when to sleep and when to eat. But we can control what we choose to do repeatedly. We can create new neural pathways in the brain. Instead of letting the world batter us, we can put ourselves back in the driver's seat."

In these early sessions, I see little challenge to this emphasis on self-regulation and making better choices. At least one participant, Josh, openly embraces these ideas, noting, "I think mindfulness helps people not to make bad choices. It's unlikely that anyone who is being mindful will end up back here." This is particularly interesting because later in the class, at least three participants openly contest the legitimacy of their own incarceration, insisting that it is unwarranted or unjust. But in these early sessions, no one asks: "What if I'm not here because of something I chose to do?" Instead, the notion of individuals requiring regulation seems to meet with approval, at least by those who do speak up. Ed in class B vigorously agrees with the description of the fight-or-flight response: "Yeah, that's exactly what it felt like when the shit hit the fan, I remember my hands started shaking, I was trembling, I couldn't believe I was getting so angry and upset, it sounds like exactly what you're talking about." Jay offers his own experience in response to the claim about neuroplasticity: "I was in prison for twelve years, and I was told by the staff there that I had become unfit to be in society. It had altered the sense in my brain of what was appropriate and what wasn't."

After some discussion, Chaplain Eric introduces a technique called "straw breathing" to down-regulate the nervous system. Participants are invited to breathe in through the nose and out through the mouth through pursed lips, as though breathing out through a straw: four counts in on the inhale, extending the exhale to make it twice as long, to a count of seven or eight— and eventually, even longer. Over time, Chaplain Eric says, "we might find that our breathing slows down. We can breathe into our belly, and just notice any physiological shifts."

Chaplain Eric ends by encouraging participants to use this technique in their challenges pertaining to incarceration: "I've talked to a number of people here who use this especially when they're going to court, while you're on the bus, or in the holding pen.[11] You need to be clear and focused in court, you need to understand everything that's going on, especially if someone makes a mistake or says something that's not true, you need to be able to react appropriately. I use this practice almost every day, maybe when I'm driving and someone cuts me off, or sometimes I walk the hallways here and see stuff I don't like, so I do my straw breathing, I start to feel the effects right away." These remarks represent one of the few occasions in which the chaplain acknowledges—even if obliquely—that incarceration often entails miscarriages of justice, and that these practices may in fact be employed to react effectively to such injustice, rather than simply cope with it.

Learning to Be OK with Discomfort: Prison as a "Growth and Learning" Opportunity

In week six, using the makeshift whiteboard, the chaplain draws a diagram of three concentric circles, while passing around a handout titled "Outside the Comfort Zone" (see Figure 6.4). "So this first inside circle is the comfort zone," he notes, "a place of refuge that's nurturing, safe, and relaxing. But it's problematic if we get stuck in that comfort zone." Pointing to the outermost circle, he says, "that's the excessive risk or danger zone. We're not ready to go there, because we're not gonna learn anything, it's too soon." He gives the example of the potential trauma experienced by a piano student who is forced to perform at Carnegie hall before they are ready.

Figure 6.4 Outside the Comfort Zone Handout

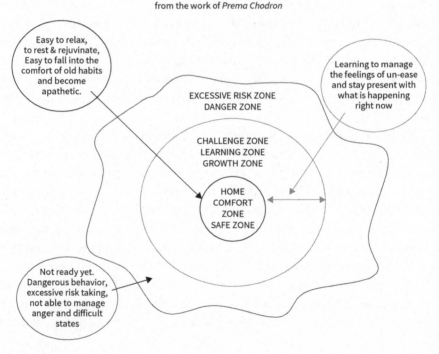

OUTSIDE THE COMFORT ZONE
Learning to travel in the challenge zone
from the work of *Prema Chodron*

Easy to relax, to rest & rejuvinate, Easy to fall into the comfort of old habits and become apathetic.

Learning to manage the feelings of un-ease and stay present with what is happening right now

EXCESSIVE RISK ZONE
DANGER ZONE

CHALLENGE ZONE
LEARNING ZONE
GROWTH ZONE

HOME
COMFORT
ZONE
SAFE ZONE

Not ready yet. Dangerous behavior, excessive risk taking, not able to manage anger and difficult states

Pointing now to the middle of the three concentric circles, he notes: "This middle zone is outside our comfort zone, but not quite the danger zone. It's the 'challenge zone' or the zone of 'growth and learning,' where we're stretching ourselves. So how does it feel outside the comfort zone?" Several participants murmur that it feels "uncomfortable" or "anxious." "Yes, its uncomfortable, that's true," the chaplain says, "but this is where we grow and develop. Personal learning happens here. So the challenge zone is not easy, but we are stretching ourselves, and maybe we can grow." Now Chaplain Eric introduces the concept of "expanding the comfort zone" in order to train ourselves to make life "more workable" and to "manage our discomfort": "It's like working out, we put ourselves through these strenuous things, because we know there's a benefit to us. Life becomes more workable when you expand your comfort zone to include what was previously outside it."

Now, he asks, "How can we relate this to being incarcerated? I would really like to know, what are the growth and learning experiences you guys have here?" In class B, Ed reports, "There's a constant flux of people coming and going, so I try to just listen and learn. Even in here, there are opportunities to learn, maybe you learn from other people's mistakes so you don't make them yourself." Logan, also a self-identified gay white man in his thirties, reports playing chess, and writing a lot: "I take my experiences outside by writing to people about them." But soon Logan begins to express frustration with the incarceration system: "I get frustrated when I see people here and this is the only life they've known, they're forty years old and have been incarcerated on and off for twenty-five years . . . where's the rehabilitation? And then when you get out, there's stigma, you try to get a job, you've paid your debt, but you can't get a job, so what are you supposed to do? You go back to doing what you did before, you end up back here . . . it's like, 'what did you expect me to do?'" Chaplain Eric nods and acknowledges that "there's some real holes" in the system, but responds again by encouraging participants to "step into the growth, learning, and challenge zone."

In class A, Mark (the only student remaining in the class by then) responds to the chaplain's question by asserting: "What's most important to me in the world are my kids and their mom—nothing else matters. How do I come back to the comfort zone if there's no way to be with them?" "Well, I obviously don't have an answer to that," the chaplain admits, "I guess you don't have much of a comfort zone to go back to." He then offers the same encouragement he offered to participants in the other class: "Growth and learning come from the challenge of managing discomfort . . . in an unfamiliar situation. We don't want to do it, but it's allowing us to grow and learn." During this session, as Chaplain Eric keeps circling back to working with discomfort through mindfulness,

Mark becomes increasingly agitated, launching into a tirade about repeated violations of his rights that have landed him in the facility and driven him almost to the brink of suicide. Eventually, the revelations become so fraught and Mark's demeanor so incensed that the chaplain asks me to step outside while he privately speaks with Mark to ascertain the risk of suicide, drawing on his chaplaincy training. (Later, I will describe in more detail the specifics of Mark's grievances, and their significance for the ideas offered in class.)

Later, Chaplain Eric re-emphasizes the notion of learning from discomfort with a story about a Tibetan lama in Kathmandu whose two sons wanted to get away from the loud, noisy capital and deepen their practice in the mountains. "You know what the lama said? *'What's the point if you can't do it here? You have to learn to practice wherever you are, let's stay in the challenge of chaos.'* So this is an incredible environment and an opportunity to practice. Of course, not one that I would choose. But you know, there's a slogan in Buddhism: *'If you are able to practice in chaos, it's the sign of a well-trained mind.'*" Here, the chaplain acknowledges that not all "learning opportunities" are chosen, but suggests that one can re-envision coercion as a growth opportunity.

Chaplain Eric offers a practice he calls a "mountain meditation" to accompany the discussion of managing discomfort. We are asked to bring to our mind's eye the most beautiful, awe-inspiring mountain, imagining its lofty peak, its snow and stone, its sheer rock faces, or forests of trees. We are asked to "become the mountain. Our head becomes the lofty peak, our sides and arms its lower hills, our pelvis and legs, rooted into the earth like its base." The chaplain then guides us into visualizing the mountain sitting still, as day passes into night and night into day, as weather patterns change, seasons pass, animals retreat, and trees lose and regain their leaves. Throughout all this, the mountain "has the intrinsic quality of awesome strength." In the same way, the Chaplain notes, "we can build our capacity to weather the storms of life. . . . As a mountain, we sit, stable. . . . The very inner core of the mountain doesn't change . . . its strength and awesomeness, rooted in earth." The chaplain then invites us to sit in silence like a mountain for a few minutes, ringing the bell three to four minutes later to indicate the end of the session.

Negativity Bias and Victim Mindset: "I Am Safe, I Am Resourced, I Am Connected"

As I noted earlier, by the middle of our ten weeks, class A has dwindled down to one participant. Mark is always vocal and engaged from day one. Once he is the only remaining participant, however, he becomes increasingly agitated, repeatedly describing what he characterizes as the violation of constitutional rights and due process in the handling of his case by prosecutors. Mark is what is known colloquially as *pro per* (short for *in propria persona*): an individual acting as their own lawyer. Mark is clearly bright and articulate enough to handle his own case, although he reports being chronically sleep-deprived, and deprived of basic healthcare in the dorm, which is reflected in the sometimes rambling and disjointed nature of his remarks. Later in our time together, he acknowledges that he probably has to "hand his case back off to the public defenders," given the impossibility of getting work done in the chaotic environment. As time wears on, it becomes clear that Mark is seeking a sympathetic hearing for his situation. He spends quite a bit of time in each session describing his litany of complaints: being chased by SWAT teams who threatened to shoot him and his children; prosecutors who have seized and sold his mobile home which contained evidence in his favor; the illegal seizure and sale of precious family heirlooms and other valuable items contained in his home; his children being sent to foster homes while he is incarcerated, and receiving news of them having bones broken; being shoved by an officer, and being denied access to medical care for the pain and ringing in his ears that results. By session seven, he reports having been put on suicide watch by the facility personnel. More than once, he insists that the system is corrupt, that it protects its own, and sets up poor and under-resourced people like him to fail. He describes the chaos and constant fighting in the dorm. He often cries throughout guided meditation sessions, later apologizing: "Every time I try to stop the flow of thoughts, I burst into tears." Both the chaplain and I react with as much compassion as we can communicate, reassuring him that there is no shame in expressing his sadness.

Despite this evident compassion, Chaplain Eric also tries to steer Mark away from his recitation of complaints, after having listened quietly and compassionately to the litany. Privately, he tells me that Mark must take ownership and responsibility for his own actions. "Taking ownership is where empowerment lies," he notes. "It's when we take responsibility and ownership that we can move out of victim mode. If he keeps waiting for the criminal justice system to change, and for other people to change, he'll just continue being a victim . . . these things don't just come out of the blue." To that end, the chaplain begins offering techniques in the latter half of the course that are designed to encourage Mark away from his negativity and "victim mindset," toward a more "positive and empowered" state of mind.

Our seventh session entails a discussion of what the chaplain calls "negativity bias." On this particular day, Mark has been particularly agitated, having been given terrible news regarding his case. During the check-in process, he describes various travesties. "It's like they're just trashing me up and throwing me away," he complains, "this criminal justice system is total shit, I'm sorry to say, I have no faith in it, it's completely corrupt." While Chaplain Eric often acknowledges these remarks with an empathetic comment, like "Yes, there are many problems with the system for sure," he also stops Mark mid-rant several times, asking him to restrict his remarks and keep them brief, to "just keep it in the room, to this time and place."

Once the check-in is complete, the chaplain offers a teaching on negativity bias: "So generally when our mind is left to wander around," the chaplain notes, "it tends to go to negativity." He calls this part of our survival system: "Back in the day, when we lived in the jungle, it was us against the saber-toothed tiger, and our number one job was always to survive. Let's say we're walking along, and we hear a '*snap-crackle-pop!*' If it's a tiger, those of us that reacted correctly, with the fight-or-flight response are the ones who survived over time, the ones who always were vigilant and afraid. Those who were relaxed and thought it was Bambi didn't survive, because they weren't vigilant the one time it *was* the tiger. So we have the negativity bias . . . we need to counterbalance this tendency, and it can just be through small things. We can find relief, and relaxation through whatever we can find to be grateful for."

The chaplain now leads us in a practice he calls "Safe, Resourced, Connected." After the usual invitation to take a posture and to tune in to our senses and our breath, Chaplain Eric asks us to repeat to ourselves the first phrase: "I am relatively safe." "Now this may bring up memories of not being safe," he admits. "We can acknowledge that. This may not be the ideal environment, it may not be perfect. But I'll encourage us to repeat, *right here, right now, the reality is that I'm safe.* And we can bring that into our body." Next, after a few moments of silent mindful breathing, we are asked to repeat to ourselves, "I am resourced." For this very moment, Chaplain Eric notes, "I have what I need, even if it's not perfect. I have a roof over my head, I have running water, I can use the facilities, I have food. . . . We're telling the mammalian brain it doesn't need to go crazy finding resources, because our needs are met." Next, after a few moments of silence, we are asked to repeat to ourselves the last phrase: "I'm connected, I'm not alone. . . . There are two people here who care about me, there are others in the facility who've got my back, others on the outside who care about me. It may not be perfect, but in this moment, there's at least one person here who cares." Mark makes a snorting noise, like muffled laughter. After another period of silence, the chaplain repeats, "I'm safe, I'm resourced, I'm connected," and invites us to end with three deep breaths, concluding the session by ringing the bell.

"So how was that?" Chaplain Eric asks. Mark responds glumly, "I felt like whatever I needed was not really there for me." "I'm not disagreeing with you," the Chaplain acknowledges, "but as a practice, can we simplify it and bring it down to just this moment? There's definitely resistance to this practice, but that's projected out into the future. We can preface each repetition with 'right here, right now.' We don't have to fix everything in order to feel ok in this moment." Mark presses further: "I feel at a disadvantage in all these mindfulness practices. Don't get me wrong, this is the highlight of my week. But since an officer pushed me into an elevator door, I have this constant headache, this constant ringing in my ears. They've tried everything, they say it's not really caused by [getting pushed into the door], but I know I didn't have it until that happened to me, and no matter what I do, there's this constant hum." There is a silence as Chaplain Eric acknowledges Mark's disgruntlement nonverbally.

The Drama Triangle: Shifting from Victim Mindset to Empowerment

In week eight, the chaplain offers a teaching on the "Drama Triangle," a model of social interaction developed and disseminated by the psychologist Mark Karpman. "This is about positive, constructive communication," he offers as a prelude, "about developing a skill set that has to do with personal responsibility and ownership." The tone is thus set with personal responsibility as the goal. Chaplain Eric draws a triangle on the whiteboard, labeling each of its three angles as "persecutor," "rescuer," and "victim." "It's important to remember," he notes, "that these are not people but mind-states. And we can all be in the victim mind-state at different times." Next, he asks rhetorically: "How do we normalize the victim mindset? We normalize it every time we're upset, and we place the reason for it outside ourselves. We say, 'I'm angry and it's your fault. Woe is me. I can't feel good until that person changes.' And that leads to powerlessness, we give our power away to something or someone outside ourselves."

From here, Chaplain Eric describes the persecutor and the hero/rescuer as both powerless victims too. The persecutor is described as "aggressive, blaming, dominating, oppressing, and criticizing," while the hero/rescuer is described as "the know-it-all, the expert," who "needs to gain power by finding people who are in need of their expertise and authority." Each archetype, he notes, is motivated by trying to gain power: "there's powerlessness and victimization at the heart of all of these, and we all gravitate toward one of these." Notably, the example offered involves an encounter with law enforcement. "So let's say you're pulled over by a cop for speeding, and you feel like a victim. Who do you think is the persecutor in this case?" In both classes, students immediately chorus: "The cop!" "Right," the Chaplain acknowledges, "you see the cop as the persecutor and then maybe you find a rescuer, like a lawyer who's going to fight your case for you. But what about from the cop's perspective? How does the cop see himself?" This produces some murmurs and cross-talk as students contemplate the question. "He sees himself as the rescuer, doesn't he?" the chaplain offers. "And who is the persecutor?" he asks. Many students immediately respond again with: "the cop!" "Actually no," the Chaplain says, "he sees the driver as the persecutor, and the victim as the public, who are endangered by this driving, and he is the one rescuing the public. So we can see how it's different from different perspectives, even in the same situation."

Following this example, students are encouraged by the Chaplain to see that all three archetypes arise from powerlessness. In lieu of this "problem-oriented mindset of powerlessness," the chaplain calls for a solution-oriented model in which we can notice irritation, anger, self-righteousness, or depression, and live from choice: "We can ask ourselves, '*What can I do when I feel like a victim? What can I do to make it different?*'" In class B, at least a few students seem responsive to this. Ed offers, "We can acknowledge and own it, when the shit hits the fan. *I put myself here, I can take myself out!*" "Exactly!" the Chaplain says. "We can make choices as we manage our neural system. Empowerment is owning our own situation. It's a choice to let go of our grievance and victimization story. Now of course sometimes it's completely legitimate, some people are horribly victimized, but how can we empower ourselves by making a choice to let go?" Chaplain Eric then offers some steps to "get off" the drama triangle, among which is the use of "'*I*'-statements to own our situation: '*I'm angry*' or '*I'm scared*,' instead of saying '*you're doing this.*' And then, once we've owned how we're feeling, we can make boundaries if necessary. Maybe we decide, '*this has to stop* or *you can't treat me this way any more.*' Sometimes, you have to call HR. Or maybe you have to call the police. But either way, we empower ourselves once we take ownership of our feelings."

In class B, most students are quite receptive. When the chaplain asks, "'*If I feel this way or that way, it's your fault.*' Who has the power in that situation?" several students offer: "They have the power!" "Yes, we've given away our power to the other person," the chaplain acknowledges. "The only thing we can control is ourself. We can't control or change other people, we can't control everything life throws at us. . . . There's a saying in Buddhism that there are 84,000 causes and conditions for any effect. So we don't really know all the things that come at us. But we can try to shift things. What we put out we get back." To this Ed responds affirmatively, "Oh yeah, definitely! You've got to be fluid and adjust to what comes your way."

In class A, however, Mark is far less receptive to this model than his counterparts in the other class. After a lengthy explanation of the drama triangle, Chaplain Eric asks Mark, "So what do you think of all that?" "It's a lot," Mark says. There is a long silence, while Mark seems to be processing. He does not jump to agree, and instead, offers some resistant remarks: "Well, from my perspective, the DA thinks she's the rescuer, but she's actually persecuting me." Chaplain Eric presses on in response: "So this is the mindset of powerlessness, it's fear-oriented and problem-oriented. If we're in the victim mentality, what can we do? We can think of positive ways to move forward. We need to do our own work. When the victim tries to get rescued, they stay a victim." "Well, I'm thinking of my situation," Mark counters, "and I can't get any help. I can't get a lawyer or anyone to help me. I'm supposed to be the persecutor, but the cop beats me up and that's OK, and I have to be in prison for the rest of my life?? It doesn't make any sense!" "Yes," the Chaplain acknowledges, "it doesn't make sense." Mark continues: "It's like the people whose job it is to rescue aren't helping. It's just been a whirlwind in my mind for these past few weeks." "So there's a lot of complexity to this," Chaplain Eric notes, "and once you start to recognize it, you'll see it everywhere. So hopefully you find something of value in there."

The conversation ends as the chaplain transitions now into another mindfulness practice. It's clear from this exchange, however, that the notion of drama triangle has not quite landed with Mark. While the chaplain encourages him to let go of his victim mindset, Mark seems to resist, insisting that actors in the law enforcement system are misusing or abusing their power. The chaplain acknowledges that there is "complexity" to this, and that Mark's situation doesn't "make sense," but continues to characterize Mark's mindset as one of victimhood and powerlessness, encouraging him to "do his own work" instead of "staying a victim."

Forgiveness: Resist Reliving Trauma

In the last few weeks of the class, Mark's recitations of his trauma, anger, and betrayal by both family members and law enforcement become more pronounced. Chaplain Eric now expresses the need to offer Mark some resources to move away from his reliving of trauma. With this in mind, our final sessions in both classes focus on forgiveness, and "changing the channel" away from the trauma.

Throughout our ten weeks together, Mark has spoken lovingly about his two young children, sometimes showing us photographs of them. In the penultimate session of class A, Mark offers a particularly harrowing and tear-filled account of his situation, contemplating the possibility of being permanently deprived of custody of his children who are currently in foster care, where he believes they are subjected to abuse. He describes the suppression of evidence by prosecutors who "make me out to be an inhuman criminal monster," charging him falsely with abuse and neglect. Although it is difficult to know the truth in such matters, Mark seems genuinely devastated, crying on and off throughout the session (as he has done many other times), and offering examples of how well he had always cared for his children. He repeatedly tells us that we "have no idea" how awful his life has been, describing his pain at being falsely accused: "I'm feeling blamed and hopeless," he says through tears.

Chaplain Eric listens patiently, asking questions and offering empathetic responses. During a break in Mark's narrative, he intervenes: "Well, I would offer this: there's research that shows every time we re-tell our traumatic experience, hormones and neurotransmitters send that all into the blood system, and we're basically re-traumatizing ourselves. You have a lot ahead of you, and you need your wits about you. It's not helping to re-live the grievance. The skill in mindfulness is, instead of rumination, we can change the channel." "I can't control this," Mark insists. "It starts when I wake up, and goes on all day until I go to bed." Chaplain Eric persists: "Every time you go back through these stories, agitation comes up in the body. This is the realm of choice, where we can ask ourselves, '*is that healthy for taking the next step? How can I be of most benefit to myself?*' So let me ask you, what practices would help you right now? We need to bring the prefrontal cortex back on line, and re-engage the executive function." Clearly too wrapped up in his own misery, Mark shrugs and says, "Whatever's on the program is fine." Chaplain Eric leads us into a basic breath-centered practice.

In the next and final session the following day, Mark seems rather more subdued. He proudly brings us more photos of his children, and reports some sadness at the class coming to a close. In this session, Chaplain Eric offers a teaching on forgiveness. "We often need forgiveness in relationship to some injustice or betrayal. It's a choice we make to empower ourselves to move forward. Can we make that choice, yet again, to suffer less? The past is done, we can't change it, we can only move forward. Forgiveness is becoming a part of the solution, it's putting our attention on good things." The chaplain now leads us in a forgiveness meditation, inviting us to remember a situation in which we think we cannot forgive ourselves. Holding that situation, we are asked to repeat slowly and silently to ourselves: *"I forgive myself for whatever I did in the past [and it's ok if this rings hollow, or you don't quite believe it]; I forgive myself for my actions; I forgive myself for my words that caused pain or hurt; If I cannot forgive myself now, may I be able to forgive myself in future. May I be happy and find peace."* Throughout this practice, Mark cries quietly.

Checking-In: Statements of "Learning, Appreciation, Insight," and Feedback

Before each practice, participants are invited to "check-in" and let us know how they are doing. After each practice, they are invited to offer statements of "appreciation, learning, or insight." We hear a wide range of things in response, and I learn much about participants' daily lives. Perhaps the most common reactions during check-in are constant reports of stress, anxiety, and depression: worries about court dates, release dates, or the health of family members while being cut off, along with worries about finding employment or housing once released. Some speak of learning about the deaths of beloved family members during their incarceration. Many report simply spending long months (or even years) in the facility awaiting trial or sentencing, seeking news of which prison they will eventually be transferred to. Others describe endless waits for court appearances, often being woken up in the middle of the night, put in a "holding pen" for hours and eventually on a bus to court, only to find out their case has been postponed through continuance yet again. Common complaints have to do with the strains of life in close confinement: the unpredictability, chaos, constant lighting, noise, freezing cold, and thin mattresses that make it difficult to get any sleep; negligent and sometimes violent behavior by correctional officers; lack of access to medical treatment despite repeated requests; being fed foods such as bologna stamped with the label "not for human consumption"; and many other daily humiliations. "We're like caged animals here," Ed says during one check-in.

I witness the more mundane indignities regularly on my weekly visits. For instance, when walking down corridors or more public areas, incarcerated men often have to call out "walking," or be loudly announced as "walking" by the officer escorting them, in order to ensure maximum segregation from civilians. Although I find this jarring and demeaning at first, I become inured to it eventually. More challenging are occasions when I hear reports of—or come close to witnessing—serious degradations. On one occasion, as we are meditating in class, we hear the sound of a loud, collective *"Hunh!"* grunt in the hallway. A little later, we are quickly ordered by officers to cut our class short and leave with some urgency, since the facility is going into lockdown. As we walk out, the chaplain speculates whether the loud grunting might have been cavity searches. I shudder, wondering if some of our students may have been cavity-searched in the hallway right outside our classroom. On another occasion, our classes are delayed because of "extractions"—situations in which recalcitrant or mentally-ill individuals with behavioral issues are extracted from their cells and sent to mental health wards or solitary confinement. On these occasions, the floor—or the entire facility—can be temporarily locked down. As we wait for our floor to open, I peek through a partial opening in the door and see someone being wheeled away on a stretcher in what an officer has just described to us as the "human taco": a new protocol in which a person is wrapped in layers of blankets for maximum immobility as well as protection, and then strapped onto the gurney.

Despite my initial discomfort with it, I eventually end up spending some time looking into the dorms that are down the hall from our classroom. The first few times we walk by, I avoid looking in. But by the time we get a few weeks into our class, our visits to the dorm become fairly routine for the purpose of speaking with participants about logistical issues. Chaplain Eric is well versed in this routine. We approach the grilled entrance area, and as we peer in, the "house mouse"—an informal elected representative—comes up to ask, "Who can I get for you?" We give him the names of students, and he walks around the dorm, calling out names, either bringing them back to meet us, or letting us know that they are in court, meeting with a lawyer, or in class, etc. He is always unfailingly polite. "Anything else I can do for you?" he always asks before we leave. My glimpses of the dorms on these occasions are fleeting, but indelible. The "dorm" is in fact a large concrete-floored room with no windows, harsh fluorescent lighting, and bunk beds crowded in to accommodate hundreds of men. The scene is a sea of white: white bedsheets hanging from bunks in an attempt at privacy, white uniforms (different from the color-coded ones worn when leaving the dorms), white towels wrapped around waists, and white lighting. There is a common area closer to the door, where TVs are mounted on the ceiling and round steel tables with stools are affixed to the concrete floor around them for viewing. Some guys are talking on payphones along one wall, some are talking or watching TV around the tables. Some are sleeping in their bunks with towels across their eyes to block out light. Some are exercising in one area, using sturdy steel stationary "pull up" and "dip" bars, or doing push-ups, sit-ups, leg raises, and so on.[12] Others are bare-chested, and most are in white. The smell of hundreds of bodies in close confinement seeps through the window, and the noise is deafening.

Despite brief glimpses into these circumstances, I am also witness to many moments of kindness, compassion, and humor, both among our students, and between officers and our students. I notice that many of our students are quite friendly with Officer Gomez, who escorts them to and from their dorm—Gomez occasionally reciprocates their camaraderie by goofing around. I see Officer Ortiz, the most senior officer on the floor, treating the teenaged trustees in an almost fatherly manner, speaking to them with an avuncular kindness in his voice and gesture. And, our students offer us many reports of leaning on each other for care and support. When some cry during class, or share a particularly difficult memory or anxiety, others sometimes gently rub their backs. I also hear reports of creative ways to meet the drudgery of life in the facility. During one class just before Christmas, I ask the guys in class B how things are going in the dorms, and they eagerly share reports of the holiday spirit: "There's a Christmas tree and nativity scene they made in our dorm," they tell me. "What's it made of?" I ask. "Soap," they all chime in. "You should see the size of the baby Jesus," Josh says, using his hands to demonstrate a baby Jesus who clearly dwarfs Mary and Joseph, while everyone laughs. "There's doves and everything in that nativity scene," Ed reports.

In the midst of this chaotic and sometimes dehumanizing environment, our students report on their attempts to practice the techniques on their own. While many report being able to practice consistently in the dorms (either individually or in pairs), we also hear that the chaos makes it difficult if not impossible. Others report reading the little books that Chaplain Eric hands out at the end of class (Buddhist classics by teachers like Pema Chödrön and Thich Nhat Hanh in miniature form), sometimes many times over. Post-practice check-ins vary from very enthusiastic to mumbling, discouraged, tired, or low-energy.

Three main themes emerge when participants describe the purpose and value of the practices. Perhaps the most common theme is using them to cope with the stresses and strains of life in confinement, with particular emphases on noise, violence, and preparation for trial. Angel is a soft-spoken young Latino man in his twenties. "I've been reading the book *Start Where You Are* [by Pema Chödrön]," he tells us. "It's helping me to be in the present moment, and to block out the constant noise in the dorms. I'm getting close to my release date, and I'm trying not to get stressed about what I'm going to do when I get out. I'm taking it day by day, one step at a time, and trying not to overthink it." Even Mark, our lone remaining participant in class A who sometimes seemed disgruntled and less receptive in moments of agitation, says, "This is my sanctuary, it's the only thing we get besides school and church."[13]

"For me," he says toward the end, "it's a way to dump everything, and achieve inner peace and inner health. . . . Using the breath to bring myself back to the here and now, to feel safe, and close out any negativity, just for this moment." Logan, another committed participant who stays till the very end, tells us, "It got a little crazy here over New Year's Eve," so "I've been practicing the mantra '*I'm here*,' and also working with '*be at peace*.' I'm also practicing walking meditation, and working on doing it laying down." Later, Logan also reports using the practices when going to court: "These practices have been really helpful. I've used them before court, I do the body scan, I do the breath counting . . . it just allows me to be in the moment instead of getting anxious and panicking." Logan also reports on using these practices to cope with anger in the face of injustice. After the mountain meditation, he offers this: "I feel upset that I'm being scapegoated by the system, I found myself going in a really angry direction, but then I calmed down and realized I'm just weathering the storm. I was thinking how the mountain isn't unchanging, there's the process of erosion and weathering, which makes it stronger. So it's been really helpful when I get angry at the situation I've been placed in, it's calming me, keeping me grounded."

The second major theme is the use of meditative practices as a coping mechanism for health issues, particularly when access to medical care is scarce. Daniel, a young Black man who reports having ADHD, is very enthusiastic in the first couple of weeks: "I never did it before, but it was really cool . . . instead of pills, I want to experience *this*! My mind was going to a million places but coming back to one place." Benjamin, a Latino man in his forties, is vocal and engaged during the first five or so sessions of the class, although he later drops out. He reports early on that the practice helps him cope with the physical pain for which he is barely given any treatment: "I have kidney stones, and the doctors and nurses treat me like garbage. I have to beg them for pain meds, because the pain is vicious. [With this practice], I can tolerate more and more pain. I fall asleep, and when I wake up, it's much better."

The third theme has to do with what we might call self-development or self-improvement, beyond simply coping with stress. One of our most vocal and engaged participants Josh, who identified himself as a "Jew-Bu" and reports having practiced meditation on and off for many years, says, "These practices make you see inside yourself. . . . I find that these practices make me a better listener. Normally I'd already be preparing my rebuttal, but now I actually listen." On another occasion after the holiday season, Josh reports, "I've been practicing *metta* [lovingkindness], calling a person's name and sending love to them. I've also been trying to work on mindful eating."

As the ten-week course draws to a close, the few remaining participants all emphasize that they don't want the class to end. They are emphatic in their gratitude for the class, and for having their voices heard. In our penultimate session of class B, Ed notes, "It's really an honor that my story is being heard. Instead of this being a negative thing, it's turned into something positive. Maybe it can help someone else down the road, so it makes me very happy. People always ask me how the class is going, and I always say, '*you guys missed out on something amazing.*'" Several participants also remark on the interesting—and perhaps ironic—disjuncture between the practices and the environment in which they are being offered. Peter, who was very engaged in class A, was released within a few weeks of the class commencing. "I keep thinking what a trip this is for me to be here in this facility, doing mindfulness meditation," he says to us before he leaves. "But it's been really meaningful. I'm really appreciative of you guys, and I wanted to thank you." Daniel, who earlier described his struggles with ADHD, jokingly remarks before his release, "Maybe I'll catch another case so I can do this again." "Please don't catch another case," the chaplain pleads, to much laughter. "There's plenty of other ways to find these practices on the outside, for free."

On the final day of class, Chaplain Eric awards a certificate of completion to each participant, as the rest of us applaud. At the end, I also ask our three remaining participants to fill out anonymous, open-ended surveys commenting on how, if at all, the practice affects their experiences of incarceration, and what benefits it has brought. "Meditation greatly helps me with living in despair, surrounded with negativity, after losing everything that I love," writes one. "The best benefit I get from meditation is overcoming thoughts of suicide. . . . This class session is time out of the housing unit, an outlet to be free from all the negativity in our surroundings, 24/7." "I feel that [meditation] has helped me to better control my mental state," writes another. "To be more conscious and aware of where I am mentally. It has also been helpful when I need to still my mind or elevate my mood from a bleak place. It has made this experience [of incarceration] more tolerable, and provided me with a constructive outlet and coping skills. It has been a class I look forward to each week, and the skills are useful in the prison setting." In response to the question, "do you have any concerns or issues with the teaching of meditation in prison?" none of the respondents raised any concerns. Two of the three stated they had no issues, and instead offered suggestions for improving the class, such as larger class sizes, more regular attendance by participants, and more frequent practice sessions. For the most part, all explicit feedback is mainly positive, speaking to the benefits of these practices. No challenges seem to be offered to the ideas being taught in this class.

Race, Class, Demographics, and Attrition

As we have seen, the ten-week course underwent tremendous levels of attrition. The most obvious explanations for this attrition are the transitory nature of the population, and the competition with other accredited classes. Previously, I had also speculated that the dense, legalistic language of the consent form might have driven a few participants away. There were also moments during the class which pointed to its lack of accessibility to certain participants. There were several instances where Latinx participants were clearly not following along very well, especially during more technical discussions of the consent form or the neuroscience sessions. In one instance, when the chaplain launches into his teachings on neuroscience, Ernesto, a Latino man who clearly seemed to be having trouble comprehending, suddenly stands up, saying "I gotta pee," leaving the room on his own. Despite several attempts to invite him back, we never see him again. On another occasion, Julio, a man who attends class A twice and often looks blank or confused, later confesses privately to the chaplain that he cannot read English. Although the chaplain encourages him to continue attending, and assures him that his literacy challenges will be confidential, we do not see Julio again. In fact, the next time we attempt to visit him in the dorm, Julio asks the officer to relay to us that he wants to drop the class, and is willing to sign a form if necessary. It seems likely, then, that the class content posed some linguistic, social, or cultural barriers that may have discouraged participants whose native language was not English, or who had lower levels of education.

In contrast, the participants who remain committed to the end are all white and Anglo, with higher levels of education and English fluency. In fact, some of the more educated participants made oblique reference to these class differentials in their experience of dorm life. Toward the end of the course, both Logan and Ed in class B, who present as white, native English speakers, begin to complain about their fellow incarcerated persons. Logan, in particular says: "There's very little common decency and courtesy in there. People here are just so aggravating and annoying. These are grown people who should know better." Earlier, Logan had provided some astute commentary on high recidivism rates due to legalized discrimination against formerly incarcerated individuals. Now, in a striking contradiction, he complains, "For a lot of these people, they've been in and out of this place for years, it's a homecoming of sorts. It's like, *'you got out, why the fuck are you back?'* . . . [Most of them] come from a really different arena of life than we do."[14] In these remarks, race and class differentials among the incarcerated population become evident, offering a possible explanation for those who completed our course as opposed to those who dropped out.

Conclusions

The most unambiguous conclusion at the end of these ten weeks is that mindfulness clearly played a crucial *ameliorative* role for our incarcerated students. Without a doubt, it offered them important tools for coping with or enduring the strains of incarcerated life: to withstand physical pain, anxiety about the future or about family members, stress about their legal situation, and other basic forms of chaos, alienation, and violence. Again and again, our participants thanked us for offering these techniques, and told us of the relief they provided—no matter how temporary—in what one described as a "pure hellhole." Central to this ameliorative component was the chaplain's emphasis on self-compassion and self-care, especially at the beginning of the class: the gentle, uncritical language of self-acceptance combined with a lack of commands and a reassurance that there was no "right or wrong." Repeatedly, participants heard that they were all human, and that no one needed fixing or advising. In an often brutal atmosphere, the chaplain's gentle, nonjudgmental perspective provided much-needed relief and humanization. He communicated much respect to his incarcerated students, congratulated them on the "great job" they were doing, and strongly advocated for self-worth and self-acceptance.

At the same time however, this nonjudgment and self-acceptance eventually dovetailed with something quite different: an encouragement toward making different choices, taking responsibility and ownership. As implied by the very name of the course, participants were also encouraged—albeit gently—to change and improve themselves, their choices, and attitudes. The course seemed to suggest they could retool their reality and reframe it as more "workable," once it was seen as a product of their own choices. "One of the reasons we do these practices," Chaplain Eric says, "is to develop our ability to have more choices, to see the consequences of our choices, to take responsibility for our choices." Although the word "rehabilitation" was never used, it was more than implied: Incarcerated individuals must transform themselves, learning to function better within—and perhaps even adjust to—their situation.

For instance, in the sessions on neuroscience, self-regulation, and choice, the chaplain acknowledged the unique and severe loss of control entailed by incarceration. He offered self-regulation through mindfulness as a coping mechanism for this challenge ("we are all developing our coping skills the best we can"), but also as the classic meditative remedy for difficult external circumstances: focus on the internal causes of suffering, rather than external ones. The language of rewiring the brain and regulating oneself seemed to imply that what caused each participant's incarceration must be a failure of neural wiring and/or good choice-making. Meanwhile, in the sessions on learning from discomfort, incarceration was reframed as an opportunity for "growth and learning," an opportunity to expand one's comfort zone and to make life more "workable." Certainly, the chaplain did acknowledge challenges from participants who pointed to the unjust nature of the system. But he also continued to offer the suggestion to "learn and grow" from discomfort, to use it as an "opportunity" for learning and personal development.

In the sessions on negativity bias, Mark had described to us (from his perspective at least) egregious miscarriages of justice. In response, the chaplain offered a practice that invoked feeling safe, resourced, and cared for. I wondered about invoking such feelings without acknowledging the traumatic, unjust context that made them so necessary—a context in which someone had just described being physically abused, living in fear, and being denied their rights by a chronically corrupt system. I was not able to interview any of the participants or to probe their views in any detail, but I wondered how they would respond to the suggestion that they reframe their feelings and re-train their brain toward relaxation, safety, and abundance, while experiencing trauma and oppression. Of course, I had no doubt that it would be beneficial for anyone in Mark's position to *feel* safe, resourced, connected—in control of themselves and their circumstances—in order to take productive action. In fact, I desperately hoped this course would provide Mark the wherewithal he needed for the fight ahead. I recalled the feedback our students gave about the strength and stability they had gained from the practices in the face of the overwhelming challenges they faced. I took comfort in remembering how they described the inner states of calm, peace, and refuge they were able to find, holding onto their sense of self while caged in a system seemingly intent on eliminating their existence. Yet, I struggled to understand: Could they truly feel strengthened, cared for, and resourced if we swept the systemic oppression they faced under the rug, remaining silent on it, and instead encouraging them to make the best of their situation?

In the session on the drama triangle, incarcerated students were taught that "feeling victimized" by law enforcement is simply one perspective. They were encouraged to shift that perspective, to see that they could just as easily be seen as a "persecutor" victimizing the public. Each time Chaplain Eric tried to offer this suggestion, students instinctively responded that the cop was the persecutor. The chaplain acknowledged their feeling of victimization, but immediately followed this with encouragement to "make a choice to let go," a choice that was presented as "empowering." I wondered whether this version of empowerment unwittingly ensured that people simply coped with and adjusted better to oppression and victimization, which could then become more normalized and less questionable.[15]

I came away from the course with a deep appreciation of the chaplain's compassion and gentleness, which served as a model for my own work in prisons. I learned a great deal from his invitational approach to meditative instruction, which I incorporated into my own teaching. I admired his unflinching commitment to providing students with resources to bolster their sense of self in the hellhole that was their life. He exemplified the duty of care toward the most vulnerable among us, and I remained in awe of the obstacles he regularly overcame to spend hours of his time volunteering at significant personal cost, bringing kindness and light to so many who were routinely dehumanized. But I was also left grappling with a series of concerns. I wondered about the repeated emphasis on individual changes in choice, attitude, and perspective, which seemed to frame everything as a personal problem with a personal solution. Meditative practice was taught as a route to accepting inequity and structural difficulty through the development of resilience and equanimity. As one activist notes, the language of resilience "puts the onus on the person to fix what should be a civic priority . . . there's an expectation that we're supposed to bounce back and that's the American way, [which] takes the power structures off the hook."[16]

I was troubled by the "bootstrapping" logic of a rugged individualism entailed in these messages of resilience and empowerment. The heroic individual seemed expected to empower themselves with a "no matter what, *I* can overcome" attitude—taking responsibility, choosing to see their circumstances differently, locating the source of their dissatisfaction in their inner world rather than in external circumstances, and ultimately transforming themselves. I worried, as one critic notes, that "you're so resilient" can become code for "'*You're on your own.*' . . . What about [focusing on] systemic racism, poverty, and inadequate educational and social supports? Are we fixing the right problems when we are teaching the importance of resilience?"[17]

Conversely, I found that the course remained largely silent on social, structural, or systemic causes of suffering, emphasizing mainly personal transformation as the solution to such suffering. Little was said about mass incarceration, other than an oblique reference to "a big conversation happening about criminal justice reform," and "skyrocketing" incarceration rates. This seemed particularly notable, given that the prison is, a sense, the most political of spaces—social, political, and legal structures are crucial contributors to incarceration, as research has repeatedly shown. Certainly, there were moments in the course that encouraged an active approach to one's situation, rather than a passive or quietist one. Notably, in the drama triangle sessions, participants were exhorted to make boundaries, challenge the status quo when necessary and take necessary action, including reporting the antagonist to human resources or—with no hint of irony—the police.[18] But overwhelmingly, the practices presented in this class did not seem designed as tools to either acknowledge or address systemic inequity or difficulties arising from social injustice. As the weeks wore on and we became increasingly familiar with our students, some used the check-in time to share detailed information on their cases, in the process offering strong critiques of the justice system. In response, the chaplain made clear in a variety of ways—through voice, gesture, and conversational redirection—that systemic critiques may not be welcome or appropriate in the class setting. In these moments, his stance was one of studied, apolitical neutrality: Despite a vague acknowledgment of the system's many "problems," he firmly but politely steered the conversation in another direction, on at least one occasion cutting someone off mid-sentence. In the face of claims regarding unjust or wrongful arrest, he typically responded with a neutral remark such as, "Well, the hope is that we can develop the capacity to navigate and move through life the best we can," shifting the discussion.

Of course, I considered the possibility (which I further explore in chapter 8) that the risk of losing access leads volunteers like Chaplain Eric to be cautious about political statements that staff may disapprove of. But his silence regarding structural issues went hand in hand with an undeniably enthusiastic advocacy of individual choice and ownership, which was sincere, and not simply pragmatic. Certainly, no mindfulness class could last long if it devolved entirely into political critique. But conversely, could mindfulness really address psychic stress without at least acknowledging the context of systemic oppression which served as the root cause of so much psychic stress? In Chapter 4 we saw how therapeutic, rehabilitative programming can function to keep the already-excluded in their place, teaching them to parrot the prison's message of their own blameworthiness based on flawed individual choices and "lack of discipline." Chaplain Eric was at pains to avoid such logic in the early part of the course, instead expressing kindness, respect, and admiration for our participants, encouraging them away from self-blame and shame. But in marrying some of the practices to the prison's own logic of individual responsibility—while staying notably silent on systemic causes of suffering—the mindfulness course seemed eerily consonant with the prison system's messaging; namely, that incarceration results from flawed individual choices and behaviors.

After the course ended, Chaplain Eric and I met to debrief and exchange our impressions of how the course went. Once again, we found ourselves in the café down the street from DFM. There, in our very first conversation years ago, the chaplain had expressed his reformist views regarding law enforcement and prisons. "What else is there [besides reform]?" he had asked at the time. "I'm not an anarchist, we can't throw all the doors open. . . . I don't think there's a conspiracy within the criminal justice system to clear the streets," he had said, noting that the fundamental intention of the justice system is "producing safety." He had also expressed empathy for police officers, who are just "doing their job," but without "the tools to deal with their stress and hypervigilance." He was enthusiastic about his involvement in a variety of pilot programs teaching mindfulness to police officers, offering tools that might allow them to listen instead of reacting instinctively.

Now, as we met in the same cafe to discuss our respective post-class assessments, I raised some of the issues that troubled me. I asked whether there was a potential tension between holding that "no one is broken," while advocating for personal transformation by incarcerated persons. "Yes, it's a fine line to walk and it's tricky" the chaplain admitted. "It's true that no one is broken, but in the end, what was the title of the course?" he asked rhetorically. "I only meet and work with people who want to transform something in their lives." I sensed he was not delighted with this line of inquiry, but continued. I pressed him on the course's strong emphasis on personal responsibility and individual ownership, while pointing out the relative silence on issues of structural or systemic injustice. "Personal responsibility is not the same as blame," he responded, "there's a huge difference." He then offered incisive critiques of racism and socioeconomic inequity, showing how keenly aware he was of these issues. "I have a limited amount of time with them," he asserted. "I have to offer them what I can do." He also noted the importance of "cultural humility" in not presuming to lecture incarcerated persons on systemic injustice: "It's not my place to tell them how the system is stacked against them, or to make them see it clearly. They see it already, they live it every day." This was a concern I shared: I too had felt nagged by whether it was my place to offer a perspective on systemic inequity to people who experienced it far more intensely and routinely than I ever had. He described his own brush with poverty many years ago—becoming somewhat emotional during this retelling—noting that it was nothing compared to what many of his students have experienced. "It would be condescending for me to tell them about that," he insisted. "Maybe that's part of my privilege, that I don't know what it was like to grow up like that."

I asked why discussions of systemic injustice were not encouraged even when students made clear they wished to move in that direction. "Yes, because I saw how quickly they could devolve into the details of one's grievance story," he said. He also argues for the importance of neutrality when working in law enforcement: "We can't have an agenda." I offered some suggestions and ideas from fellow volunteers on the importance of marrying individual self-improvement lessons to discussions of systemic issues. Chaplain Eric replied that this may not jibe fully with what incarcerated participants want for themselves: "If some want to become social justice warriors, that's up to them to find meaning. Maybe they'd rather just be with their families, or go live on an island. I can't be the one to decide what is meaningful for them. My hope is that as mindfulness and awareness develops further, as self-compassion and a sense of unshakable self-worth blossoms, we each in our own individual way find and pursue what is meaningful for us in our lives." Our conversation came to a close with Chaplain Eric re-emphasizing the importance of individual transformation: "I think the work has to happen one individual at a time, that's the only way. I can't do the work of addressing social structures, it's not what I know how to do. I can only offer what I know how to offer. The only empowering space for action occurs at the individual level, that's all I've got. It's that simple."

Months later, as this book came closer to fruition, I sent Chaplain Eric a draft of the full manuscript, offering him the opportunity to provide feedback as part of the "member-checking" process (outlined at further length in the Methodological Appendix). Chaplain Eric offered several interpretive challenges and clarifications to the claims in this chapter. In response, I have modified the language in a few passages here, and discussed his clarifications in greater detail in the concluding chapter of this book.

SECTION III
TEACHING INSIDE: VOLUNTEER COMMUNITIES AND PERSPECTIVES

7

The World of Prison Volunteers

It is 6:30 am on a cold Sunday morning when my alarm usually goes off. After snuggling in the warmth of my bed for a few extra minutes, I begrudgingly drag myself out. This is far earlier than I would normally rise. Bleary-eyed, I dress myself (skipping my morning shower),[1] and make sure to eat something small but protein-filled, enough to get me through the next six or seven hours. I move slowly, often groggy because I never sleep well before I have to wake up early. Half an hour later, I get in my car and make the almost hour-long drive out to a prison, where I volunteer with an organization that brings yoga to incarcerated women. By the time I am on the road, I have gotten over my early morning lethargy, and am looking forward to the time I will spend with my incarcerated students. There is rarely any traffic at that hour, and the drive becomes a time of contemplative solitude. Gazing at the morning light filtering through the sky, I recall that first moment of resistance when the alarm goes off, and I long to sleep in. But by the time I reach the prison, I am energized—eager for a morning yoga practice with my incarcerated students, and glad to offer something that, in the words of one student, "makes [them] feel human enough and valued enough to be offered that experience."

Between August 2016 and March 2020, this became my routine on many mornings. Between the drive, the lengthy entry and exit security procedures at the prison, the class itself, and the post-class chitchat with fellow volunteers and incarcerated students, it was often well past lunch-time before I returned. Over almost four years, I made weekly visits—some-times once a week, sometimes more—to different prisons and jails to offer yoga or meditation classes. I became immersed in the landscape and logistics of prison life, learning about the differences between different types of facilities, their routines and protocols, while getting to know many of my incarcerated students. In facilities where our students were serving longer sentences, many attended our classes consistently. We would have time for small personal interactions after class, as they shared with us various aspects of their lives—asking advice about dealing with aches, pains, and ailments, sharing news and excitement about release dates, and even occasionally showing us pictures of children or grandchildren. Other facilities where people were being held pretrial or serving shorter sentences were more

Freedom Inside?. Farah Godrej, Oxford University Press. © Oxford University Press 2022.
DOI: 10.1093/oso/9780190070083.003.0007

of a revolving-door: We would see some students repeatedly, but others would vanish after a few times, as each class brought new faces. Here too, some of us volunteers would have short friendly chats with students after class whenever possible. In some cases, we became familiar with prison staff through repeated encounters, exchanging greetings and conversations either while being escorted within the facility to and from the classroom (a requirement in some but not all facilities); or during the entry and exit security and sign-in protocols; or simply during casual run-ins while making our way within the facility. In no case were any of the classes I taught ever directly monitored or surveilled by facility staff. Eventually, I began to take on a greater leadership role in two volunteer organizations, learning much more than I had ever expected about the inner workings of this world, from the perspective of an insider.

How does the world of the prison intersect with that of the volunteers? How do volunteers confront the prison system, and what do they believe, learn, or think they know about it? Along with my immersion in local volunteer communities, my extensive interviews and conversations with fellow volunteers gave me a way to learn about the relationship that volunteers have with the system they serve, and how they understand the context and conditions of their volunteer work. In this chapter I examine the various forms of messaging—both from the prison and from volunteer organizations—that volunteers receive, showing how vastly different messages can end up offering vastly different lessons. I show that what volunteers learn, know, and come to believe about the prison context can be heavily mediated by prisons themselves. While some volunteer organizations offer their own trainings to counteract the prison's messaging, others offer little by way of training, leaving volunteers to cobble together their own views about the prison system.

In this chapter, I move back and forth between what I learned through interviews and my personal experiences as a prison volunteer. Through my personal experiences, I reflect on the largely apolitical tone of many prison volunteer organizations, including the ones I participated in. I found, for the most part, that enthusiasm for politically oriented yoga or meditation was limited among fellow volunteers, leaving me with few politically engaged models to draw on. I also found that their largely apolitical stances sometimes led volunteer organizations to replicate the prison's messaging about the subordinate status of incarcerated persons (even if unwittingly). Many volunteers retained traditional notions of leadership and authority from their yogic training, and few seemed to believe that the prison context was unique enough to rethink how yoga or meditation should be taught. As a result, incarcerated students were largely seen as objects of discipline, rather than as co-equal partners in learning.

Lessons from Prison Trainings: Where the Messaging Begins

I described in Chapter 2 how I initially connected with local organizations serving jails and prisons. With the support of group leaders, I was approved to start volunteering at four facilities, which first required undergoing a security clearance. The only other requirement was a training offered by each prison or jail, which mainly addressed the facility's rules, regulations, and security protocols. Once I passed each facility's clearance process and attended their respective trainings, I was able to start accompanying fellow volunteers into prisons, and co-teaching with them. Like other beginners, I was asked at first to observe the teaching of more senior volunteers. But I soon became comfortable offering classes my own, which I discovered was not unusual for many experienced volunteers.[2]

Early on, I learned that prisons seemed to care only about two aspects of the volunteers' role: the background check, and their attendance of the training run by prison staff, focused largely on security issues. Other than this, they left the work of training, vetting, or recommending specific volunteers to each organization (or to groups of volunteers, loosely organized), taking a largely hands-off approach. One of the most important events shaping the volunteer's encounter with prisons, therefore, is the training session required by each facility. These sessions last between two and four hours, depending on who conducts them.[3] The staff running these trainings were sometimes civilians, at other times correctional officers (COs).[4] Most facilities require trainings to be renewed annually, so each volunteer ends up sitting through these virtually identical training sessions once per year.[5]

Over the years, I attended a total of six required volunteer training sessions held by different prisons and jails. These trainings were meant to present the institutional perspective to civilians seeking to volunteer inside prisons and jails. At these trainings, I met fellow volunteers preparing to serve in a variety of programs: chaplains in training from different religious groups (Buddhist, Muslim, Christian, and even Native American), AA or NA volunteers, as well as volunteers for a variety of religious, educational, and self-help programs such as restorative justice, writing programs, and other therapeutic programs. In contrast to both COs and civilian staff who are employees of the prison, many, if not most, of the prison volunteers I encountered—including those who taught yoga or meditation—were unpaid, and therefore, outsiders to the system.[6]

Regardless of whether they were run by federal, state, or county facilities, the common themes of the prison trainings rarely varied: First and foremost, they were designed to give volunteers a run-down of the security protocols and procedures in each facility. These ranged from everyday issues like entry and exit procedures, protocols for escort, to rules and regulations about interactions with incarcerated persons. Some facilities insisted on a blanket no-touch policy, while others allowed handshakes only, with a strong recommendation against touch. There were strict regulations about materials that could be brought in to the facility for distribution to incarcerated persons—most facilities allowed books and other paper-based materials with prior approval, although dire warnings were given about everyday objects (such as pens, pencils, or staples) that were prohibited because they could be turned into weapons. Most facilities did not allow volunteers to accept anything from incarcerated persons, including cards or handwritten notes.

In addition to these rules and security protocols, every single training I attended emphasized the idea of the prison as a space of never-ending threats to one's person, and the need for constant security and vigilance due to the very nature of those it controlled. Repeatedly, we volunteers were warned not to fraternize excessively with incarcerated persons, to remember that they were "bad people" who had done "bad things," to keep a polite distance and be on our guard against their inevitable attempts at manipulation and rule-breaking. These warnings were given both by COs and by civilian staff such as prison psychologists. At some sessions, prison staff threw in cautionary tales about inmates who had tried to compromise, injure, or manipulate both volunteers and staff through a variety of means—asking them to call or mail something to family members, attempting to obtain money or other resources from them, and employing sweet-talk or even seduction. One facility produced an extensive slideshow of all the weapons confiscated from cells, made from everyday objects. Some facilities discussed lengthy protocols for hypothetical crisis situations, such as a fight—or worse, a hostage situation—breaking out during volunteer programs, inevitably the most tense moments during the training.

During these sessions, many of my fellow attendees reacted with visible shock and sometimes alarm. At one training, a woman about my age produced regular gasps and wide-eyed sounds of disbelief when the officer presented the "weapons" slideshow and discussed potential hostage situations. Many other attendees nodded vigorously in agreement when the training officer spoke about avoiding fraternization, and some raised their hands to offer their own insights—although notably, no volunteer ever offered a story of being manipulated or pressured by an incarcerated person. Once, during a discussion of the hostage-situation protocol, I raised my hand to ask how often such situations had come to pass in that facility. The officer conducting the training racked his brain, and finally admitted that there had in fact been no such events that he could recall. Still, these dire warnings seemed to drive a few people away: I later found out that at least one potential yoga volunteer had been too "freaked out" by the training and had subsequently decided against volunteering in prisons.

Overwhelmingly, the volunteers who attended these trainings represented a service-oriented ethos. At the same time, the institutional perspective presented at these trainings seemed designed to both encourage yet moderate their "do-gooding" impulses: "by all means come in to to help our prisoners," they seemed to say, "but don't forget that these are bad people who do bad things." While these institutions allow volunteers to offer opportunities for rehabilitation, they also continue to warn volunteers that the prison itself largely exists to control and contain those who may be irredeemable, cautioning us to be on our guard against them.

Strikingly, none of the local organizations I joined offered their own training to counteract, complement, or otherwise moderate these very specific messages offered by the jail or prison (at least at the time that I arrived). In the local organizations I joined, volunteers were screened by leaders, but this screening focused mainly on their level of familiarity with yogic or meditative practices, a reasonably competent and mature demeanor, and the ability to abide by the prison's rules. There was little occasion for volunteers to critically examine or interrogate the prison's rules and messages among themselves. There were no meetings or conversations with new recruits to discuss what was taught at the prison training; there were no collective discussions of what we volunteers were to make of the prison's lessons.

I soon learned that this was not the norm in all organizations. Later in this chapter, I will discuss how other, larger and more well-established volunteer organizations conduct their own trainings in addition to the prison's training, and disseminate clearer systemic messages to their new recruits. From attending their trainings, I learned that these organizations disseminated very specific messages about the prison, its narratives, and its rules, rather than leaving volunteers to cobble together their own private beliefs about the prison system based on the system's own messaging. In contrast to these more established organizations, the local organizations I joined gave volunteers relatively few resources for understanding the system they were about to enter, apart from what they were told by the prison.

Dealing with a "Dysfunctional Bureaucracy"

Soon after becoming a member of local volunteer organizations, I was asked to take on more leadership and responsibility, whether formally—through serving as a Board member or a Co-Executive Director—or informally, through liaising with both fellow volunteers and prison staff in the daily management and administration of prison programs. Many of the tasks I took on were relatively routine, such as weekly logistics, scheduling, and eventually recruitment of new volunteers. But as I became more centrally involved in leadership, I also became privy to more fraught scenarios entailing closer involvement with the administration of programs, and more regular communication with prison staff.

At every facility, we adhered to different—though equally complex—security procedures and navigated relationships with staff in order to keep our programs running smoothly. I began accompanying group leaders to meetings with prison administrators in order to discuss the continuation of existing programs—or, in some cases, the establishment of new ones. Some of these meetings involved tense negotiations over stalled programs. Often, prison staff would randomly cancel the day's yoga class, leaving us with miffed volunteers who had driven long hours to the prison and were denied access for no discernible reason. Other times, our programs were indefinitely put on hold, subject to the whims of administrators who cited various logistical issues that never became fully transparent or comprehensible to us.

I learned about the strict military hierarchy in prisons, and found that nothing would move smoothly if we did not respect this command structure in our dealings, being careful to defer to the right people—and use their correct titles—without overstepping. When prison staff turned over, our programs were inevitably affected, as new administrators instituted new rules, or simply had no idea how to keep a previously authorized program running. Many prison staff were friendly and enthusiastic, and did whatever they could to help us. Many expressed gratitude for our commitment, and told us how much they valued our work. But other staff members often seemed too overwhelmed, sleep-deprived, underinformed, or simply lacking the bandwidth to be able to assist with programs that were clearly considered a low priority in the grand scheme of things. Over the years, I learned that the work of keeping any volunteer program going inside a prison—not to mention starting a new one—entailed constant uphill battles, navigating often-inconsistent, byzantine rules and regulations (which inevitably differed from one facility to the next), while understanding staff's own limitations, and working around personality quirks and conflicts.

My interviews with fellow volunteers deepened my understanding of these phenomena. Many of my respondents were barely involved in the administration of programs, and did not communicate with prison staff more than minimally necessary. Their participation was of what we might call an "in-and-out" variety: They signed up to teach regularly (usually once or twice a month) at a given facility, which entailed showing up on the designated day, following the security protocols for entry and exit, and teaching their class. These volunteers admitted they paid little attention to the system, and did not seem interested in commenting on larger contextual or systemic issues. They appeared to be largely siloed in their experience. In contrast, leaders of volunteer organizations had far more to say about the systemic context. They had typically worked closely with prison staff to establish their programs, which required complex negotiations to establish a regularly functioning class schedule.

Some leaders spoke at length about the challenges of launching these programs and keeping them running smoothly. Many told me that prison staff had been openly skeptical about the value of yoga or meditation, and that finding an insider contact had been crucial to their ability to get their foot in the door. Even then, it often took months to get the attention of the correct staff members to establish a program. Victoria describes the persistence required for this task: "[There were] lots of doors being shut in my face . . . we weren't welcome, we weren't facilitated, and [yet our yoga program] managed to survive." She describes repeated phone calls being evaded by her staff contact: "I learned through experience that it would take about six calls to get through. . . . After that I just started driving downtown and showing up in his office . . . they would never have called me back if I didn't show up there in person . . . if we had disappeared, nobody would even notice."

Like Victoria, many volunteer leaders expressed frustration with the chaotic, mystifying, and often inconsistent manner in which prison staff implemented rules, regulations, and procedures. Having volunteers go through a security-clearance process was usually the very first step in establishing a program, and many reported that the clearance process could be confusing or disorganized. Applications were often lost, sometimes multiple times, forcing applicants to reapply at personal expense (if documents required notarizing). Some volunteers were cleared virtually overnight, others waited months until they eventually gave up and moved on to other opportunities.

Describing the "trials and tribulations" of the clearance paperwork, one volunteer leader stated that no organization has "figured out a way to make this work easy." Different facilities require different forms and paperwork to be submitted, and background checks often involved social media checks to scrutinize the online profile of a potential volunteer. Another volunteer described the security clearance process as intentionally ambiguous: In some cases, a detective calls a potential volunteer's employer or shows up at their home to verify their address, "which is just a code word for living in a certain neighborhood." In other cases, volunteers whose class status or other credentials are easily verifiable sail through clearance with no extra scrutiny. "That's by design," asserted Claire, a white woman in her thirties, describing the ease of her own clearance and the "politics of respectability": "I don't know anyone in a prison. I'm not related to anyone who's been incarcerated. I don't correspond with anyone who's incarcerated." What some experience as chaos or inconsistency is seen by others as an intentionally vague process that allows the prison system to carefully control who enters, without offering any transparency into its own decision-making: "They get to look at the hell out of you, but you get no look on the inside of what they're doing," Claire pointed out.

Even after yoga or meditation programs are established in prisons or jails, obstacles seem to abound. Entry into the prison, even for cleared volunteers, is never guaranteed. Anyone entering and exiting a prison in any capacity is subjected to total control, seen as a potential threat to order and security, and scrutinized or disciplined accordingly. Marie Gottschalk recounts her experience in a prison education program, as she and her students waited through the usual entry protocols: "While waiting to clear security, a correctional officer declared that the sweater a . . . student was wearing violated the facility's dress code. The student's polite entreaties that she had worn the sweater into the jail several times without a problem were futile. Directly challenged, the correctional officer used his enormous discretion to warn that other students waiting behind her in line might also be in violation of the dress code." Visitors to prisons routinely report that clothing is strictly policed through dress codes, allowing prisons to humiliate visitors, or worse, turn them away after long hours of travel. Many report being treated as though they are incarcerated: "It's horrible because it makes you feel like one of them. . . . That just teaches you a lesson."[7] Volunteers are no different: Like Gottschalk and her students, I and many other volunteers were often told—in arbitrary and completely inconsistent manner—that something we had worn previously would not pass muster on this particular day, with this particular CO. A forgotten driver's license would often end up resulting in a wasted two-hour drive, for no one can enter the institution without identification. Clothing became a constant source of anxiety: Were our yoga pants too tight or form-fitting? Had one of us mistakenly put on one of the many forbidden colors while dressing ourselves in the fog of the early morning? Would our underwire bras set off the metal detector? Would the officer known for being extra-strict be on duty and refuse to let us in? To add to the anxiety, the dress codes inevitably varied across different facilities: what worked in one had almost no relationship to what worked in another.

Beyond the discretionary scrutiny of one's clothing, many volunteers report that there are other reasons for being denied entry. Some tell me that their entry-authorization documents mysteriously disappeared when they would show up at the facility to check in for class. Others report being let in one week, but not the next, with officers claiming their name was "not on the list" of approved volunteers. The most common complaint was the arbitrary cancelation of yoga or meditation class, often for no discernible reason, or for reasons that seemed entirely preventable (such a scheduling mistake or a lack of escort personnel), and typically without prior warning—"sometimes I would drive 100 miles," said Morgan, a white woman in her thirties, "and they'd say '*sorry no yoga today*,' with no explanation and no logic." Morgan's story was far from atypical: Victoria reported that volunteers from her organization would arrive promptly for an early morning class (often having woken up hours earlier in order to make the drive and get through the routine entry protocols), only to find that their assigned time-slot had been taken over by a staff member dispensing medications, or haircut/grooming time, or any number of other activities that took precedence. One leader, Hannah, reports a period during which her group's yoga classes were canceled for six weeks in a row—in her words, "usurped"—resuming only after she had written to complain to a high-level contact at the state department of corrections, much to the chagrin of her staff coordinator at the prison. Victoria reports having to jostle with a competitor volunteer group when the regular, long-established time-slot for her yoga program was suddenly given to another organization without warning. Leaders like Hannah and Victoria emphasized the delicate balance between being a "squeaky" enough wheel to fight their way through a system strewn with obstacles, while being careful enough not to complain so loudly as to make enemies. Eva, a white woman in her fifties who founded a major prison yoga program, describes the prison bureaucracy as "dysfunctional," "complicated," and "convoluted."

Relations with Prison Staff and Other Volunteer Groups

Despite these reports of frustration, inconsistency, and general chaos, many volunteers insisted that their experience with the prison system had been relatively smooth, and their relations with prison staff were often friendly, cordial, and respectful. "They seem fairly well-intentioned," said Marissa, representing the views of many who did not take a critical tone. Some volunteers took pains to insist that the work of corrections was difficult and stressful, and that everyone was doing the best they could in an under-resourced and overwhelmed system. Thalia described corrections department and prison officials in her state as "progressive," while Eva acknowledged that the response of correctional staff to yoga and meditation programs varied by state and jurisdiction. Others made a distinction between high-level administrators (such as a warden) and on-the-ground officers or staff: "You might have prison administrators that recognize the value of yoga," said Mason, who has founded a nationally recognized prison yoga organization. "Where you run into the difficulties is with the people who basically run the day-to-day operations of the prison. Those are the ones you have the most contact with . . . and they're the least open [and] informed." Mason characterizes this as a "cultural divide": These officers' perception of yoga is that of "white women in beautiful yoga clothing chanting in a studio. . . . They're just like, 'come on, gimme a break, we're giving these convicts yoga?'" Like Mason, many volunteers characterized upper administration as supportive, but ground-level staff encountered in daily dealings as skeptical and even antagonistic. Victoria notes that a sympathetic prison official once warned her that yoga or meditation organizations would not find "many welcoming people in the criminal justice system." And, for Morgan, despite some support from prison staff, her attempts to sustain a yoga program were like "pulling teeth."

As volunteers described relations with actors in the prison system, two groups emerged as most antagonistic to their work. The first, as we see, were COs with whom they worked most closely on a daily basis, and who were tasked with facilitating their programs. The second were the Christian volunteers in the prison, who often saw yoga and meditation as a competing faith. Anecdotes about the skepticism and hostility of COs toward volunteer programs were ubiquitous: Overwhelmingly, volunteers reported COs expressing the view that incarcerated persons are "there to be punished" and do not "deserve" programs such as yoga and meditation. The vast majority reported officers stereotyping incarcerated persons as worthless, and one volunteer quotes a CO asserting that they should all be "electrocuted." Charlotte, a white meditation instructor in her fifties, confesses that she avoids interactions with prison staff because they are so negative about incarcerated persons. In describing the "culture of hostility from the guards," Hannah says, "they treat us like prisoners . . . because we're naive and we don't understand the criminal mind, we're so easily manipulated." Many report that officers "delight in telling you you're wasting your time," because incarcerated people are "not sincere" in their pursuit of any self-improvement. Such reports were by no means universal: Even those who expressed frustration with these forms of stereotyping noted that some COs could be friendly, respectful, and supportive. They also emphasized the importance of recognizing the tremendous stress of working in corrections—resisting the urge to demonize was often seen as part of one's own yoga or meditation practice, in which no one was to be made into an enemy. "The culture as a whole is hard and demeaning and punitive, and people are treated like a sub-human," according to Courtney. For some volunteers, the system itself served to harden prison officials, eventually stripping them of their humanity and leaving them with, in Thomas's words, "a suspicious and controlling attitude toward prisoners."

The relationship between yoga or meditation programs and Christian chaplains in prisons also seemed somewhat fraught, though in a less overt way. Courtney, a white meditation instructor in her fifties, describes many of these Christian volunteers as "territorial": despite attempts to present meditation as compatible with any faith commitments, Christian chaplains "see it as a competing faith." She reports that some of her students "feel negatively judged by the chaplains" for attending meditation, and are told that they are "not a real Christian" if they attend. Some yoga volunteers reported hearing from their incarcerated students that Christian chaplains believe yoga is "the work of the devil." Buddhist meditation volunteers sometimes discovered that Protestant chaplains refused to minister to or otherwise serve incarcerated persons if they were also seeing Buddhist chaplains or participating in meditation. Even though volunteers taught these practices as either secular or compatible with any faith, incarcerated students routinely reported to them that Christian chaplains opposed their attendance. Some volunteer leaders also heard from prison staff that religious programming—and particularly Christian programming—got special priority in the prison (although it is unclear whether this was official or unofficial). In a system where time, space, and resources for volunteer programming are severely limited, many found their yoga or meditation program's space or time-slot arbitrarily given away to a Christian group. Jane, a white woman in her thirties, reports systematic bias in favor of Christian volunteers at the facility she served: Yoga instructors often had to wait over an hour for an officer to escort them into the facility, while Christian volunteers sailed past immediately. "It was really challenging," she says. "It definitely felt like we weren't really valued for the contribution we were making." Jane also believes that the Christian volunteers had enough influence with prison staff to pressure them to warn yoga volunteers not to proselytize or convert prisoners to Hinduism or Buddhism. Although no one reported any direct confrontation with Christian chaplains, some did report frosty interpersonal interactions when their paths occasionally crossed. "I would get a little of the side-eye," says Julia, a yoga volunteer, describing her occasional encounters with Christian volunteers while they all waited at the front desk to be checked-in.

Who Shows Up and How? Relations with Incarcerated Students

Who shows up in yoga or meditation classes in prisons and jails, and how is their attendance determined? For the most part, volunteers noted that attendance in such programs was mostly voluntary, unlike in many other prison programs—such as, say substance-abuse or anger management—where attendance is often court-mandated by the terms of sentencing. This meant that those who attended yoga or meditation classes usually self-selected. Very occasionally, yoga and meditation programs were accredited for "milestone" credits, or other forms of "points" that allowed for sentence-reduction.[8] But this was largely the exception rather than the rule: In the vast majority of cases, students received no credit for class attendance, and attended simply out of interest. Even so, some volunteers reported that the discretion of COs sometimes tended to determine who actually was able to attend. Several noted that they saw staff using their classes as a form of control, as a privilege to be granted or denied, deciding who they deemed to be well behaved enough to "deserve" yoga or meditation. For precisely this reason, Charlotte said, she is loathe to report any students who may demonstrate behavioral issues in her class: "The last thing I'm going to do is go to the administrators," she said emphatically.

Volunteers also experienced widely varying levels of surveillance for their classes and students. Depending on the facility and its protocols, students were either escorted to the class by officers, or allowed to independently arrive at the room designated for the class. Many volunteers reported that no prison staff monitored or supervised their classes: One stated emphatically that she preferred to close the door to her classroom and be left alone with her students, without staff supervision. Other volunteers report that a CO is often stationed in the room where they teach yoga or meditation. Because jail populations tend to be transitory, classes in jails had much higher turnover than in prisons, and those who taught in jails reported it was common not to "see the same person twice." Some volunteers found this frustrating or dispiriting, especially if they had developed relationships with their students. "You see some people for months or years, others not more than once, and there's no way to know," said Charlotte. Many other volunteers taught far more stable populations in prisons, where people tended to have longer sentences: Some reported that such students had been attending their classes for a decade or more.

In Chapters 6 and 9 of this book, readers get more detailed accounts of yoga or meditation classes in incarceration facilities. But in describing their classes and their students, many volunteers generally noted that teaching in prison is often no different from teaching in a yoga studio or a meditation center in the outside world: Students enter the space, take their seats (or roll out mats, in a yoga class), and the volunteer facilitator leads everyone in the daily practice. They describe their students as highly motivated, attentive, and disciplined in their practice, especially those with long years of commitment and experience. "Smart," "capable," "bright," and "enthusiastic" were words used by many to describe their students. More than one volunteer shared this assessment by Morgan: "I feel like I get through to inmates at a way higher percentage and level than any of my 'outside' yoga classes . . . in terms of their motivation and adherence to practice. There are some serious practitioners and serious searchers in there . . . a lot of them are not going to get out, they're not going to see freedom, so the spiritual component becomes important to their life." Julia echoed this view: "I feel like they're more attentive and willing and respectful, almost more than people on the outside who are paying their twenty bucks for their classes." Hannah described her prison program as a truly "yogic environment," where some incarcerated students have even started teaching yoga to others within the prison. "I obviously love my students," said Thalia, with passion. "I think they're amazing and I learned a lot from them, more probably than I can ever teach them, about the incredible resilience of human beings . . . it's really an honor to be in the room with them." Alice similarly describes teaching "high-security" students in freestanding cages: "I thought I'd be intimidated [or] a little afraid, and I never was. In fact, I absolutely loved teaching the gentlemen that were in the [cages], because they kept asking me questions about the *Bhagavad-Gītā*, and then they had questions about the postures, and they were just eating it up."

But other volunteers offered a different perspective, characterizing their incarcerated students as undisciplined, disruptive, dysregulated, and disinterested. "The vast majority don't know what yoga is," said Victoria, "in the beginning they looked at me like I was talking about alien abduction." Victoria had perhaps the strongest views about the lack of discipline she encountered in her prison yoga classes: "I would go crazy with them on a permanent basis. They don't have any self-control or regulation. . . . They won't be quiet . . . most of them don't get it, and they still talk [during class]. I'll correct them, I'll say, *'you guys can stop talking now, please.'*" They just have never been required to exhibit any form of self-discipline. I get people who get up and leave, they can't deal with it. Whether it's striking a nerve, or they're lazy." Some volunteers described their adult students as "childlike": "[they're] a little bit like children," said one; "it almost feels like having a troubled child," said another, of her incarcerated students. Some reported various forms of disruption through cross-talk or laughter, behaviors almost never seen in mainstream yoga studios or meditation centers, where silence tends to be the norm during practice. "They're just dysregulated," says Vivian, describing many of her female students, although like many others, she acknowledges that this typically results from the long histories of trauma, violence, and abuse that most incarcerated persons—particularly women—share. Vivian is the only volunteer to report witnessing a fight while teaching in a jail or prison. Those who taught in juvenile facilities especially found that disruption was not unusual, particularly given the histories of trauma, abuse, and sex-trafficking that their students had suffered. These histories equally often resulted, especially among the younger teen students, in a lack of enthusiasm or flat affect. Alice describes her experience teaching yoga at a juvenile facility: "We would go into the one unit where they're on meds because they tried to kill themselves . . . there's just a huge disconnect there. They're not able to show certain emotions . . . they really have no one that they're close to, except for the family that's pimping them out . . . they're so wound up that they don't know how to relax . . . [or] they'd be zoned out on meds."

Regardless of the difficulties they reported with disinterested, apathetic, or disruptive students—and one very rare report of sexualized or inappropriate behavior—most volunteers overwhelmingly reported positive experiences and relationships with incarcerated students. All volunteers, including those who taught in the highest-security units or with populations labeled most "difficult," report being met with tremendous gratitude. "They tell us thank you, that they're happy to see us," says Ethan. "Just an overall attitude of gratitude," says Julia, echoing the majority of my respondents, who described easy and smooth relationships. Many report that tears are not uncommon expressions of gratitude: "They want to hug me," says Victoria, "because I give them a lot of love and affection" during class. Claire, however, warns that these often intense, tearful reactions say more about the brutality of incarceration than anything else: "You get treated as a saint for a very, very low bar," she says wryly, "for meeting [someone] as human." Some volunteers do report having to fob off attempts by incarcerated students to obtain their contact information—"Where can I find you when I get out?"—gently informing them that they are not allowed to share such information, instead offering more general suggestions for yoga or meditation classes in their community.

Lessons from Volunteer Trainings: Where the Messaging Continues

Soon after I entered the world of prison volunteers, I came to see that my local volunteer work did not represent the full scope of conversations happening nationally around the teaching of yoga or meditation to severely marginalized groups. The more I learned about leading national organizations doing this work, the clearer it became that I needed to attend their trainings in order to compare what goals, priorities, and values were being communicated to prison yoga or meditation volunteers elsewhere. I attended trainings at three comparable organizations, with national profiles. From attending these trainings—and interviewing leaders of these organizations—I found that there were stark differences in the cultures of prison yoga or meditation organizations. In particular, I found that while established national organizations gave very specific recommendations for how to revise traditional practices for the prison context, the leadership of the local organizations I joined demonstrated little interest—and in some cases, reluctance—to re-examine long-standing practices and norms. There were three important dimensions to these disagreements: the emphasis on larger structural political issues; the revision of traditional notions of yogic authority and discipline; and rethinking issues of consent for touch. Attending the national trainings made clear to me that teaching yoga or meditation to marginalized groups required attentiveness to these core themes. As I became increasingly involved in leadership positions, I began to report back to local volunteers and group leaders about what I had learned in these national trainings. I also began to cautiously experiment with introducing some of these values and priorities into our local practices, with mixed success. For the most part, I found myself largely outnumbered in my desire to re-examine these important topics for the prison context.

Political Commentary about the Prison System

First, I found that local volunteer groups evinced little interest in larger structural or systemic issues, or in the political dimensions of mass incarceration. Organizational priorities seemed focused mainly on keeping programs running smoothly without running afoul of prison regulations, and volunteers were left to make what they wanted of the prison trainings they had attended. There was no discussion of how we might think about the messages we had been given at the prison or jail's trainings, or about the system we were entering. No one seemed interested in addressing the more fundamental structural issues about how it was that so many people ended up in prisons in the first place, or that the vast majority of them seemed poor, Black, or brown. In stark contrast to what I heard at the three national trainings, it seemed as though none of my local organizations—or their leaders—gave any clear messages about the system we were entering.

The first training I attended was held by an organization called Yoga in Prison (YIP), which offered a nationally recognized form of accreditation that anyone seeking to volunteer in prisons can avail of. At their training, the founder of the organization—a white man in his sixties named Mason—presented a series of slides titled the "Failure of the US Prison System," running through well-rehearsed figures: The United States has 5 percent of the world's population but 25 percent of its prisoners, 2.25 million people are incarcerated, six hundred thousand of them for nonviolent offenses, the majority are people of color, 60 percent recidivate within three years of release, and so on. Mason called the system "broken," but almost immediately cast the solution in terms of individual responsibility. The purpose of "bringing yoga into prisons and jails" was cast as "teach[ing] personal responsibility and accountability for harm caused . . . adapting traditional yoga practice to behavioral issues, acting out, harming people . . . which can be the difference between committing another crime and not." In a room full of mostly white women (with a smattering of men, and few participants of color), no challenge was offered to this view. One Black woman did interject to offer that society has failed incarcerated persons, but agreed with Mason that such people "need to be moralized, they need to be taught a spiritual core." The thrust of the message from this organization was that teaching yoga and meditation to people in prisons was the solution to a structural problem—a solution which teaches damaged, traumatized populations to manage their reactions better, so as to develop the emotional intelligence to transform themselves.

I then attended trainings by two other organizations, Freedom for the Incarcerated (FFI) and Social Justice and Yoga (SJY), which offered far more critical views of the prison system. At FFI's training, people of color seemed to constitute about half the group, and many of the Black and Latinx participants identified as formerly incarcerated or system-involved. The facilitators included two white women, an openly gay Black woman and a formerly incarcerated white man. The leadership and involvement of people of color and system-impacted persons seemed to be a high priority. Facilitators required participants to read *The New Jim Crow* in advance. They critiqued the prison system as fundamentally inequitable, and did not use any language of "taking responsibility" or "encouraging behavioral change." Instead, they emphasized the systemic, disproportionate criminalization of Black and brown people, and asserted that doing prison work would require volunteers to examine their own inaccurate views of marginalized populations. They reexamined the logic of individual choice, noting that systemic disadvantage usually has "nothing to do with how hard you worked, it has to do with what opportunities you get, the decisions that get made, which makes the deck stacked." In contrast to YIP's goal of providing tools for behavioral modification and impulse control to address "acting out" and "committing crimes," FFI's training taught that the purpose of teaching yoga in prisons was to provide support and healing through humility, kindness, nonjudgmental acceptance, and affirmation: "undoing shame" through "acceptance" and improving "self-worth."

While FFI had certainly offered a far more critical message than YIP, the most radical political commentary was offered by SJY, an organization which held its trainings online. SJY's co-founder, Adina, offered the same critique that I had heard at FFI: "the system is biased against people of color," she noted, minutes into the training. "It's built into the laws and the sentencing." From here, SJY's political messaging went on to be far more direct and coherent than any other organization I had trained with, connecting yoga and meditation to the dangers of colluding with an unjust system. "When we suggest that [people] calm down and breathe, it's almost like silencing them," said Adina. "They should be angry, they should be indignant . . . [being incarcerated] has nothing to do with the fact that they '*made a bad choice.*' People from all walks of life make bad choices, but if you're a person of color, if you're low-income, you're more likely to be criminalized for that bad choice." Next, Adina zeroed in on the ways in which self-help and wellness interventions could exacerbate these inequities: "psychology, social work, mental health are all guilty of perpetuating a blame-the-victim mentality, '*oh these folks have trauma, this is why they're acting XYZ,*' without understanding that they live in a system that's not giving them access to basic resources that allow them to function." Adina was also emphatic that volunteers should "get an education" about the communities they worked in: "Try to consider the historical, ancestral, political roots of why the people you are working with are in the circumstances they are in." Without understanding these contextual factors, Adina warned, "we can further someone's internalized sense of oppression. . . . This is how these systems work, they don't need to be enforced from the outside because we will embody them."

Certainly, both the YIP and FFI trainings had made standard references to the systemic oppression of mass incarceration. But SJY's training was far more explicit about understanding the collective, systemic causes of trauma such as race or poverty, instead of reducing everything to "individual" actions or choices. They were also unique in raising an issue on which all other organizations had remained silent (a crucial issue that I examined in Chapter 4): well-meaning self-care and wellness programs, SJY noted, ran the risk of reinforcing oppression, silencing marginalized individuals by asking them to "calm down" and focus solely on their "bad choices." In their trainings and public communications, SJY repeatedly emphasized the importance of cultural humility by those entering marginalized communities—they recommended learning from the leadership and involvement of system-impacted, disadvantaged communities and people. Their "yoga and social justice" training modules were designed to provide holistic understandings of oppression (both historical and contemporary), while yogic philosophy and meditative practices were presented as integrally connected to—and not detached from—social and political justice. These modules connected yogic and meditative teachings to issues such as racial inequality, slavery, white supremacy, settler-colonialism, gender and sexuality inequities, and a variety of civil rights movements.

Clearly, FFI and SJY both had strong critical, political commitments that motivated and undergirded their volunteer work, though SJY's were communicated far more directly and coherently. YIP, in contrast, offered a standard critique of the "failure" of the prison system, but eventually went on to offer a message completely in keeping with the system's own logic: Incarcerated persons must be taught to transform themselves; this was the solution to the problem of an unjust system.

None of these political, systemic issues had been raised in my local prison volunteer groups. There was little to no guidance from local organizations about how we were to interpret the prisons' messaging. There were no conversations mentioning mass incarceration, much less any political stance or commitments in regard to it. There was little discussion of race or other forms of inequity, and no views were expressed about the nature of the system volunteers were preparing to enter, much less about the political issues that shaped its context. The national trainings I attended gave me a further clue about the vastly disparate perspectives on the prison system held by the volunteers I both interviewed and worked with. Certainly, many expressed frustration and criticism—they were antagonistic toward the prison system, inclined to characterize it as corrupt or inhumane, to criticize the unaccountable manner in which prisons operated, and the conditions their incarcerated students endured. But for every volunteer who expressed these criticisms, there were plenty more who took a more neutral stand, remaining silent on the systemic issues, or professing a lack of knowledge. Particularly when their experience was relatively siloed, some volunteers appeared to have little appetite for engaging with systemic issues.

Many expressed views like Marissa, who restricted her volunteer work to one yoga class in one facility, and had little administrative experience or larger contextual engagement. "I doubt how much I really know," she said, "I might be floating on a little bit of a cloud." Marissa also withheld judgement on the content of the prison's trainings, stating that if she had seen "even one instance" of the sort of behavior she was warned about in the trainings conducted by the prison, "[Maybe I'd] say, '*Oh, yes. We definitely need more of your type of rules.*'" Like Marissa, some volunteers were prepared to identify with and internalize the system's lessons.

I saw how such views made sense if the only systemic message a volunteer had received was the one provided by the prison itself, about remaining wary of incarcerated persons and the dangers they represented. When organizational leaders remained largely apolitical, or offered no critical examination of the prison's perspectives, it stood to reason that volunteers might develop a relatively neutral understanding of the prison and its narratives. The prison's perspective, along with its strict rules and security measures, could seem far more reasonable to those who had not been given much training on the overall context, especially given popular depictions of prisons and of incarcerated persons.

As I took on more of a leadership role in my local organizations, I did my best to inject a more political tone and to offer a more critical, political perspective on the system to fellow volunteers. In one case, an organization I had joined began to require a four-hour training of all new recruits. When I was asked to co-facilitate these trainings, I made brief presentations about mass incarceration. I made reference to the main factors determining incarceration, such as race and poverty. I cited *The New Jim Crow* and recommended it as required reading of anyone who wanted to enter a prison. Modeling my remarks on SJY's training, I also discussed how the language of rehabilitation and "behavioral modification" fed into the stereotypes of incarcerated persons being circulated by prisons and by popular public discourse. While my interventions were mostly well received, not many people—including the new recruits—seemed particularly interested in these issues.

My attempts to infuse a more political tone into the organization were further stymied by the anxiety that the prison's monitoring of political activity induced in some volunteer leaders. When I suggested, for instance, that one organization consider taking a more explicitly political public stand against mass incarceration on its website and in social media posts, a colleague demurred, saying, "we mustn't be too critical, or they will pull the plug on us." Of course, this was not wrong; prisons are not welcoming of political activity of any kind. At least one of the facilities we worked in required volunteers to reveal on their clearance application whether they had ever been involved in civil disobedience. We advised volunteers never to lie on their clearance applications, particularly if the facts could independently be verified through media or public records. But we also found that at least one applicant with a record of political activism was denied clearance. In frustration, I watched as some of our most politically active applicants were weeded out of the pool, either through outright denial, or through the chilling effect of the application alone.

For the most part, my attempts to take the organization in a more political direction remained largely on the margins of its priorities. In some ways, I may have pushed the organization to become slightly more political—one colleague later emphasized that I had had an impact on "shaping the organizational culture." But I also came to see that raising political issues during a training event or pushing for more public political statements was not going to change the culture very much. Without a more thoroughgoing commitment woven into the organization's priorities, the issues I raised remained a small, one-off component. Meanwhile, the nonprofit priorities of fundraising, publicity, brand-management, and organizational expansion remained far more important. The leadership was more interested in raising funds in order to hold more classes in more facilities, staff these classes, and find more volunteers to reach more incarcerated people. Given these priorities, my explicitly political vision for the organization was mostly sidelined, and re-orienting the organization in a more political direction did not gain much traction.

Trauma-Informed Yoga, Authority, and Discipline

The second crucial issue that emerged from attending national trainings was that of "discipline" and "rigor," which ended up being more contentious than I had anticipated. I discovered that my local organizations were far more wedded to traditional ideas of authority and discipline than the three national organizations I had trained with. At the three trainings I described earlier, all of the national organizations advocated for a "trauma-informed" approach to teaching incarcerated populations. Although I came to see that "trauma-informed" meant different things to different people, in the trainings I attended the focus appeared to be on several key things. First, it meant that students were to be given invitations to practice, rather than being commanded. Rather than being told what to do in a pose—"place your right foot here and your left foot here"—the leaders of these organizations encouraged the use of invitational language. Language such as "if it feels right to you, you might consider placing your right foot here" was considered preferable. Second, options were to be offered, rather than insisting on any one "correct" way to perform a pose, allowing the student to choose for themselves and exercise their autonomy. In contrast to mainstream yoga practice, which sees the teacher as the expert source of authority, and expects students to follow along with the teacher's sequence, the trauma-informed model encourages incarcerated students to make their own choices for what works best for them. This may mean doing something quite different from what the teacher is offering. Third, and perhaps most important, trauma-informed yoga strongly advocates against touching any students inside prison—this means never offering any physical adjustments.

These trauma-informed principles stand in strong contrast to much mainstream yoga, which follows the guru-disciple model of the Indian tradition, in which the student submits fully to the teacher's guidance and instructions. Stories are told of legendarily authoritarian Indian gurus like B.K.S. Iyengar and Pattabhi Jois, who were famous for their forceful teaching styles, often employing corporeal discipline, aggressive physical adjustments, even slapping and shouting at their students.[9] (B.K.S. Iyengar is thought to have been nicknamed "Bang, Kick, Slap."[10]) To a lesser degree, the same was true of famous Asian meditation teachers such as Soen-Sa Nim and Trungpa Rinpoche, who began to accrue Western disciples: they employed forceful, unorthodox methods of teaching that required students to follow instructions closely. Of course, much of this traditional discipline was watered-down when these practices took hold in the West, and had to be softened in order to appeal to a Western consumer audience.[11] Even so, the cultural expectations of yoga studios and meditation centers are very much in keeping with the ethos of rigor defined as silence, self-discipline, and compliance.

For national organizations like FFI and SJY, practices like yoga and meditation needed to evolve in authoritarian contexts such as prisons, when taught to marginalized populations. "We're already going into a whole structure of discipline and authority," said Eleanor, one facilitator, "so we don't need to replicate that by setting up expectations of discipline." Keisha characterized most mainstream yoga as overly harsh in its disciplinary expectations, to the point that students now demand and expect aggressive styles from yoga teachers. "That discipline and rigidity of yoga, I thought it was the way it should be . . . that's a power I don't want [now]." For FFI facilitators, keeping yoga tethered to its classical discipline only reinforced the discipline these students were already facing—often in extremely harsh and violent forms— by an authoritarian power structure. Their view was that yoga and meditation needed to evolve beyond "classical" forms, into something softer, gentler, and less disciplinary, inviting students to make a variety of choices in how they practiced, giving up expectations of compliance and even silence. Adina, the co-founder of SJY had noted, the "container of discipline can be oppressive" for some students. Keisha shared that in her prison classes, "each student was doing something different," including laughing or talking loudly, which she welcomed.

When I discussed these issues with my local organizations, I found that traditional expectations were still very much the norm, and when pressed, few volunteers wanted to deviate much from them. I asked some local leaders about the commitment to refrain from disciplining or silencing students— even disruptive ones—in prison. Hannah, who had founded a prison yoga program rooted in the Iyengar school of yoga—and considered herself a "sub-versive person"—was not enthused by this, calling it "very antithetical" to her training. "I understand it politically," she said, "but I don't think it translates well into the yoga room. . . . I think [the students] benefit so much from the quiet." Not only did these leaders resist the idea that one might need to rethink these practices in the prison context, they went even further, asserting, as Hannah did, that the New Age movement has made yoga too "floaty and airy," causing it to "lose its essence." Victoria, the founder of another local organiza-tion, was even more emphatic on this point: "Yoga has already been defined," she said. "We don't need to redefine the basic tenets, which [are] cleanliness, structure, purifying discipline, silence, being precise, that's what yoga is. Not some flim-flam thing. . . . I feel very strongly about that."

Both Hannah and Victoria also asserted that discipline was particularly important for incarcerated people: "Once they learn some inner discipline, it contains the wildness and helps explain the past a little bit," Hannah said. "They're learning to have a discipline . . . to focus, and set goals . . . inmates need that more than anybody. . . . If you can just give them a step-by-step path inside, that's where they can clean up." Victoria offered a similar view: "A lot of these [incarcerated] people have zero boundaries, they just don't have any personal discipline, because they were never taught what that even means. That's why they're talking while you're talking, [it's] why they did all the things that they did. They need to have an authority figure whom they can admire and look up to, who is a role model, who can show them that learning some discipline is a good thing . . . [that's why] I do go in with authority." In these remarks, local organizational leaders construed incarcerated persons as wild, lacking discipline, and being in need of role models to teach them how to "clean up." Not only would there be no learning from the leadership of system-impacted persons in these organizations, on the contrary: Leadership still seemed to belong to the mostly white volunteers who brought yoga and meditation to system-impacted people and communities, who were seen as being need of learning discipline from authority figures.

Once I began to teach solo in prisons, I did my best to reverse these traditional models of hierarchy and authority. I found myself moving fully into invitational—instead of commanding—language. My language became softer, and my guidance less authoritative and more invitational. I described poses in the first person, rather than telling students what they should be doing. "If it feels right to you in your body," became a constant refrain of mine, and I always offered several different versions of the pose, from the most basic to the more advanced. I would repeat phrases like "I'll invite you to consider whether it feels good to do this, and if not, maybe try the other version." At least once, Hannah complimented me on my teaching—"your poses are beautiful, Farah"—but also said she didn't think I needed to give students so many different options. "You might consider that just doing what you're told really quickly might work for some people," she suggested. I continued to find ways to express my political commitments while teaching inside prisons. I tried to decenter the authority of the so-called expert by "invit[ing] incarcerated persons into a joint exploration of the inner world," rather than "directing" or "teaching" them.[12] But I found myself once again in the minority—many of my fellow volunteers seemed more interested in our students "doing what they were told."

I found that much the same was true among the meditation volunteers I encountered, where old-school, didactic, or authoritative approaches were still the norm.[13] Several meditation volunteers "preached" at incarcerated students, describing meditation as a way to learn from their "bad choices" and urging students to "transform themselves" via these practices. One volunteer went even further, urging students to use meditation to become more accepting of the prison, even when it appeared unjust. "I tell them, *'try not to perceive injustice here, no matter how bad it seems,'*" they reported to me later. "When they have negative feelings toward the prison staff, I tell them *'stop that, don't do that!'* There are a lot of things you can't change in prison: your work, your roommate, the staff, the officers, but you can change your perspective, and refrain from feeling injustice." Many volunteers seemed eager to "talk at" incarcerated persons, to preach to them about the value of self-transformation, or to urge them to avoid controversy or resistance of any kind. These volunteers seemed to have internalized the prison's logic of "flawed individuals" needing "behavioral transformation." Treating incarcerated students as empowered equals—much less adopting a posture of humility or cultural learning about the context of marginalized communities—scarcely appeared to be the norm.

Touch, Consent, and Autonomy

Third, I found that I did not end up seeing issues of touch, consent, and autonomy in prisons in the same way that many of my fellow volunteers did. In the studio setting, teachers physically adjusting students' bodies in a pose—usually without requesting or obtaining consent—was still *de rigueur*, at least at the time that I began doing this work.[14] In my twenty years of practice in India and the West, countless yoga teachers had physically adjusted me without ever asking whether such touch would be welcome. Until I began teaching in prisons, I never thought to question this expectation. When I first began volunteering, I saw that physical adjustments were given without second thought: Volunteers rarely asked for consent when touching students, and if they did, it was perfunctory. On one occasion, I saw a volunteer reach out to adjust a student's hips and then pause, asking almost as an after-thought, "Can I adjust you?" In that moment, it was impossible to tell whether the student's quickly whispered "yes" was an expression of genuine consent, or a habitual reaction in a context where saying "no" often came with severe consequences.

After I had begun to take trauma-informed trainings, I began to feel increasingly uncomfortable about touching incarcerated students. I struggled when I saw a student doing something that brought their body out of alignment and increased the likelihood of injury: an overarched lower back, or a hyperextended leg putting too much pressure on a knee joint. My instinct was always to prevent injury, so I began experimenting with offering verbal rather than physical guidance. I offered suggestions rather than giving commands—"try taking a longer stance between your feet maybe?" I began to swear off touching students once I learned more about how prison staff were required to touch them invasively and without consent. I felt less and less confident that I would know when my touch could unwittingly cross the line from healing and supportive into harsh or triggering.

I also began to be more vocal about the issue of consent for touch with local organizations. I had little doubt by then that yoga traditions needed to be modified to respond to a severely authoritarian context. I worried that our students were already taught to be overly compliant by an institution that rewarded docility and punished resistance of any kind. I became concerned with how to offer some measure of control over their own bodies to people who had very little bodily autonomy. Some of the local organizational leaders I worked with were attentive to concerns about overly harsh or aggressive adjustments, particularly for victims of trauma. On balance, however, they were quite reluctant to modify yoga's traditional expectation of adjustment by the teacher. One insisted that nonsexual touch could be "healing," "loving," or "enlightening," another said that a stringent no-touch policy was too militant, and that she had only ever seen "tears of gratitude" from those she had touched: "They feel like I treated them like a human being." Having seen no evidence of students being triggered by touch, she felt that taking away loving, nonsexual touch would be to "throw the baby out with the bathwater." I was not unsympathetic to these arguments—I had personally experienced some of the intimacy, rapport, and camaraderie between volunteers and incarcerated yogis, fostered by compassionate, healing touch.

At one point, I consulted with a group of incarcerated women to ask how they felt about being adjusted during yoga. Most of them unequivocally stated that they preferred not to be touched without consent. Some described their experiences with volunteers who "adjusted very aggressively": "I don't like being touched in that way," said one woman plainly. "I am always so relaxed during yoga, [but] when she teaches is the only time that my body is completely unrelaxed . . . she kept trying to push my knee in a direction it didn't want to go." They also noted that they would prefer to opt-in to touch rather than have to opt-out. As I suspected, no one wanted to publicly identify themselves as uncooperative in a prison setting, by being asked "who does *not* want to be touched?" and having to raise their hands. These students asked if there could be a more discreet way for people to opt-in rather than opt-out of consent.

Based on this conversation, I experimented with a consent card system in which I asked students to place a white notecard on the edge of their mat if they wanted an adjustment. I found many students eagerly opting-in to the notecard, sometimes waving me over to explicitly ask for adjustments. I was pleasantly surprised by how much more comfortable I felt offering adjustments once I knew that they were welcome. I also felt it was a way of attributing agency to incarcerated yogis, to offer them what I hoped was a meaningful opportunity to give genuine consent, a sorely needed corrective in prisons. As an ethical matter, I felt it important that volunteers stand in resistance to the routine bodily violations our students experienced. And, in centering the recommendations of our incarcerated students in decision-making, I tried to follow the principle of allowing system-impacted persons to lead. But I was the only local volunteer who ever seemed preoccupied with these issues. The consent card system I started in one prison eventually fell by the wayside. Most of my fellow volunteers—especially those trained in more supposedly "rigorous" schools of yoga—did not seem interesting in experimenting with these issues or thinking about them much. My push to re-examine traditional understandings of touch and adjustment for the prison context was met mostly with reluctance or indifference.

Conclusions

Prisons can and do exert a great deal of influence on volunteer understandings of systemic issues. Volunteers are taught that all incarceration results from personality flaws and/or personal shortcomings, that incarcerated persons constitute an ongoing threat, and that compliance with the total control of the institution is a necessary means to neutralize this threat, both for volunteers and for inhabitants of the prison. The prisons set the narrative, and appeal to the volunteers to identify with prison staff, rather than with their incarcerated students; in fact, they strongly encourage volunteers to disidentify with incarcerated people. Absent any sustained challenge to these ideas, the prison's discourse can become a baseline form of political education that is internalized by volunteers, shaping their understanding of the prison system.

Still, in many cases, volunteers I interviewed seemed to have developed more critical understandings of the prison system. When I attended trainings by several national prison yoga and meditation organizations, I learned why this might be. These organizations offered messages that sometimes complemented but more often counteracted those disseminated by the prison system. In stark contrast to my experience of being invited to join volunteer organizations with little to no training from the organizations themselves— and a lack of any structural commentary regarding the system we served— these organizational trainings provided behind-the-scenes disruptions of the prison's narratives.

In the years that I regularly volunteered in these facilities, I found myself in the minority on a variety of fronts. Although I was given a position of some seniority and leadership responsibilities, I also often found myself raising difficult issues and staking out positions that were not always resonant with the views of others. In particular, my attempts to make our groups more politically attuned gained little traction. There were a few cases in which I was able to push an organization to be more political, by changing language on websites, or offering more politically nuanced understandings of yoga and meditation for the prison context. But by and large, these efforts remained on the margins of organizational priorities.

In particular, I appeared to be alone in my commitment to using yoga or meditation as ways to counter the prison system's logic and messaging. The more time I spent in prisons and the more I learned about how the system worked, the more I became committed to reversing the hierarchy at the heart of yogic and meditative traditions. Traditional emphases on the expert authority of teachers stipulate that the teacher knows the student's body (or mind) better than the student can understand their own. Many of the volunteers I encountered rarely questioned these assumptions. Yet, as Adina—the leader of SJY—noted, yoga students need the space to trust their own bodies: "You [as the teacher] don't know their life experience, and you don't know what's happened to that body." Still, there is a tendency in the yoga world for teachers to think students are not "yogic enough, not spiritual enough, and not disciplined enough," perpetuating the idea that the student is "doing yoga wrong." I came to the conclusion that power hierarchies and historical forms of oppression that impacted our students—both in their pre-incarceration lives, and in the prison system—required us to re-think how yoga and meditation should be offered.

This viewpoint, however, did not seem to have much resonance with others. They did not seem to begin—as I did—from the presumption that the prison context was a set of authoritarian power relations in which our students were forcibly enmeshed. Neither did they see yogic and meditative practices as ways to counter this system through choice, bodily autonomy, and opportunities for consent. For them, yoga or meditation as healing, therapeutic practices remained largely apolitical, having little to with the ways in which power was exercised. To me, it seemed obvious that teaching *anything* in prison is as much about power, hierarchy, and authority as it is about the therapeutic goals of the practices being taught. But few seemed to share this perspective.

These disagreements underscored how debates in the yoga world sometimes percolated into the prison world. Dogmatic modes of yoga or meditation, I came to see, were not for every *body* (literally). And, I also came to see that being attached to the so-called Indian roots of yoga was not always appropriate for the prison context. Concerns that yoga would be diluted, watered down, or made impure by introducing softer, more compassionate styles seemed to go along with narrowly conceived notions of "correct" ways to practice, or the insistence on the teacher's authority. I was often the only South Asian practitioner in most yoga or meditation spaces, including in prisons. Yet, I also found myself the most vocal proponent of modifying traditions for the prison context. I had initially been skeptical of trauma-informed yoga's departure from traditional models, wondering if it was too removed from yogic principles. I struggled with what it would mean for yoga or meditation to neglect its origins in a culture of submission to discipline and expertise. Eventually, however, I began to care far less about fetishizing the transmission of a tradition, and far more about ensuring that it was adapted to the needs of those it was supposed to reach. But I never convinced fellow volunteers to explore these commitments more thoroughly, and was continually baffled at how controversial they sometimes seemed. The organizations I joined seemed much less interested in dismantling systems of power than in teaching therapeutic or healing practices. There was little attention paid to the ways in which these practices could subtly reproduce power relations, through underlying relationships of authority and expectations of submission.

These local volunteer communities left me with few models of politically engaged prison work to draw on. Meanwhile, in the course of my interviewing, I learned about another local organization which was apparently more explicitly committed to critical political views about the prison system and the status of incarcerated people. Although leaders managed to keep these commitments under the radar, I learned that this organization took an explicit political stand, dedicating time at volunteer trainings to addressing political issues, and expecting all volunteers to approach prison work with these commitments. I attempted to contact group leaders in order to learn more about their approach. But my repeated attempts to learn what a politically engaged organization looked like never came to fruition. After a variety of scheduling issues prevented me from having a personal conversation with group leaders, I signed up to attend this organization's training, so as to learn directly from them. But in March of 2020, two months before the scheduled training, the pandemic arrived—all volunteer programs in prisons and jails were immediately shut down, as were trainings by prison volunteer organizations.

8

"Making them Better Human Beings" or "Stirring the Pot"?

Interviews with Volunteers

In the conference room of a small university library, I sit across the table from Sankar, a Buddhist monk who was raised and trained in the monastic life in Southeast Asia. Along with several others from a Buddhist organization, he now teaches meditation in prisons in California. When I ask Sankar to reflect on the purpose of this work, he offers his view that practices like yoga and meditation "reform" the incarcerated person to become "a better human being": "people who go to prison, they are associated with the worst people . . . all the underworld and drug dealers . . . doing all those bad things. If somebody can teach them . . . show them the path." Contrast this with Adina, a woman of Middle Eastern origin, whom I also interviewed on this same topic. Adina has also taught yoga and meditation to incarcerated youth. In response to this same question, she asserts that working with incarcerated people must entail "helping them [to] have a critical view of the system." Yoga, she says, is "a form of self-regulation—*not* so that we can be okay with things that are wrong, but so that we can develop strategies for liberation in a more effective and sustainable way. . . . If we have just stopped with tolerating discomfort, we become a tool for keeping people down."

Sankar and Adina's views typify two very different narratives about the purpose of teaching yoga or meditation to incarcerated persons. When I first began exploring these issues, I was struck by how closely the literature and public information of leading prison yoga and meditation organizations converged with the perspective expressed by Sankar. The predominant response to "Why teach yoga or meditation in prisons?" seemed to be: "to make prisoners better and reduce crime," so that incarcerated individuals can improve themselves through better choices and more responsibility. But this was not the only story I found. Another story was developing, one that emphasized the social and political inequities at the heart of mass incarceration. Instead of "improving" incarcerated persons through "responsibility" or "better choice," this story emphasized an unjust system that constrained people's choices, and

Freedom Inside?. Farah Godrej, Oxford University Press. © Oxford University Press 2022.
DOI: 10.1093/oso/9780190070083.003.0008

suggested yoga or meditation as tools for oppressed individuals to navigate this system.

This chapter asks, how (if at all) are these two narratives about the purpose of prison yoga or meditation reflected in the views of organizations and volunteers? I explore this question through interviews with volunteer yoga and meditation instructors. But I also show that these narratives are not innocuous: They are more than simply a set of perspectives that volunteers hold. They each do a kind of political work that shapes yoga and meditation programs in important ways, and they each have implications for the growth and protection of these programs in prisons. We will see in this chapter that the first narrative is far more prevalent among the majority of volunteers I interview, who internalize and replicate the prison system's view of incarceration as the result of bad choices by flawed individuals needing improvement: individual reform leads to reforming the system. A minority of respondents express the second narrative, which challenges this logic by pointing to systemic inequity as the root cause of incarceration. These respondents describe yoga and meditation as tools to allow incarcerated persons to develop a consciousness in opposition to the prison system and its logic. The prison system itself encourages the dissemination of the first narrative—and, it sometimes actively works to discourage and even shut down expressions of the second narrative, which can rarely be expressed as openly as the first. My interviews demonstrate the prevalence of the former: While a small minority of respondents interpret these practices as tools for recognizing and challenging injustice, the majority tend to reaffirm the logics supporting an unequal, biased system, allowing powerful institutions to continue putting the burden of systemic change on deeply disadvantaged individuals.

The Predominant and Dissenting Views: Similarities and Differences

Let us examine the two narratives circulating about the purpose of yoga or meditation in prisons. Early in my exploration, the website of the Prison Yoga Project (PYP), perhaps the best known organization of its kind, celebrated the "rehabilitative value of yoga," which "address[es] . . . behavioral issues," and "increase[s] . . . empathy for others."[1] PYP, an organization based in the Bay Area, pioneered a long-standing yoga program at San Quentin prison which began in 2002—since 2010, it has offered weekend training programs for those interested in teaching incarcerated populations, in partnership with various other institutions that provide space for training. Trainees report that

PYP's approach "enable[s] offenders to recognize the harm they have caused and accept full responsibility for their wrongdoing."[2] Yoga and meditation were described as "necessary services to prevent future crime," providing the ideal conditions for self-transformation and successful re-entry.[3] PYP's mission statement has recently softened to include references to restorative justice, and harm as the result of trauma. Yet, it continues to describe incarcerated people as needing to "take personal responsibility" and "[behave] in a different way,"[4] learning to make "positive personal and pro-social choices."[5]

This emphasis on individual responsibility is even more pronounced in the literature of the Prison Mindfulness Institute (PMI) and its associated organizations, including the Engaged Mindfulness Institute and the Mindful Justice Initiative. Formerly known as the Prison Dharma Network, PMI was founded in 1989 by a Buddhist then serving a fourteen-year sentence in a federal prison for drug trafficking. Subsequently, PMI spawned a network of contemplative ministry and outreach programs teaching mindfulness throughout the criminal punishment system, including offering training to corrections staff. In the PMI literature, meditation in prisons is geared toward the "efficient management" of incarcerated populations, and the development of "prosocial attitudes and behaviors."[6] Incarcerated people are described as suffering from a lack of self-awareness and emotional self-regulation, vulnerable to antisocial personality and procriminal attitudes.[7] The focus of the practice is on changing the dysfunctional mindset of these individuals, and fostering their eventual ability to take responsibility for their actions.[8]

These influential public accounts of yoga and meditation in prisons rely on an idea of improving incarcerated individuals fully in keeping with the prison system's logic, as we have seen from Chapter 4. But I soon found a somewhat dissenting narrative about the purpose of prison yoga and meditation in *Best Practices for Yoga in the Criminal Justice System*, a collectively authored manual for prison yoga organizations.[9] Published in 2017 by the Yoga Service Council, a nonprofit organization dedicated to making yoga and mindfulness practices accessible—and supported by the Omega Institute for Holistic Studies—the manual brought together twenty-five experts in education, psychology, medicine, and policy in order to create a guide to developing and implementing yoga programs in the incarceration environment.[10] Although the manual was initially little-known and unheard-of in my volunteer circles, it has increased in visibility over the years since it was published. This manual is characterized by the remarkable absence of "rehabilitation" or "personal responsibility" language. Instead, it emphasizes the inequities entailed in incarceration. It raises questions of social justice, calling on volunteers to "critically examine [their] own social position," and suggesting that such positions confer privileges and instill biases.[11] It warns against one-dimensional or in-accurate views of incarcerated individuals, and notes that they are likely to have been impacted by social marginalization or discrimination.[12] In contrast to the view of PYP and PMI, which uses terms such as "perpetrators," this manual rejects pejorative terms like "criminals" and recommends "respectful forms of address for incarcerated persons."[13] Instead of using yoga or medita-tion to rehabilitate incarcerated persons, the manual calls for such practices to foster autonomy and empowerment among incarcerated students in an op-pressive and disempowering system.[14]

Before turning to my interviews, I note that the two views I've described here are not entirely opposed to one another. They share some important assumptions and overlap in important ways, so the differences between them should not be overstated. In fact, at least one person associated with the pre-dominant narrative was also involved with the *Best Practices* manual—for this reason, our concern is with narratives rather than with people. Both narratives discuss the inequities at the heart of mass incarceration, including systemic harm to communities of color through policing practices, and legal inequities caused by prosecutorial discretion and sentencing laws. Both also discuss the need for "trauma-informed" yoga or meditation.[15] Incarcerated persons are seen as victims of trauma in two senses: the actions resulting in incarcera-tion are seen as the result of historical trauma, while the prison environment is itself seen as causing further trauma. Yogic, meditative practices support healing and resilience in this environment, through self-awareness and self-regulation, which reduce mood disorders, substance abuse, and so forth.

But despite these similarities, the most significant difference is this: The predominant view offers yogic and meditative practice as a way for incarcer-ated people to accept their own role in creating their circumstances. Social and political change requires inner change by individuals.[16] The second, dissenting view offers the same practices as a means to skillfully navigate an unjust system by preserving one's own sense of self. It emphasizes inner change by individuals, but has a very different understanding of this inner change, and insists on situating it within an acknowledgment of systemic in-justice. Drawing attention to systemic injustice does not necessarily mean that incarcerated individuals must become political activists, or engage in some manner of political resistance; as we saw, such action can be counterproduc-tive, impossible and even dangerous for many in their situation. Instead, the forms of resistance emphasized by this second narrative are largely internal, pertaining to the ways that incarcerated persons can understand themselves and their own situations, without allowing the prison and its logic to shape their views and perspectives. The dissenting narrative contains a much more direct assessment of the prison system as an unjust power structure, and the ways in which those enmeshed in it might oppose this structure, at least within their own minds, even if not through their outward actions.

For the predominant view, addressing individual behavioral issues is the solution to an unjust system. Structural inequities, including trauma, are thought to *cause* bad individual choices, and practices that increase responsibility are solutions for navigating unequal social and political conditions. That is, if people are unable to "choose well" due to poverty, trauma, discrimination, and so forth, the solution is to make them more mindful, so that they can choose differently. The "greatest gift" to incarcerated persons is to offer them the "freedom to choose certain behaviors over others," by recognizing that "we create and invite much of what happens to us."[17]

The founder of PMI, perhaps the greatest advocate of such an approach—and a formerly incarcerated white man[18]—acknowledges the vastly unequal nature of the system, as do so many others. "Through systematic legislation and prosecution," he admits, "this country has been incarcerating the disowned, undesirable, impoverished, undereducated, mentally ill and non-white members of our society."[19] In practically the same breath, however, he describes the organization's curriculum in this way:

> Most of the people in prison are there because they've made bad choices. . . . We want them to take responsibility for their choices, and we give them the tools to make better choices. We call this "radical responsibility." . . . Through meditation, prisoners come to recognize their conditioning as their own and take responsibility for it, and ultimately step outside of it.[20]

Or, as a recent fundraising appeal by PYP stated: "The system is changing. Incarcerated people have more and more opportunities for transformation and growth." Again, inner change by incarcerated individuals is equated with systemic change.[21] There is very little assessment of the prison system as a power structure, and no interrogation of how the equation of individual change with systemic change might reinforce the prison's own logics.

Contrast this with what I am calling the "dissenting" view in the *Best Practices* manual, where there is little language of changing or "improving" incarcerated people. A blog post by a related organization insists: "Without condoning [the] action, we also don't want to ask for accountability. We'd just be part of the same mental and social system that creates the problem."[22] The point of healing trauma is not to teach people more accountability. Instead, this view seems more interested in how to resist the "coercion," "domination and control" of the "alienating, dehumanizing"[23] prison system. It recommends that volunteers counter oppressive prison culture by refusing to give commands during yoga or meditation classes, instead offering students a variety of options for their practice. It focuses on the incarcerated person's severe loss of freedom, and offers opportunities for decision-making and autonomy in a rigidly controlled environment.[24] In this second, dissenting view, references to "changing" people usually refer to improvements that allow individuals to understand themselves apart from the prison's messaging, as more worthy, capable, and powerful than the system may allow them to feel.

One might wonder whether what must be said publicly in order to appeal to prison administrations may be different from what volunteers believe the actual purpose of their work to be. Public discourse often needs to be palatable in what Katherine Blee calls the "front-stage," while veiling more radical commitments that stay "backstage."[25] No doubt organizations serving jails and prisons must learn the vocabulary that circulates within the penal sector, to be considered credible and given entrée to operate.[26] As we saw in Chapter 7, getting a foot in the door of the byzantine prison bureaucracy can be an uphill task, and several volunteers confirm in private conversations that they are keenly aware of the need for "double-speak" in order to get in the door. Through confidential interviews with thirty-six volunteer yoga and meditation instructors, I found that the idea of redeeming incarcerated persons by modifying their behavior is more than simply a "front-stage" performance to demonstrate credibility. Rather, many volunteers genuinely see these ideas as fully consistent with the practices they advocate. A minority of volunteers do see yoga and meditation as tools to challenge the system's logic, but the vast majority of my interlocutors interpret yoga as a resource to encourage self-reflection and better "choice," largely reaffirming the ideas supporting mass incarceration. In what follows, I show how the views of my respondents converge with the two narratives I have described here.

My findings fill an important gap. Most programming in prison and jail settings is provided by the "voluntary" sector—individuals and groups who provide an array of supportive programs, although they do not work directly for correctional agencies.[27] These include therapeutic, educational, skills training, and spiritual services. Despite a flourishing role for these volunteers in prisons, we know little about them, "who they are, and what their experiences are as they navigate their role in correctional settings."[28] There is little research on these various "stakeholders," namely, the education, mental health, nonprofit, and spiritual providers whose perspectives inform practices in the prison system.[29] This chapter brings to life the voices and perspectives of those who provide healing, spiritual, and mental health support to incarcerated people.

The Interviews

Over three years, I interviewed thirty-six fellow volunteer yoga or meditation instructors. At the time, this accounted for almost every volunteer who taught yoga or meditation in area jails and prisons I volunteered in, as well as eight leading figures in nationally recognized organizations.[30] Of the twenty-eight volunteers from my local organizations, only four were trained by or otherwise allied with one of the national organizations—the rest were only associated with local organizations, and had no contact with (or even knowledge of) the national organizations. There was wide variation in the organizational structures these volunteers worked in: In some cases, they were part of informal, loosely affiliated networks of a few individuals banding together; in other cases, their organizations had wider membership and more formalized structures such as 501(c)(3) status. The length of time that each of these respondents had volunteered varied from anywhere between a few months to ten years. Given the sensitive nature of prison work, I have taken measures to ensure confidentiality, and have changed or removed all identifying information. Table 8.1 gives us basic demographic information on interviewees, showing that the vast majority were Caucasian and female.

Table 8.1 Basic Demographics of Interviewees

Age	
20–29	2
30–39	6
40–49	13
50–59	7
60–69	8
Gender Identity	
Female	28
Male	9
Race/Ethnicity	
Caucasian	28
Black	3
South Asian	1
East or Southeast Asian	1
Middle Eastern	1
Biracial	2

Motivations: "Helping" versus "Social Justice"

What motivates volunteers to offer yoga and meditation in prisons, and what brought these individuals to this work? Overwhelmingly, most of my respondents cited being motivated by a personal desire to serve, to be of assistance, or to "give back." Many shared the view that yoga or meditation had helped them, and that they felt it could help others: As Thomas, a white male in his sixties, said, "I wanted to share something of what had brought me so much joy and happiness." Yoga or meditation were often seen as inaccessible, and many spoke of their desire to make these practices more accessible to populations who were particularly in need of them yet rarely had access to them. The desire to alleviate suffering was extremely common, and some cited wanting to work in a capacity similar to a mentor or a therapist. Like Marissa, a majority of volunteers envisioned incarcerated populations as "need[ing] more on a mental, psychological and spiritual level," given that addiction, trauma, mental illness and abuse were seen as highly prevalent in their lives. Many also described their own spiritual journeys, or their own personal or familial struggles with mental health, addiction, or abuse, feeling a sense of kinship with others facing similar issues. One volunteer turned to teaching in prisons after her son was incarcerated, another after he found himself "in a dark place" at the end of a relationship, and several others had struggled with addiction or trauma and found yoga or meditation to be a refuge. Hannah shared that her parents were Holocaust survivors, which sensitized her to the brutality of incarceration and "the needs of people who have nothing." Eva had suffered severe abuse and trauma as a sex-trafficked child, and identified deeply with incarcerated persons. For many, the desire to work in prisons arose from a personal connection to trauma, abuse or addiction, which they saw as pathways to prison, connecting their own life-stories to those of incarcerated persons. Tan, a Buddhist monk, wanted to do something "more satisfying in terms of personal achievement" toward attaining enlightenment. Many, like Sondra, "just wanted to do something" in light of their own privilege: "Maybe I feel a little guilty that I've had it so good." Most often, their desire to volunteer was spurred by a flyer they had seen posted in their yoga studio, a personal connection to someone who was already volunteering, or to an educational/chaplaincy program that was affiliated with prison volunteer work. Others were inspired by an article they had read, or a film or TV clip they had watched, like Ethan, who found himself contemplating "the help [these people] need" after reading a magazine article about incarcerated persons. Several, like Vivian and Sarah, admitted that they did not know why there were drawn to this work. Sarah even said that she continually struggled for an answer when asking herself this question. "I just try to help where I can," said Vivian, upon further reflection.

In all but four cases, the motivations mentioned for undertaking prison volunteer work were entirely personal, rather than systemic, structural, or political. That is, even if respondents claimed to be familiar with critiques of mass incarceration, there was no mention of activism or social justice as motivating their volunteer work. One notable exception was Jackson, a white male in his thirties, who described being inspired by the engaged Buddhism of Thich Nhat Hanh, to understand trauma "on the individual level as well as a collective or historical level," and thus to "[embody] social justice" in prisons. Courtney, a white woman in her fifties, described perhaps the most activist motivation, having previously worked with the ACLU to document the systematic denial of mental health treatment in jails. Already politicized by this work, Courtney later re-entered the jails as a meditation volunteer. For Courtney, the political work of documenting systematic injustice functioned as the stepping-stone to her work as a meditation volunteer. As we will see, many other respondents demonstrated a keen understanding of social, structural, and systemic issues. But these four were outliers in describing their motivations for prison work as explicitly political, activist, or justice-oriented, in contrast to the majority, who cited personal motivation—we will later see the significance of this point.

Common Themes across the Board: Coping, Surviving and Healing through Yoga and Meditation

Volunteers were also asked to describe the purpose or goal of yoga and meditation in prisons. The most predominant theme emerged as a therapeutic one: coping with the significant stresses and strains of prison life. Every single respondent believed they were offering healing, self-care, and survival tools in an inhumane and brutal environment. Some saw this as a basic humanization and restoration of personal dignity: "bringing self-respect," or "making it survivable with your self intact." Others used the language of alleviating stress, suffering, or discomfort in a chaotic and constrained environment: "how to bring some relaxation to their bodies and minds while they're locked up in there." "I just want people to be at ease while incarcerated, to have meaning in their life," says Maria. The language of self-care was extremely common: "Yoga is essential to teaching people how to care for themselves."

Volunteers were familiar with the inhumane conditions of confinement, which they either directly witnessed or learned about from their students.

In the face of such conditions, some cast the practices as more pragmatic in nature, helping to cope with everyday physical aches and pains. Others described the practices as mechanisms to cope with "grief and loss, like grief of being separated from family." Relatedly, many wanted to offer incarcerated persons a network of support and guidance: "give [them] the sense of not being alone," "feel[ing] loved and supported and cared for." Many saw healing and self-care as crucially connected to offering a positive sense of self-worth: "We're teaching them self-love, self-acceptance, self-forgiveness, positive emotions to counteract the negativity they've been given." Others characterized this as helping them to "feel better about themselves, be less reactive and judgmental [toward] themselves." A few yoga volunteers went even further in stating that they wanted students to recognize their connection with the divine, although this language was by no means universal. Some volunteers stuck to a more secular and scientific reasoning, articulating the benefits of yoga or meditation in neurological terms such as the stimulation of the parasympathetic nervous system, moving away from fight-or-flight and toward relaxation. Nora, a white woman in her fifties, gave perhaps the most articulate summary of the psychotherapeutic benefits:

> If you connect with that peaceful, safe, deeper sense of self, [and if] feelings of fear or psychological pain come up . . . you can feel [them] without having them take over. You can process them and let them release. Learning to work with the yoga tools, they've learned to regulate those feelings, so that [they] are not overwhelmed by them.

We see, then, that every respondent viewed yoga and meditation as having ameliorative or therapeutic effects. Although they expressed these goals in a variety of ways, they were all connected to alleviating the suffering of incarceration, whether through secular/scientific means or spiritual ones. These ameliorative goals ranged from mundane ones such as coping with back pain or mobility issues, to deeper emotional ones, such as healing from trauma through unconditional self-love, and occasionally to the loftiest ones such as realizing one's divinity or connecting with a universal force. Despite the variations in the range of goals expressed, what was common across all respondents was the expression of care, concern, and kindness, and an emphasis on gentle, healing thoughts toward the self. The word "trauma" may not have been used by every respondent, but all expressed the desire to relieve their students of the layers of trauma brought on by past abuse, negative conditioning, lack of resources, and other factors.

Despite this common emphasis on alleviating suffering, there was a striking variation in how respondents saw incarcerated persons in relation to the system that incarcerated them. From the broad consensus on therapeutic effects, the responses began to diverge into roughly two kinds of narratives, consistent with the predominant and dissenting narratives I described earlier. In the predominant set of narratives expressed by the majority, incarcerated persons were seen in ways that replicated the prison's own logic. The second, dissenting narrative, more characteristic of a smaller minority of respondents, sought to challenge the prison's perspective, either subtly or overtly. While I do divide my respondents into two groups, not all respondents fell squarely into one group or the other, defying a clear-cut distinction. Out of the thirty-six interviews, thirty sorted cleanly into one narrative or the other, but in six cases, I found widely differing and somewhat inconsistent ideas and shifting views within a single conversation. Of those six, all were people who initially appeared to express the predominant narrative, but made comments more in line with the dissenting one later on. In what follows, I focus on the themes that emerged from each narrative, and the ways in which the dissenting narrative differed from the predominant one. Again, both groups had many goals in common. Both were concerned with empowering their students—offering them opportunities for change, in ways that allowed them to overcome past conditioning, to see themselves anew, and to develop capacities for creative and self-determined action. But there was a divergence in the precise meaning that each set of respondents gave to empowerment and self-development, either interpreting these concepts in accordance with—or in opposition to—the prison's logic.

The Predominant Narrative: "Becoming Better Human Beings"

The majority of respondents (22 out of 36) interpreted the purpose of teaching yoga or meditation in prisons as some form of rehabilitation, personal transformation, and behavioral management: impulse control, self-regulation, self-discipline, making better choices. Despite the strong emphasis on goals like self-love, self-compassion, self-forgiveness, and so on, this first group of respondents all saw yoga or meditation as changing the incarcerated individual, aligning with the prison's goal of making them more responsible, accountable and better-behaved. I call this the predominant narrative.

Mason is a white male yoga teacher in his sixties who has founded a prison yoga organization. He says, "Yoga and mindfulness practices serve as a behavioral rehabilitative aid for prisoners. How can you manage yourself in a way that relieves you of suffering? Self-control, impulse control [is] a big one. My intention is that my students find yoga to be an opportunity for personal transformation." Eric, another white male in his sixties, has served as a Buddhist chaplain in jails and prisons for five years, while Jessica, a white woman in her forties, teaches yoga to juvenile teens. They all use the language of "staying out of trouble," "calming down," and "controlling [their] reactions." "They're able to recognize and subvert their anger," says Eric. "They're becoming accountable to themselves, and their community," says Jessica.

Many respondents who expressed this narrative similarly described incarcerated persons as having made bad choices, as prone to anger and violence, and as being in need of change through self-control. Here, I found both a more nuanced and a more reductive version of this idea: The most reductive and simplistic version came from respondents like Sankar, quoted at the beginning of this chapter, who simply assumed that all incarcerated persons were "criminals" or "bad guys" who needed to be taught to behave better. Vivian, a Black female yoga teacher in her 60s (and one of only three Black respondents), connected this to preventing repeat offenses: "We punish them and they get out and go back to what they did before, 'cause that's all they know. They'll be living right next to us, so you got to help them get it together, become productive citizens, stop being criminals."

A more nuanced version of this idea was offered by those who recognized the high preponderance of trauma among this population, and the need for self-awareness and self-regulation through more attunement to the mind-body connection. Angela is a white woman in her mid-20s who has been teaching yoga in prisons for several years. Many shared her view that yoga gives people "an opportunity to reflect on their habits and behavior," by being "present with emotions as they arise" and being "less impulsive," which in turn would "prevent violence." Tan, the monk who teaches meditation in both men's and women's prisons, says: "the more you meditate, the better you will be at identifying your own subtle emotion. . . .they are much more aware of their feelings and anger." Jessica also notes that her students "became very aware . . . of their actions, aware of their personal dialogue. . . to know when they were having those thoughts or were about to take that street drug." These respondents emphasized self-compassion, self-valuing, or gentle non-judgment of self. Yet, their references to self-regulation assume that their students are incarcerated due to bad behavior or lack of self-control.

Taking Responsibility and Accountability

Those who adhered to this predominant narrative suggested that taking more responsibility and making better choices will fix the problems that plague incarcerated people. Sondra, a white female yoga teacher in her fifties, notes: "If people aren't going back to jail, because they're starting new and better practices, they're actually just taking responsibility for their lives. And it's not asking the government to fix it all for them: they're a participant in their own reform." Nicole emphasizes offering "unconditional love" to her incarcerated students, but also says, "The only thing you can control is what you can choose. . . . You can forever be a victim of what happened to you [and let that] shape your justification for things. [Or] you're choosing how you're gonna respond to stuff that happens around you, and not let that define you." In these remarks, all problems are assumed to be resolvable by individuals taking control of their own fate, instead of "asking the government to fix it all" or forever remaining "a victim." As Sondra says, "If individuals are transformed, they start changing their thought patterns or destructive behaviors . . . it's part of the idea of reform." Notably, these views on personal responsibility seemed fully congruent with the concern for self-love, self-compassion, and self-care expressed by all respondents.

"Real" Rehabilitation instead of Punishment

Across the board, all the respondents in this group expressed frustration that prisons were punitive and retributive rather than rehabilitative, and many in this group characterized the prison system as "corrupt," "inhumane," or "barbaric," as described in Chapter 4. But those who represented the predominant narrative saw yoga or meditation as a way to therapeutically "educate" those incarcerated in an overly punitive and harsh context. "They're being punished for something they did . . . [for] bad behavior," says Hannah. "And there really aren't a lot of tools for becoming a different person who wouldn't do that." Like so many others in this group who emphasized self-compassion, Tiffany is a proponent of making her incarcerated students "feel happy and good and feel love inside." In the same conversation, she notes, "There's no rehabilitation [in the system], they don't care about it. I don't think just locking somebody up is going to teach them anything . . . it really starts with education and therapy." For these respondents, the goal was to reform an inhumane system into one that was better able to educate those in need of personal reform. Sondra exemplifies this view. She characterizes the system as "barbaric" and "inhumane," and hopes for a "redesigned approach" to "real rehabilitation": "I think people should be punished, but . . . [we need to] do a lot more to make people more productive members of society when they're in prison." Even while considering themselves resistant to the system, these respondents ulti-mately reverted to the prison's logic of personal transformation as the solution to a systemic issue.

Social Order and Compliance in Prisons

Many respondents in this group connected the benefits of yoga and medita-tion with better behavior toward correctional officers, and making the work of corrections easier. Alice, a white woman in her sixties, offers, "You notice a much calmer population, a less reactive population, like [one of the officers] said . . . that's gotta make their lives easier." Sankar too states that "[Prison staff] are happy because these guys are not trouble-makers anymore . . . they see these people are improving." Tan notes that it allows his students to avoid prison sanctions such as solitary confinement, or longer sentences. Several respondents share the system's emphasis on a governable, obedient prisoner, as well as its goals of social order and compliance within prisons. In fact, many reported that their incarcerated students seem to have internalized the goals of self-regulation by accepting their circumstances. "[They say things like] '*I've learned a lot about impulse control in yoga and meditation.*' . . . They feel calmer, less angry, more peaceful, more accepting . . they're seeing things differently."

Pathologizing "Broken, Undisciplined" Individuals

Judah Schept reminds us that the work of punishment is to "deem some people normal and others deviant and requiring social control."[31] Schept quotes a judge who describes incarcerated individuals: "They have seldom been responsible or accountable . . . they are usually self-centered, focused on immediate gratification, have less empathy for other people." Among the twenty-two respondents who expressed the predominant narrative, we see precisely this stereotyping at work: sweeping generalizations about incarcer-ated individuals playing a "moralizing role for a class of people who need in-struction about living in society."[32] These generalizations were made in the same conversations where respondents insisted on self-compassion, self-acceptance, self-forgiveness, and self-love. Victoria, a white woman in her sixties who has also founded a prison yoga organization, emphasizes that it is based in "love and compassion": "I want every woman to feel better about herself when she walks out the door." In the same conversation, she calls her students "just so undisciplined," with no self-control or regulation: "Yoga is such a marvelous way of taking a broken, undisciplined individual, who hasn't been properly parented, and [giving them] some guidance . . . some of them are like little puppies [at the pound] . . . we want to go in and socialize them."

Sondra offers the most dramatic version of this stereotyping: "It's great to feel good that we're helping people . . . even if someone is evil or an animal or unevolved." Certainly, many respondents acknowledge the preponderance of trauma and abuse in the prior lives of their students, combined with social and economic disadvantage. They acknowledge that "prisoners are at the bottom rung of the social ladder," that the vast majority "come from . . . abusive backgrounds, child abuse, sexual abuse, abandonment," and are "abusing drugs and alcohol to numb the pain of their existence." But despite these concessions to structural and social inequities, my respondents tend to describe what Schept has called a "population both economically and morally impoverished and liable to various . . . pathologies."[33] Their recognition of trauma remains at a superficial level: They acknowledge the role of structural inequity, but stress that the solution is individuals learning to "behave better" and changing themselves, a narrative taught and reinforced by the prison.

Addressing Mass Incarceration

Among other things, I explored what political understanding of mass incarceration appeared to underlie the volunteer's commitment to teaching in prisons. How, if at all, did instructors see the purpose of their work in relation to systemic injustice? Respondents were asked about their views on mass incarceration, and whether they felt that the work of teaching yoga or meditation was connected to addressing this issue. The conversational, open-ended style of interviewing allowed for a range of views—often contradictory—to emerge within the same conversation.

Among the twenty-two respondents who enthusiastically endorsed the predominant narrative, two patterns emerged. One subset of six admitted they did not get into the politics of the situation, and just tried to "help wherever they could." One respondent, the monk Sankar, described political commitments as "part of our attachment or desire" in Buddhist thought, and thus refrained from making any judgment on such issues. These respondents were avowedly apolitical, confessing that they either did not know much—or did not care to learn much—about the structural or political aspects of mass incarceration.

The remaining subset of sixteen in this group of respondents all acknowledged that mass incarceration was structurally unjust. Despite these acknowledgments, their emphasis was overwhelmingly on the need for individual behavioral change as the appropriate response to an unjust system. Here, I saw three patterns: First, some of them felt powerless to take on systemic injustice (or resisted taking it on). Second, some insisted that their volunteer work was a form of social justice work because by changing themselves in prison, individuals could demonstrate that they did not "deserve" incarceration. Third, some saw prison volunteer work as social justice work, but for a different reason: because changing individuals in prison would have ripple effects outward in society.

Resisting Systemic Critique

Eric, the Buddhist chaplain, demonstrates the first pattern among this subset of sixteen respondents, one of hesitation at addressing injustice. He acknowledges the existence of injustice and systemic racism, which he says we have "no control over." He describes himself as left-leaning, and subscribing to standard critiques of the prison-industrial complex. Yet, he insists:

> I don't think there's a conspiracy within the criminal justice system to clear the streets. Obviously there is a lot of oppression, inequality, dysfunction. But crime's gonna happen, what do you do with people who are really violent? It's beneficial to look at the fundamental intention of what the justice system is trying to do, it's trying to produce safety, right? It's easy to lose that and see it as oppressive, hierarchical, and top-down.

Like Eric, several other respondents acknowledged the systemic issues at the heart of mass incarceration, but did not think addressing these issues was the purpose of their volunteer work—either because the system is intractably broken and can't be fixed, or because we have no control over injustice, or because there are good reasons to resist being too critical.

Making People More "Worthy"

Ethan is a white male in his thirties, a graduate student studying Buddhist theology, while volunteering to offer Buddhist meditation at men's prisons. He illustrates the second pattern among the subset of sixteen respondents who acknowledge mass incarceration as a structural issue: He critiques the system, and claims that prison work addresses social injustice by helping individuals "prove" they do not deserve to be incarcerated. "I feel like there's a call for me to redress the social situations that are causing people to end up there," says Ethan. When I ask how, he says: "Hopefully, [meditation] can help them be equanimous towards their living conditions, help them change their attitudes and behavior . . . perhaps be recognized as non-threatening and maybe as, *'This guy's not just a dog who needs to get locked up'* . . . showing that these people may be worthy of reconsideration, or consideration in the first place . . . perhaps be treated better." If incarcerated people accept their fate, Ethan suggests, they may be considered more worthy of good treatment. And, despite his strong statement about "social situations" that contribute to incarceration, Ethan later insists, "People are there as a result of—most of the time—doing some crime. . . . I mean there are certain laws that can be changed, but I don't think that's my concern so much, the sentencing aspect." Here, Ethan rejects the focus on systemic change, and focuses instead on changing the behaviors of incarcerated individuals. For him, as for many others, this constitutes social justice work. Sondra shared Ethan's view that yoga or meditation practices would constitute a response to mass incarceration by making individuals "more worthy" of consideration. She calls mass incarceration a "continued form of slavery," but insists, "if people aren't going back to jail . . . they will prove they're not part of mass incarceration, that they've actually just been taking responsibility for their lives."

The Ripple Effect: From Individual to Structural Change
The third subset of sixteen respondents also saw teaching yoga or meditation as synonymous with social justice activism against prisons. When pressed, these respondents interpreted activism to mean that self-improvement by incarcerated individuals would have ripple effects outward into society. Structural, political change was again seen as the cumulative result of individual changes. Jane, a white yoga teacher in her thirties, notes, "The best way for me to be an activist is to look at who's in front of me . . . [not to] get too caught up in the larger scheme. It's an individual process . . . that's the social justice piece." Julia, a white yoga teacher in her forties, who initially describes the prison system as a form of "slavery," emphasizes the principle of "each one teach one": "I think if each one of us can do something for someone else, that would change the whole system."

Like other respondents in this subset, Alice considers herself an extremely political person and expresses anger with mass incarceration, calling it "archaic and violent and awful." The view that people "deserve to be in there" is "just lunatic," she asserts. But when asked if yoga was a response to this injustice, she insisted, "You're . . . giving tools to help people who are incarcerated to change on some level. And then when the people in charge see those changes, [they say], 'Okay, this does make a difference. There's less fighting on the yard.' I do feel it's a form of social justice. The incarcerated themselves are changing from within, and everybody around them feels that change. It's a ripple effect." Alice, Maria, Julia, and Jane all assert that social justice consists in changes brought about through "one person helping another person." Individual changes ripple outward, producing large-scale behavioral changes in society.

"Empowering" People to Change

Another idea mentioned by respondents across the board was that of "empowering" incarcerated people. But respondents who held the predominant narrative gave a specific meaning to the notion of empowerment. They saw themselves empowering incarcerated individuals to change in keeping with the prison's logic, seeing mass incarceration as a problem of badly behaved individuals. Eric notes, "My longing is to offer people tools to become empowered on their own . . . to heal and transform themselves to live in civil society." The suggestion here is that to empower incarcerated individuals is to make them fit for society. For Sondra, incarcerated people needed to "be empowered to turn things around in a constructive way." Nicole is explicit about rejecting a focus on any systemic critique: "We're not focused on talking about what's not right with the system, we're focused on teaching and learning skills to become more self-aware, become more self-empowered." She calls this the "only real version of rehabilitation": "Until then, they're just a victim of circumstances and choices." For Nicole, like many others, speaking about empowerment required a focus on individual choices and a pivot away from critiquing the system, in terms that matched the prison's narrative.

Here once again is Mason, the founder of a leading prison yoga program, who was also deeply critical of mass incarceration. He strongly supports sentencing reforms that would change mandatory minimums for nonviolent offenses, particularly for those with substance-abuse or recovery needs. But, he also insists that "reform" requires "a person [having] the opportunity to learn skills that are going to prevent them from re-offending." His perspective is shaped by working with many life-sentenced persons who had lived "criminal lifestyles that resulted in their taking somebody's life." He shares stories he heard from prisoners, attesting to their own criminality: "*I was lost in a lifestyle. I was completely in denial. I was basically living the classic convict code. I had no concept of the harm that I had caused.*' And then, being able to go through [yoga or meditation] programs and come to grips with, '*I take responsibility for causing this harm*'—how that can set an individual free."

Mason's interview represents the patterns that emerged among the twenty-two respondents who endorsed the predominant narrative: Even while questioning the legitimacy of mass incarceration, Mason stated that he "absolutely, beyond a doubt" sees rehabilitation as a key factor in addressing it. Addressing structural injustice is achieved partially by addressing the need for penitence and responsibility for criminal behavior, changing individuals through yoga and meditation. Like these twenty-two respondents, Mason acknowledges that the problems with the system are structural, but holds that the solutions are individual.

The Dissenting Narrative: Yoga or Meditation as Tools for Resistance and "Stirring the Pot"

In contrast to those who emphasized a version of rehabilitation fully consistent with the goals of the prison system, a minority of fourteen respondents describe yoga and meditation in ways quite resistant to the logic and goals of the system. They reject the idea that it is solely incarcerated individuals who need "fixing" or betterment. Instead, they emphasize the effects of race, poverty, and socioeconomic/legal disadvantage in incarceration, and encourage a critical orientation toward the system among their students. They also express discomfort with the notion of compliant or governable prisoners. A few attempt to combine yoga or meditation with political education and consciousness-raising (with mixed success). Instead of expecting people to self-regulate in order to "become better individuals" or "reduce propensity toward crime," these respondents insist on a political purpose for yoga and meditation. They link the teaching of self-care to an internal awareness of systemic injustice. For them, yogic and meditative practices can serve as forms of self-regulation in opposition to unjust structures. Below, I describe the themes that emerged from conversations with those who expressed what I have called the "dissenting" narrative. Recall that in six of my conversations, respondents expressed views that initially seemed compatible with the predominant narrative, but later appeared to veer more toward the dissenting one. I categorized these respondents with the earlier group of twenty-two, but in what follows, I occasionally identify ways in which they express dissenting views closer to the second group of fourteen. It bears repeating, then, that the distinction between these two narratives—and the groups of respondents who express them—is not entirely clear-cut, because some respondents pick up the threads of both narratives, often shifting fluidly between them in the course of a single conversation.

Choice as Empowering, and Yoga as a Political Vehicle

When asked to elaborate on the purpose of their volunteer work, every one of the fourteen respondents in this group described furthering the personal control or agency of the incarcerated individual. They described the prison as an unjust context that offers little opportunity for such control or agency. Rather than making people less inclined to "commit crimes," the volunteers in this group focused on offering choices for poses or meditative techniques. Yoga and meditation in the "outside" world are based largely on following the commands of a teacher: instructions to close one's eyes during meditation or place one's hands in a certain position; instructions to shape one's body in a particular way during a yoga pose, and so on. But the *Best Practices* manual points out that incarcerated people have few choices to exercise personal choice in their daily lives, and strongly recommends yoga and meditation as a much-needed opportunity to exercise such control. "It is preferable to say, '*If you feel comfortable closing your eyes, I invite you to do so. If not, you can perhaps let your gaze soften and move downward*,' ... As opposed to simply saying '*Close your eyes*.'"[34] Like the manual, every volunteer in this group strongly advocated for "trauma-informed" methods of teaching in prisons: eschewing commands in favor of a more invitational style, offering students options to decide the form of the practice for themselves, instead of directing them toward a method, pose or technique. In so doing, they rejected the prison's discipline, and refused to assume positions of authority over students. Instead, they argued that this more egalitarian approach would have transformative effects for those caught in systems of oppression.

"They're being yelled at and ordered around all day," says Naomi, a white female yoga instructor in her forties. "Instead, I'll offer you a choice, like '*eyes open*' or '*eyes closed*.' I want to give them a little of their power back." "It's a very radical shift," says Thalia, a white woman in her thirties, "it's about the internal locus of control." Eva, the founder and director of a prison yoga organization, is a white woman in her fifties. The trauma-informed approach, she says, "[offers] a different experience in power-relations. . . . There's no difference between us and our students. We're not there as experts. [It's a] nonhierarchical paradigm of [unconditional] acceptance and nurturing." Eleanor, a white prison yoga instructor in her thirties, described this as "empowering," "radicalizing," and "giving [them] back . . . agency:" "In a way, our system is built on people . . . not knowing their own power, right?" she asks. Keisha, a Black woman in her thirties, calls this approach "revolutionary": "I do sometimes wonder," she muses, "if they knew how powerfully transformative it could be, would [the system] allow it? You'd have a whole bunch of people perhaps questioning what's happening [in prisons], maybe questioning the medication that gets shoved down their throat, why things are the way that they are. It can be very disruptive." It is this disruptive potential that Morgan, a white woman in her thirties, calls "yoga utilized as a political vehicle: something that could stir the pot a little bit, that would engage in more feelings of rights and awareness, [more subversive feelings]." Thomas, a white meditation instructor in his sixties, also insists that meditation can help people to be more assertive, instead of being "over-submissive," or not standing up for one's rights.

Notice that the concept of empowerment as defined by this group of respondents stands in contrast to the one emerging from the predominant narrative. Rather than supporting the prison's logic of changing students to make them more accountable, this concept of empowerment is focused on making students agents of their own lives, through "feel[ing] more in charge of their own experience." This version of empowerment entails encouraging students to cast critical scrutiny on the prison's logic and messaging, to steal moments of freedom and agency in a system intent on denying these experiences.

"You Are Giving the Man Your Power"

Instead of expecting people to self-regulate in order to "reduce propensity toward crime," this group of respondents insisted that not reacting to oppressive conditions was a form of resistance to an unjust system. Jade, a Black yoga volunteer, confesses to teaching this perspective to incarcerated youth, albeit covertly, away from the gaze of staff: "I'm like, '*don't fucking come back. You are giving the man your power. . . . Your ancestors worked so hard to move out of enslavement, and you are choosing to put yourself back into it.*' . . . Use a practice to create space between being triggered and reacting so that you don't get locked up." Adina too confesses to sharing this political perspective with youth of color in juvenile facilities. The world, she notes, "wants to see Black men angry": "[I tell them] *it's not that you are broken or can't be regulated—the system is actively trying to harm you.* So we use these tools to not become who the system wants us to be." The dissenting narrative urges incarcerated persons to see themselves in opposition to the prison's messaging about who they are: strong, worthy and capable, rather than broken, dysfunctional or dysregulated.

Three respondents of color—Keisha, Jade, and Adina—found self-care to be a radical political act, especially for certain communities. Jade cites Audre Lorde's view that Black women are expected to care for others instead of themselves: "I'm not being self-indulgent . . . I am making a political stand to nurture myself. This is about my survival." Keisha shared with her incarcerated students that she had heard Angela Davis speak of self-care as an act of revolution: "And two COs looked at me. That's when you see the system cringe a little bit . . . if people take care of themselves, they take care of other people and that's when you can incite great change."

"Seeing Yourself as a Worthy Equal"

Perhaps the most basic task in promoting self-care was to induce messages of self-worth, in contrast to the messages received from the prison system and from society. Courtney refers to the demeaning culture of imprisonment, which treats people as subhuman and penetrates their self-understanding: "Meditation can be this oasis where you can get back in touch with who you really are, [instead of being] confirmed in the idea that [you're] basically bad." Thomas also sees this work as countering the social messages that dehumanize incarcerated individuals: "We communicate some sense of valuing them as people and valuing their dignity . . . that they are deserving of our time and of these practices." "I think it's an activist stance," Naomi asserts. "I'm standing up to the system, I'm going to be kind to people that you're throwing away, treat them like human beings, smile and look them in the eyes." Many felt it important to communicate that they saw their students as no different from themselves. As Naomi noted, "We're all one crime away from being in there, what stops us is our skin color or gender or socio-economic status." In fact, Morgan asks, "Maybe that's the scary thing, right? That everybody is just a person like you, [and] they're not some crazy, wild-eyed criminal?"

This theme was echoed by several respondents who initially advocated for the predominant narrative, but gradually appeared to change their stance later in the conversation. Jane began to resist and refine the predominant view as our interview progressed: "I wanted to create a space where everyone . . . felt comfortable to be themselves and felt equal," she says. She wanted to offer her students a self-conception that resisted the prison's attempts to control incarcerated persons by telling them who they were. Jane explains this as a kind of empowerment that allows students to "step out" of their past narratives, dispelling the power of these patterns to structure their identity:

> I wanted to provide a space where everyone felt valued regardless of past circumstance . . . a space where people feel free and able to step out of that trauma-informed [personal] narrative or identity that we all have. . . . Yoga is absolute eradication of judgment and meeting oneself with love and kindness and compassion. And that is empowerment in the greatest sense, to see yourself outside of your circumstance . . . and past experience.

Jane emphasizes that this view of empowerment goes far beyond the prison's goals of social order and compliance: "I think to say, '*oh there will be less fights in the prison*,' [that's an] over- simplification. It's so much more than that, are you kidding me? We are breaking [certain] norms . . . radical self-inquiry and courage to question and re-formulate what [you] want [your] life to be, trying to cultivate a nonjudgmental escape from the world's expectations and normalized priorities." With these remarks, Jane goes in a far more subversive direction than she had initially implied, encouraging her students to oppose the standard messaging of both the prison and of society.

Rehabilitation as a "A Nice Form of Oppression"

Many respondents in this group rejected the language of rehabilitation. They insisted they did not see incarcerated people as "broken" or requiring "fixing," and that structural inequity was a strong causal factor in incarceration. "I'm not sure that [they] needed rehabilitation as much as . . . support," Morgan insists. "The things that got you in there such as prostitution and drug use were not things you had control over, because you didn't get choices. Given a different set of [situations], they wouldn't necessarily have found themselves there." Like Keisha, who earlier quoted Angela Davis, many noted that the focus on rehabilitation reinforced the systemic oppression of mass incarceration, by ignoring its race- or poverty-based character: "If you're not really addressing the deeper cause, then you're only putting in place another form of oppression—it may be nice oppression, but it's still oppression." Instead of expecting people to change, Eva suggests, these practices focus on encouraging each student to see their own already-perfect nature: "Yoga and meditation view a person as already perfect . . . seeing the wholeness and the light that's already there and reflecting it back."

"Keeping the Slaves Happy?"

Those who expressed the dissenting narrative were deeply concerned that yoga or meditation might result in overly docile, submissive, or pacified prisoners. Perhaps the most direct statement comes from Jackson, a white Buddhist meditation teacher in men's prisons, who compares the prison to a slave-plantation:

> The idea that you can make a slave on a plantation happier, but he's still a slave on a plantation. We're just teaching them how to deal with their anxiety or their anger, so they're feeling better and they're less likely to come back to prison because they've been able to deal with their stress. But they haven't necessarily been able to understand and respond to the collective causes of what's going on. So the slave doesn't necessarily wanna ask tough questions about slavery . . . to a point of revolt. If I was letting somebody over-blame themselves, or if someone started speaking about collective issues and I didn't support that, I would feel like [it was] problematic.

Morgan confesses to having struggled with the idea of creating "a crowd that's easier for guards to handle": "I don't feel good about making a population who's just resigned to their fate," she sighs. "I don't want to add to that blind compliance, that slavery."

Here too, some of the respondents who had initially advocated for behavioral management began to express discomfort with this idea. Jane, earlier quoted within the predominant narrative, later says that mass incarceration is "obviously an attempt to control the social distribution of what are no longer minority populations." Similarly, both Julia and Marissa, who were initially categorized with the predominant narrative, began to raise questions about social control through pacification. "True yoga is not just a tranquilizer," Julia insists. "[The goal of yoga] is not to become more docile, it's. . . . I would say even speak your truth. I do not think that yoga is making people just accept their circumstances." Marissa says, "An empowered inmate may not be good as a submissive inmate." I ask her to elaborate which of those goals she is pursuing. "I know which one I'm spiritually aligned to," she responds without hesitation: "the empowerment of the individual. If I didn't feel that—if I felt like I was going in there to check a box for rehabilitation—I would not be spending my weekends doing that." From here on, she becomes increasingly emphatic. "[It's] not the purpose of yoga to become compliant and docile and submissive. No, no, no," she insists. "Discipline of your own self, to become empowered . . . that ultimate spirit of freedom and self-awareness. [It's about taking] control back in a positive way of their own souls and of their own destinies."

Challenging "Personal Responsibility" and "Individual Choice"

The fourteen respondents who expressed the dissenting narrative saw systemic inequity as crucially related to their work, in many cases preempting my questions about mass incarceration. Not only were they more politically astute and informed, they openly challenged conventional assumptions about incarceration. Many used the language of complex systems that were structurally stacked against their students, producing constrained choices. Others critiqued the capitalist structure, with particular emphasis on debtors' prison, and the warehousing of the poor, the mentally ill, or the homeless. They pointed to excessive prosecutorial discretion, and laws that incentivize the criminalization of marginalized populations, making for longer sentences with less possibility of parole, compounding the effects of intergenerational trauma. They criticized the recidivism-inducing effects of punitive incarceration, particularly on those struggling with addiction or mental illness. Unlike most of the respondents in the previous group, they had read texts such as *The New Jim Crow*, or required it in their organizations.

Jackson insists, "They may have done something immoral, but then the overall context could be seen as immoral . . . if you look at the trauma or the addiction and poverty that they're coming from. How much of that is their own individual responsibility, versus how much is the collective responsibility?" Claire, who works in restorative justice groups, is perhaps the most critical of this phenomenon: "The greatest liberation is when folks who are experiencing incarceration can say, '*It wasn't all my fucking fault.*' [And] the pushback against it—I call it the '*AA'ing*' and the '*NA'ing.*' It's mostly older, white volunteers who go in and talk about accountability to young people of color. . . . The overwhelming load of responsibility gets put on the person who is incarcerated, without an acknowledgment of structural or communal realities."

Turning the "Panoptic Gaze Back on Itself"

Among these fourteen respondents who expressed the dissenting narrative, a small minority of four had tried to combine yoga or meditation with political education and consciousness-raising in prison. This included introducing discussions of structural injustice in their classes, and in some cases, engagement with the communities feeding into the prison pipeline. These respondents saw yoga or meditation as necessarily—and not just incidentally—connected to political awareness. In Claire's words, it was to "think of yourself as a resource serving the destruction of mass incarceration."

Charlotte and Jackson both insist that meditation must be taught in a way that allows for, in Charlotte's words, an "open acknowledgment" of injustice: "acting from clear-sightedness, acknowledging, not denying, keeping your eyes open." Jackson described his experimental forays into discussing "systemic and structural racism" with his incarcerated students: "What are the conditions that lead to violent crimes and what are the structural issues? What's individual karma, what's collective karma? What personal cycles do I keep being reborn in, but what are the collective cycles [like racism or mass incarceration] that keep being reborn?" Claire goes even further, insisting that the failure to raise such questions makes one complicit with the system: "If I'm not doing something inside that turns that panoptic gaze back on itself . . . to systematically undo mass incarceration, then I can't do this. It's collusion. You're just reinforcing messages about them being defined as criminal."

But even those few respondents who had contemplated—or experimented with—incorporating political education into their prison classes acknowledged that yoga or meditation alone could not achieve this. The practices would need to be combined with an educational setting in which ideas could be discussed. Jackson admits that he has been unable to fully explore political education in prisons, citing Malcolm X and groups like Critical Resistance as models for such work in the future. Teaching meditation in prisons, he suggests, could be combined with broader education and political critique: "If we were more vocal about mass incarceration and involved in activism, if the curriculum we teach includes a more social justice component to it. And then, if we start building relationships with the community outside the prison . . . connecting inside and outside." Nora describes a model she is familiar with, in which postural yoga is combined with philosophy and political ideas: "like *'how could I work with the resourcing I got through yoga to build relationships, to create community, to develop ideas for more radical change?'*" But on the whole, she laments, "the ideas component is probably not given as much time and effort as it should."

The Empowerment of Internal Freedom

Respondents who held to the dissenting narrative also offered an understanding of freedom that did not require overt resistance, and did not wait for social, political, or structural issues to be resolved. This was a reshaping of the mind, an internal strength through "work on the self" that allowed people to feel free despite being demeaned or victimized by unjust structures. Keisha, a queer Black woman who supported the dissenting narrative, offers the most eloquent summary of this:

> Toni Morrison always had this stance that . . . true liberation and true transcendence of oppression comes from a deep knowledge and love of the self. So, regardless of the circumstances, you can liberate yourself. I can work to change and end mass incarceration, but in the meantime, I wanna live my life, not in response to the way that white America treats me. I wanna live my life free. Period. It doesn't mean we have to accept the circumstances we have [or] that things are okay. But if we're constantly operating in opposition to what is happening, we never liberate. You can still have a way that you see yourself, and it doesn't matter what other people say. . . . And when I teach, that's what I want people to understand about themselves.

Keisha notes that she previously used to disagree with this perspective: "I used to think [it] was a bunch of bullshit, like *'how can she say that*??'" But she is now at pains to clarify that Morrison's view is not "the same as *'pull yourself up by your bootstraps'*": "'cause I also think that's bullshit . . . [this] is a very different proposition." In a similar vein, Jade offers,

> These teachings have liberated me. I don't feel trapped, or bullied, or pushed. I don't feel like I am a victim of what happens to my life. There is a sense of being fully in control, and empowered. I can be any way that I want to be in this world. For

me, that's a huge political statement. Especially as a Black, queer, woman: to feel that strong.

Here, the divergence between the definitions of empowerment offered by the predominant and dissenting narratives comes into stark relief. Keisha rejects the "bootstraps" message that exhorts people to simply "try harder" to get past structural obstacles. Instead, she and Jade both offer a window into a sense of internal freedom that can flourish despite such obstacles, despite the reality of confinement. Or, as Courtney puts it, "I wanted to offer something that is of value that can't be taken away. As you begin to develop your mind and create more strength and stability and openness, you're not as incarcerated as you were . . . [You] can navigate and feel free within [a system] that is completely stacked against [you]." This understanding of an internal freedom and agency that did not depend on society's recognition of one's humanity was most prevalent among this minority group of fourteen. But it was also occasionally glimpsed in the views of a few respondents from the predominant narrative. It's "teach[ing] them to be free within," says Matteo, "recognizing [their] own power," says Cecilia, through "an embodiment [that allows for] strength and stability," in Julia's words.

"North American Yoga Culture Is Largely Uninformed about Social and Political Issues"

The respondents in the minority dissenting group all acknowledged that barriers to political work in prisons were high. The most oft-cited barrier was other individuals in their organization, who resisted overtly political understandings of yoga or meditation. A few, like Nora, reported a parting of ways with their organizations, after the leadership resisted or ignored their suggestions that questions of race, poverty, power, and inequity be integrated into prison classes: "I guess I had a more ambitious vision that didn't really become accepted. . . . Volunteers [shouldn't just go] in as yoga teachers, but should have a lot more social and personal awareness."

A common theme was, as Nora characterized it, North American yoga culture as "largely uninformed about social and political issues and not deeply interested in them." Social and political education are not part of mainstream yoga training, Nora notes, and yoga culture "has a tendency to think of yoga as something . . . apolitical." Adina echoes this view: "I see a lot of yoga being used as spiritual bypass," she says. Yogic ideas such as *everything happens for a reason* or *that's their karma* are used to bolster an "apolitical and anti-intellectual" yoga culture with "not a lot of critical thinking. . . . Just these fluffy ideas about the world where we don't have to confront ourselves too much."

Jackson, meanwhile, works with an organization that identifies itself with "engaged Buddhism," but criticizes them for not being "engaged" enough: "Going to a prison could be seen as 'engaged,' as opposed to just sitting at the temple somewhere," he admits. But he calls this version of prison work "medium-engaged," and insists that "high-level" engaged Buddhism would adopt the more radical vision he earlier described, engaging with social justice and critique. Jackson reports that none of his colleagues objects to his activist vision, but no one seems particularly interested in it either.

Jade notes a remarkable absence of issues such as race or systemic inequity in trainings held by prominent prison yoga and meditation advocates during her early years. "It's beyond being unconscious," she says. "It's not even on their radar. . . . I don't know that they see the connection [between yoga or meditation and political issues] in the first place. How many people have they harmed, in ten or fifteen years [of doing these trainings], by not having that lens?" She often found herself to be the only person of color at these events, and eventually, this lack of political awareness caused her to withdraw from prison yoga and meditation altogether. "After ten years of being optimistic, like, *'Yeah! We can create systemic change!'* I was like, *'I'm not fucking changing the system from doing direct service.'*" Claire also parted ways with a leading restorative justice group she previously worked with, for not being radical enough. Their curriculum she notes "had been mass approved by the corrections department." As a result, "its own non-profit-complex, of getting funding from the Department of Correction, leads [the organization] to be nonpolitical about the Department of Corrections itself."

"The System Works to Protect Itself" and the Importance of Pragmatism and Caution

Many in this minority group reported that it was difficult to raise political issues in the prison setting without attracting scrutiny from staff. Surveillance and potential loss of access to prisons were barriers to overtly radical political work. Claire notes, "The system works to protect itself. I watched people be removed for saying or doing something that the prison doesn't like. If somebody goes rogue, they get reined in and kicked out by the organization before the prison can get involved." Thalia shares that her organization sometimes visits legislators at the state capitol to speak with them about the challenges their students face: "When we did that this year, we immediately got an email from the Department of Corrections asking us what we were doing down there." Another respondent (who emphatically asked that this information not be accompanied by any identifying information) reports receiving a thinly veiled warning from a senior prison administrator after they had brought in political materials to share with students, pertaining to nonviolent forms of resistance by prisoners. Given these forms of monitoring, Thalia insists that in order to keep the yoga program accessible to incarcerated students, "it's best to not go into those kind of conversations [about political issues] . . . I don't want to lose access."

For similar reasons, at least one respondent regrets not having voiced political concerns strongly enough to her incarcerated students. "I absolutely feel that I've held back on voicing my political opinions," says Morgan. "I felt that I would very quickly be removed should I be subversive. . . . I've weighed that a million times." She expresses the ardent wish, in retrospect, that she had more openly expressed her political views to her students: "I do wish I had said, *'here's where I stand. . . . It's not you being a person who needs to be fixed, or who did something so unforgivable. This is a system flaw . . . think about how few choices you had . . . we're doing wrong by you.'*" Thalia, in contrast, insists that expressing political positions can be done subtly, without any explicit discussion of political or social issues, particularly given how fraught such discussions could be within the prison environment: "It's how we show up. It's in the handouts that we hand out. It's in the kind of language that we use. I think that a lot of the students know that we are doing more than just yoga."

Such caution was evident among the respondents who had worked on the *Best Practices* manual. The book's introduction skirts around critiques of mass incarceration. I interviewed several key contributors, one of whom confessed that there was some disagreement: "There was a lot of discussion about what to call the book. People didn't like 'criminal justice system,' because we don't like calling people criminals, and we don't think it's just. But, we want to reach people who work in the system, [like] potentially sympathetic administrators. [One of our reviewers said] *'Every single person who works in that system, they're going to see that [you're not comfortable with 'criminal justice'] at the beginning, [and] they're gonna stop reading.'*"

For this reason, many agreed that there are pragmatic reasons to adopt the language of rehabilitation. Naomi is blunt about this: "That word [rehabilitation] is used to appease the people that let us come in . . . it's the language of the system, we use it to manipulate the system." Thomas confesses, "[When prison officials] see how our program is helping with rehabilitation—that's great. [But] our thinking behind what we're doing is a little different." Eva laughingly acknowledges, "I don't say to the administrators [that we are not there to rehabilitate]. I'm not lying to anyone. I'm just not gonna maybe use the word 'subversive,' you know. Just be diplomatic." Claire notes that this is precisely why she became excited to join a new, more radical organization: "[Our new founder] was like, "*If I'm with this group of people, I frame it this way. . . . If I'm with that group of people, I frame it that way.*"

Nora addresses the practical barriers to combining yoga or meditation with discussion. She notes that building an organization with political goals is difficult from a logistical perspective: "It's a very difficult process of building up from the pragmatic level to the organizational level to the educational level to the politically relevant level. In the absence of infrastructure and resources to work with. . . . The rational thing to do is to feel overwhelmed and completely hopeless." Similarly, Thalia and Eva both acknowledge that it is difficult to combine service work with policy work or political advocacy, both because of the logistical burdens, and because of the perception that nonprofit organizations are governed by rules that prohibit political activity seen as "partisan," a common misconception.[35]

Conclusions

Judah Schept finds in his research that those who repeatedly condemned the institutionalized racism of the prison system also spoke of incarcerated persons as though their actions were freely chosen outside of any structural constraints.[36] "The very people they were quick to identify as victims of past abuse, addiction, cyclical poverty, structural inequality, and historical racism"[37] were also seen as being in need of personal transformation. In his study of reentry organizations, Reuben Miller notes that such organizations focus on "people-changing": seeking to treat, reform or remake individuals, encouraging offenders to "look within" for the answers to their problems, rather than focusing on the deeply unequal social or economic conditions within which their choices are made.[38] And, in her study of rehabilitative programming at a women's prison, Jill McCorkel writes that incarcerated persons are expected to "take ownership of their problems and resolve them by learning to make the 'right' choices even when, in many instances, the situations they find themselves in are not an outcome of choice."[39]

In much the same way, the predominant narrative expressed by the majority of my interviewees gave a vision of reforming prison into an opportunity for positive personal change, making prison time "productive, introspective and redemptive." Yoga or meditation became part of a "virtuous detention experience that perform[s] the necessary work of making people responsible and saving them."[40] My respondents were overwhelmingly white and female. It is worth noting also that the leadership of the major national service organizations offering yoga and meditation in prisons (at least at the time of my research) was almost entirely white, and there was almost no-one in their ranks who identified as formerly incarcerated or system-impacted.[41] Admittedly, it is difficult (though not impossible) for someone with a record to gain security clearance to volunteer in prisons. Still, in my countless hours of immersion within the volunteer world—and in my study of prominent national organizations—I found little evidence of practices in which the views of formerly incarcerated persons from system-impacted communities or communities of color were prioritized (or even sought) in giving direction to organizational goals. And, volunteers of color were few and far between. In the time-honored tradition of the white savior who heroically redeems the benighted Others,[42] many of my respondents who expressed the predominant narrative pathologized their students as "criminal," "undisciplined," "unevolved," or even "childlike," claiming the mantle of "serving" or "helping." Most of these same respondents were quite apolitical, purely concerned with service and not politics. Others claimed to be familiar with critiques of mass incarceration as systemically biased or unequal. Among those who did acknowledge structural issues, some expressed resistance to activist work, insisting that systemic issues were things they had no control over. Others saw themselves as activists, interpreting their teaching of yoga or meditation as an act of social justice. Yet, when asked to specify the social justice impact of this work, they linked it with teaching people to "better themselves." Social justice was interpreted in individualistic terms, teaching self-improvement to incarcerated individuals, through one-on-one interactions. Their work advocated personal, cognitive change by incarcerated persons through addressing perceived individual deficits,[43] and rarely addressed issues of structural or systemic inequity.

The minority group of respondents expressed support for what I have called the dissenting narrative: they rejected the idea that simply making individuals "better" would equal social justice. To be clear, these volunteers were not opposed to teaching incarcerated individuals greater self-regulation, self-awareness, or self-discipline; they acknowledged that some may have caused harm, or could benefit from self-reflective practices. But they had a far more political purpose in mind for the self-discipline they were teaching. They believed such individual improvement had to include awareness of—and resistance to—mass incarceration. Note that this was rarely conceived in terms of explicit political action: It was more often an internal sense of freedom and agency, a way to feel free and empowered even while confined and dehumanized by a manifestly unjust system. Incarcerated people could be encouraged to be subversive, disruptive, and less submissive—that is, less accepting of the prison's authority, at least in their outlook if not their actions. Without this component, yoga and meditation would become, in Adina's words, "a tool for keeping people down," or, in Jackson words, a way of "keeping slaves happy on the plantation." Any self-management teachings that did not include an understanding of systemic inequities ran the risk of "colluding," in Claire's words, with the prison system.

For these volunteers, the refusal to confront difficult systemic issues, especially inside such a politically determined space, constituted a failure—even a misunderstanding or misinterpretation—of the practices of yoga and meditation. Several of the more political respondents expressed frustration that the organizations they worked with did not hold a critical position on mass incarceration, or expect volunteers to share, internalize, and disseminate these political values. As a result, they eventually parted ways with them. Most of the politically minded respondents had all withdrawn from prison yoga or meditation work (well before the pandemic shutdowns), citing frustration with the general lack of political consciousness.

My findings shed light on little-explored aspects of the "voluntary" and "nonprofit" sectors in prisons. Among other things, these interviews uncover the ways in which correctional discourses of punishment and social control influence volunteers, who can then become agents of penal management and control, perhaps unwittingly, as they reproduce and disseminate the system's own messaging.[44] They also point to the paradox of what has been called the "nonprofit industrial complex": a structure that flattens resistance and tends to suppress the radical ideas that drive social justice movements, by making nonprofits more beholden to career-based modes of organizing, to the pursuit of their own organizational goals, and as a result, to large corporate donors and other powerful institutions invested in the status quo.[45] Nonprofit work thus tends to be inherently cautious and relatively conservative, as activist energies are watered down and redirected into uncontroversial projects that rarely challenge power structures or transform society in radical ways. Of course, not all the volunteers I interviewed were part of formal nonprofit organizations. Regardless, they all faced pressure to conform to the prison's expectations: Even if there was no explicit "litmus test" for allowing volunteers into the system, we saw previously that the system works to train volunteers to identify with its perspective, and volunteer organizations vary greatly in the extent to which they offer counter-messages to their own members. Some are explicit about rejecting the system's logic, but many offer little opportunity to collectively examine the prison's messaging. Given these pressures, the predominant tendency of many volunteers to repeat the prison's logic—even among those who understood themselves to be opposed to it—does not seem so puzzling.

These interviews also uncover the difficulty of "doing politics" in prison: Through both surveillance and messaging, volunteers are warned to steer clear of any political statements or critiques in prisons. The few respondents who have attempted political work inside prisons report doing so either subtly (without being too explicit about their views) or covertly (away from the gaze of prison staff, whenever possible). They report that the relative lack of supervision by both the prison and the volunteer organization has occasionally left them in the extremely rare position of having a degree of autonomy with their students, at least for a time. But such reports are extremely rare—both because such lack of surveillance is rare, and because most volunteers do not seem drawn to such work. Part of what these interviews teach us, then, is that prisons tend to push yoga and meditation in an apolitical direction. But simultaneously, we also see that even before they entered the prison, the majority of interviewees simply did not see teaching yoga and meditation in prisons as a political endeavor. In all but four of thirty-six interviews, social justice or political activism were given very little mention as priorities that motivated prison work. One possibility, therefore, is that prison makes yoga and meditation apolitical, and serves to defang the radical politics that may accompany these practices. But another possibility, explored in Chapter 7, and confirmed here by some respondents, is that yoga and meditation are already so depoliticized that most practitioners don't see them as having political relevance to begin with. Even politically determined spaces such as prisons seem to draw a preponderance of yogis and meditators with apolitical attitudes, already socialized to decouple these practices from anything overtly political. The largely white, middle-class makeup of most prison volunteer organizations, along with their relative disengagement from system-impacted communities and leadership, underscores this.

SECTION IV
REVOLUTIONARY EXPERIMENTS

9
Yogic Philosophy, Nonviolence, and Resistance in a Women's Prison

With the coauthorship of Reighlen Jordan and Maitra

In the summer of 2016, I joined a group of volunteer yoga teachers at an incarceration facility for women in California.[1] Though I am not certified to teach *āsana* (physical or postural yoga), I have a long-standing personal practice, and a deep familiarity with yogic philosophy as part of my scholarly career. After a lengthy conversation, Rachel, the program's founder, invited me to join the group of volunteers, facilitating my smooth entry into the prison. Several months later, I was approved to obtain an identity card which allowed me to walk around the prison grounds unescorted, to escort other volunteers, or informally facilitate groups of incarcerated persons.[2] A few months later, several of the incarcerated yoga students approached me. They wanted to start an "inmate-led self-help study group" on yogic principles and virtues, and asked if I would like to join in and facilitate the group. They planned to meet informally every week after the yoga class ended, but prison rules dictated that they could only meet if a volunteer was present. Serenity Jones was the leader of this group; she had written a proposal outlining how yogic principles and ideas could assist these women in their journey. I immediately agreed to facilitate, which would involve staying an extra hour after the *āsana* portion of class ended. This chapter is a collaborative endeavor, coauthored with two formerly incarcerated women who attended the group during that time. Although much of the chapter is written from my perspective as a volunteer, my coauthors have written large sections in their own voices, and provided their perspective of studying yogic philosophy while incarcerated.[3]

A typical morning begins with the *āsana* portion of yoga class around 8:45 or 9 am. A fellow volunteer and I co-teach the class for about ninety minutes, to a group of anywhere between ten to thirty women of varying ages and races. No staff members are present. We lead the class through a sequence of poses—typically one of us instructs, while the other models the poses, or walks around the room offering individualized attention to certain students, via modifications or adjustments. We end the class by leading students in

Freedom Inside?. Farah Godrej, Oxford University Press. © Oxford University Press 2022.
DOI: 10.1093/oso/9780190070083.003.0009

chanting "Om" three times, followed by greeting each other with the traditional "namaste." Before we break up, I quietly remind everyone that our yoga class is to be immediately followed by our study group. Those who want to stay should keep their mats, I say, and we will reconvene in a circle. The silence pools for a few moments as everyone sits still in the darkness. I am always privately glad when we can preserve the stillness for a few extra moments.

Within moments, the lights go on, and the room starts buzzing as everyone gets up to clear away their mats, put their props away, put their shoes back on, and collect their belongings on their way out. A few incarcerated leaders assume their usual roles in stacking the props neatly in the storage area. During this time, several students come up to thank us for teaching, a few to say a quick "hi" or "bye," others to give an update on their lives, and some to report changes in their mental or physical states. Some approach us to ask about a particular pose they had trouble with, to ask for help in dealing with specific injuries, or recommendations for practicing on their own. Like the beginning of class, this is also a time for friendly chit-chat and catching up, filled with expressions of gratitude, quick waves, and calls of "See you next time!"

During this time, we also transition from the physical *āsana* class to the study group, which is themed around nonviolence. The leaders of the group—Serenity, Reighlen, and Maitra—set up their mats in a circular formation and prepare their materials, while my fellow volunteer and I wrap up all the post-class logistics: locking up the props closet, discussing any future schedule changes with our sponsor, and so on. Finally, having completed these formalities, I join the group sitting on yoga mats on the floor.

Phase I: Rehabilitation through Yogic Nonviolence

At first glance, the proposal for the group is fully in line with the prison's messaging. Although it does not directly mention rehabilitation, it casts the purpose of the group as "address[ing] personal character defects, personality traits or behaviors that need changing in order to be a whole, healed and healthy person." It provides examples of intention-setting, such as "My focus remains on positivity, productivity, and good health." It purports to engage in "self-work" and "goal-setting" with a focus on "improving personality characteristics" through affirmations such as "I will be slow to anger"; changing habits such as "I will be on time" or "I will not overeat"; making intentional longer-term choices such as "I will attend one self-help group this month"; and eventually on "life-direction goals" such as "when I am released, I will go to court to gain custody of my child." As such, it seems to appeal to the dominant logic that circulates within the prison, assuming that everyone is incarcerated due to character flaws or criminogenic tendencies that require self-improvement. However, I later find out that for some of the group leaders, this proposal was something of a performance. Reighlen, one of the group's co-founders, tells me, "Everyone knows what you have to say to the prison administration to get a program going. We all know 'rehabilitation' is just the excuse they need to keep us all locked in here. But we also know what we have to say in order to get out." As we will see, Reighlen's analysis of how rehabilitation works in prison is astute.

The group as conceived by its leaders is part self-help, part group therapy, part yogic philosophy. The leaders define yogic nonviolence as "non-injury and non-harming toward self and others." They have composed a handout based on their research, in which they explain key yogic principles. They typically kick off class by reading from this handout, emphasizing certain concepts and ideas, throwing out questions, and opening the floor to discussion. Questions might range from "Can you identify how you got to thinking of yourself in a certain way?" to "What is our *sankalpa* (intention) for this week?" or "How can we stay grounded in our own highest truth, especially when things are not going well in here?" Participants offer suggestions for yogic practices such as becoming aware of one's thought-stream, learning how to breathe in difficult situations, cultivating yogic virtues such as *muditā* ("friendliness toward the joyful") and learning to witness one's own repetitive, self-destructive thought patterns. The discussions inevitably turn personal. Women use the opportunity to relate yogic concepts to their own lives, with an emphasis on coping with the many challenges of prison life. Occasionally they relay stories of their pre-prison lives, families, children, jobs, and so forth. But for the most part, the group becomes about coping with prison life through yogic principles, while improving and transforming oneself.

In the first few months of facilitating, I notice two—possibly contradictory—patterns at work. On the one hand, the discussions involve much talk of accepting responsibility for rehabilitation and accepting the consequences for "bad choices" that landed one in prison. This language echoes what they are told by the prison: that incarcerated persons are "criminals" who deserve their incarceration. Women talk about having only themselves to blame for where they are. The theme of prison as "an incredible growth opportunity" comes up often: Prison is the "best thing that happened to me," many of the women say. Some report trying to "reframe" their prison term as an opportunity to get free education, without the pressure of feeding anyone, paying bills, or parenting. Yogic practice becomes a further opportunity for self-improvement through "becoming more aware of thought patterns," "learning to develop better habits," "learning to be less reactive," and so on.

On the other hand, the group leaders subtly emphasize themes that resist the logic of the prison. They emphasize learning to forgive themselves through self-acceptance and self-compassion, despite the labels the external world puts on them. They insist on not identifying with negative self-talk or self-image, and refusing to punish themselves despite being punished by society. They also refuse to "believe the labels, faults, imperfections and judgments that society puts on us." Instead, they focus on seeing the divine within themselves, seeing their highest Self as strong, powerful, and innately good. Many times, Reighlen says, "I refuse to be defined by the worst thing I have ever done." "Seeing the beauty in ourselves" also becomes a common theme, as does developing equanimity, detachment, and compassion in the face of the terrible treatment they receive and witness in prison. The group discussions often cohere around themes of supporting and caring for one another in solidarity to withstand the brutality of incarceration. Concepts such self-forgiveness and overcoming negative self-talk often have a subversive subtext. The discussions of self-care take on an indirectly political tone—that is, even though no one ever directly discusses mass incarceration or the prison-industrial complex, the questions being raised and the ensuing discussions resist the messaging of the system that incarcerates them. As Reighlen states, "There are all kinds of expectations set up for us about who we're supposed to be, and so our group is really about not allowing those to dictate to us. . . . it's about letting go of other people's labelings of who we are. We are not who they say we are. We have to figure out who we are for ourselves."

During this period, I find myself enthused by, yet also concerned about, the self-care emphasis of the group. Feminists like Angela Davis and Audre Lorde have reminded us that self-care can be a political act: Simply taking care of oneself, when considered disposable, unworthy or subhuman, can be an act of resistance. Even talking about such ideas in prison can be a form of resistance. To take care of the self is to treasure the self, to insist on one's self-worth, and to make time for work on the self. This could be construed as a somewhat political act for these women who are otherwise labeled as criminals, inherently flawed, and unworthy of care. But I was uncomfortable with the individualized emphasis of this self-care—there didn't seem to be much discussion of the inequitable social and economic structures which tended to constrain people's choices. Was this group in danger of reaffirming the fiction that improving *oneself* alone somehow leads to improving society? As ever, I worried that yogic philosophy and practice would remain a "band-aid" that would allow incarcerated women to cope, all the while seeing their fate as solely the result of their individual actions. I began to contemplate whether— and how—I might intervene, by subtly shifting the tenor of the discussions. Could I introduce a space for discussion of structural or political issues, and could these discussions legitimately complement the goals that the women had for their own class?

Phase 2: Creating Space for Structural, Political Commentary

From my volunteer interviewees in Chapter 8, I had learned that yogic or meditative practice could be combined with discussion about larger social, economic, and political structures that feed into incarceration. And at least some of my formerly incarcerated interviewees in Chapter 5 had insisted that volunteers needed to combine yoga or meditation with critical inquiry, challenging dominant preconceptions and encouraging radical political action. That said, I had few concrete models for such work. One volunteer respondent, Claire, had offered the following guidelines for how discussions of accountability and ownership may occur within the context of—rather than in detachment from—discussions of systemic or social harm:

> We're working in the 200% reality. The 100% reality is that you [the incarcerated person] caused harm. The other 100% is that you also were nested in a system that you had no control over. And it wasn't your fault, what happened to you wasn't fair. We actually care more about what's going on when we acknowledge that both of these things are true. When we overemphasize your responsibility, the community is taking less responsibility. . . . It's not that your violence is the issue. Your violence was a response to something that was the real issue. So [we can ask], "*what could have been the injustice that my family experienced, that I feel and that I acted on, and that I don't need to carry as my fault?*" The radical experience here might be that you get to choose what you personally feel ready for: What feels true in your ownership? And then we cheer you on. Rather than, "*You need to hold yourself fully accountable.*" [And finally] "*How do I want to take care of myself and stay alive in a world that seems to cause me a lot of harm?*" If anything's possible in a prison in terms of liberation work, I feel like it's that.

With this in mind, I began, cautiously yet intentionally, to offer suggestions for discussion. This led to a second phase of the yogic philosophy group, which began after about three months of my attendance. This phase was initially launched by a change in leadership, as one of the group founders was released, and a new cohort of leaders took over. Meanwhile, I began to experiment with interjecting a more critical, challenging tone into my conversations, to explore whether yogic practices could have more political effects.

During this phase, I proceeded with caution, testing the waters by raising questions and only continuing if I sensed interest. When I sensed such interest, I began to gently interrogate the prison's messaging. I raised questions about the structural inequities that may have landed the women in prison, and asked them to contemplate these issues. I asked whether they felt that their incarceration was justified, and whether they felt that they bore the full responsibility for it. I asked them whether they thought "rehabilitation" was a legitimate goal, and what the concept meant to them. And, I asked those who seemed most interested to respond to some of these questions in writing, turning the class into a collaborative endeavor between myself and incarcerated colleagues.

Some of the women were extremely responsive to my suggestions, but only a few from the leadership group were truly galvanized by them. I found that my interrogation of the rehabilitative model did not necessarily "land" with all of my interlocutors. Some expressed enthusiasm for such issues, but others remained silent and participated only in the less controversial aspects of the conversation. It became clear that the explicitly political questions I tried to introduce did not resonate with every member of the group, and perhaps even induced discomfort in some, for whom "doing time" entailed keeping one's head down and not causing trouble. Rather than changing the direction of the class, I encouraged the two group leaders to take the class in the direction they chose, while inviting those who were interested to offer written and verbal reflections privately. The leaders continued to set the agenda from their own concerns about prison life, while incorporating my suggestions for considering political and structural issues. I made sure to hang back and listen, deferring to what the group leaders found important, and what struck them as worthy of being addressed. In their written reflections, they responded with vigor to my provocations, occasionally integrating these issues into their group work.

Phase 3: Yoga as Transformative and Not Simply Ameliorative

Today, a day like any other in the spring of 2018, the group consists of the two incarcerated leaders, four or five other incarcerated participants, and myself. It has now been about nine months since our group began, and in the interim,

I have started to notice a shift in the tenor of the group. Today's session exemplifies this shift, as group leaders foster discussions of the systemic inequities in society, which feed into mass incarceration. The class typically opens with a quote, a story, or a passage from a yogic text to launch the discussion. Today, Reighlen says, "I want to share this great story that I heard the other day." She proceeds to tell the story of a "little person" incarcerated repeatedly at this facility:

> She did really great while she was in here, because she kept going to all this programming. But every time she got released, she kept showing up here again. Finally, one of the officers asked her, "*You're doing so great in here, why do you keep coming back?*" and she told the officer that she had to take a bus to go check in with her parole officer because she didn't have a car. And she kept missing the bus because the bus drivers couldn't see her and would drive right by the stop!

The story brings forth exclamatory gasps from the rest. I wonder aloud what the story teaches us. Maitra, who has recently become more vocal and stepped into a leadership role, connects the story to an article I had recently shared, in which the author had compared prisons to corporations. "An incarcerated person is like a customer or a client," she says. "We consume goods and services at taxpayer expense. So, you could say that we are like the repeat clients of this corporation, they always want us to keep coming back." I am momentarily stunned by the aptness of the analogy, and the women even giggle among themselves at this. "They have to make everyone believe that we all keep coming back here because we're such bad people," Reighlen says. "But it's really because their jobs depend on it, and the whole system works to make it so that people end up back here no matter how hard they try."

I ask the women to elaborate and share further. Reighlen speaks of the prison penpal she has been corresponding with: "He comes from a racial minority group, he grew up poor, then he went into the marines. But he had PTSD from everything that happened, and then he did something that caused him to end up in prison. All of our stories are the same: We ended up in here because we needed help. Why couldn't we have gotten the help we needed instead of getting locked up here? It's job security for the guards, we all know that." After a brief pause, she continues, "If I had gotten the help I needed, I wouldn't be here. It's true that I've used prison as a time for self-growth and improvement, but why did I have to be locked away for that to happen? It's just that we all grew up in different circumstances and had different things happen to us, that caused us to make bad choices. People are in here because of society."

Nine months into the class, the focus has shifted away from simply discussing strategies for individual growth and self-improvement. Now, the leaders are occasionally addressing the ways that inequity accounts for incarceration. Along with this critical examination of social and economic structures, some are also eager to re-examine the concepts of individual responsibility and rehabilitation. "Every 'rehabilitation' program is just here to make sure that we all accept responsibility for our crime," Reighlen insists, adding the scare quotes when she speaks. "We get these rote messages from all the rehabilitative programming we take in prison. It's really easy to just internalize the messages instead of thinking beyond them for ourselves."

But not everyone in prison accepts the power of "rehabilitative" logic. Reighlen tells us the story of a restorative justice group at this facility. "This group was all about recognizing how you hurt your victims, but when women who had attacked their abusive husbands had questions about what got them there in the first place, no one really had answers to those questions, and people started to leave the class." She offers another story: "My roommate got twenty-eight years for attempted murder of her abusive husband who was a cop. She didn't do it, she only said she *wanted to kill him,* . . . but of course the system protects its own, and the only reason she's here is that her husband's a cop. Meanwhile, he's out there, alive and well in the world. She comes up for parole every year, but she refuses to admit responsibility for her crime, because she didn't do it. She keeps getting told that she won't parole until she accepts responsibility."

These excerpts show us how mass incarceration relies on ensuring that its targets are acculturated to accept their own responsibility. But more crucially, they show us that those who refuse to accept this logic often do so at great cost, because parole or other forms of early release are predicated on acceptance of this responsibility. And, by sharing these stories with each other, the women also artfully engage in resistance against such logic, reminding everyone of the social and systemic causes of what often gets labeled as crime.

As these political conversations deepen, I ask the group leaders to consider whether yoga—and yogic principles more specifically—can encourage incarcerated people to be more accepting of personal responsibility, at the cost of being critical and resistant toward the system that incarcerates them. Below is one excerpt from a reflective essay by Reighlen:

> For me, the term "rehabilitate" tells me that I am to be restored to a previous state. Like my crime was a random act, not stemming from years of preparation. Who I was before incarceration is NOT who I want to be when I leave, so what are they rehabilitating or restoring? . . . I have taken 95% of the rehabilitation programs offered

to female prisoners and they all have a lot in common: Take responsibility, control your actions, and do not break the rules is pretty much the gist of their content. Like being a criminal is a personal choice we make one morning while brushing our teeth. None of the groups really take a deeper aim to promote true change. The ladies I see every day are hurt and broken down so much, they will believe anything. So they walk into these groups for change, and they leave with a band-aid.

Yes, I would agree that these groups aim to control us. Give us time off for taking the groups, time off for being robots that comply with any rule they make up. And we do it, we comply so that we can have the time off and go home sooner, but where does the cycle heal? How can we achieve true healing? . . . I believe yoga and meditation, as it is currently structured in the prison system falls directly under the "rehabilitation" initiative. . . . I feel like having yoga is only going to teach us as inmates how to deal with our circumstances, not improve them. The many injustices happening everyday are shadowed by the illusion of yoga classes. Naturally, the prison system will promote fundraising, the "happy" groups they offer, the few success stories that occur. But they cover up staff suicide, inmate murder, inmate mental health needs, the abuse of power that is displayed daily. . . . *Yoga can be shallowly practiced and runs the risk of feeding into the illusion* [emphasis added]. I've seen this before in class. The system has brainwashed people so deeply, they believe the prison system is here to help. Stockholm syndrome at its finest. In this case yoga becomes an aspirin, just lifting the pain temporarily, maybe just long enough to make it to dinner. . . . Without a class like [this,] yoga remains a band-aid.

Similarly, Maitra writes:

I have a problem with the word "rehabilitate." According to Webster's II, it means to "restore to a former state." This implies that our downfall happened when we committed our crimes and that the goal is to restore us to what we were before that time. The fact is, most of us were broken before we committed our crimes, so what will "rehabilitation" accomplish? I prefer the word "transformation" because I feel that is what needs to happen. To me, the language of rehabilitation means responsibility, but *a hobbled sort of responsibility* [emphasis added], that doesn't involve empowerment to make real choices. It's just "program or else," "lock in or else," "pick up your medication or else." What kind of a choice is that? Luckily, we have some choices that we can make, and yoga is one of them. In that sense, yoga can be a positive force for change of course, once you change yourself on the inside. The next logical step that occurs to you is to change the world around you. That is a frightening prospect for administrators, who would prefer that we stop at the development of personal "coping skills" that don't threaten the system they have put in place.

In another exchange, Maitra notes, "I've only ever done one bad thing in my life, I never did anything before that, I've never done anything after that, and I'll never do anything like that again. But for the rest of my life, I'll be labeled as an offender, and this one bad thing I did will define me for the rest of my life. . . . Rehabilitation makes no sense unless they actually believe we *can* be rehabilitated. But there doesn't seem to be any point to it, because we're going to be forever suspect, all the judges, prosecutors, and lawyers who are involved in mass incarceration talk about it as 'keeping the public safe.' . . . How does it help to make us forever suspect?"

Through these exchanges, the group leaders were increasingly rejecting the notion that "rehabilitation" was designed to improve a flawed individual, or that incarceration was the result of personality flaws, negative traits, or criminogenic tendencies. Maitra immediately identifies the contradiction at the heart of incarceration: It claims to be "rehabilitative," but legalized discrimination against ex-offenders ensures that they are not considered capable of being truly rehabilitated. Both Maitra and Reighlen have astutely argued that mass incarceration relies on the reproduction of public sentiment in which both the public and incarceration officials must accept the logic that only chronically "bad" people end up in prison. Rejecting this narrative, they reveal that incarceration is often the result of a few incidents or bad decisions, sometimes based on what Reighlen calls "a lifetime" of preparation through repeated disadvantage. Maitra also skillfully questions the kind of "responsibility" that accompanies the prison's rehabilitative logic, calling it "hobbled" and devoid of any real choice. She contrasts this with the more meaningful choice entailed in using yoga to direct individual self-improvement toward larger systemic change, which she views as threatening to those in power.

In a subsequent class where we continue in-depth discussions of these issues, Maitra also demonstrates a concern with the "shallow" teaching of yoga, both in prison and on the outside. "Well, it depends on how these practices are being taught," Maitra says. "Are they being taught in a kind of shallow, superficial way? But if they're being taught in a deep way, like we're doing here, then we have to talk about things like right action, and right speech, and ethics and justice." In a written essay, she elaborates:

> There is something missing from mindfulness when it is separated from ethical precepts such as those laid out by the Buddha. Meditation, when broken down into its component parts, consists of concentration and awareness, or mindfulness. But, the Buddha stressed that we must cultivate *right* mindfulness and *right* concentration [emphasis in original]. Otherwise our awareness may become the awareness of the assassin and our concentration the concentration of the burglar.

In another essay, she explores the same issue with respect to yogic practices:

> People will likely tire of the McYoga approach, disillusioned by its promise of
> benefits that are both superficial and ephemeral, and its lack of deeper meaning....
> Some may have seen issues of *Yoga Journal* and perused its articles, all the while
> being bombarded by images of youth, whiteness, and thinness. Articles on medita-
> tion, spirituality, and ethics are book-ended by advertisements for yoga mats, cute
> yoga clothes, essential oils, jewelry, and expensive yoga retreats. Very few take it
> upon themselves to penetrate this veil of consumerism, to the deeper teachings of
> yogic philosophy.

The conversations we have and written materials we exchange during this
period all suggest a path toward deepening our engagement with these
questions. Over time, I start to ask my collaborators whether the shallow or
purely ameliorative forms of yoga they have identified are the only option
for incarcerated persons. Can yoga serve as anything other than a shallow
practice, a band-aid or a coping mechanism? Is there some other way in
which these practices can be interpreted in the incarceration environment?
I am pleasantly surprised by the conviction with which I see them respond
in no uncertain terms: Having acknowledged that yoga *can* make people
passive or docile in the face of injustice, they insist that *their* interpretations of yogic practice are anything but compliant or quietist. Rather, these
women interpret yogic principles as active resistance to injustice, often
invoking Gandhi, Martin Luther King Jr., or Thich Nhat Hanh. They insist
on interpreting yogic philosophy as a tool for both personal and social/po-
litical transformation.

Phase 4: Yoga as a Tool for Political Transformation

Later that same spring, group leaders raise the issue of interpreting nonviolence in a particular way: acting when necessary in the face of injustice, instead of remaining silent or passive. Reighlen opens discussion one day by
asking, "How [can we] remain calm in the face of injustice but also act when
we need to? How can we use the principles of yoga without numbing out to
everything that's happening?" This day's session stands out as one in which
the women were most vocal against passivity or quietism as the purpose of
yoga or meditation. Many of them insist that remaining calm does not mean
being passive in the face of chaos or injustice. "Being a doormat is not being
nonviolent toward yourself," one woman emphasizes. Another woman, a lifer,

tells of how she joined a group of incarcerated women in taking the prison system to court in order to have their Wiccan religion recognized: "We have to be warriors too," she insists. "Knowing when to speak is a really important skill," Reighlen notes. "I know I sometimes stay silent in the face of injustice. It's easy to be passive in the face of all this oppression. I recently read this quote by MLK: '*In the end, we will remember not the words of our enemies, but the silence of our friends.*'"

Another session soon after begins with the distribution of a few photocopied pages from Nicolai Bachman's *The Path of the Yoga Sutras: A Practical Guide to the Core of Yoga*. Reighlen begins by reading a quote from Gandhi, which serves as the epigraph at the beginning of the chapter she is presenting. As Reighlen continues reading, the group flags a passage on the injunction against wrong action resulting in suffering and ignorance. "But what about inaction?" Maitra insists, "Isn't that as important to avoid as wrong action?" Without having read much of Gandhi beyond these few pages, Maitra instinctively gravitates to the importance of action in the face of injustice as central to nonviolence. In a written essay, she later asserts,

Yoga, like Buddhism is nondualistic—it values oneness. That can be taken to mean that if one of us suffers, we all suffer. . . . In both, there is the concept of service. Mahayana Buddhists take a *bodhisattva* vow, and likewise there is *karma-yoga* for yogis. This implies we have concern for others' suffering. It seems reasonable that the logical conclusion is to not only address suffering, but to take action to prevent it, and to do so for as many people as possible, which points one in the direction of political activism. You don't need to abandon equanimity, or to hate those who oppose you, but like MLK, you may hate what they stand for . . . perhaps we are so worried about alienating anyone that we have become completely apolitical?

Because the class is still in an informal, drop-in format, there is little consistency in attendance. Some participants attend once or twice, a few others attend consistently, and the two group leaders are the most regular and consistent attendees. Nonetheless, the group continues to meet regularly through the spring and summer of that year, and the leaders become more committed to exploring the convergence between yogic philosophy and nonviolence. Our conversations and written collaborations continue to take on more political overtones, as the leaders respond to these issues with greater frequency and enthusiasm in their written work. Meanwhile, they also take more initiative to raise political issues during group discussions.

Phase 5: Yoga as Skill in Action

One class session stands out as a striking example of this shift in tenor. Maitra has chosen an article from *Yoga Journal* to kick off the discussion on this day, handing out photocopies to everyone, and reading aloud from it. At first, the article seems as though it repeats the narrative of finding peace within by not reacting to perceived injustice, disagreement, or ill-treatment. But Maitra has clearly put some thought into the choice of this article. I immediately see that the article's central question is a "spiritual conundrum: How do you not succumb to outrage and alienation, yet keep your passion and motivation to fight for justice and social good? . . . How do you let go of anger, bitterness, and blame while at the same time standing up for what you believe to be right?" This question generates a great deal of nodding, affirmation, and enthusiastic discussion.

As Maitra continues reading aloud, the focus of the article shifts to the practice of "reconciliation." Some of the women ask whether reconciliation means just accepting whatever happens, and Maitra says, "But wait! It's not what you think." She reads on:

> When you practice reconciliation, you are reconciling yourself to the truth that in this moment there are painful differences or polarities. [R]econciliation practice is . . . to be reconciled with this moment just as it is. It doesn't involve resignation or defeat. [It] does not mean you have to forsake passionately advocating for what you believe to be right.[4]

This passage generates much enthusiastic discussion. Many of the women insist that accepting something "doesn't mean not acting for change." Another woman notes emphatically, "Being reconciled doesn't mean doing nothing, it just means acting from a place of love and compassion." Maitra responds by reading the following line aloud from the article: "Being shut down by anger or hate is not an effective position for working toward change." This leads to a discussion of the difference between positive, change-driven actions that are skillful, as against unskillful ones that are driven by negative emotions like anger or hate.

One of the women asks for clarification: "What exactly do we mean by skillful behavior?" Maitra tells a story to illustrate that reacting with anger to an unjust situation is never productive or skillful. "I was walking on the yard minding my own business, and this female officer decided to harass me, she searched my bag, she asked me where I was going, why I was going there, why I had this stuff in my bag . . . she basically just gave me a really hard time.

I didn't react at all, and another officer walked by to ask her how she was doing, and she said, '*Oh, I'm bored.*' So she basically admitted that she was harassing me out of boredom. But I made sure not to react. I always regret it when I react to something with anger, but I never regret it later when I react with calm. Instead of reacting in the moment, I use 602 forms[5] [inmate grievance forms] to make complaints or requests after the fact, using my writing skills."

Reighlen shares a similar story of being harassed by an officer, which she later elaborates on in writing:

> I was really close to my dad and he was very ill. The day he died, I got called into speak to one of the Lieutenants. I knew in my heart why I was being called in. My whole world stopped. . . . I walked in a daze to the Lieutenant's office so he could "*make sure I was ok.*" (Ha, a phony protocol designed to reassure prisoners' families that we are being "cared for.") When I got to the door of the Lieutenant's office, I was met by another officer on a power trip. . . . Who was I to need to see the Lieutenant?? he demanded. He made me repeat who I was multiple times, reminding the world and everyone watching that I was indeed an inmate. Say it, he repeated. I'm an inmate, I repeated. He smiled while he belittled and degraded my essence.
>
> That night could have gone two ways. The first is the most common in prison. I could have let my emotions win, got defensive, express[ed] my right to be there, defend[ed] my position. This would have propelled him even further, giving him ammunition to degrade me further, and grounds to do so—my disobedience. I could have done what was an acquired instinct, to punch him in the face. Oh, everything inside of me just wanted to sock him really good, which would have earned me more charges and a longer prison term, more time to endure the power differential between us and the guards.
>
> Before that night, I didn't even know I had another option inside of me. I had my *sankalpa*, I had my breath. I cultivated every principle I practiced on the mat in that moment. Every time he spoke, I breathed in and breathed out. My whole body was cold and covered in chills. I breathed. He degraded me and I breathed. He tried his hardest to disrupt my sense of self. But I breathed. In that one instant I chose to breathe rather than to let my reactions take over and give him what he deserved, a black eye that would ultimately hurt only me. I breathed in and out so much I actually started to let compassion for him absorb inside me. I held on to God inside me and the awareness I have found to be eternal. When he was done I walked away. And in that moment, I discovered why I love yoga.

In these conversations and written collaborations, Reighlen and Maitra describe forms of nonreactivity and acceptance that do not equate to docility, quietism, or inaction. Rather, they show that skillful nonreaction to injustice in the moment is fully compatible with advocacy and pursuit of justice in the long term. In sharing these stories, the women are not counseling each other to develop compliance or acceptance toward the system that incarcerates them. Rather, they model forms of skillful, yogic action without being side-tracked by unproductive emotions. "Anger doesn't really help you act," Maitra insists. "To truly act to transform something, you have to be free of anger, because anger just makes you stuck. . . . Accepting something in the moment doesn't mean accepting that it's always going to be this way."

Maitra also insists that freedom from negative emotions is liberating, rather than confining or restricting. She is vocal about how free and empowered she feels because she has controlled her reactivity and nothing can touch her:

> When I was on the outside, I was a really different person: I identified a lot with material things, I had a lot of stuff, and it really mattered to me. As Americans we really identify with our material possessions, we are pressured to be achievers. But now I have almost nothing, and literally nothing can touch me. I am completely free. Besides that, I used to get angry very easily. Yoga and meditation have allowed me to calm my anger, but that doesn't mean that I don't see things for what they are or cannot act when it's necessary. If anything, these practices have given me the tools to be able to act. I have never felt so empowered and so liberated in my life.

My interlocutors also insist, "There is a difference between simply using yoga and meditation to relax, to become passive, to just feel better about your situation, and using it to meet challenge in a constructive way." Reighlen provides the example of warrior II, a yoga pose in which the front knee is bent to 90 degrees, the back leg is straight and strong, and the arms are held out straight and parallel to the ground. Many such poses require standing in discomfort for quite some time. "I remember one of the yoga teachers giving us instructions about holding warrior II one day, and she talked about recognizing your discomfort, but then using that discomfort to meet challenge, by developing your own knowledge. We're not just using yoga or mindfulness to accept the discomfort, but to take that and to have clearer vision, more defined vision, to see things for what they are and to be able to meet challenges head-on."

Reighlen further distinguishes between being compliant toward an officer who is treating you badly, and treating them with compassion. "Just being compliant means you're not really seeing the situation as it is, to think about what are the reasons that person is allowed to treat you that way. Whereas if you can have love and compassion for that officer, you can also have the clear vision to think about what allowed that to happen." Here, Reighlen demonstrates that nonreactive compassion allows one to step back from a situation and view it within the overall context of structural injustice. In this way, one can sharpen one's vision in order to see the incident—an officer treating an incarcerated person badly—as more than just isolated or individualized, but rather as part of a systemic whole.

Reighlen also insists that as a result of such practices, one's relationship with others and the world around us might become more—rather than less—antagonistic. "In fact, sometimes these practices make things harder because you become more aware." What do you mean? I ask. "Well," she says, "before I started practicing yoga, I would numb out. I spent so much of my life running from my emotions and disconnecting from my body and mind. Eventually I became an unemotional zombie. I spent over a decade of my life not crying. Even when I found myself on the bus, shackled and headed toward prison, I couldn't find emotion within myself. I was numb without the help of drugs. Now I'm more aware of the pain. Yoga and meditation make you feel your feelings more clearly. You can't numb out any more, and you have to confront what's going on within you and around you."

Similarly, Maitra asserts that engaging in yogic practices "doesn't mean you'll never have conflict. Your life's not going to be 100% perfect, and everyone's not going to love you. *It's not the job of these practices to erase conflict, but rather to give you tools to work with them* [emphasis added]. . . . I think that any yoga instructor worth her salt recognizes that the practice is more than just exercise and relaxation techniques, at least I would hope so." In this conversation, both Reighlen and Maitra seem to agree that yogic and meditative practice result in the very antithesis of docility, compliance, or acceptance. Rather, in making one more aware of one's internal state, they offer resources to remain attentive to both the inner and outer world. As Maitra reminds us, they do not *suppress* conflict—rather, they make it possible to become aware of negative emotions and situations, while navigating them skillfully.

Interestingly, even as our conversations became more critical and political, I found that my interlocutors continued to embrace the language of yogic and meditative practice as self-improvement and self-enhancement. But just like my respondents in Chapter 5, they embraced this self-improvement as a crucial aspect of resistance. "We can refuse to accept what the prison tells us," Reighlen notes, "but we can also strive to be something other than what we are. I'm not letting this prison and this experience of being imprisoned define me. We have all these false expectations put on us here, and we learn conformity. So one of the things that meditation had helped me with is not accepting other people's messages about who I am; to really come to my own understanding of my identity instead of allowing others to have any influence on that."

"I took prison as an opportunity," Reighlen emphasizes. "Here, we have no control over anything, you're told when to eat, when to sleep, when to shower, and when to shit. . . . Maybe they keep us dependent and out of control here on purpose, maybe they make it easy here so that it's harder for us to adjust to the difficulties of life on the streets. . . . It's so easy to get institutionalized in this place. . . . But I took this as an opportunity to get to know myself without all the labels, without all the roles and responsibilities that I would have on the outside." In this way, Reighlen reframes yogic and meditative practice as a way to resist the institutionalization fostered by prison life through "working on myself, improving myself and getting to know myself." For some of these women, yogic self-enhancement and self-improvement can be opportunities for resisting the effects of incarceration on their self-understanding and identity. For Reighlen, the equanimity gained from this perspective is emancipatory: Reframing prison as an opportunity for growth is consistent with a resistant position toward incarceration.

In one memorable conversation, Maitra shares, "On a mundane level I guess I was meant to come here to pay for my crime. But on a spiritual level, I came here because I was meant to witness suffering. It's like this huge big secret, what goes on inside prisons. And I would never have known had I not come here." Reighlen agrees vigorously: "Coming here has changed the entire scope of my life. I actually can't imagine not having been here, it changed what I knew about our society." I ask both women if they knew anything about mass incarceration before arriving at the prison. Maitra: "Yes, but I never thought it could happen to me, it was always something that happened to someone else." Reighlen agrees: "It gives me compassion for all the other people out there who are ignorant about it, just like I was ignorant before. I knew absolutely nothing, and now it's changed my life to know all this. It's been this amazing opportunity to figure myself out, but also to see cruelty, incompetence, and negligence firsthand, and to see how people's hope and drive is completely crushed and lost."

Perhaps the most tangible political effect of the group is the creation of community and solidarity among these women. In a prison where, by the women's own admission, there had historically been almost no political action of any kind ("we've never had hunger strikes, protests or anything like that here"), our small group increasingly bands together not simply to express empathy, but to confront difficult issues together, and engage in collective discussion and resistance. Reighlen reports recent moments of solidarity in which the women have started questioning the racialized aspects of mass incarceration, building solidarity with each other around the concept of an oppressed class instead of emphasizing race divisions within prison. "Isn't that precisely what the prison doesn't want us to do?" she asks. "They want to divide us against each other so that we fight and they can justify their jobs. Are we resisting that when we build community and stay empathetic toward one another and refuse to fight with each other?"

In a written essay, Reighlen insists that when accompanied by groups like this, which include explicit discussions of structural injustice, yoga can awaken political action rather than passivity.

> Bringing an element of awareness through yoga, maybe it will awaken the fight inside them that has been suppressed by society. Maybe it will lift the cloud of lies we've been fed, and that most of us believe. But this is contingent on how the inmate practices. We need yoga to become a tool that backfires on the system. I think the more we educate people, the less likely they will continue to be brainwashed. The *āsana* portion gives people a chance to look within themselves, but then what? What do they do with it? *Without a class like this, yoga remains a band-aid* [emphasis added]. By illuminating truth, through groups like this, maybe we can reverse the illusion of yoga to "rehabilitate," and [instead] use it for true change. Allowing yoga to remain just a coping mechanism, a tool to make prison look like a better place—that would contradict yogic nonviolence. Educating people on how inaction is harming may make them take action. I feel that we need to manipulate their illusion of the system to fight injustice—and that's yogic nonviolence.

In an essay titled "What Are We Accomplishing?" Maitra offers a pointed critique of the retributive logic underlying the entire enterprise of imprisonment, and suggests that yogic and meditative practices can illuminate the futility of such retributive incarceration:

> What does rotting in a prison cell year after year have to do with ending the suffering of the victims, assuming that the crime has produced victims? What is the point of burdening a largely indigent population with restitution payments, the majority of which the victims will never see? Why ask taxpayers to contribute hard-earned tax dollars in return for the illusion of safety provided by "border walls" separating our prison cities from them? How does police violence in the form of unprovoked tackling, kicking, shooting, punching, chokeholds, and high voltage tasering discourage violence in others? How is the public really protected when the ways in which felons may be legally employed is severely limited? How does the enforcement of additional ninety-day prison sentences for violations of silly rules within prison (hanging curtains, missing an appointment, not picking up medication on

time) foster a respect for the law? The pointlessness of these practices can only occur to the spiritually aware person, not the person who dwells in *avidyā* [Sanskrit for ignorance]. Time will tell whether spiritual practices such as yoga or meditation will resonate with people in the long term and pierce this veil. Otherwise, we may continue to be persuaded by seemingly logical arguments that encourage and perpetuate injustice.

For Maitra, yoga and meditation, rather than fostering acceptance of an unjust status quo, may allow practitioners to "pierce the veil" that keeps the very logic of mass incarceration in place, both for its victims and for the public.

Epilogue

I eventually sent a draft of this chapter to Serenity, the group's founder, who had been released long before the group took its political turn. The draft provided Serenity with her first real update on what had happened to the group she founded after she left the prison, and I wanted to make sure she had a chance to express her views. Serenity also wanted to make sure we understood her motivations for proposing the group. "A lot of groups [in prison], they are very much about being broken and wanting to fix yourself," she says. "[But] I wanted [this group] to more be about accepting yourself, loving yourself right where you are." Serenity had studied many different religions including Christianity, and found yoga to be "different from other faiths": "Other faiths teach you to love yourself because God made you, but they also teach you are bad because you did this or that." In contrast, she says, yoga made her "more tranquil and accepting of myself, in a place where you're just searching for something to make you feel OK. . . . I was passionate about how yoga had empowered me, given me confidence, self-worth, respect, made me more stable."

For Serenity, yoga was clearly a mode of resistance. She describes the multiple forms of violence, abuse, and trauma she endured at the hands of law enforcement and the prison system. She shares with me stories of the demeaning treatment she experienced in prison, including being forcibly cavity-searched vaginally every time she returned from a visit with her family, leaving her humiliated and in tears. "They basically strip-search you and drug test you," she says, "but it's not just peeing in a cup. They make you lift up your breast, spread your legs, squat and cough, spread your cheeks . . . [pause] It was like an assault. . . . They make you feel like you're not human at all." In the face of a violent and seemingly immovable system that routinely dehumanized people,

Serenity says, "yoga was helping me to realize that there was kind of a little super-hero inside of me." Serenity wanted to share this with other women whom she saw similarly mired in despair: "I wanted to empower women in a place where I saw so much self-loathing and giving up." Serenity emphasizes that she always found the system to be unjust. "[But] when you're in there and you're being abused, like it's kind of hard to . . . you know, you go in and the first couple of months, it's very '*Oh my god, I'm so horrible. What did I do?*' . . . I think maybe there was a moment where I thought, '*I'm the biggest piece of shit ever.*' It doesn't help if you are bombarded with people shoving that at you, whether its attorneys or courts or COs. . . . But then it starts to become clear how unjust it is. I didn't have the tools, if I would have had the tools . . . ." she says, trailing off. She then resumes: "It was about me looking back and wishing I could do something different. . . . I wanted to empower women, I wanted to open their eyes through the practice of yoga and meditation . . . to be at peace with themselves, make them stronger . . . opening their eyes to the super-hero within, not letting anybody tell them different."

Serenity is at pains to clarify that her concept of empowerment was in opposition to the prison's logic and messaging: "In no way was I like '*let's be part of this system,*'" she insists. "We're not just putting these rose-colored glasses on and, you know, '*Ommm.*' . . . That's not it. . . .I don't want people to get the wrong impression about [yoga]. Just like roll over and play dead. . . . I don't think that kind of submission is the true meaning of yoga." I ask her to elaborate. "[It's] the weapon of love," she insists, quoting Martin Luther King Jr. "Peaceful resistance, but standing up, through *āsana* . . . being present, not lying down . . . if you're accepting all this mistreatment, that goes against the principles of yoga."

By the time of this writing, Serenity, Maitra, and Reighlen have all been released. The group we all participated in eventually fizzled out due to lack of interest and leadership. Soon after, in March of 2020, all volunteer programs at prisons were suspended due to the pandemic—as of this writing, they have yet to be resumed. While incarcerated, Maitra and Reighlen had both expressed eagerness to get involved in anti-prison work in the future. Reighlen connected with a prison abolitionist organization, and was excited to attend their meetings. Maitra had proposed conducting a research project to expose the "inherent problems involved with the current philosophy of rehabilitation," using oral histories and interviews of fellow incarcerated persons to demonstrate how mass incarceration "threatens our American values of democracy." In different ways, both Reighlen and Maitra appear to have been politically radicalized by the experience of being incarcerated—in part due to the small but powerful group discussions on yoga and its relationship to nonviolent resistance. None of the women engaged in any explicit acts of re-sistance while they were in prison. Serenity is most explicit about this: "I knew I was getting out. . . . I had young children, and I did not want to do anything to make anybody mad." But she clarifies that starting the group and coming together in solidarity was itself an act of resistance to the prison: "It was us just connecting and forming a sisterhood and not accepting the bullshit around us . . . aligning physical strength with emotional resilience." For now, all three women are focused on getting off parole or figuring out their educational and professional goals for the near future. Reighlen is working construction, and thinking about returning to university for further education, as well as a yoga teacher training certification. Maitra is also training to become a yoga instructor. Serenity is working at a restaurant, fighting a legal battle with her ex-husband for custody of her children, while also teaching free yoga classes.

10
Conclusion

It has felt virtually impossible to "conclude" a book like this. Having spent several years immersed inside prisons, my volunteer work came to an abrupt end in 2020, when the COVID-19 pandemic swept across the globe, and prisons and jails shut down all volunteer programs virtually overnight. As of this writing, I have no idea whether or when I will be able to return to prison volunteer work. To say that I miss the work would be a gross understatement. I often joke to friends and colleagues that I am among the few who are sad to have been kicked out of prison. But in truth, as the pandemic wore on, and it became clear that it could be months (if not years) before I would see my incarcerated students again, I was left with a kind of heartache. I felt keenly the loss of the unique privilege of nurturing and accompanying so many, of building relationships of solidarity and intimacy that defied the prison's warnings not to become "overfamiliar." Friends and colleagues have asked me to theorize explicitly about the cultivation of relationships that happened in those spaces. I still struggle to fully articulate this phenomenon. It is difficult to capture the enormity of what it meant to attach, connect with, and accompany my students: to nourish them, to share in their suffering, yet focus on seeing the best in them, rather than defining them by the worst thing they had ever done (or that they had been accused of doing). The labor entailed in this work of relationship-building is immense, and the experience of vulnerability and intimacy in those spaces still too raw for me to fully process or give voice to. "Privilege," as one friend and colleague noted, is simply too thin of a word to describe it.[1] "In less grandiose terms," Joshua Price calls this "the intimate calculus of accompanying a person well or poorly, of staving off despair in oneself or another, in offering a platform for collective engagement."[2]

Of course, this is precisely the reason that prisons exhort volunteers to maintain their distance, to remain wary of incarcerated persons—the bonds forged through this kind of work make it impossible to consider the criminal punishment system as an abstraction. Instead, as the lives and feelings and stories of the human beings it cages become increasingly real to us—as we allow ourselves to witness the suffering so many have endured—it becomes steadily more difficult to square this with any notion of "justice." But many volunteers continue to cultivate a posture of neutrality when working with

Freedom Inside?. Farah Godrej, Oxford University Press. © Oxford University Press 2022.
DOI: 10.1093/oso/9780190070083.003.0010

incarcerated students, heeding the prison's warnings to remain polite but detached. One training manual, while encouraging meditation volunteers to "see the humanity of each person," also discourages them from "taking sides," becoming "prisoner advocates," or "overidentifying with prisoners as innocent victims."[3] This makes perfect sense if one has a relatively conventional understanding of prisons, and of the people who end up in them. And, it is not as though I found the emotional bandwidth and fortitude for relationship-building in prisons overnight: It takes months of consistent, painstaking effort to move past stereotypes, to remain open and porous, willing to relate differently to people who are cast as the "worst of the worst" (many of whom end up carrying this as their self-belief). I cannot claim that my perspective was somehow more evolved, nor can I fault those who firmly abided by the prison's recommendations, rarely connecting with students beyond polite, superficial "hello's" and "goodbye's," and sticking to an official understanding of the rules.

As one volunteer insisted, "We can't have an agenda" when volunteering in prisons. But remaining "neutral" in the face of massive injustice never felt like a viable option to me—how, I wondered, could we be doing anything but giving it our tacit approval and making it function more effectively, if we remained neutral? Instead, I found myself entirely in agreement with the volunteer who insisted that working to dismantle mass incarceration should be the most important priority of anyone seeking to volunteer in prisons: "to think of yourself as a resource to serving the destruction of [an unjust system]." The nurturing and accompanying relationships I built were just one tiny piece in the landscape of such efforts, which are of course happening in prisons and jails everywhere. And, as I found myself in the rare position of creating space for political education inside prisons, I felt freed from the confines of operating solely as a social scientist, of speaking and writing in a scholarly voice. Instead, I could relate to students as a teacher and an activist, through the lens of caregiving. In so doing, it is my hope that I was able offer them a space of freedom—no matter how fleeting—from the brutality they endured.

As I warned at the outset, the many complex narratives I have uncovered here point to the difficulty of drawing firm conclusions. Binary narratives about whether yoga and meditation promote acquiescence or resistance do not adequately describe the range of meanings that people give to these practices, as they interpret and employ them in a wide variety of ways. Over the years, I encountered many moments in which yogic or meditative practices seemed to serve as a palliative to justify the social ills of a deeply unequal society. I saw firsthand the ways in which a "self-help" spirituality separate from social justice might become "a sedative for coping with an oppressive and difficult world."[4] I heard incarcerated persons proclaim that prison had been "a blessing" to them, giving thanks that they had learned to accept their own flaws, and improve themselves as a solution to their woes. I watched as volunteers offered some version of the advice to "deal with yourself, not with society," celebrating the individual's freedom to create their own reality.

For most spiritual practitioners, acceptance is a foundational goal. I knew from personal experience that "accepting what is" is the first step to trans-formation. All too often, though, I watched as teachers and students inside prisons treated acceptance as the end goal of these practices, neglecting to mention that acceptance need not mean resignation, reconciliation, or pas-sivity toward injustice. I saw many examples of this "neutered, apolitical" ap-proach, in which teachers of mind-body practices said little or nothing about the systemic difficulties people lived with, but rather offered tools for them to function better within and adjust better to structural obstacles.[5] Several for-merly incarcerated persons confirmed to me that in the face of overwhelming messaging from prisons, acceptance and adaptation often became the path of least resistance. Sandra confirmed that she and many others repeatedly heard the message from prison staff that "it's your responsibility to correct yourself, we didn't bring you here . . . you created your reality, this is all your fault." This messaging, she noted, often brings about a compliance borne of weariness: "If we tell our truth . . . that makes those who have the power more resistant to us. . . . [So] some may say, '*it is all my fault, there is nothing I can do about it*,' and leave more disempowered than when [they] came in. '*Maybe I just better go along with it and be done with it. . . . [I] don't want to make any waves*.'"[6]

But I hope to have shown that this was not the only story worth uncovering. I also learned how multivalent these practices could be, and how effectively they could invite participants into a mindful attention to the collective causes of suffering and oppression. I learned of rare instances in which prison volunteers offered these practices to deepen participants' understandings of the choices available to them, without relying on standard prison indoctrina-tion about choice as entirely removed from structural constraints. I learned from incarcerated people who reported feeling empowered, not simply be-cause they were taking responsibility for self-improvement, but because they were able to articulate how social, political, and legal arrangements constrained their ability to "simply choose not to commit crimes."[7] I saw how lessons of tolerating physical discomfort during the practice of yoga poses could be geared toward building strength to face challenge, rather than being passive or docile. Occasionally, through writing and discussion, I saw incarcerated persons develop new forms of attentiveness to—and less reac-tive, more considered responses to—the world around them, that went far beyond their default modes of perception. I learned how yogic and meditative practices could be change-oriented in a way that defied rather than repeated the prison's logic, illuminating well-worn habits, negative self-images, and past conditioning resulting from oppression.[8]

Many of the incarcerated and formerly incarcerated people I worked with, talked to, and read about sincerely endorsed the prison's narrative of individual choice, ownership, and responsibility. I think of one in particular who vigorously defends these ideas in a book titled *Radical Responsibility*, insisting that they are different from "blame": "Ownership," he insists, "is not another form of self-blame but a radical act of self-empowerment."[9] But many others who have lived in prisons found nothing empowering in this logic: They pointed out the contradiction entailed in harping on ownership, while refusing recognition of structural obstacles that shape and constrain these choices, often over generations. "The truth is, everything is not in my control," said Sandra. "There is an individual and societal responsibility. No matter what I'm being told, I know that I'm responsible for my part, but that's not the whole story . . . it's like domestic violence on a systemic level. You know how a man may beat you or abuse you or assault you, and then he says '*you made me do it*?' [The system] is like that. I put all these different instances together [of severe oppression and marginalization], and then the law says, '*you should have done this, you should have done that*.'"

It can be tempting to imagine that we must adjudicate among these two perspectives, or figure out which is the "correct" option. It is not anyone's place to judge why certain kinds of messages might have resonance, what forms of comfort they may provide, and how they may allow people to cope with brutal circumstances (in ways that may entail creative dissembling and the appearance of conformity). Rather, my goal has been to probe both kinds of views more deeply. Thinking through the lens of yogic and meditative practices allows us to see nuances that may not emerge as clearly if we remain stuck in the binary of individual and structural responsibility. Importantly, I found that the horizon of what was possible inside prisons could not simply be explained by these dualities between "compliant" and "oppositional" modes of practice.

In some instances, people opposed the prison's messaging through a kind of self-improvement that rejected conventional views about imprisonment. This posture or approach did not always meet the definition of traditional political involvement: Instead, it was often found "in daily acts of oppositional behavior and defiance,"[10] and even internal beliefs and thoughts, which expressed resistance to a dominant system. Resistance in prisons operates in a multitude of ways, from riots and hunger strikes, to writing, practicing jailhouse law, serving on inmate councils, and doing theater, to developing personal codes of conduct and belief.[11] But here I have attempted to elaborate on a richer and more expansive vocabulary for understanding resistance, which goes beyond these activities. Even when incarcerated yogis or meditators turned fully inward rather than undertaking any systemic critique or challenge, they found a space of healing, renewal, refuge, and rebuilding, which allowed for an internal sense of freedom to flourish, regardless of how outwardly confined they were. Still, what I am referring to here is something fuller than simply an internal sense of freedom. Elsewhere, I have given the name "spiritual" resistance to these inner states, which are grounded in a felt conviction of self-worth, of being a person who is worthy of embodying the fundamental, meaningful, and positive value of freedom. There is also a sense of having the agency to contain, structure, and direct that freedom (to the degree possible within the constraints one faces). Even among those who declined the language of resistance or subversion, these practices offered resources for survival and greater control over their situation. Joshua Price calls them "practical [activities] that [provide] a method and a means . . . to sustain [oneself]," through "creative engagement in tactics of everyday survival in the face of massive state violence."[12] Or, as one of my interviewees, Serenity, offered, "You wanna find those little realms of escape [sigh] . . . the system is so invincible that it takes super-human will . . . you can't control all the stuff that's happening around you, at least you can control yourself. . . . I can control whether I allow this to break me."

It should be clear that the goal of teaching these practices inside prisons is not to push all incarcerated persons to become political activists, to insist that they immediately model themselves on George Jackson, Assata Shakur, or Angela Davis. We have seen that outright political resistance inside prisons is the exception rather than rule. Political activity and expression in prisons is a long-standing tradition—but it can also be dangerous because of the discretionary authority that prison staff wield, and the many forms of retaliation that await those who speak out. The people we have met in these pages have outlined for us these risks: Having the length of one's sentence increased is the minimum sanction one might expect, and being thrown into solitary confinement for the least infraction is not at all unusual. In very few cases have we seen that yogic and meditative practices—even if taught in a political way—have translated into actual activism, whether during or after incarceration. Large-scale systemic change may yet be too ambitious and unlikely to result from teaching yoga and meditation in prisons—few incarcerated yogis or meditators may turn into full-fledged political activists, and it is likely that many of them may not have the resources or energy to do so. But rather than investigating the direct political effects of these practices, I have been interested here in the meaning that these practices have for the people who engage in them.

Yet, it is also a key premise of this book that those who bring therapeutic, healing practices like yoga and meditation inside prisons can think more carefully about the political messages they disseminate to incarcerated persons, whether intentionally or otherwise. They can bring critical attention to how the practices are taught, and how their benefits might inadvertently turn detrimental. Practices such as yoga and meditation contain political undertones, depending on how they are communicated. These undertones can reinforce deeply entrenched patterns of alienation, inuring entire groups of people to their second-class status. We know that prisons are places of political sedation, where lessons of unequal citizenship are taught and reproduced, where people are taught what to expect for themselves, to internalize and accept their subordination. The curriculum of the prison is one in which compliance and silence are rewarded. Or, as Serenity put it, "those people who are like *just get through it*," when they get out, they [may] carry that same self-loathing and ugly guilt. It's crippling. . . . It's fear, keeping [your] head down."

When prison volunteers reaffirm the idea that self-improvement is the only appropriate response to incarceration, they may exacerbate this political sedation, further circulating these ideas in public discourse. These volunteers enter a context where a state-sponsored apparatus of pacification, control, docility, and compliance is at work. Of course, much of what we saw suggested that what practitioners receive does not always align perfectly with the intentions and actions of those who teach. In fact, Chapter 5 suggested that we have little evidence as yet for a causal connection between what volunteers teach and what people end up believing. Still, volunteers should consider the potential impacts of teaching inside prisons as an ethical matter, paying attention to the political meanings that are being made. It seems unfair to simplistically applaud and encourage choice, ownership, and responsibility to those who have so few choices in life, and who are virtually guaranteed to continue being denied these choices by massive structural obstacles. It seems unethical to reductively teach incarcerated persons that they can change anything through the power of their mind, and the power to own their own thoughts and actions, when in fact the world is systematically stacked against so many of them, and will continue to be so after their release. As Sandra reminded us, "We've been shown and told over and over again how powerless we are, and then to turn around and say, *'you have the power, it's your fault*,' it's hard to reconcile those."

It bears repeating that advocating for systemic change does not preclude promoting individual growth—in fact, for many activists, the two necessarily go together. There is little doubt that everyone can benefit from the change, personal growth, and self-improvement that yogic and meditative practices offer. But one goal of this inquiry has been to think through precisely what kind of "growth" or "transformation" we might want to see among those who are forced to live in prisons. Such transformation cannot come with the nonnegotiable price tag of having to deny the very forms of oppression that may have contributed to one's predicament. The question is not whether anyone should have to take responsibility for personal change, but whether the concept of responsibility can be made richer, more robust, and more meaningful, without being hamstrung by absurd denials of structural obstacles. The call to responsibility becomes "hobbling" (in Maitra's words) in a system that has monopolized "responsibility" as a tool to bludgeon and blame,[13] while continuing to insist that people live in a world of unconstrained choices. Despite all of this relentless messaging, we have been able to unearth the voices of those who are exploring more expansive forms of self-improvement, recreating and asserting their own agency, and in the process, teaching us something about yogic and meditative traditions.

These traditions are not solid, static, or ossified. Rather, they are alive, continually being reinterpreted in a wide variety of ways. Depending on how they are interpreted, and by whom, they have supported a variety of political goals and purposes. The practices do not operate in a vacuum; instead, they routinely absorb culturally available ideas and values, which direct them toward certain goals and give them certain meanings.[14] An environment geared toward control, pacification, and neutralization of populations—replete with the discourse of "rehabilitating criminals"—might mold the direction that yogic and meditative practices take, inclining them toward these ends rather than more subversive ones. But many other religious and spiritual traditions—not to mention self-help programs—provide tools to help control one's mind in ways that are pacifying and apolitical. So-called resilience strategies that exhort individuals to focus only on themselves and their own role in bringing about their suffering can be seen in religious programs, jobs training programs, substance abuse programs, and many forms of counseling and therapeutic discourse, all of which are "on the menu" in prisons. Rather than seeing yoga or meditation as uniquely available to be mobilized as a pacification tool, I have examined these practices as part of an entire system of pacification happening within the prison environment, as practitioners take the canvas of yoga or meditation and paint a variety of messages onto it.[15]

The meaning of yogic and meditative practice is being made and remade daily in these sites of terror and captivity.

Member-Checking: Research Participants "Talk Back"

I offered all research participants the opportunity to read and offer correctives to draft manuscript chapters before this book went to press (I reflect on this "member-checking" process at greater length in the Methodological Appendix). Although few actually read my work, I outline here some of the key responses. Victoria, who read an entire draft of the manuscript, offered the suggestion that I add "just one clarifying sentence that shows that you are not completely unaware of the fact that prisons house violent people." The scholar-activist Joshua Price describes how his commitment to end violence against women sometimes tested his anti-prison commitments, particularly when he encountered sex offenders or others accused of violence against women.[16] Like Victoria, readers may feel I have not sufficiently grappled with these contradictions, or that I have been too quick to paint incarcerated persons as victims rather than as perpetrators. Victoria noted that she felt there had been a "kind of softening of the fact that many of them *have* done bad things (regardless of the reasons)." She cited Shane Bauer's book *American Prison*, in which the author goes undercover as a prison guard, "cultivat[ing] feelings of sympathy for one guy in particular . . . [who] was released but is now back for sexual assault on a ten-year old." She relayed the story of a well-respected yoga student at one prison where she volunteers regularly, who was "spinning . . . about his innocence," after which she was warned by a staff member that he had "killed three people in cold blood." She thinks about this a lot: "Is it okay for us to teach yoga and bring love and compassion to rapists (when I actually think of the terror and life-altering experience)? I don't have an answer. I go in with a neutral attitude."

The critiques of volunteer work I offered generated a combination of careful consideration and counter-arguments. The few research participants who offered feedback mostly emphasized how much they enjoyed reading the draft, and found its arguments valuable overall. Still, there were ideas and passages that they found controversial or difficult. Victoria said the manuscript gave her "much to think about." She found it "sad and disturbing/enlightening to know that our students see us (white) volunteers as looking down at them and judging them." She vowed to address these issues in upcoming volunteer trainings. "I see your argument throughout about yoga being a tool of the prisons to perpetuate a slave mentality," she noted, adding that she had "never thought about that as a motivation. . . . No one I approached or worked with in the prison system voiced embracing yoga as a way of pacifying prisoners." She also clarified: "When I think about subduing the chaotic nature of those who lack self-discipline, I think about the fact that jails and prisons are their homes, especially lifers, [who] do not want to live in a constant state of disruption." Victoria found some of the critiques of volunteer work "hard to read in light of how much we all do in hopes of making even a small difference in the never-ending cycle of incarceration." She admitted to being "somewhat taken aback by" the ongoing argument about the lack of political emphasis in her organization, expressing skepticism about "how it would ever work" to address structural issues, in light of the many logistical difficulties facing volunteer organizations.

Hannah had a different set of concerns. She also prefaced her remarks by noting that she "totally respected" my views and agreed fully with many of them. She did, however, want to re-emphasize her commitment to the Iyengar method discussed in Chapter 7, including the centrality of physical adjustments: "My adherence to Iyengar yoga comes from the belief that the full, traditional practice leads to a broader consciousness," she noted, "to 'seeing more' . . . maybe not as quickly or obviously as political consciousness-raising, but no less deep." She also acknowledged that while "probably not everyone loved [physical] adjustments, it is a deep yogic tool . . . my priority was always to give [students] the real deal—not out of tradition, but out of honoring the depth of my own path." Describing her own experience with physical adjustments, she notes, "I soon learned that not only was my body being protected from injury, but *much more* importantly, I had access to more of myself. Areas that were asleep began to awaken . . . and I could very literally breathe into places to which I had no previous access. That was a magical gift pretty early on in my practice and that is why adjustments are important to me as a teacher . . . you [learn] more about parts of yourself previously hidden." Hannah emphasized the idea of "trusting the process": "If you stick with yoga, you will see more . . . It may take years, but you cannot open your body without also eventually having the rest of yourself get 'enlightened' too."

Mason, the founder of the organization Yoga in Prison which I described in Chapter 7, felt that this book "presents very important considerations for bringing yoga and meditation into carceral settings and . . . for appropriately serving incarcerated individuals." Mason wanted to emphasize that his organization's approaches to teaching and training volunteers had "evolved significantly" since I had first encountered them. "Much of it is a reflection of the re-emerging importance of addressing social justice issues in this country, and the role yoga can play in that," he noted. After eighteen years of teaching in prisons, "[we are now] looking at the incarcerated population as a concentration or distillation of all of the inequalities that exist in American society." He noted the organization is now stressing these issues of inequity in teacher trainings: "If you don't get this, if you're not coming in with this level of understanding and empathy, unless you get this issue, that prisons and jails basically house a concentration of the social inequities of society, you don't deserve to be teaching with us . . . What about the pain and suffering that society inflicts on people, particularly marginalized people? It's a very important thing to acknowledge in the work we do, it's going to become more important." Mason also noted that there has been an evolution in terms of the purpose of the teaching: "What we are attempting to provide . . . are actually skills for healing that turn into empowerment. We're not just, 'well here are some tools that are going to make you feel better.' [Rather], out of feeling better and feeling stronger you are going to feel a sense of empowerment as an individual." Mason now critiques previously dominant ideas such as "anger management": "[It's] a misnomer, you have every right in the world to be angry if you're incarcerated, if you live in this culture and this society with inequities, how can you not harm yourself and others with your anger? You certainly have to feel it and find ways to express it . . . [although] there's a different way to demonstrate strength and masculinity than how you were conditioned."

Chaplain Eric read a draft of Chapter 6, and challenged several of my interpretive claims regarding the mindfulness class I participated in. In response to these challenges, I modified some passages in that chapter. The Chaplain also clarified that all the information he presented was intended to "be of a supportive and instructive nature," re-emphasizing the need to "step out of the blame and shame paradigm altogether." In particular, he pushed back against my critiques of his teachings on neuroplasticity and self-regulation. "I do not encourage participants to directly reflect on and review past personal actions, choices, and decisions," he noted. "They have plenty of opportunity to do that on their own. My tone was hoped to open up possibilities of seeing 'life ahead' in a more expansive way. None of us 'sees all that is there' in the open field of data. At best we have a limited read, of a limited set of the data . . . the nature of human (and all) life is one of constant change, cradle to grave. As we move forward in our lives, day to day, month to month, year to year, we have the opportunity to explore creative and varying responses and approaches to all that we encounter, externally and internally."

Ultimately, Chaplain Eric offered the following important clarification to my interpretation of his work with incarcerated students. I quote him directly and at length, in order to preserve the integrity of his remarks:

> In mentioning my respect for cultural humility, I had hoped to encompass what seemed to me—and seemed to you—to be the unshakable, unmistakable truth of the wretchedness within the walls of that [facility]. One cannot spend but a few minutes on the secure side of the sally-port without being struck directly to the heart with the injustice, inhumanity, degradation, disrespect, inequality, racial disparities, unhealthy, unclean, and unconscionably deplorable state of that home [where those] men go to sleep and wake up every day and night. . . . Each has traveled his own path through all of the challenges—familial, cultural, emotional, systemic, political, financial—that has ultimately allowed them to lie down their head on one of those bunks. The development of increased mindfulness and awareness results in clearer, more direct seeing into our inner and outer worlds, bringing into focus that which is real in our life, as hard and as beautiful as it may be. I believe it is only through deep personal knowing of these multiple landscapes that one can be an effective agent of change in life. As the veils clear, hearts, minds and eyes see more and more of that which is real in that [facility], and the multiple forces at play that keep it full, on a general and on a personal level. I believe teaching mindfulness and awareness to these men is a radically subversive act. As the world and society evolve, it is those who are able to live from the place of connection and embodiment of our human inheritance, innate wisdom, intelligence and loving heart that will continue to bend the arc of justice in a positive direction.

Possibilities for Political Change

Readers may also ask, was any lasting, concrete, political change achieved by any of the activities described in this book? In Chapter 8, I described the frustration that caused many of the more politically minded volunteers to part ways with the organizations they served, citing the lack of interest from fellow volunteers, and the general lack of political consciousness in their organizations. Many volunteers (myself included) also learned firsthand the difficulty of "doing politics" in prison, where volunteers are often encouraged to steer clear of political statements. Politically critical, emancipatory work inside prisons must be largely covert and implicit, relying on stolen moments away from the gaze of prison staff and the rare lack of supervision. There are many factors—not least of which are the system's own priorities, but also the priorities of so many organizations and fellow volunteers—that push in apolitical directions. Meanwhile, the more conventional (and as a result, politically con-servative) forms of teaching are relatively common and easy to implement. As a result, the examples of radical work that I (and a few others) describe re-main largely tentative and experimental. Like others who have attempted po-litical consciousness-raising in prisons or with formerly incarcerated persons, I found that such organizing was episodic, intermittent, and difficult to sus-tain.[17] While Reighlen and Maitra consistently showed up for—and brought their leadership and voices—to our yogic philosophy group in prison, such continuity was rare. Many other students dropped in and out frequently, occasionally engaging in our discussions as and when they were able. Most yoga and meditation programs in prisons do not qualify for the "good-time" credits or other "milestone" points that count toward earlier release, which disincentivizes attendance (although Reighlen and Maitra maintained that there was a silver lining to this—they felt that only people who were truly in-terested in and dedicated to the practices would show up). Without consistent attendance or leadership, these groups fizzled out easily, as the more com-mitted leaders cycled through their terms and out of prison.

There was no doubt that the work we did together had transformative effects on individual self-consciousness, as well as our personal relationships with one another. It is less clear that it had systemic effects (recall that we have been saying all along that personal change is no substitute for systemic change). While I am hopeful that the collaborations I described had some ripple effects in the lives of those I worked most closely with, I also saw firsthand how the difficulties of post-prison re-entry (and the effects of state-sponsored discrim-ination) leave people to struggle endlessly with basic needs such as housing, employment, and child custody. It is difficult to engage in political work when one is fighting to regain custody of one's children, or trying to put food on the table, or trying to find a job while repeatedly being turned down because of a record, or trying to meet the many convoluted requirements of parole and probation that often threaten to send people back to prison, for violations as simple as not having transportation to the next meeting with a parole officer. While the students I worked most closely with demonstrated great enthu-siasm for the politically infused work we did together, none of them could af-ford to become activists after their incarceration. And, as we saw in Chapter 5, few of the formerly incarcerated persons who were politically attuned have translated that into ongoing activism.

Perhaps the skeptic will ask, given that yogic and meditative practices seemed to have little tangible effect on political life, why keep bothering with them if the goal is to dismantle mass incarceration? Assuming it would even be allowed, why not just shoot for straightforward political education that teaches incarcerated persons more concrete ways to aim for systemic change upon their release: how to get involved in political movements that target prisons and policing, how to work for legislative change by lobbying to change sentencing laws such as mandatory minimums, how to connect with organizations that work to address the different manifestations of the problem, like Banning the Box, fighting against the construction of new facilities, ending cash bail, changing the conditions of parole and probation, and so on? Put more bluntly, if individual change does not equal systemic change, why bother with practices that appear (at best) to impact only individual consciousness?

I have spent much time contemplating whether our efforts inside prisons are misdirected when focused solely on service and self-care projects like yoga and meditation. Like Joshua Price, I have felt defeated and worn down by the lack of political progress.[18] I have shared the frustrations of Jade, the volunteer from Chapter 8 who withdrew from prison volunteer work after realizing how deeply apolitical most organizations were, and how little impact "direct service" had on systemic change. I have found that the leadership of formerly incarcerated persons is no guarantee that prison volunteer organizations will take a stand on systemic issues. I served on the Board of one organization that taught meditation in prisons, which included at least one formerly incarcerated Board member of color. During the Black Lives Matter protests in the summer of 2020, I tried to convince Board members that our organization should make a strong statement of support on its website. Some (including our formerly incarcerated colleague) replied that they did not believe systemic racism was a problem; others felt there was little need for such a statement; and some expressed the view that organizations working inside prisons should not be vocal in criticizing law enforcement. I learned the hard way that even organizations which include the leadership of formerly incarcerated persons can end up reproducing conventional political views.

However, it is clear that yogic and meditative practices—even when they are not explicitly geared toward political ends—provide invaluable support for inner life, self-worth, and self-understanding to people in grueling circumstances. They can allow people to connect with their inner selves in deep and even defiantly positive ways. Even if not every incarcerated yogi or meditator turns into an activist, these practices allow many to pursue forms of inward-oriented spiritual pursuit denied (or possibly unknown) to many people in society. They foster the creation of critical mental distance between the self and the institutions in which one is caged. In Jarvis Jay Masters's words, "prison walls disappeared" and he could "find freedom no matter where [he] dwelled."

We can acknowledge that the subtle and complex forms of resistance we have seen in this book may not be explicitly political, while considering the possibilities for pushing in more political directions. Yoga and meditation programs occupy a rare space within the prison system (assuming an end to the pandemic and the eventual resumption of volunteer programming inside prisons). Not only are they among the few avenues for alleviating its horrific suffering, they are also one of the few ways for people on the outside to engage directly with system-impacted persons, to undertake forms of inside/outside solidarity. The findings in Chapter 8 may not portend a particularly optimistic outcome for such solidarity—we saw there that a majority of volunteers who taught regularly inside prisons were quick to traffic in stereotypes. Engaging regularly with incarcerated persons, as we saw, is no guarantee of feelings of sameness—"they're just like us" or "this could have been me" moments were few and far between. But what if volunteers were trained in different and more capacious ways, to think differently about the system they were entering? What if volunteer organizational trainings were focused on highlighting the social control function of prisons, and the ways in which rehabilitative pro- gramming reproduced this control? What if organizations trained volunteers in the deeply entrenched patterns of subordination and deep alienation that are reproduced by prison discourses? What if they studied the notion of prisons as places of political sedation, and their hidden curriculum of compli- ance and silence, which reinforces what Michelle Alexander calls the "genius of the current caste system?"[19] What if volunteer organizations paid critical attention to the political undertones of yoga and meditation, and the beliefs, meanings, and self-understandings that these produce among custodial citi- zens? What if they contemplated Emile's exhortation to attend to the forms of "erasure" that result when volunteers purport to bring "healing" to incarcer- ated persons without acknowledging the damage done by systemic oppres- sion? Volunteers could work to establish the accompanying study groups of the sort I participated in, combining the study of yoga postures or meditative practices with discussions of systemic injustice. In such groups, meditative practices could focus on moment-to-moment awareness of structural injus- tice; participants could consider how one's personal self-improvement could be skillfully combined with efforts toward social or political change, through the lens of say, Buddhist concepts such as "right speech" or "right action." The existing structure of yoga and meditation programs provides a set of channels and opportunities for political education and subversion, by transforming the meaning and purpose of self-care and self-discipline (even if only subtly).

The value of what I have called "spiritual" resistance may also be fruitfully applied to other practices, beliefs, and programs, both within and beyond prisons. Within prisons, other forms of programming beyond yoga and meditation could be geared toward maximizing emancipatory potential through parallel commitments. While much prison programming reproduces the oppressive logics of "rehabilitation" we have examined, this need not necessarily be so: In principle, a variety of programs—educational, therapeutic, counseling, or treatment—could work within the sort of frameworks I have identified (insofar as they have the freedom to operate outside tightly controlled official boundaries). Of course, a rare set of conditions may need to line up correctly for all of this to be possible, including the ability to engage in subversive messaging without attracting scrutiny. And, we would also have to hope that openly discussing these issues will not itself result in increased scrutiny or even termination of such programs by prison administrators. These and many other issues would need to be contemplated more carefully by those who do this work.

More broadly, the findings here point beyond simply prisons—they show how practices of wellness, self-care, and self-cultivation can constitute acts of radical opposition by members of marginalized communities. Practices of health and wellness can be co-opted by powerful forces perpetuating the ideology that you can be whatever you want to be, and therefore, if anything bad happens, it is "no one's fault but your own."[20] Wellness and self-care, in their neoliberal iterations—pitched by health magazines and self-care gurus, and commodified through buzzwords like "productivity," "gratitude," or "positive thinking"—can encourage people to withdraw into individualized pursuits, rather than focus on social or political oppression. They call on us to "embrace the glorious fact that your life is in your hands," while also accepting that misfortune is your own fault,[21] ignoring the large, structural problems that affect everyone's health and well-being, while zeroing in on the precious individuality of those who can afford to subscribe to such services.[22] But increasingly, we also see that for those who come from communities that have spent generations in captivity and servitude—their bodies and minds deemed expendable and disposable—self-care can be a radical, oppositional act. In directing care toward themselves, people in a variety of unjust circumstances can understand their own minds and bodies as "worth caring about."[23] They can reclaim or "steal back" their minds and inner lives for self-directed growth, often resulting in experiences of empowerment and authentic self-assertion. In a world replete with narratives of diminished citizenship and unequal status—and experiences of the self as an object of control and discipline— finding value in oneself and cultivating one's mind and body to find strength, self-worth, and dignity are crucial acts of defiance.

What Next? Beyond "Reformist" Reforms

In the end, not many of the people I worked with in prisons—including both volunteers and incarcerated persons—imagined that addressing the many harms of incarceration required thinking much beyond "reforming" the system. "What else is there?" asked one volunteer, when confronted with the concept of prison reform. Most moderate critics believe that the prison system can be reformed to become more efficient as well as humane, so that only those who truly "deserve" punishment are incarcerated.[24] Reformists argue that much of what is wrong with prisons can be solved by reorienting them toward improving individual behaviors rather than simply punishing people, through educational, vocational, and therapeutic programming, including twelve-step recovery and other self-help programs. The real problems, on this reformist view, are the "excesses" of imprisonment, prison-backed policing,[25] and an overly harsh and punitive system that ends up making people more violent, increasing recidivism by turning novice offenders into career criminals.[26] Reformists call for changing the conditions of incarceration, making prisons more therapeutic and rehabilitative, by increasing opportunities for self-improvement. Despite all evidence to the contrary, reformists assume that prison can prepare people for reintegration into society.[27]

But here, I have followed the many scholars and activists who argue that the system is not "excessive" or "broken"—rather, prisons are doing exactly what they are meant to do. Making prisons more therapeutic and rehabilitative by offering programs for wellness, self-care, and self-improvement, they argue, makes them no less instruments of social control. My inquiry has taken its cue from those who note that "reform" is a way to keep the current system going in new guise. Instead, they assert, our society must address the underlying suffering that animates harmful behavior, in ways that do not rely on captivity and caging. Why, asks Ruth Wilson Gilmore, do we think we can solve social problems by repeating the kind of behavior that brought us the problem in the first place?[28] Many scholars and policymakers now agree that such a system is morally untenable, and must be dismantled: The state must stop using prisons as a tool of exclusion and control, and instead invest in meaningful solutions to social problems that systematically disadvantage certain individuals (and their communities).[29] "Improvements" that cast prisons as sites of caring social service and therapeutic programming, they argue, are wholly inadequate measures, designed to repackage an unjust system and whitewash the reality that it serves to control marginalized populations.[30]

But these debates are complicated by the fact that even those who are most fiercely opposed to prisons—such as the abolitionist Angela Davis—argue in favor of some rehabilitative prison reform.[31] Not all prison reform, they remind us, necessarily reproduces its punitive, exclusionary, control-and-containment effects. Until large-scale systemic change is achieved, we must give incarcerated persons tools to survive what is universally acknowledged to be a brutal and inhumane system, and even to "flourish and create a meaningful life" behind bars.[32] These critics argue for what they call "non-reformist" reforms—measures and policies that have the effect of reducing or diminishing rather than strengthening the system in the long run. For this reason, some of the harshest critics of the prison system advocate for prison education programs, particularly if they have a political component. Unlike some rehabilitative programs which lend themselves more easily to the prison's goals of conformity and obedience (such as substance abuse or anger management), educational programs may have the opposite effect. Education can be a subversive undertaking, especially when it encourages incarcerated persons to engage in a study of power—"determining who gets what and why," often by reading the works of other incarcerated authors such as Malcolm X and George Jackson.[33] If those behind bars can avail themselves of resources to understand, navigate—and possibly change—a world stacked against them, such programs may end up having a far more revolutionary effect than intended. In fact, political education inside prisons has a long history of producing incarcerated thinkers, writers, and activists who challenge and resist— rather than passively accept, adjust to or comply with—the system, despite the tremendous repression they have faced.[34]

As a longer-term solution, we might ask ourselves what options exist for dealing with harm that do not entail punishing, caging, and captivity. We can ask, as Ruth Wilson Gilmore does, whether we need organized state violence as a response to harm. Perhaps the most crucial shift we can effect is to challenge the language of "individual choice" when it comes to thinking about harm and with it, the hyper-individualism that is "baked into our culture and society."[35] In part, I hope to have cast some critical light on the pervasiveness of the message—perpetuated by the entire punitive apparatus, not to mention society at large—that incarceration only ever results from freely made individual choices. American political discourse has always favored a moralistic view of crime perpetrated by "willful" individuals, casting criminal behaviors as the result of choices made by lone bad actors, while ignoring social and structural constraints.[36] As a result, we have an impoverished vocabulary for understanding responsibility, because we think of it as solely individualized, enmeshing it with concepts of moral blame and religious notions of sin.[37] The law enforcement system is the very epitome of this hyper-individualism: It sees harm as largely perpetrated and suffered by individuals, and views violence as only harming one person (or set of persons). It seeks to resolve this harm and violence in a bureaucratic fashion, by restoring the rights or sovereignty or sanctity of the person harmed, through enacting state-sanctioned vengeance against those who have done the harm. But this, one scholar pointed out, does not "resolve the violence, or the pain that animates those who do violence, often in order to survive." Instead, it merely "bandaids the sets of interrelations that compel people to act violently."[38] As such, it is a shortcut to wrestling with the pain of these relations. Nor does incarceration do anything to make restitution or restore anything to victims—most forms of punishment offer no assistance of any kind to victims.[39] But once we start to think about harm and violence as collective and structural, we may be able to think about mechanisms of community accountability for such harm. Leading abolitionist scholars and activists have produced a rich array of literatures that show us how imprisonment begins to seem far less compelling and necessary once we do so. This shift would involve "transforming ourselves and some of our most deeply held ideas and practices about blame, responsibility, and desert."[40] Collective, structural harms include systems of oppression such as racialized law enforcement, unequal social and economic institutions, and lack of educational and socioeconomic opportunities and supports that leave people without options for livelihoods, all of which often frame the context for individualized harms. But we tend to think of imprisonment as reserved for "evildoers," Angela Davis tells us, allowing the prison to function ideologically as "an abstract site into which undesirables are deposited, relieving us of the responsibility of thinking about the real issues afflicting those communities from which prisoners are drawn in such disproportionate numbers . . . especially those produced by racism and, increasingly, global capitalism."[41]

Of course, we are unlikely to see an overnight shrinking of the carceral state. In the interim, many activists are deeply involved in policy work to reduce the scope and footprint of the prison-industrial complex through painstaking grassroots organizing: stopping new prison construction, closing prisons and jails one facility at a time, ending solitary confinement and the death penalty, eradicating cash bail, organizing to free people from prison, opposing the expansion of punishment through hate crime laws and surveillance, pushing for universal healthcare, and for laws and policies that lead to the gradual decarceration of more and more people.[42] Even if we cannot come around to the vision of a world where prisons are rendered obsolete—despite the fact that an array of distinguished scholars such as Angela Davis, Ruth Wilson Gilmore, Michelle Alexander, James Forman Jr., and many others advocate for it—these thinkers and activists model how to advocate for an interim set of strategies that bring about incremental change.

At the outset, I noted that this book is not about whether or not yoga and meditation should be taught in prisons. Rather, it is about *how* they are taught. As I hope to have made clear, this is not an argument against all prison reform—rather, it asks us to consider which kinds of reforms work to incrementally diminish the system in the long run, and which kinds of reforms end up bolstering or supporting it. Throughout this book, I have tried to show how those who see themselves as working against the system may end up offering reforms that reproduce the system's own logic. I have also tried to show how yoga and meditation practitioners can present challenges to carceral thinking, even if these challenges do not look like outright political resistance, and instead remain implicit and internal, rather than explicit and external. If these traditions can teach us other vocabularies for responding collectively to harm or injury, taking us beyond the languages we currently have, they can become part of the incremental work of dismantling the prison-industrial complex. As Gilmore, Davis, and others might say, their practices can serve as "non-reformist" reforms: "reduc[ing] rather than strengthen[ing] the scale and scope of policing, imprisonment, and surveillance,"[43] and destabilizing an unjust system from the inside.

Methodological Appendix

Sampling and Access: Volunteer Communities

In Chapter 2, I described how I gained access to the world of prison volunteer communities. My immersion in this world came about relatively quickly and smoothly. Most scholars who require access to a community note that the process of establishing relationships with organizations must be mutually beneficial. I endeavored to create such reciprocal relationships with the organizations I was given access to. Although I initially approached leaders as an outsider seeking to learn about their world, I soon became part of their world, and was able to learn by doing what community members did. Still, I was keenly aware that I could not simply come in to "take what I needed and leave,"[1] and began volunteering my time to help with administrative and leadership tasks. Given how under-resourced these organizations were, and how much logistical and administrative coordination was often required to keep their programs going, my efforts were warmly welcomed. These efforts also ended up giving me a far deeper understanding of prisons than I otherwise would have had.

As I describe in Chapter 7, I became involved in a range of activities, starting with more mundane tasks, and eventually taking on a leadership role. Throughout the almost four years that I remained immersed in this world, the boundaries between my researcher and volunteer leader roles became increasingly fluid. It soon became clear (both to myself and my fellow volunteer leaders) that I was not simply doing this work for the sake of reciprocity, or to "earn" my insider status as a means to my larger research goals; rather, the work became valuable in and of itself, regardless of the research that had brought me to it. Had the pandemic not intervened—and assuming I would be allowed to continue doing so after the publication of this book—I would still be doing this work after the conclusion of my research, further shaping (and hopefully reshaping) the role that these organizations would play in prisons.

As I came to understand the missions and leadership of these organizations by becoming part of their landscape, I attended (and in some cases, eventually co-organized) their trainings. I also attended volunteer trainings held by other, more established organizations. I analyzed their websites and their other publicly disseminated information. I read training manuals and other materials disseminated by these organizations to their recruits. And, my participation in this world allowed me to recruit thirty-six yoga or meditation volunteers as interviewees. This combination of interpreting public discourse, in-depth interviewing, and participation allowed me to triangulate and cross-reference my findings.

Interviewing, Sampling, and Access: Volunteers

Many of my interviewees in Chapter 8 were fellow volunteers within the organizations I had joined. My initial conversations with organizational leaders led to introductions to other respondents, who in turn introduced me to others—a method known as "snowball" sampling. As a result, in many cases, my interviews were "relational"—that is, I had established relationships with many respondents through co-teaching with them at a jail or prison (or through attending trainings or other informal gatherings of the organization). What emerged in these conversations was a result of the relationship and experiences I shared in common with respondents—the fact that I was a fellow volunteer, immersed in the very communities I was studying, encouraged a collaborative approach to knowledge-production.[2] My approach combined interpretive methods such as relational, ethnographic, and active interviewing, in which both parties to the interview are actively involved in meaning-making. In this orientation, researchers acknowledge the positionality and views of both interviewers and respondents, and incorporate these into the production and analysis of the data.[3]

I conducted the interviews using a semistructured, open-ended approach. The conversations were wide-ranging, ranging in length from 60 to 180 minutes. While each interview was guided by a set of scripted questions, many veered into unexpected territory, directed by the respondents' interests. Rather than aiming for consistency, I found that I learned more about respondents' values and priorities by allowing them to direct the conversation, while loosely following my script. In this way, I allowed what was important to emerge from the respondents' elaborations. Semistructured open-ended interviews allow for "an exploration of people's views of reality while permitting the researcher to maximize discovery and description through the production of nonstandardized information."[4] This dialogical approach makes for a far less rigid and formal structure.[5] Like many other qualitative scholars, my interviews did not proceed as a replicable survey, with "each question being asked the same way and in the same order."[6] Rather, in each conversation, I asked the same general questions, and brought the conversation back to the script as often as possible. For this reason, different respondents emphasized different aspects of the same issues. I did not offer any compensation for my interviews with volunteers.

Interviewing, Sampling, and Access: Formerly Incarcerated Persons

Recruiting formerly incarcerated individuals to interview is no easy task, given the obvious issues of both social stigma and legalized discrimination against those who have been to prison. I attempted—unsuccessfully—to advertise with organizations that offer housing or employment assistance to these populations. I found eventually that I was far better off relying on my contacts in the prison yoga and meditation world. Volunteers I had either interviewed or volunteered with were able to connect me with formerly incarcerated practitioners.[7] Once I established rapport and credibility with an interviewee, they were often able to introduce me to someone else in their network. In this way, despite the largely uphill task of recruitment, I was able to speak at length to twenty-five such participants through "snowball" recruitment. I used the same interview methods I described earlier: open-ended, semistructured interviews directed loosely by a script, but more so by the respondents' interests and preoccupations. I informed all participants that I would be using pseudonyms in any published research. Four of the respondents in this group insisted that they be identified by their real names. Since these participants were not in any way linked to any other respondents, and since I did not use the names of any of the facilities they were incarcerated at, I determined it would pose no risk to other respondents to use their real names.[8]

Over time, the extent of my contact with each respondent varied greatly. I attempted to stay in touch with all my interviewees, contacting them for updates from time to time. While several of them fell off the radar, my relationship with others deepened. In some cases, I kept in regular contact, even writing support letters for pardon applications, recommendation letters for college or graduate school, and collaborating on public events relating to mass incarceration. In this way, my work here was also "relational," emerging dynamically from the relationship between researcher and interviewee.

I never asked any respondent the reason for their incarceration.[9] If in the course of the conversation they wanted to reveal it, I made a note of it (and chose to include it if relevant). Some referred obliquely to "my crime," while others offered long re-tellings of events that landed them in prison or jail. Some respondents openly put their prior selves into the category of "criminal"; others insisted that they had done nothing wrong; and still others referred to their past without going into detail. Given the stigma around incarceration, I was committed to not asking for any information about harm caused, which could be seen as assigning blame or assessing moral worth.

Given my limited research budget, as well the many bureaucratic constraints on the use of University funds at a public institution, I was able to offer each participant a $25 gift card in exchange for their time, which was mailed to them after the interview. In contrast to my volunteer respondents who were largely white and economically relatively secure, these participants tended to be far less comfortable. Most were taking time away from important activities such as employment (or job-hunting) in order to speak with me, and many were facing the usual frustration and legalized discrimination encountered by those who emerge from a prison term. Scholars agree that it is important to compensate research participants from vulnerable or marginalized groups for their time and energy. In Chapter 2, I elaborated on the dilemma of compensation: I felt awkward reducing the knowledge these participants shared with me to a mercantile exchange. The paltry amount I offered could scarcely be seen as a true measure of the "value" of their time and knowledge, given everything they had been through. Yet, I ultimately felt it was important to recognize their time, energy, and knowledge, even if symbolically. Many participants later let me know that they appreciated this gesture.

Methods of Interview Analysis

Like other scholars of qualitative data, I read carefully through the transcribed interviews several times, and "pulled out common themes and tensions."[10] My first "pass" at the interview data was deductive—that is, I sorted interviewees according to the predominant and dissenting views eventually presented in Chapters 5 and 8. These two views had already emerged from a variety of other data such as websites, as well as through my fieldwork. This deductive sorting was not 100% "clean," as I have already noted. After this "sort," my analytic technique was classically inductive, drawing out themes for each group. Rather than systematically "coding" the interviews (i.e., what percentage said this or that), I focused on identifying broader themes that emerged within each set of views.

In order to further validate my research findings across different sources, I subjected them to triangulation, which entailed presenting the findings to a wide variety of audiences including academics, activists, and others who work in communities impacted by incarceration, while also reviewing accounts of the incarceration experience from different sources. Like other prison researchers, I used these strategies to "corroborate [my] findings . . . [through] the experiences of other prisoners, and to the testimonies of those who work closely with or who are intimately related to individuals with a history of imprisonment."[11] As a further check on my findings, I also engaged in a process called "member-checking," which I describe in further detail later.

Ethnographic Methods: Participant Observation and the Role of the Researcher

The participant observation (or rather, "observant participation"[12]) of a mindfulness class described in Chapter 6 also came about as a result of my combined efforts in recruiting interview participants, while immersing myself in the local world of prison volunteer communities. Through the snowballing sampling that led me to volunteer respondents, I had met Chaplain

Eric. I had initially interviewed him as part of the research described in Chapter 8. Meanwhile, I had increasingly become embedded as a volunteer in local communities, and broached to him the possibility of accompanying him as a participant-observer in his prison classes. Unlike many other ethnographers, anthropologists, and social scientists, I had little hope of reducing my own influence as researcher on the social setting under study, given the obvious ways in which I stuck out in a men's detention facility. Here, I offer some reflections on the impact of my own presence on the community I was studying, and on the ways that I might have been read or perceived by my participants.

Once the course began, Chaplain Eric and I would arrive into the classroom together. At the beginning of the course, he introduced me to the participants, and gave me the floor to introduce myself and say a few words about my research project. I introduced myself by first name and institutional affiliation (without using a title such as "Professor"), explaining my research project. I tried to keep my explanations as simple as possible, partly out of alertness to the relatively low literacy levels in incarceration facilities, but also in order not to take up too much precious time, aware of how the class and the practices offered would be a rare respite in an otherwise hostile and difficult environment. Of course, this had to be balanced against ensuring that everyone understood exactly what they were signing up for. I also wanted to avoid sounding overly cerebral or intimidating. I felt awkward about the legalities introduced by my consent form, and hyperaware of the power differentials that might lead me to be perceived as an authority figure, or result in anyone feeling coerced into joining the course, no matter how subtly. I had been volunteering in prisons long enough by this point to feel relatively comfortable in interpersonal exchanges within that environment. Still, like Cheryl Mattingly, who describes the consent-signing process as something to be approached with trepidation, I too felt apologetic and stumbled through this part of the process, trying to "translate written words that sound as cold as any lawyer's into some kind of human conversation," and to "convey the impression that I [was] not the person behind this unfeeling language."[13] I attempted to minimize my own conspicuousness by striving to be as friendly, down-to-earth and relatable as possible. I tried to reassure everyone that I was there to learn from them and their experiences, and that there was no pressure at all to sign the form or join in the project.

I was relieved—somewhat paradoxically—during the explanation of the consent form in an early session, when one person loudly declared he was not interested in participating, and asked to leave the classroom, an incident I describe in footnote 10 of chapter 6. The fact that at least one potential participant openly voiced their refusal to join the project with no apparent fear of consequence made it seem more plausible that the rest were exercising some agency in participating willingly. I hoped therefore that my sincerity in requesting rather than compelling their participation had gotten across. And, as the course went on, the fact that so many participants later dropped out also indicated to me that they seemed to fear no particular consequence from nonattendance. All of this offered me some reassurance that I might have managed to communicate to participants that neither the project nor I were part of the coercive state machinery that controlled their lives.

Once everyone seemed to understand my purpose and the course got started, I eventually became part of the scenery to some extent. My goal was not to be an entirely inconspicuous "fly on the wall,"[14] which would have been impossible in the prison environment in any case. Rather, I participated in the course like any other member of that community, and learned by doing. This meant that I inevitably stood out in some ways, even as I aimed to be unremarkable in others. I endeavored to be unremarkable by participating in all the meditative exercises Chaplain Eric taught, like any other member of that community. I chatted informally with our students just as Chaplain Eric did, making friendly small talk at the beginning and end of class. When the time came for check-ins, I took my turn in the circle like everyone else. I talked about my own challenges just as others did, describing my state of mind or sharing the day's ongoing preoccupation, whether it was a stressful situation or a mundane thought. But of course, I could not simply blend into the background, for more than just the obvious reasons. On several occasions, I felt embarrassed that the things Chaplain Eric or I shared as "challenges" during our respective turns at check-in paled so obviously in comparison to what our students were dealing with. Meanwhile, sharing some particularly good news during these check-ins also felt inappropriate to me, for the same reasons. And, despite my attempts to blend in, no one had an opportunity to forget my role as a researcher, given that I took notes throughout, furiously scratching them out on pen and paper while people talked around me, and trying to write down almost everything I heard and saw. (Neither cell phones nor any other recording devices were permitted in any incarceration facility I have ever been to. After I got home each day, I spent four or five hours transcribing my chicken-scratched, shorthand-filled field notes for the day's class session onto my laptop, filling in details and nuances from memory, and eventually producing approximately 300 single-spaced pages of field notes for this chapter alone.) Eventually, as the class wore on and we got into a groove, Chaplain Eric asked if I would lead a few yoga poses. During the final few sessions, I led everyone in several simple poses that required no props other than a wall, such as tree pose, chair pose or downward dog at the wall. These brief sections of class led by me lasted no more than fifteen minutes at a time, and students often expressed their gratitude later, reporting that they had felt new muscles they had never known they had, and that they were practicing the poses in their dorms to feel stronger.

Another important issue that emerged in conversation with research participants was the issue of sharing research results with them—a few said they would be keen to see these results. During negotiations, prison administrators had made clear they did not want me to share my contact information with incarcerated participants. I was told to state on the consent form that research results would be made available on request, and that participants should contact facility staff to ask for such results. During the discussion of the consent form, participants laughed out loud at this clause, reminding us that it was virtually impossible to get the custodial staff to respond to their most basic needs, including requests for medical care—given how badly they were treated, why did we think prison staff would be responsive to their requests for access to research results? (Such claims of mistreatment by prison staff are confirmed in much of the research I cite in Chapter 4.)

I decided it was incumbent on me to try and find a better way to make research results available to participants without forcing them to plead with already-unresponsive prison staff. After several conversations with IRB administrators on my campus, we arrived at a compromise: I persuaded IRB officials to serve as the liaison between myself and any incarcerated participants who might ask to see research results. The IRB's contact information (including their office phone number) was already listed on the consent form signed by each participant. I told incarcerated students they could call that number, identify themselves as a participant in my research, share their contact information, and ask to have results sent to them. Meanwhile, IRB agreed to have a staff person alert me if they received any such phone calls and facilitate sending my results to anyone who might request it. This seemed to satisfy the participants, while also satisfying the prison officials' request for minimizing contact with incarcerated persons. As with so many other issues, I was left with no choice to follow the prison's directives in my ability to engage with my research participants. I was hopeful, however, that at the very least I had done my best to be responsive to participant concerns within the limits of these constraints. Ultimately, I never received any notification from the IRB office regarding research participants contacting them.

Confidentiality and Anonymity

Following many researchers who work on politically fraught topics, including prison-related research, I have decided to obscure the name and any other identifying characteristics of the geographical area in which I did my volunteer work and my interviews. Additionally, the names of all individuals, organizations, and institutions have been anonymized, with the exception of those mentioned previously. In a few cases, I have created composite characters to further minimize the risk of identification.[15] I have deleted or altered references to information that could identify my participants. With regard to the incarceration facilities I have visited or volunteered at, I have purposely obscured details that could lead even inadvertently to participants being identified. I have kept precise records of all the pseudonyms I have used, ensuring that I did not choose pseudonyms that approximated a person's real name in any way.[16] My commitment to protecting the identities of respondents and participants does cause me to sacrifice a textured analysis of the area in which I did my work, as well as its demographics and representativeness, and the various different facilities I volunteered in.

Of course, many scholars note that it is difficult to obscure identities entirely, to the point where participants and other members of their communities would not be able to recognize themselves or others,[17] especially in small communities of the sort I was involved in. The sociologist Will Van Den Hoonard notes that "every person is identifiable by a unique set of expressions and experiences that set him or her off from other human beings."[18] Descriptive details—biographical information such as race, gender, age, and occupation as well as other unique mannerisms or experiences—are crucial in painting as vivid and accurate a picture as possible of the communities and their members. Scholars must constantly balance the professional goals of such accuracy against privacy concerns. Four respondents who read manuscript drafts correctly identified themselves (while a fifth made an incorrect guess). Yet, it is extremely unlikely that anyone else from their communities—much less a prison staff person or official—would be able to identify them or their organizations. In cases where some more textured analysis has been offered (such as in Chapter 6), I have taken care to ensure that any descriptive details would make participants recognizable to very few people besides themselves (such as prison staff or other volunteers who were already aware of their participation). In this instance, the opacity of prisons favors the anonymity of research participants: Very few people who are not already familiar with the workings of a facility can know much about what goes on inside it, enough to identify those who are described.

This commitment to anonymity is also the reason that I do not offer more detailed and specific information on the volunteer organizations I worked with. Given concerns about prison retaliating against volunteer programs—and given that I volunteered with several different organizations in different facilities—my goal was to make it difficult to trace my involvement with specific organizations, people, or facilities. For the same reason, I do not offer any biographical details that would render my coauthors in Chapter 9 (or the facility they were incarcerated at) identifiable.

Member-Checking

In interpretive scholarship, the practice of "member-checking" (sometimes known as "member review") requires that all research participants be given an opportunity to offer correctives to the research results, serving as a check on the author's interpretive lens. By "invit[ing] readers who are research participants to have a say in the characterizations and generalizations made about them and their worlds,"[19] member-checking can be among a set of "reflexive practices that compel researchers to subject their interpretations to challenges from a range of subject perspectives, reexamining them in light of the received responses."[20] Providing research participants the opportunity to review the research narrative also "honors their right to know how their world is being rendered for public . . . consumption and to voice their perspective. Thus, it expresses fairness and reciprocity in the research relationship and restructures it in a way that acknowledges participants' rights and capacity to critically interrogate research writing."[21] The intention, simply put, is to "see whether the researcher has 'got it right' from the perspective of members 'native' to the situation or setting under study."[22]

Despite the general consensus on member-checking as a "best practice" in qualitative scholarship, there is little agreement on the specifics.[23] What precisely should be shared with research participants: interview transcripts? The quote(s) cited from their interview(s) in a manuscript draft? Should only the portions paraphrasing their quotes be shared? Or, should the entire manuscript be shared? Additionally, researchers debate the question of when these materials should be sent: Should transcripts be sent immediately after the interview? Should drafts be sent as soon as they are ready? Or should the author wait until the entire manuscript is ready to be shared? Scholars also note that member-checking practices can introduce issues of power differentials, both among the researcher and the research participants, as well as among differently situated research participants, who may be more or less powerful relative to one another. In cases where research participants are more powerful relative to the researcher, they may try to influence the thrust of the research results. Researcher interpretations may be embraced by some actors in the field, but vigorously rejected by others, and "seamless" agreement about whether the researcher has "got it right" may be virtually impossible.[24] In some cases, if participants are displeased with certain aspects of the research results, they have been known to try and obstruct the publication of the resulting research.[25] Meanwhile, revealing what those in lesser positions of power have shared can be ethically problematic if the drafts are shared with participants who are in greater positions of power or authority.

As a result, member-checking can be a fraught enterprise. This was particularly true in my case: I was a scholar-activist who had worn multiple hats, and had ultimately ended up writing somewhat critically about some of the communities I had been embedded in. My immersion in these volunteer communities had begun several years before the writing of this book. As I have detailed, I had been warmly welcomed, and had eventually begun to play a central leadership role in several of these communities. Although the pandemic brought a natural end to our volunteer activities in prisons approximately a year before I completed writing, I remained in contact with most community leaders (and a few other community members) in the interim. All of these participants were aware from the very beginning that I was writing a book based on my immersion within their communities, and I had repeatedly reminded them of this fact over the years.

I had sixty-one research participants and two coauthors. Because I ultimately felt that the arguments in my book were complex enough that any one piece could not be understood outside the context of the whole, I elected to wait until closer to the completion of my manuscript to share draft chapters with all research participants. Thus, in some cases, years had elapsed between when I had first interviewed some participants, and when I eventually felt that drafts were ready to share.[26] I made case-by-case decisions about whether to send the entire book manuscript, or select draft chapters that were pertinent. In cases where I had worked very closely with participants, I sent the entire manuscript, since I felt that any single chapter needed to be read in the context of the overall arguments.[27] Alternatively, if I had not had much close contact with a participant beyond the interviews, I sent the pertinent chapters where excerpts from interviews were quoted (usually accompanied by the introductory chapter for context).[28]

I informed all participants that all names of participants, organizations, and institutions were anonymized. Using pseudonyms and removing identifying information, however, does not always ensure that research participants will be anonymous to organizational insiders—some individuals may still be recognizable by the social position they occupy, or by their ways of speaking about events, issues, and people.[29] By reviewing their own representations, research participants can monitor their own anonymity.[30] Particularly given that I was writing about occasionally sensitive and confidential issues, I wanted to give participants—especially those with whom I had worked closely—the opportunity to ensure that they did not feel compromised or endangered by anything in the manuscript.

I found, however, that the matter of asking participants for feedback was far more delicate than most scholarship acknowledges. When contacting participants, I was careful to clarify that while I was keen to integrate participant feedback into the final draft, this was optional, and that participants were under no obligation to read or respond. This was important since I was contacting people in the midst of an ongoing pandemic. I felt awkward about adding more to their plates at a particularly challenging time when many were overburdened, isolated, possibly grieving losses, or otherwise facing any number of difficulties. As an academic who had myself been overworked and exhausted during the pandemic, while having worried incessantly about the health of family members, I knew how it felt to have yet another request put on my plate. That said, I ensured that all the leading research participants who were prominently featured (or who were relatively prominent within their own communities) had an opportunity to read at least their own depictions.

Like Locke and Velamuri, I "believed that subjecting my case narrative to member review would enhance its quality by allowing organization members to challenge my account."[31] Yet, I was keenly aware that any such challenges would need to be carefully navigated. Member-checking may generate interpretive differences that potentially put research results at risk—research participants may retroactively withdraw their consent to participate if they feel they have not been portrayed in a manner they agree with. Allowing participants the opportunity to review and edit depictions of them raises the question of "what kinds of representations they might be comfortable with."[32] Research participants may "press researchers to reshape their narrative so that it better accords with their perspective," or ask for changes to the final manuscript that make their own representations more "palatable."[33] When participants contest the researchers' explanations and narratives, this raises the question of "interpretive privilege," that is, "whose perspective best represents them and their organization more clearly,"[34] rubbing up against the autonomy of the researcher to present her own arguments.[35] Given the explicitly critical tone of some of my work, I was prepared for various forms of contestation or challenge. I was also prepared to honor the voice of my participants by integrating the crux of any disagreements into the text of the final draft while retaining my own perspective and integrity as interpreter and author, rather than allowing these challenges to "flatten or sanitize" my accounts.[36]

Responses from research participants varied. Researchers who undertake member-checking usually report that the most common response from research participants is no response at all.[37] Accordingly, relatively few of my participants actually responded or read the drafts I sent. Among the interviewees from volunteer communities, ten participants simply responded to congratulate me on the completion of the book, while four other lead participants—including two community leaders with whom I had been most closely embedded—read the entire draft and offered feedback, which I have detailed in the concluding chapter. These responses served as an important source of triangulation and corroboration in order to validate the findings.

Among formerly incarcerated interviewees, six participants responded after having read the drafts I sent, and reacted positively. In two cases, correctives to minor factual errors were offered, but none offered any substantive correctives to my interpretive accounts. All reported having enjoyed the draft chapters, and told me how honored they were to participate and have their voices included. Here too, constraints on member-checking are under-recognized in academic literature. As we have seen, formerly incarcerated persons often lead extremely difficult lives; additional labor-intensive requests to read my work felt particularly extractive to me, and left me torn about asking for feedback. Yet, I eventually erred on the side of giving my participants the opportunity to engage in member-checking if they chose, while attempting to make clear that I respected their time and did not expect them to devote more of it to my work.

Notes

Chapter 1

1. These quotes are exact transcripts, excerpted (and lightly edited) from interviews on which I report in further detail in Chapter 5. While Lee is a pseudonym, Michael has specifically asked to be identified by his real name. For more information on interview methods, as well as considerations of confidentiality and anonymity, see the Methodological Appendix.

2. See Wendy Sawyer and Peter Wagner, "Mass Incarceration: The Whole Pie," Prison Policy Initiative, https://www.prisonpolicy.org/reports/pie2020.html#dataheader, accessed June 2, 2021. As of 2018, the U.S. Department of Justice estimated that 6.4 million people were held in prisons or jail, or were on probation or parole. See Laura M. Maruschak and Todd D. Minton, "Correctional Populations in the United States," U.S. Department of Justice, August 2020, https://www.bjs.gov/content/pub/pdf/cpus1718.pdf, accessed May 3, 2021. The Prison Policy Initiative estimated the number at 6.7 million in their 2018 report. This number is higher because it includes 20,295 people who are involuntarily committed and 48,043 confined youth. See Alexi Jones, "Correctional Control 2018: Incarceration and Supervision by State," Prison Policy Initiative, December 2018, https://www.prisonpolicy.org/reports/correctionalcontrol2018.html, accessed May 3, 2021. The Prison Policy Initiative reports that these population numbers do not capture the more important phenomenon called "jail churn": the staggering number of people admitted to jails each year, which is now thought to be 10.6 million. See Sawyer and Wagner, "Mass Incarceration: The Whole Pie."

3. Congressional Research Service, "American War and Military Operations Casualties," July 29, 2020, https://fas.org/sgp/crs/natsec/RL32492.pdf, accessed June 2, 2021.

4. The Prison Policy Initiative estimates that 1 in every 37 people in the United States is under correctional control. See Jones, "Correctional Control 2018." These numbers, however, do not include people in immigration detention, community sanctions, drug courts, and many other forms of supervision, which leads some scholars to suggest that the total number is above 8 million, or one in twenty-three adults. See Marie Gottschalk, *Caught: The Prison State and the Lockdown of American Politics* (Princeton, NJ: Princeton University Press, 2016), pp. 1, 285.

5. Kelly Lytle Hernández, Khalil Gibran Muhammad, and Heather Ann Thompson, "Introduction: Constructing the Carceral State," *Journal of American History* 102(1) 2015, p. 18.

6. See Brian Elderbroom, Laura Bennett, Shanna Gong, Felicity Rose, and Zoë Towns, *Every Second: The Impact of the Incarceration Crisis on American Families* (Washington, DC: FWD.us, December 2018), https://everysecond.fwd.us/downloads/EverySecond.fwd.us.pdf, accessed June 2, 2021: "Socioeconomic and racial disparities are also intertwined. . . . For white people in the United States, socioeconomic status is a major indicator of exposure to family incarceration. . . . The difference is smaller for black people, who experience family incarceration at higher rates than white people regardless of socioeconomic status,"

p. 30. See also "Criminal Justice Facts," *The Sentencing Project*, https://www.sentencing project.org/criminal-justice-facts/, accessed June 2, 2021; Jeremy Travis, Bruce Western, and F. Stevens Redburn, *The Growth of Incarceration in the United States: Exploring Causes and Consequences* (Washington DC: National Academic Press, 2014), https://doi.org/10.17226/18613.

7. Elderbloom et al., *Every Second*.

8. Gene B. Sperling, "The New Debt Prisons," *New York Times*, February 16, 2021, https://www.nytimes.com/2021/02/16/opinion/politics/debt-america.html?action=click&module=Opinion&pgtype=Homepage, accessed June 2, 2021.

9. Referring to the "indigent defense crisis," Marie Gottschalk quotes a legal journalist as noting, "[T]here is no meaningful right to counsel for Americans too poor to afford their own attorney." Andrew Cohen, "The Lies We Tell Each Other About the Right to Counsel," Brennan Center for Justice, March 13, 2013, https://www.brennancenter.org/our-work/analysis-opinion/lies-we-tell-each-other-about-right-counsel, accessed December 12, 2021, cited in Gottschalk, *Caught*, p. 11.

10. Sawyer and Wagner, "Mass Incarceration: The Whole Pie."

11. Roy Walmsley, "World Prison Population List," Institute for Criminal Policy Research, 2018, https://www.prisonstudies.org/sites/default/files/resources/downloads/wppl_12.pdf, accessed June 2, 2021.

12. John Gramlich, "Only 2% of Federal Criminal Defendants Go to Trial, and Most Who Do Are Found Guilty," Pew Research Center, June 11, 2019, https://www.pewresearch.org/fact-tank/2019/06/11/only-2-of-federal-criminal-defendants-go-to-trial-and-most-who-do-are-found-guilty/; Jeffrey Q. Smith and Grant R. Macqueen, "Trials Continue to Decline in Federal and State Courts: Does It Matter?," *Judicature* 101(4) 2017, https://judicialstudies.duke.edu/wp-content/uploads/2018/01/JUDICATURE101.4-vanishing.pdf, accessed June 2, 2021.

13. This phrase was first coined by the cultural theorist Mike Davis, and has since been popularized. See Mike Davis, "Hell Factories in the Field," *The Nation* 260(7), February 20, 1995, p. 229.

14. Sawyer and Wagner, "Mass Incarceration: The Whole Pie"; Keesha Middlemass, *Convicted and Condemned: The Politics and Policies of Prisoner Reentry* (New York: NYU Press, 2017).

15. Chris Uggen, Ryan Larson, Sarah Shannon, and Arleth Pulido-Nava, "Locked Out 2020: Estimates of People Denied Voting Rights Due to a Felony Conviction," *The Sentencing Project*, October 30, 2020, https://www.sentencingproject.org/publications/locked-out-2020-estimates-of-people-denied-voting-rights-due-to-a-felony-conviction/, accessed June 2, 2021.

16. Gottschalk, *Caught*, p. 2.

17. Joshua Price, *Prison and Social Death* (New Brunswick, NJ: Rutgers University Press, 2015), p. 12.

18. Rosa Brooks, *Tangled Up in Blue: Policing the American City* (New York: Penguin, 2021), p. 18.

19. Amy E. Lerman and Vesla M. Weaver, *Arresting Citizenship: The Democratic Consequences of American Crime Control* (Chicago: University of Chicago Press, 2014), p. 230. See also Reuben Jonathan Miller and Amanda Alexander, "The Price of Carceral Citizenship: Punishment, Surveillance, and Social Welfare Policy in an age of Carceral Expansion," *Michigan Journal of Race and Law* 21 (2016), pp. 291–314.

20. Gottschalk, *Caught*, p. 6; James Forman Jr., "Racial Critiques of Mass Incarceration: Beyond the New Jim Crow," *NY Law Review*, February 26, 2012, pp. 114–115.

21. Forman, "Racial Critiques of Mass Incarceration."

22. Michelle Alexander, *The New Jim Crow: Mass Incarceration in the Age of Colorblindness* (New York: New Press, 2012), p. 215.

23. Lerman and Weaver, *Arresting Citizenship*, pp. 162–169, 179–196; Jill McCorkel, *Breaking Women: Gender, Race and the New Politics of Imprisonment* (New York: NYU Press, 2013); Loïc Wacquant, "Crafting the Neoliberal State: Workfare, Prisonfare, and Social Insecurity," *Sociological Forum* 25(2) 2010, p. 214; Gottschalk, *Caught*, p. 15.

24. Marie Gottschalk, "Conservatives against Incarceration?" *Jacobin*, December 23, 2016, https://www.jacobinmag.com/2016/12/carceral-state-mass-incarceration-conservati ves-koch-trump/, accessed June 2, 2021. "Problems such as crime, poverty, mass unemployment, and mass incarceration are no longer viewed as having fundamental structural causes that can be ameliorated by policies and resources mobilized by the state. Instead, these problems are regarded as the result of fate or individual choice."

25. Alexi Jones, "Reforms without Results: Why States Should Stop Excluding Violent Offenses from Criminal Justice Reforms," Prison Policy Initiative, April 2020, https://www.priso npolicy.org/reports/violence.html, accessed June 2, 2021. "Many key risk factors for violence are related to social and community conditions, not individual attributes. Poverty, inequality, high unemployment, high rates of neighborhood change, and lack of educational and economic opportunities all contribute to violence in communities."

26. There are varying accounts of the origins of yoga and meditation programs in US prisons. Although these practices had arrived in the West by the early twentieth century, the countercultural "hippie" movement of the 1960s and 1970s, which brought many Indian spiritual teachers to the West, led to a boom in their popularity. Around this time, several individuals and organizations began establishing a presence in prisons. Given the highly decentralized nature of US prisons, however, there is no single "origin story" for these programs in prisons: One is more likely to find loosely organized groups operating locally in discrete fashion, some of which have subsequently coalesced into well-established organizations. One well-recognized source of these programs is the Human Kindness Foundation, formerly known as the Prison-Ashram Project, co-founded by Bo and Sita Lozoff in the early 1970s. The Lozoffs were influenced by the famous American spiritual teacher Ram Dass (formerly known as Richard Alpert), who had sent thousands of free copies of his book *Be Here Now* (San Cristobal, NM: Lama Foundation, 1971) to prisons across the country. Initially financed by Ram Dass, the Lozoffs built an organization designed to "help prisoners use their cells as ashrams, and do their time as 'prison monks' rather than convicts." See Lozoff, *We're All Doing Time* (Durham, NC: Human Kindness Foundation, 1985), p. xvii. Having served as consultants to the US Bureau of Prisons, the Lozoffs began offering classes on yoga and meditation in prisons, and found that "prison doors . . . suddenly flew open." By word of mouth, they began receiving letters from incarcerated persons, in turn sending pamphlets, tapes, and books, while visiting many prisons across the country, offering workshops and classes. One report claims that *We're All Doing Time* has been sent to over 30,000 incarcerated persons. See Fleet Maull, "The Prison Meditation Movement and The Current State of Mindfulness-Based Programming for Prisoners," Prison Mindfulness Institute, See https://www.prisonmindfulness.org/ mindful-justice-conference and https://afc724b7-5fdd-4ef2-92bf-6d2ad2de05d4.files usr.com/ugd/8ea141_052233c39f154ba7ae2bd41da4a88911.pdf, accessed May 7, 2021,

p. 2. The SYDA foundation (also known as Siddha Yoga)—led by the charismatic yogic teacher Swami Muktananda—established its Prison Project in 1975, focused mainly on offering correspondence courses on Siddha Yoga teachings. See https://www.siddhayoga. org/syda-foundation/prison-project, accessed May 26, 2021. Other individuals and organizations who initiated prison yoga or meditation programs in the early years include Hogen Fugimoto, Stephen Levine, and the Transcendental Meditation (TM) movement. More recently, in the 1990s, Fleet Maull, an incarcerated Buddhist, founded the Prison Dharma Network, now known as the Prison Mindfulness Institute (PMI), which serves as an umbrella organization for many different prison contemplative organizations that have proliferated in the intervening years. See Maull, "The Prison Meditation Movement." Meanwhile, the Prison Yoga Project (PYP) was founded in 2002 by James Fox, who began teaching yoga classes at San Quentin prison—it has now spawned an array of prison yoga programs across the globe, established by PYP-trained teachers. Key films that heightened awareness of prison contemplative programs include *Doing Time, Doing Vipassana* (chronicling the work of female Inspector-General Kiran Bedi in bringing meditation to Indian prisons) and *Dhamma Brothers* (an account of meditation practices at a high-security prison in Alabama). See https://www.karunafilms.com/doing-time-doing-vipassana-c1wy3 and http://www.dhammabrothers.com, accessed May 27, 2021.

27. Farah Godrej, "Nonviolence and Gandhi's Truth: A Method for Moral and Political Arbitration," *Review of Politics* 68 (2) 2006, pp. 287–317; "Ascetics, Warriors, and a Gandhian Ecological Citizenship," *Political Theory* 40(4) 2012, pp. 437–465.

28. Rev. angel Kyodo Williams, Lama Rod Owens, and Jasmine Syedullah, *Radical Dharma: Talking Race, Love, Liberation* (Berkeley: North Atlantic Books, 2016); Tara Brach, *Radical Acceptance: Embracing Your Life with the Heart of a Buddha* (New York: Bantam, 2004); Lama Rod Owens, *Love and Rage: The Path of Liberation through Anger* (Berkeley: North Atlantic Books, 2020); Rita Gross, "The Wisdom in the Anger," in Melvin McLeod (ed.), *Mindful Politics: A Buddhist Guide to Making the World a Better Place* (New York: Simon and Schuster, 2006).

29. Ron Purser and David Loy, "Beyond McMindfulness," Huffington Post, July 1, 2013, https://www.huffpost.com/entry/beyond-mcmindfulness_b_3519289, accessed May 12, 2021.

30. Ronald Purser, *McMindfulness: How Mindfulness Became the New Capitalist Spirituality* (London: Repeater, 2019).

31. David Forbes, *Mindfulness and Its Discontents: Education, Self and Social Transformation* (Halifax: Fernwood Publishing, 2019); Daniel Simpson, "From Me to We: Revolutionising Mindfulness in Schools," *Contemporary Buddhism* 18(1) 2017, pp. 47–71.

32. Matthew Remski, "Modern Yoga Will Not Form a Real Culture until Every Studio Can Also Double as a Soup Kitchen, and Other Observations from the Threshold between Yoga and Activism," in Carol Horton and Roseanne Harvey (eds.), *21st Century Yoga: Culture, Politics, Practice* (Chicago, IL: Kleio Books, 2012), p. 118.

33. Farah Godrej, "The Neoliberal Yogi and the Politics of Yoga," *Political Theory* 45(6) 2017, pp. 772–800.

34. Wendy Brown, "American Nightmare: Neoliberalism, Neoconservatism, and De-Democratization," *Political Theory* 34(6) 2006; *Undoing the Demos: Neoliberalism's Stealth Revolution* (Cambridge: MIT Press, 2015); Lisa Duggan, *The Twilight of Equality? Neoliberalism, Cultural Politics, and the Attack on Democracy* (Boston: Beacon Press, 2003); Joe Soss, Richard C. Fording, and Sanford F. Schram, *Disciplining the Poor: Neoliberal Paternalism and the Persistent Power of Race* (Chicago: University of Chicago Press, 2011).

35. Derrick Jensen, "Forget Shorter Showers: Why Personal Change Does Not Equal Political Change," *Orion Magazine*, https://orionmagazine.org/article/forget-shorter-showers/, accessed June 2, 2021.

36. While recognizing that jails and prisons serve different functions, I use "prison" as short-hand for both.

37. For reasons of confidentiality and requirements of anonymizing, I offer no geographic details about where these facilities were located.

38. Marie Gottschalk, "Yosarian Meets 'Up the Down Staircase': Teaching the Politics of Crime and Punishment at Penn and in the Pen," *PS: Political Science and Politics* 52(1) 2019, p. 2.

39. I am indebted to Mark Golub for clarification of this point.

40. Private communication, Tiffany Willoughby-Herard.

41. I owe this very succinct formulation to the generous reading of Naomi Murakawa.

42. Joshua Eaton, "American Buddhism: Beyond the Search for Inner Peace," *Religion Dispatches*, February 20, 2013, https://religiondispatches.org/american-buddhism-beyond-the-search-for-inner-peace/, accessed May 11, 2021.

43. Michelle Alexander, "Let Our People Go," *New York Times*, May 13, 2020, https://www.nytimes.com/2020/05/13/opinion/coronavirus-prison-outbreak.html, accessed June 2, 2021.

44. Dylan Rodríguez, https://www.caseygrants.org/freedom-scholars/dr-dylan-rodriguez, accessed November 24, 2021.

45. Dvora Yanow and Peregrine Schwartz-Shea, *Interpretive Research Design: Concepts and Processes* (New York and London: Routledge, 2011), p. 4.

46. Yanow and Schwartz-Shea, *Interpretive Research Design*, p. 105.

47. Yanow and Schwartz-Shea, *Interpretive Research Design*, p. 52.

48. See Lerman and Weaver, *Arresting Citizenship*, for examples of this kind of causal inference.

49. Mary Woods Byrne, "Conducting Research as a Visiting Scientist in a Women's Prison," *Journal of Professional Nursing* 21(4) 2005.

50. Michael Hames-Garcia, *Fugitive Thought: Prison Movements, Race, and The Meaning of Justice* (Minneapolis: University of Minnesota Press, 2004), p. 155.

51. Lerman and Weaver, *Arresting Citizenship*, p. 16.

52. McCorkel, *Breaking Women*, p. 162.

53. Pat Carlen and Jacqueline Tombs, "Reconfigurations of Penality," *Theoretical Criminology* 10(3) 2006, p. 356.

Chapter 2

1. The title of this chapter references a passage from the work of James Baldwin: "If one really wishes to know how justice is administered in a country, one does not question the policemen, the lawyers, the judges, or the protected members of the middle class. One goes to the unprotected—those, precisely, who need the law's protection most!—and listens to their testimony." James Baldwin, *The Price of the Ticket* (New York: St. Martin's Press: 1985), p. 527. I thank Tiffany Willoughby-Herard for drawing my attention to this passage.

2. On immersion as a method for in-depth learning about a community while engaging in its everyday routines and practices, see, for instance, Clifford Geertz, *The Interpretation of Cultures* (New York: Basic Books, 1973); James Clifford, "On Ethnographic Authority," *Representations* 2 (1983) 118–146; Edward Schatz, "Ethnographic Immersion and the Study of Politics," and "What Kind(s) of Ethnography does Political Science Need?" in

Edward Schatz (ed.), *Political Ethnography: What Immersion Contributes to the Study of Power* (Chicago: University of Chicago, 2009); Lisa Wedeen, "Ethnography as Interpretive Enterprise," in Schatz (ed.), pp. 75–93; Timothy Pachirat, "The Political in Political Ethnography: Dispatches from the Kill Floor," in Schatz (ed.), pp. 143–161; Ellen Pader, "Seeing with an Ethnographic Sensibility," and Samer Shehata, "Ethnography, Identity and the Production of Knowledge," in Dvora Yanow and Peregrine Schwartz-Shea (eds.), *Interpretation and Method: Empirical Research Methods and the Interpretive Turn* (New York: Routledge, 2015), pp. 194–208 and 209–227. See also Timothy Pachirat, *Every Twelve Seconds: Industrialized Slaughter and the Politics of Sight* (New Haven: Yale University Press, 2013).

3. Many system-impacted people argue that words defining human beings by their crimes and punishments are dehumanizing. A 2015 survey revealed that 38 percent of 200 respondents preferred "incarcerated person," while 23 percent preferred "prisoner" and 10 percent preferred "inmate." See Blair Hickman, "Inmate.Prisoner.Other: Discussed. What to Call Incarcerated People: Your Feedback," *The Marshall Project*, April 3, 2015, https://www.the marshallproject.org/2015/04/03/inmate-prisoner-other-discussed, accessed May 5, 2021. See also "The Language Project," *The Marshall Project*, https://www.themarshallproject. org/2021/04/12/the-language-project, accessed May 5, 2021. Throughout this book, I use "incarcerated person," based not only on these reports but also on conversations with multiple incarcerated individuals who expressed a preference for this term. The occasional use of terms such as "prisoner" or "inmate" occurs mainly when quoting other writers or conversations.

4. Keramet Reiter, "Making Windows in Walls: Strategies for Prison Research," *Qualitative Inquiry* 20(4) 2014, pp. 417–428.

5. Reiter, "Making Windows in Walls," p. 420. See also Loïc Wacquant, "The Curious Eclipse of Prison Ethnography," *Ethnography* 3(4) 2002, pp. 371–397; Yvonne Jewkes, "Foreword," in Deborah H. Drake, Rod Earle, and J. Sloan (eds.), *The Palgrave Handbook of Prison Ethnography* (London and New York: Palgrave Macmillan, 2016), pp. ix–xiv; Kelly Hannah-Moffat, "Criminological Cliques, Narrowing Dialogues, Institutional Protectionism and the Next Generation," in Mary Bosworth and Carolyn Hoyle (eds.), *What Is Criminology?* (New York: Oxford University Press, 2012), pp. 440–455.

6. The mid-twentieth century was thought to be a period of relative flourishing in qualitative or ethnographic approaches to studying prisons in the United States. Classic qualitative prison studies during that era include Donald Clemmer, *The Prison Community* (New York: Rinehart, 1958); Gresham M. Skyes, *The Society of Captives: A Study of a Maximum Security Prison* (Princeton, NJ: Princeton University Press, 1958); and Erving Goffman, *Asylums: Essays on the Social Situation of Mental Patients and Other Inmates* (London: Penguin, 1963). The exponential growth of the prison-industrial complex in the late twentieth century seemed to coincide with the steady disappearance of qualitative or ethnographic studies in US prisons, with access for researchers becoming increasingly difficult, and precedence being given to quantitative studies that are relatively uncritical of prisons. See, for instance, Wacquant, "The Curious Eclipse of Prison Ethnography;" Lorna Rhodes, "Toward an Anthropology of Prisons," *Annual Review of Anthropology* 30 (2001), pp. 65–83. The rare contemporary studies that have obtained an "insider" view of a US prison, or have engaged directly with incarcerated persons in the United States, include Ann Chih Lin, *Reform in the Making: The Implementation of Social Policy in Prison* (Princeton, NJ: Princeton University Press, 2000); Kitty Calavita and Valerie Jenness, *Appealing to Justice: Prisoner Grievances,*

Rights and Carceral Logic (Oakland: University of California Press, 2014); Lorna A. Rhodes, *Total Confinement: Madness and Reason in the Maximum Security Prison* (Oakland: University of California Press, 2004); Jill McCorkel, *Breaking Women: Gender, Race and the New Politics of Imprisonment* (New York: NYU Press, 2013); Sharon Dolovich, "Two Models of the Prison: Accidental Humanity and Hypermasculinity in the L.A. County Jail," *Journal of Criminal Law and Criminology* 102(4), Fall 2021, pp. 965–1117; Russell K. Robinson, "Masculinity as Prison: Sexual Identity, Race and Incarceration," *California Law Review* 99 (2011), pp. 1309–1408. It is worth noting that qualitative and/or ethnographic prison studies have flourished (relatively speaking) in several non-US contexts (primarily Canada, the United Kingdom, and Europe), where access to prisons is less rare. See, for instance, Drake, Earle, and Sloan, *The Palgrave Handbook of Prison Ethnography*; Michael Adorjan and Rose Ricciardelli, *Engaging with Ethics in International Criminological Research* (London and New York: Routledge, 2016); Ben Crewe and Yvonne Jewkes, "Introduction," *Punishment and Society* 13 (2011), pp. 507–508; Mary Bosworth, *Engendering Resistance: Agency and Power in Women's Prisons* (London and New York: Routledge, 1999); Alison Liebling, "Doing Research in Prison: Breaking the Silence?," *Theoretical Criminology* 3(2) 1999, pp. 147–173; K. Beyens et al., *The Pains of Doing Criminological Research* (Brussels: Vrije Universiteit Brussels Press, 2016); Mahuya Bandyopadhyay, *Everyday Life in an Indian Prison: Confinement, Surveillance, Resistance* (New Delhi: Orient BlackSwan, 2010); Ben Crewe, *The Prisoner Society: Power, Adaptation and Resistance in an English Prison* (Oxford: Clarendon, 2009); Yvonne Jewkes, Ben Crewe, Jamie Bennett, *Handbook on Prisons* (London and New York: Routledge, 2016); Lila Kazemian, *Positive Growth and Redemption in Prison: Finding Light behind Bars and Beyond* (Abingdon, Oxon: Routledge, 2020); Kelly Hannah-Moffat, *Punishment in Disguise: Penal Governance and Federal Imprisonment of Women in Canada* (Toronto: University of Toronto Press, 2001); Andrew Jefferson, "Conceptualizing Confinement: Prisons and Poverty in Sierra Leone," *Criminology and Criminal Justice* 14(1) 2014, pp. 44–60; Sacha Darke, "Inmate Governance in Brazilian Prisons," *Howard Journal of Criminal Justice* 52 (3) 2013, pp. 272–284; Thomas Ugelvik, *Power and Resistance in Prison: Doing Time, Doing Freedom* (London: Palgrave MacMillan, 2014); Thomas Ugelvik, "Prison Ethnography as Lived Experience: Notes from the Diaries of a Beginner Let Loose in Oslo Prison," *Qualitative Inquiry* 20(4) 2014, pp. 471–480. The Prisons Research Centre at the University of Cambridge catalogs extensive publications resulting from qualitative, UK-based prison research at https://www.prc.crim.cam.ac.uk/publications, accessed April 26, 2021.

7. Mary Bosworth and Sophie Palmer, "Prison: Securing the State," in Molly Dragiewicz and Walert S. DeKeseredy (eds.,) *Routledge Handbook of Critical Criminology* (London and New York: Routledge, 2011). For examples of ethnographic research based directly on the experience of being incarcerated, see Michael L. Walker, "Race Making in a Penal Institution," *American Journal of Sociology* 121(4) 2016, pp. 1051–1078; Rik Scarce, "Doing Time as an Act of Survival," *Symbolic Interaction* 25(3), 2002, pp. 303–321.

8. Ted Conover, *Newjack: Guarding Sing Sing* (New York: Vintage, 2001); Shane Bauer, *American Prison: A Reporter's Undercover Journey into the Business of Punishment* (New York: Penguin, 2018)

9. See for instance Lin, *Reform in the Making*, Appendix 1 and Appendix 2, pp. 175–194. On the necessity—and challenges—of building institutional "insider" relationships, and establishing connections and credibility with administrators for prison access, see Reiter, "Making Windows in Walls"; Andrew M. Jefferson, "Performing Ethnography: Infiltrating

Prison Spaces," in Drake, Earle, and Sloan, *Palgrave Handbook of Prison Ethnography*, pp. 169–186. On the role of "serendipity" in prison research, see Valerie Jenness, "From Policy to Prisoners to People: A 'Soft Mixed Methods' Approach to Studying Transgender Prisoners," *Journal of Contemporary Ethnography* 39 (2010), pp. 517–533.

10. Every university has an IRB: a group of faculty, staff (and occasionally outside community members) whose role is to formally review and monitor any research involving human subjects. IRBs have the authority to approve, require modifications to, or refuse to approve research, according to their understanding of the protection of the rights and welfare of human research subjects.

11. Reiter, "Making Windows in Walls," p. 422. See also Ruth Armstrong, Loraine Gelsthorpe, and Ben Crewe, "From Paper Ethics to Real-World Research: Supervising Ethical Reflexivity When Taking Risks in Research with the 'Risky,'" in Karen Lumsden and Aaron Winter (eds.), *Reflexivity in Criminological Research: Experiences with the Powerful and Powerless* (New York: Palgrave Macmillan, 2014): "Powerful institutions can utilise ethical procedures designed to both define and protect 'the vulnerable' to inhibit research that aims to encounter these individuals within the risky realities of their lives," p. 207. See also Mark Israel, "A History of Coercive Practices: The Abuse of Consent in Research Involving Prisoners and Prisons in the United States," in Adorjan and Ricciardelli, *Engaging with Ethics in International Criminological Research*, p. 80: "Research ethics regulations have enabled corrective services to portray their refusal to allow external researchers access to prisons as being in the best interest of prisoners. The ambition . . . to limit independent research might be less serious if it were not accompanied by a general lack of disclosure and transparency."

12. Kevin Haggerty, "Ethics Creep: Governing Social Science Research in the Name of Ethics," in Adorjan and Ricciardelli, *Engaging with Ethics in International Criminological Research*, p. 14.

13. Paul Atkinson and Martyn Hammersley, "Ethnography and Participant Observation," in Norman K. Denzin and Yvonna S. Lincoln (eds.), *Handbook of Qualitative Research* (Thousand Oaks, CA: Sage, 1994), pp. 248–61; Kathleen M. DeWalt and Billie R. De Walt, *Participant Observation* (Walnut Creek, CA: AltaMira Press, 2011).

14. "Approval to conduct research within a prison . . . often involves layers of formal and informal approval. . . . Delays may be experienced in each step of the process." Lynne Roberts and David Indermaur, "The Ethics of Research with Prisoners," *Current Issues in Criminal Justice* 19 (3) 2008, p. 312.

15. See Israel, "A History of Coercive Practices," in Adorjan and Ricciardelli, *Engaging with Ethics in International Criminological Research*, pp. 69–86; and Roberts and Indermaur, "The Ethics of Research with Prisoners." See also Heather Ann Thompson, "Attica: It's Worse Than We Thought," *New York Times*, November 19, 2017, https://www.nytimes.com/2017/11/19/opinion/attica-prison-torture.html?action=click&pgtype=Homepage&clickSource=story-heading&module=opinion-c-col-right-region&region=opinion-c-col-right-region&WT.nav=opinion-c-col-right-region&_r=4, accessed April 25, 2021.

16. Roberts and Indermaur, "The Ethics of Research with Prisoners," p. 310.

17. Roberts and Indermaur, "The Ethics of Research with Prisoners," p. 316.

18. See Adorjan and Ricciardelli, *Engaging with Ethics in International Criminological Research*; Lumsden and Winter, *Reflexivity in Criminological Research*.

19. Private communication, Keramet Reiter.

20. Stuart Henry, "The Threat of Incarceration Does Not Deter Criminal Behavior," in J. Haley (ed.), *Prisons* (Farmington Hills: Green Haven Press, 2005), pp. 41–48, cited in Alan Mobley, Stuart Henry, and Dana Plemmons, "Protecting Prisoners from Harmful Research: Is 'Being Heard' Enough?" *Journal of Offender Rehabilitation* 45 (1–2) 2007.

21. Israel, "A History of Coercive Practices," p. 70.

22. See Barrie Thorne, "'You Still Takin' Notes?' Fieldwork and Problems of Informed Consent," *Social Problems* 27(3) 1980, pp. 284–297: "asking each member of a setting to sign a consent form . . . seem[s] overly legalistic, formalized, and intrusive in the more fluid context of field research" p. 286. "The abstract, universal and individualistic assumptions of informed consent limit its ability to help resolve . . . ethical dilemma[s]. The doctrine of informed consent does not take account of ethical dimensions of the knowledge a researcher may seek. . . . By itself, the doctrine of informed consent does not do full justice to the complexity of the ethical judgments fieldworkers confront," pp. 293–294.

23. Mary Woods Byrne, "Conducting Research as a Visiting Scientist in a Women's Prison," *Journal of Professional Nursing* 21 (4) 2005, p. 225. See also D. J. Moser et al., "Coercion and Informed Consent to Research Involving Prisoners," *Comprehensive Psychiatry*, 45 (2004), pp. 1–9.

24. The ethical principle of beneficence assesses potential research risks in light of expected societal benefits, by recognizing the longer-term benefits that may result from the improvement of knowledge for society at large. See National Commission for the Protection of Human Subjects of Biomedical and Behavioral Research, "The Belmont Report: Ethical Principles and Guidelines for the Protection of Human Subjects of Research," Washington, DC: Department of Health, Education, and Welfare Publication No. (OS) 78–0012, 1978, https://www.hhs.gov/ohrp/regulations-and-policy/belmont-report/read-the-belmont-rep ort/index.html ,accessed May 3, 2021.

25. See James B. Waldram, "Anthropology in Prison: Negotiating Consent and Accountability with a 'Captive' Population," *Human Organization* 57(2) 1998, pp. 238–244; Thorne, "'You Still Takin' Notes?'"; Murray L. Wax, "Paradoxes of 'Consent' to the Practice of Fieldwork," *Social Problems* 27(3) 1980, pp. 272–283.

26. Israel, "A History of Coercive Practices," p. 71.

27. We eventually found a way to ensure that these written records would be destroyed, but this was reliant on the prison staff agreeing to destroy these records. Although I cannot confirm whether this was done, I took measures to anonymize all my research participants so that it would be virtually impossible to trace anything directly back to a specific participant, so as to eliminate the risk of retaliation.

28. The prison researcher James Waldram describes "walking away" from a proposed research contract with an incarceration facility which he found "unacceptable," both because it stipulated that the government would own all research and because it gave the right to prison staff to examine all records and supporting data, thereby making it impossible to maintain participant confidentiality. See Waldram, "Anthropology in Prison," p. 243: "Ethical sensibilities dictate that, where an [agency] insists on breaching fundamental ethical principles such as confidentiality of participants, we must walk away."

29. Roberts and Indermaur, "The Ethics of Research with Prisoners," pp. 309, 311. Another scholar writes that procedures and requirement for signed consent can become "meaningless rituals rather than improving the ethics of field research." See Thorne, "'You Still Takin' Notes?,'" p. 286. The noted prison researcher Mary Bosworth writes that academics are taught to seek refuge in procedures such as "informed consent" as a way to evade

their larger affective, emotional, and interpersonal obligations to research participants. See Mary Bosworth, Debi Campbell, Bonita Demby, Seth M. Ferranti, and Michael Santos, "Doing Prison Research: Views from the Inside," *Qualitative Inquiry* 11(2) 2005, pp. 249–264, p. 258.

30. Israel, "A History of Coercive Practices," p. 79.
31. See Waldram, "Anthropology in Prison," p. 243: "A correctional system that insists on maintaining absolute control over inmate participation in research, to the exclusion of inmates' wishes, is not a healthy place for ethical social science."
32. Mobley, Henry, and Plemmons, "Protecting Prisoners from Harmful Research," p. 35.
33. Rod Earle, "Insider and Out: Making Sense of a Prison Experience and a Research Experience," *Qualitative Inquiry* 20(4) 2014, pp. 429–438, p. 432.
34. Drake et al. note that for people who do research in prisons, "immersion" is bound to be relatively shallow. The same is true for volunteers, who, like researchers, remain outsiders to many facets of prison life. See Deborah Drake, Rod Earle, and Jennifer Sloan, "General Introduction: What Ethnography Tells Us about Prisons and What Prisons Tell Us about Ethnography," in Drake, Earle and Sloane, *Palgrave Handbook of Prison Ethnography*, pp. 2–3. Other prison researchers have noted that their work should be considered "semi-ethnographic in recognition that it is impossible for any 'free-world' researcher to become completely immersed in, or truly experience the realities of, the prison." A. Stevens, "'I Am the Person Now I Was Always Meant to Be': Identity Reconstruction and Narrative Reframing in Therapeutic Community Prisons," *Criminology and Criminal Justice* 12 (2012), pp. 527–547. p. 530. On the limitations and difficulties of outsider "immersion" in prisons, see Earle, "Insider and Out"; Liebling, "Doing Research in Prison"; Alison Liebling, *Prisons and Their Moral Performance: A Study of Values, Quality, and Prison Life* (Oxford, UK: Oxford University Press, 2004); Alison Liebling, "Moral Performance, Inhuman and Degrading Treatment and Prison Pain," *Punishment and Society* 13 (2011), pp. 530–551. However, it is important to note the stark differences in levels of access granted to prison researchers in different national and subnational settings: for instance, some prison researchers in the United Kingdom and Europe describe being given free access to wander about within certain prisons (or sections of prisons), coming and going as they pleased, being given their own sets of keys to various parts of the prison, talking to any incarcerated person as they pleased without official approval, both in common areas and inside cells, and occasionally even joining them for recreational time such as exercise, TV-watching, or playing games. See Ugelvik, "Prison Ethnography as Lived Experience," and Bosworth, *Engendering Resistance*. Such levels of access for researchers are virtually unheard-of in contemporary US prisons, and also greatly exceed the severely limited access and mobility I was allowed as a volunteer.
35. For accounts of insider ethnography or "complete-member-research" by a formerly incarcerated sociologist, see Walker, "Race Making in a Penal Institution."
36. Mobley, Henry, and Plemmons, "Protecting Prisoners from Harmful Research."
37. Several US-based scholars have been able to achieve this to some extent, but this is exceedingly rare. See, for instance, Rhodes, *Total Confinement*; McCorkel, *Breaking Women*; Lin, *Reform in the Making*, and Calavita and Jenness, *Appealing to Justice*. For examples outside the US context, see, for instance, Bosworth, *Engendering Resistance*; Ben Crewe and Jamie Bennett, *The Prisoner* (London and New York: Routledge, 2012)
38. For other examples, see Carmella J. Braniger (ed.), *Critical Storytelling from behind Invisible Bars: Undergraduates and Inmates Write Their Way Out* (Boston: Brill, 2020);

Bob Gaucher (ed.), *Writing as Resistance: The Journal of Prisoners on Prisons Anthology* (Toronto: Canadian Scholars' Press, 2002); Michelle Inderbitzin, Joshua Cain, and Trevor Walraven, "Learning and Practicing Citizenship and Democracy Behind Bars," in Laura S. Abrams, Emma Hughes, Michelle Inderbitzin, and Rosie Meek (eds.), *The Voluntary Sector in Prisons: Encouraging Personal and Institutional Change* (New York: Palgrave Macmillan, 2016), pp. 55–83; Bosworth et al., "Doing Prison Research." The *Journal of Prisoners on Prisons*, established in 1988, encourages submissions from currently—and formerly— incarcerated persons. Supported by an editorial board of academics, activists, and advisers, the journal publishes twice yearly peer-reviewed issues, and fosters collaborative writing projects between established prison academics and those who are currently (or have been) imprisoned.

39. Byrne, "Conducting Research as a Visiting Scientist in a Women's Prison," p. 226.
40. Mobley, Henry, and Plemmons, "Protecting Prisoners from Harmful Research," p. 43.
41. Price, *Prison and Social Death*, p. 12.
42. Price, *Prison and Social Death*, p. 17. See also Paul Apostolidis, *Breaks in the Chain: What Immigrant Workers can Teach America About Democracy* (Minneapolis, MN: University of Minnesota Press, 2010).
43. Bosworth et al., "Doing Prison Research," pp. 261, 250.
44. Bob Gaucher, "Inside Looking Out: Writers in Prison," *Journal of Prisoners on Prisons* 10(1&2) 1999, pp. 14–31, p. 14. Scholarship by those who write from a background of being imprisoned and employ their experiences of imprisonment is sometimes referred to as "convict criminology." See Gaucher (ed.) *Writing as Resistance*; Greg Newbold et al., "Prison Research from the Inside: The Role of Convict AutoEthnography," *Qualitative Inquiry* 20(4) 2014, pp. 439–448; J. I. Ross and S. C. Richards (eds.), *Convict Criminology* (Belmont, CA: Wadsworth, 2003). S. C. Richards and J. I. Ross "The New School of Convict Criminology," *Social Justice* 28 (2001), pp. 177–190; Earle, "Insider and Out." So-called convict criminology now flourishes in countries outside the United States, including the United Kingdom. The American Society of Criminology has a division of Convict Criminology (https://www.concrim.org, accessed May 2, 2021) that specifically highlights the contributions of system-impacted scholars. Some use the term "convict criminology" to refer to formerly incarcerated persons who have gone on to receive academic training and become prison researchers, while others use it more broadly to include writings on prisons and imprisonment by currently incarcerated persons.
45. Justin Piche, Bob Gaucher, and Kevin Walby, "Facilitating Prisoner Ethnography: An Alternative Approach to 'Doing Prison Research Differently,'" *Qualitative Inquiry* 20(4) 2014, pp. 449–460.
46. Piche et al., "Facilitating Prisoner Ethnography," 452.
47. Piche et al., "Facilitating Prisoner Ethnography," 450.
48. Bosworth et al., "Doing Prison Research," p. 251.
49. Piche et al., "Facilitating Prisoner Ethnography"
50. Bosworth et al., "Doing Prison Research," p. 258.
51. Price, *Prison and Social Death*, p. 10. See also Ruth Wilson Gilmore, *Golden Gulag: Prisons, Surplus, Crisis and Opposition in Globalizing California* (Oakland: University of California Press, 2007), p. 27; Judah Schept, *Progressive Punishment: Job Loss, Jail Growth and the Neoliberal Logic of Carceral Expansion* (New York: New York University Press, 2015).
52. The prison researcher Thomas Ugelvik asserts, "As long as you are writing about a prison, you are either taking a critical position about what is happening in it or you are

not . . . [therefore] neutrality is practically impossible. The best we can hope for is to show the readers of our research results what having chosen a position means, so that they can decide whether or not it influences the results in an unacceptable manner." *Power and Resistance in Prison*, p. 36. Sociologists, ethnographers, and other qualitative social science researchers vigorously debate the values of objectivity and neutrality in ethnographic work. On this topic, see Loïc Wacquant, "Scrutinizing the Street: Poverty, Morality, and the Pitfalls of Urban Ethnography," *American Journal of Sociology* 107, 6 (May 2002), pp. 1468–1532; Mitchell Duneier, "What Kind of Combat Sport Is Sociology?" *American Journal of Sociology*,107, 6 (May 2002), pp. 1551–1576; Elijah Anderson, "The Ideologically Driven Critique," *American Journal of Sociology* 107(6), May 2002, pp. 1533–1550. Criminologists who do research inside prisons and with incarcerated persons also grapple with these issues: see, for instance, Howard Becker, "Whose Side Are We On?," *Social Problems* 14(3) 1967, pp. 239–247; Ben Crewe and Alice Ievins, "Closeness, Distance and Honesty in Prison Ethnography," in Drake, Earle, and Sloan, *Palgrave Handbook of Prison Ethnography*, pp. 124–142; Alison Liebling, "Whose Side Are We On?: Theory, Practice and Allegiances in Prisons Research," *British Journal of Criminology* (2001) 41, pp. 472–484; James Sutton, "An Ethnographic Account of Doing Survey Research in Prison: Descriptions, Reflections, and Suggestions from the Field," *Qualitative Sociology Review* 7(2), August 2011, pp. 45–63; James B. Waldram, "Challenges of Prison Ethnography," *Anthropology News* 50(1) 2009, pp. 4–5; Waldram, "Anthropology in Prison." In this book I follow the lead of scholars such as Joshua Price and Judah Schept, who inhabited both researcher and activist roles, and as such, were explicit about their critical, activist commitments regarding the prison system. See Price, *Prison and Social Death*; Schept, *Progressive Punishment*. On critically engaged research practice, see Kamari M. Clarke, "Toward a Critically Engaged Ethnographic Practice," *Current Anthropology* 51 (Supplement 2) 2010, pp. S301–S312; Soyini Madison, *Critical Ethnography: Method, Ethics, Performance* (Thousand Oaks, CA: Sage, 2012), p. 5: the critical scholar "use the resources, skills, and privileges available to her to make accessible . . . the voices and experiences of subjects whose stories are otherwise restrained and out of reach . . . contribut[ing] to emancipatory knowledge and discourses of social justice." For examples of qualitative, ethnographic research inside prisons from an explicitly critical perspective, see McCorkel, *Breaking Women*, and Rhodes, *Total Confinement*.

53. On the need for performance, ambiguity, and identity-management in obtaining research access to prisons, see Jefferson, "Performing Ethnography."

54. Price, *Prison and Social Death*, pp. 3–4.

55. Piche et al., "Facilitating Prisoner Ethnography," p. 456; S. Richards and J. I. Ross, "Introducing the New School of Convict Criminology," *Journal of Prisoners on Prisons* 13 (2004), pp. 111–126. "Good-time credits" refers to credits received in prisons for participation in rehabilitative programming, which lead to an advancement of one's parole eligibility or release dates.

56. G. McMaster, "Maximum Ink," *Journal of Prisoners on Prisons* 10(1&2) 1999, pp. 46–52.

57. Jon Marc Taylor, "Diogenes Still Can't Find His Honest Man," *Journal of Prisoners on Prisons* 18(1&2) 2009, pp. 91–110.

58. Dvora Yanow and Peregrine Schwartz-Shea, "Framing 'Deception' and 'Covertness' in Research: Do Milgram, Humphreys, and Zimbardo Justify Regulating Social Science Research Ethics?," *Forum Qualitative Sozialforschung/Forum: Qualitative Social Research* 19(3) 2018, pp. 1–31; and "Reforming Institutional Review Board Policy: Issues in

Implementation and Field Research," *PS: Political Science and Politics*, July 2008, pp. 483–494.

59. On transitioning between researcher and practitioner roles in prisons, see Lilian Ayete-Nyampong, "Changing Hats: Transiting between Practitioner and Researcher Roles," in Drake, Earle, and Sloan, *Palgrave Handbook of Prison Ethnography*, pp. 307–325.

60. On the importance of reflexivity and reflections on author positionality, see Charlotte Aul Davies, *Reflexive Ethnography: A Guide to Researching Selves and Others* (London: Routledge, 2007); Pierre Bourdieu and Loïc Wacquant, *An Invitation to Reflexive Sociology* (Cambridge: Polity Press, 1992); Mats Alvesson and Kaj Skolberg, *Reflexive Methodology: New Vistas for Qualitative Research* (London: Sage, 2000); Carolyn Ellis and Arthur P. Bochner, "Autoethnography, Personal Narrative, Reflexivity," in Norman K. Denzin and Yvonna S. Lincoln (eds.), *Handbook of Qualitative Research* (Thousand Oaks, CA: Sage, 2000), pp. 733–768; Gillian Rose, "Situating Knowledges: Positionality, Reflexivity and Other Tactics," *Progress in Human Geography* 21 (1997): pp. 305–320; Yanow and Schwartz-Shea *Interpretation and Method*; Abigail Rowe, "Situating the Self in Prison Research: Power, Identity and Epistemology," in Drake, Earle, and Sloan, *Palgrave Handbook of Prison Ethnography*, pp. 347–370. See also Yanow and Schwartz-Shea, *Interpretive Research Design*, defining reflexivity as "active consideration of and engagement with the ways in which [the researcher's] own sense-making, and the particular circumstances that might have affected it . . . relate to the knowledge-claims [s]he ultimately advances in written form. . . . Reflexivity includes considerations of how the researcher's own characteristics matter. . . . [It] strengthens their personal responsibility for the research and its outcomes," pp. 100–101. On the relative lack of reflexivity in criminological research, see Coretta Phillips and Rod Earle, "Reading Difference Differently? Identity, Epistemology and Prison Ethnography," *British Journal of Criminology* 50 (2010), pp. 360–378.

61. Two of these offered yoga, while the third offered meditation under the umbrella of "engaged" Buddhism. (The fourth organization of meditation volunteers was juggling too many logistical obstacles for me to be able to join immediately, but my relationship with them eventually led to the collaboration described in Chapter 6.)

62. Marjorie De Vault, "Ethnicity and Expertise: Racial-Ethnic Knowledge in Sociological Research," *Gender and Society* 9(5) 1995, p. 612–631.

63. Private communication, Tiffany Willougby-Herard.

64. Price, *Prison and Social Death*, p. 14

65. Lee Ann Fujii, *Interviewing in Social Science Research: A Relational Approach* (New York and London: Routledge, 2017), p. 91

66. Price, *Prison and Social Death*, p. 65

67. Price, *Prison and Social Death*, p.70

68. Price, *Prison and Social Death*, p. 64. See also Deborah H. Drake, "Finding Secrets and Secret Findings: Confronting the Limits of the Ethnographer's Gaze," in Drake, Earle and Sloan, *Palgrave Handbook of Prison Ethnography*, pp. 252–270: "In the closed, secretive and often paranoid environment of the prison, some aspects of the field can remain obscured to the outsider researcher, no matter how much time he or she spends with informants or observing in the field," p. 253.

69. Private communication, Tiffany Willoughby-Herard.

70. Price, *Prison and Social Death*, pp. 71–72.

71. Price, *Prison and Social Death*, p. 72.

72. Price, *Prison and Social Death*, p. 66. See also Bosworth et al., "Doing Prison Research," p. 255.

73. These stories overlap greatly with the narratives that already exist in many accounts by incarcerated and formerly-incarcerated persons. See especially Price, *Prison and Social Death*, ch. 2; Robin Levi and Ayelet Waldman, *Inside This Place, Not of It: Narratives from Women's Prisons* (New York: Verso, 2017); Susan Burton, *Becoming Ms. Burton: From Prison to Recovery to Leading the Fight for Incarcerated Women* (New York: The New Press, 2019).

74. Ayelet Waldman and Robin Levi reveal the horrors of incarceration for women, offering oral histories, statistics and policy analysis to shed light on the ways in which women are uniquely vulnerable to certain forms of abuse, humiliation, and dehumanization in prisons. See Levi and Waldman, *Inside This Place, Not of It*, "Introduction," "Appendix II: Forms of Violence against Incarcerated Women, Part I—Sexual Abuse and Misconduct," "Appendix III: Forms of Violence against Incarcerated Women, Part II—Lack of Adequate Care," "Appendix IV: Pregnancy, Abortion, Sterilization and Shackling." "Appendix V: Access to Children, Loved Ones and Intimate Relations." "Appendix VIII: Barriers to Communication from Prisons." "Appendix IX: Rape in U.S. Prisons and How to Stop It."

75. Price, *Prison and Social Death*, pp.15–16.

76. Qualitative prison researchers write about the importance of acknowledging the emotional costs and burdens of prison research. See for instance, Yvonne Jewkes, "Foreword," in Drake, Earle, and Sloan, *Palgrave Handbook of Prison Ethnography*, p. xii: "criminology has largely resisted the notion that prisons are highly charged emotional environments and that qualitative inquiry has autoethnographic dimensions . . . [telling] stories from the field without fear of exposure as human beings capable of compassion, empathy, excitement . . . far from producing 'soft' research . . . succeed[s] in retaining epistemological and theoretical rigor while at the same time being highly reflexive. . . . Reflexive, human-centric ethnography is an important counter, not just to quantitative analysis, but to the 'official' audit culture . . . that render[s] individual prisoners anonymous targets." See also Yvonne Jewkes, "Autoethnography and Emotion as Intellectual Resources: Doing Prison Research Differently," *Qualitative Inquiry* 18 (2012), pp. 63–75; Alison Liebling, "Postscript: Integrity and Emotion in Prisons Research," *Qualitative Inquiry* 20(4) 2014, pp. 481–486; Liebling, "Doing Research in Prisons." Mary Bosworth writes, "without questions, emotions and confusion, it is much easier to present crime and punishment as simple matters of policy rather than politics, as issues that are divorced from the rest of us." Bosworth et al., "Doing Prison Research," p. 258 The anthropologist Kirschner has argued that "emotional responses in the field can constitute an important channel through which ethnographic knowledge is gathered." See S. R. Kirschner "'Then What Have I Do to with Thee?' On Identity, Fieldwork and Ethnographic Knowledge," *Current Anthropology* 2(2) 1987, pp. 211–234, p. 213.

77. Nic Beech, Paul Hibbert, Robert MacIntosh, and Peter McInnes, "'But I Thought We Were Friends?' Life Cycles and Research Relationships," in Sierk Ybema, Dvora Yanow, Harry Wels, and Frans Kamsteeg, *Organizational Ethnography: Studying the Complexities of Everyday Life* (London and Thousand Oaks: Sage, 2009) pp. 196–214; Stephen Case and Kevin Haines, "Reflective Friend Research: The Relational Aspects of Social Scientific Research," in Lumsden and Winter, *Reflexivity in Criminological Research*, pp. 58–74. See also Pierre Bourdieu, *The Weight of the World: Social Suffering in Contemporary Society* (Stanford, CA: Stanford University Press, 1999); Jane Malcolm, *The Journalist and the Murderer* (London: Granta, 1990).

78. Reiter, "Making Windows in the Walls."
79. I owe this insight to Timothy Pachirat. The interpretive scholar Lee Ann Fujii wrote of research ethics that "like most ethical moments in the field, there is no way to resolve all tensions through one set of actions. Attempts at resolving one dilemma can create new ones . . . nonactions [can have] ethical implications as well." Fujii, "Research Ethics 101: Dilemmas and Responsibilities," *PS: Political Science and Politics*, October 2021, p. 720.

Chapter 3

1. Carol Horton, "Reimagining Yoga," *Yoga International*, https://yogainternational.com/article/view/reimagining-yoga-holistic-wellness-social-connection-spiritual-revitalizati, accessed May 11, 2021.
2. Eaton, "American Buddhism."
3. Eaton, "American Buddhism."
4. David L. McMahan, "How Meditation Works: Theorizing the Role of Cultural Context in Buddhist Contemplative Practices," in David L. McMahan and Erik Braun (eds.), *Meditation, Buddhism and Science* (New York: Oxford University Press, 2017), pp. 23, 25.
5. Godrej, "The Neoliberal Yogi."
6. Andrew J. Nicholson, "Is Yoga Hindu? On the Fuzziness of Religious Boundaries," *Common Knowledge* 19(3) 2013, pp. 490–505; Andrea R. Jain, "Who Is to Say Modern Yoga Practitioners Have It All Wrong? On Hindu Origins and Yogaphobia," *Journal of the American Academy of Religion* 82(2) 2014, pp. 427–471; Wade Dazey, "Yoga in America: Some Reflections from the Heartland," in Knut A. Jacobsen, *Theory and Practice of Yoga: Essays in Honour of Gerald James Larson* (Leiden: Brill, 2005), pp. 409–424.
7. Because the goals of these practices vary depending on the practitioner and their cultural context, David McMahan notes that different practitioners may cultivate very different ways of being in the world. McMahan, "How Meditation Works," p. 24.
8. Sally Kempton, *Meditation for the Love of It: Enjoying Your Own Deepest Experience* (Louisville, CO: Sounds True, 2011).
9. Of course, transcendence is not the sole goal of yoga, given the diversity of schools. For instance, in the cases of *jñāna-*, *bhakti-* and *karma-yoga*, beneficial mental states are to be respectively complemented by wisdom, devotion, or selfless action and service to others.
10. Hinduism's yogic traditions include both meditative and physical practice. The Sanskrit word *yoga* refers to any technique of disciplined self-mastery that allows transcendence of the ordinary world, attaining a state of union with the divine. Like the mainstream of Hindu philosophy, the yogic tradition is largely renunciatory, controlling the senses and withdrawing from the material world. See Georg Feuerstein, *The Yoga Tradition: Its History, Literature, Philosophy and Practice* (Prescott, AZ: Hohm Press, 1998); Lance E. Nelson, "The Dualism of Nondualism: *Advaita Vedānta* and the Irrelevance of Nature," in Lance E. Nelson (ed.), *Purifying the Earthly Body of God: Religion and Ecology in India* (Albany: SUNY Press, 1998). Traditionally, ascetic discipline was not seen as compatible with social or political action. Rather, transcending the material world—which included householding, society, economics, and politics—was seen as more valuable. See Veena Howard, *Gandhi's Ascetic Activism: Renunciation and Social Action* (Albany: State University of New York Press, 2013), pp. 16–17; Greg Bailey, *Materials for the Study of Ancient Indian Ideologies: Pravṛtti and Nivṛtti* (Torino: Indologica Taurinensia, 1985); M. G.

Bhagat, *Ancient Indian Asceticism* (New Delhi: Munshiram Manoharlal Publishers, 1976). This led to a radical individualism in which one's private quest for liberation trumped all social obligations. The *Bhagavad-Gītā* teaches the philosophy of nondualism: Worldly distinctions between good and evil are part of the same divine consciousness with which everything eventually reunites. "All is one," in other words. The fluctuations of the mind are symptoms of the illusory material world, thus one must detach from these ever-changing physical and mental phenomena. Barbara Stoler-Miller, *The Bhagavad-Gita: Krishna's Counsel in Time of War* (New York: Bantam, 1986); Alladi Mahadeva Sastry (trans.), *The Bhagavad Gita with the Commentaries of Adi Sri Sankaracharya* (Madras: Samata Books, 1977). So too with Patañjali's *Yoga-Sūtras*, where the goal is stilling the fluctuation of the mind through practicing dispassion. All yogic practices, physical and mental, are directed toward this end: a controlled mind that has conquered sensual desires and is absorbed in the divine. See Edwin F. Bryant, *The Yoga Sūtras of Patañjali* (New York: North Point Press: 2009).

11. Buddhism shares with Hinduism the idea that the material world is ever-changing; the purpose of meditative training is a mind that rests in contentment despite unstable external conditions. The ultimate goal is to live in a timeless, transcendent state of enlightened freedom beyond human suffering, birth, life, death, and desire. McMahan, "How Meditation Works," p. 23. See also Rupert Gethin, *The Foundations of Buddhism* (Oxford and New York: Oxford University Press, 1998); Charles Prebish and Damien Keown, *The Routledge Encyclopedia of Buddhism* (London: Routledge, 2007). Most Buddhist traditions also subscribe to a version of nondualism, although somewhat different from its yogic predecessor. Largely shorn of Hinduism's belief in divinity, Buddhism insists on a fundamental emptiness: everything we perceive is prone to decay. It also famously rejects the notion of a permanent or independent self. The world around us, indeed our very selfhood, is not only unstable and impermanent, it is also a construction of the mind. Gethin, *The Foundations of Buddhism*, pp. 61–62.

12. Purushottama Bilimoria, 'Indian Ethics,'" in Peter Singer (ed.), *A Companion to Ethics* (Oxford: Blackwell, 1991), pp. 43–57; U. N. Ghoshal, *A History of Indian Political Ideas: The Ancient Period and the Period of Transition to the Middle Ages* (London: Oxford University Press, 1959); Wendy Doniger O'Flaherty, *Textual Sources for the Study of Hinduism* (Chicago: University of Chicago Press, 1988).

13. Gross, "The Wisdom in the Anger," p. 228.

14. McMahan, "How Meditation Works," pp. 26–27.

15. Classical Hinduism may have privileged renunciation over action, but other schools have contained a vast body of secular reflection, including works on jurisprudence, statecraft, ethical conduct, social norms, economic policies, and so forth. Secular, social involvement seems to have coexisted with personal spiritual progress toward liberation. Bilimoria, "Indian Ethics"; Ghoshal, *A History of Indian Political Ideas*; O'Flaherty, *Textual Sources for the Study of Hinduism*. Some read the *Bhagavad-Gītā* not merely as a treatise on personal spiritual pursuits, but also as one that urges the pursuit of collective social and political welfare. Shruti Kapila and Faisal Devji (eds.), *Political Thought in Action: The Bhagavad Gita and Modern India* (Cambridge: Cambridge University Press, 2013). Yoga is often translated as "skill in action," and the *Gītā* in fact warns us that detachment is no excuse for inaction. Others point out that Patañjali's *Yoga-Sūtras* contains an emphasis on ethical behavior and moral restraints such as nonviolence and truthfulness. Yoga, one scholar insists, need not be perceived as a "world-renouncing" tradition, and is compatible with

"engaged and benevolent social action in the world." Bryant, *The Yoga Sūtras of Patañjali*, p. 130. Similar tensions exist within Buddhism: Buddhist practice can sometimes seem goal-less and devoid of any attempt at improvement, because of the fundamental impermanence and emptiness of independent existence. See McMahan, "How Meditation Works," p. 27. Some have called this the tension between the "constructive" and "deconstructive" aspects of Buddhism: Is there a self—and a world—that we are supposed to cultivate, or do we just learn to accept everything as it is, and transcend it? Many argue that Buddhist practice has always had goals, whether transcendent (like enlightenment) or worldly (ethical and social). McMahan, "How Meditation Works," p. 45. It has given clear guidance for the states of mind, modes of living, and ethical outcomes that are most valuable and beneficial. McMahan, "How Meditation Works," pp. 26–27. Buddhism shares yoga's emphasis on ethical restraints such as nonviolence, along with other virtues such as compassion, equanimity, and lovingkindness, with a strong emphasis on collective welfare. See Damien Keown and Charles Prebish, *Action Dharma: New Studies in Engaged Buddhism* (New York: Routledge, 2003), p. 233. For many, Buddhist practice necessarily calls for an "other-directed" orientation: living one's life for the sake of all beings, not just oneself—a self that is in any case, an illusion. Rather than simply a means to personal salvation or renunciation, its ethical teachings (*sīla*) are designed to collectively end all suffering through counteracting destructive states of mind such as greed, ill-will, hatred, and delusion. Because all beings exist in a web of interconnection, uprooting our selfish attachment to an illusory self requires us to overcome our feeling of separation from others, and identify with their suffering, deepening our sense of connection with them. See Ronald E. Purser, "Clearing the Muddled Path of Traditional and Contemporary Mindfulness: A Response to Monteiro, Musten, and Compson," *Mindfulness* 6(1) 2015, pp. 23–45; Mark Leonard, "Who Is Misrepresenting Mindfulness?" *Tricycle*, November 14, 2019, https://tricycle.org/trikedaily/mindfulness-bad-experience/, accessed May 13, 2021. Hence the concept of the *bodhisattva*, the being who exists for selfless service to others as a supreme ideal. Keown and Prebish, *Action Dharma*, p. 216.

16. In fact, some say that the tantric school of practice arose precisely as an anti-establishmentarian challenge, making the practices accessible to women, lower castes, and others marginalized at the edges of Hindu society. See Farah Godrej, "Orthodoxy and Dissent in Hinduism's Meditative Traditions: A Critical Tantric Politics?" *New Political Science* 38(2) 2016, pp. 256–271.

17. Patrick McCartney, "Politics beyond the Yoga Mat: Yoga Fundamentalism and the 'Vedic Way of Life,'" *Global Ethnographic* 4 (2017), p. 1. See also Christopher Patrick Miller, "Soft Power and Biopower: Narendra Modi's 'Double Discourse' Concerning Yoga for Climate Change and Self-Care," *Journal of Dharma Studies* 3(1) 2020, pp. 93–106; and "Modi-fying Patañjali: Biopolitics and the Hostile Takeover of Bodies in an Aspiring Neoliberal Nation State," in Susanne Scholz and Caroline Vander Stichele (eds.), *Contemporary Yoga and Sacred Texts* (New York: Routledge, forthcoming).

18. McMahan, "How Meditation Works," p. 30.

19. Jeffrey Samuels, "Buddhism and Caste in India and Sri Lanka," *Religion Compass* 1(1) 2007, p. 122.

20. Nelson Foster, "To Enter the Marketplace," in Fred Eppsteiner (ed.), *The Path of Compassion: Writings on Socially Engaged Buddhism* (Berkeley, CA: Parallax, 1988), p. 51.

21. Brian Victoria, "Yasutani Roshi: The Hardest Koan," *Tricycle*, https://tricycle.org/magazine/yasutani-roshi-hardest-koan/, accessed May 11, 2021. See also Be Scofield, "Yoga

for War: The Politics of the Divine," in Horton and Harvey, *21st Century Yoga*; Michael Jerryson and Mark Juergensmeyer (eds.), *Buddhist Warfare* (New York: Oxford University Press, 2010).

22. Samuels, "Buddhism and Caste in India and Sri Lanka."
23. Lori R. Meeks, *Hokkeji and the Reemergence of Female Monastic Orders in Premodern Japan* (Honolulu: University of Hawaii Press, 2010).
24. Godrej, "Ascetics, Warriors, and a Gandhian Ecological Citizenship.".
25. Sulak Sivaraksa, *Seeds of Peace: A Buddhist Vision for Renewing Society* (Berkeley, CA: Parallax Press, 1992).
26. "There's nothing necessarily inherent in the Buddhist tradition that would lend itself to leftist politics," says David McMahan. See Max Zahn, "Sit Down and Shut Up: Pulling Mindfulness Up by Its (Buddhist) Roots," *Religion Dispatches*, July 12, 2016, https://religio ndispatches.org/sit-down-and-shut-up-pulling-mindfulness-up-by-its-buddhist-roots/, accessed May 11, 2021.
27. Scofield, "Yoga for War."
28. Horton and Harvey, *21st Century Yoga*; Andrea Jain, *Selling Yoga: From Counterculture to Pop Culture* (New York: Oxford University Press, 2014).
29. Carol Horton, "Yoga Is Not Dodgeball: Mind-Body Integration and Progressive Education," in Beth Berila, Chelsea Jackson Roberts, and Melanie Klein (eds.), *Yoga, the Body, and Embodied Social Change: An Intersectional Feminist Analysis* (Lanham, MD: Lexington, 2016), pp. 109–123; Tony Perry, "Legal Fight against Yoga in Encinitas Schools Is Finished," *Los Angeles Times*, June 12, 2015, https://www.latimes.com/local/lanow/la-me-ln-yoga-legal-fight-20150612-story.html, accessed May 11, 2021; Neil Vigdor, "Alabama Lifts Its Ban on Yoga in Schools," *New York Times*, May 20, 2021, https://www.nytimes.com/2021/05/20/us/alabama-yoga-ban-public-schools.html?action=click&module=In%20Ot her%20News&pgtype=Homepage, accessed May 20, 2021.
30. McMahan, "How Meditation Works," p. 12.
31. Carol Horton, *Yoga Ph.D.: Integrating the Life of the Mind and the Wisdom of the Body* (Chicago, IL: Kleio Books, 2012), p. 55; Ann Gleig, *American Dharma: Buddhism beyond Modernity* (New Haven: Yale University Press, 2019), p. 39.
32. McMahan, "How Meditation Works," p. 35.
33. The Editors, "Losing Our Religion," *Tricycle*, Summer 2007, https://tricycle.org/magazine/losing-our-religion-2/, accessed May 12, 2021.
34. Ronald E. Purser, David Forbes, and Adam Burke (eds.), *Handbook of Mindfulness: Culture, Context and Social Engagement* (Cham, Switzerland: Springer, 2016), p. vii.
35. Purser, "Clearing the Muddled Path"; Jeremy R. Carrette and Richard King, *Selling Spirituality: The Silent Takeover of Religion* (London and New York: Routledge, 2005).
36. Purser, "Clearing the Muddled Path."
37. Purser, "Clearing the Muddled Path."
38. Purser et al., *Handbook of Mindfulness*, p. vi.
39. Horton, *Yoga Ph.D.*, p. 26.
40. These debates also intersect with other contentious issues, such as the sometimes-tense relationship between "heritage" practitioners and "convert" communities in the West: Western practitioners tend to reject the more metaphysical or ritualistic aspects of the traditions, focusing only on the practical elements that appeal to them; while Asians and Asian Americans sometimes view Western practitioners with suspicion, and the feeling that their native traditions are being distorted or misappropriated. Gleig, *American Dharma*,

pp. 38–39; Roopa Bala Singh, "We Are Not Exotic, We Are Exhausted: South Asian Diasporic Youth Speak," *South Asian American Perspectives on Yoga in America*, https://saapya.wordpress.com/2014/11/19/we-are-not-exotic-we-are-exhausted-south-asian-diasporic-youth-speak/, accessed May 13, 2021; Chenxing Han, *Be the Refuge: Raising the Voices of Asian American Buddhists* (New York: North Atlantic Books, 2021). There is a separate debate regarding the question of whether these Western variants are "pure" or "authentic" enough. There is a temptation to think of the Asian variants of these traditions as more "pure" versions, and their modern Western versions as somehow "corrupted," but these categories are something of a myth. Scholars warn that neither Hinduism nor Buddhism were ever uniform or static to begin with, nor were they entirely unconcerned with financial well-being or material gain. So the concern is not really to criticize deviations from some purely spiritual or "authentic" ideal. See David L. McMahan and Erik Braun, "Introduction," in McMahan and Braun, *Meditation, Buddhism and Science*, p. 4; Horton, *Yoga Ph.D.*, p. 14. In Zahn, "Sit Down and Shut Up," David McMahan warns against the idealization of a mythic, pristine form of the religion: "I would be cautious about contrasting mindfulness with some kind of absolutely pure, past Buddhism in which there was no conception or concern with material well-being or financial reward." See also Godrej, "The Neoliberal Yogi."

41. Gleig, *American Dharma*, p. 70; Lynette M. Monteiro, R. F. Musten, and Jane Compson, "Traditional and Contemporary Mindfulness: Finding the Middle Path in the Tangle of Concerns," *Mindfulness* 6(1) 2015, pp. 1–13; Jay Michaelson, "New Evidence: The Science of Brainhacking," in *Evolving Dharma: Meditation, Buddhism and the Next Generation of Enlightenment* (Berkeley, CA: Evolver Editions, 2013).

42. Here too, there is complexity and nuance: Many Westerners may also value what they see as the "spiritual" dimension, while interpreting it through a "New Age" lens. Or, they may feel comfortable merging yoga with whatever religious tradition they are already part of, including Judaism and Christianity. While orthodox believers may disagree with this, more liberal believers have been known to integrate yoga with their preexisting religious commitments. I owe this point to the incisive and constructive reading of Carol Horton.

43. R. H. Sharf, "Is Mindfulness Buddhist? (And Why It Matters)," *Transcultural Psychiatry* 52(4) 2015, pp. 470–484; and "Mindfulness and Mindlessness in Early Chan," *Philosophy East and West* 64(4) 2014, pp. 933–964.

44. Slavoj Žižek, "From Western Marxism to Western Buddhism," *Cabinet*, Spring 2001, https://www.cabinetmagazine.org/issues/2/zizek.php, accessed May 12, 2021. Of course, there is something of a contradiction at work here. Many critics insist that these traditions should always be married to the higher, spiritual purposes for which they were intended. See, for instance, Purser, "Clearing the Muddled Path." But we have already seen that these traditions were often used for conservative purposes in the past, so a recognition of their "higher purposes" is no guarantee of a radical or critical political leaning.

45. Jon Kabat-Zinn, "Mindfulness-Based Interventions in Context: Past, Present, and Future," *Clinical Psychology: Science and Practice* 10(2) 2003, pp. 148–150; and *Coming to Our Senses: Healing Ourselves and the World through Mindfulness* (New York: Hachette, 2006).

46. Gleig, *American Dharma*, pp. 56–62.

47. Purser, *McMindfulness*; Purser and Loy, "Beyond McMindfulness"; Purser, "Clearing the Muddled Path"; Forbes, *Mindfulness and Its Discontents*; Bhikkhu Anālayo, "The Myth of McMindfulness," *Mindfulness* 11 (2) 2020, pp. 472–479.

48. Purser, *McMindfulness*, p. 8; Carrette and King, *Selling Spirituality*; Purser and Loy, "Beyond McMindfulness"; Žižek, "From Western Marxism to Western Buddhism."

49. Kabat-Zinn, "Mindfulness-Based Interventions in Context," p. 149; Purser and Loy, "Beyond McMindfulness"; Purser, "Clearing the Muddled Path," p. 35.

50. "How Mindfulness Became the New Capitalist Spirituality," *Radio New Zealand*, February 15, 2020, https://www.rnz.co.nz/national/programmes/saturday/audio/2018734278/how-mindfulness-became-the-new-capitalist-spirituality, accessed May 12, 2021.

51. "How Mindfulness Became the New Capitalist Spirituality."

52. Purser, "Clearing the Muddled Path," pp. 37, 42.

53. Carol Horton, "Re-Imagining Yoga, Part 2: Spirituality and Social Justice," *Yoga International*, https://yogainternational.com/article/view/re-imagining-yoga-part-2-spirituality-and-social-justice, accessed May 12, 2021. See also Jain, *Selling Yoga*; Scofield, "Yoga for War."

54. Godrej, "The Neoliberal Yogi."

55. Simpson, "From Me to We"; Zahn, "Sit Down and Shut Up."

56. Forbes, *Mindfulness and Its Discontents*.

57. Forbes, *Mindfulness and Its Discontents*; Purser, *McMindfulness*, p. 34.

58. Maia Duerr, "Toward a Socially Responsible Mindfulness," May 16, 2015, http://maiaduerr.com/toward-a-socially-responsible-mindfulness/, accessed May 12, 2021. See also Elliot Cohen, "Cutting the Buddha's Body to Fit the Neoliberal Suit: Mindfulness—From Practice, to Purchase, to Praxis," *Annual Review of Critical Psychology* 13 (2017), pp. 1–18.

59. Paul Rabinow (ed.), *Michel Foucault: Ethics, Subjectivity, and Truth* (New York: The New Press, 1997); Paul Rabinow (ed.), *The Foucault Reader* (New York: Pantheon, 1984).

60. Purser et al., *Handbook of Mindfulness*, p. xiv.

61. Natalia Mehlman Petrzela, "When Wellness Is a Dirty Word," *Chronicle of Higher Education*, May 1, 2016, https://www.chronicle.com/article/when-wellness-is-a-dirty-word/?cid2=gen_login_refresh&cid=gen_sign_in, accessed May 12, 2021; see also Carl Cederström and André Spicer, *The Wellness Syndrome* (Hoboken, NJ: John Wiley & Sons, 2015).

62. I owe this point to the insightful commentary of Naomi Murakawa.

63. Carrette and King, *Selling Spirituality*, p. 85.

64. Suzanne Moore, "Mindfulness Is All about Self-Help: It Does Nothing to Change an Unjust World," *The Guardian*, August 6, 2014, https://www.theguardian.com/commentisfree/2014/aug/06/mindfulness-is-self-help-nothing-to-change-unjust-world, accessed May 12, 2021.

65. McMahan, "How Meditation Works," p. 41. Of course, many other religious traditions explicitly reject the worldly or the material in favor of the divine, and one could argue that other religions tend just as much toward being pacifying and apolitical. The differences between liberation theology and, say, Protestant prosperity gospel in Western Christianity demonstrate how both progressive and conservative political commitments can be encouraged within the same set of religious commitments.

66. Pablo Das, "Why This Gay Buddhist Teacher Is Dubious about Buddhist Refuge in the Trump Era," *Lion's Roar*, November 17, 2016, https://www.lionsroar.com/commentary-why-this-gay-buddhist-teacher-is-dubious-about-buddhist-refuge-in-the-trump-era/, accessed May 12, 2021.

67. Gross, "The Wisdom in the Anger," p. 225.

68. The widely read American Buddhist Pema Chödrön, for instance, writes that beliefs and convictions are "an excellent opportunity to have a good laugh about the human condition."

Pema Chödrön, *How to Meditate: A Practical Guide to Making Friends with Your Mind* (Boulder, CO: Sounds True, 2013), p. 159. Another teacher holds that a "strong attachment to our own views" is the source of most political problems. G. K. Gyatso, *How to Solve Our Human Problems: The Four Noble Truths* (Glen Spey, NY: Tharpa, 2007), p. 4.

69. bell hooks, "Buddhism and the Politics of Domination," in McLeod, *Mindful Politics*.

70. Gleig, *American Dharma*, pp. 70–72.

71. Horton and Harvey, *21st Century Yoga*; Jain, *Selling Yoga*.

72. Andy Hoover, "Don't Just Sit There—Act," *Lion's Roar*, September 2019; Chenxing Han, "The Invisible Majority," *Lion's Roar*, May 2019; Roshi Pat Enkyo O'Hara, "Gender and Sexuality: From 'Other' to Others," *Lion's Roar*, May 2019; Ann Gleig, "Beyond the Upper Middle Way," *Lion's Roar*, May 2019; Crystal Johnson, "The Infrastructure of Inclusion," *Lion's Roar*, May 2019; Ruth King et al., "Power & Heart: Black and Buddhist in America," *Lion's Roar*, May 2019; Gleig, *American Dharma*.

73. hooks, "Buddhism and the Politics of Domination."

74. Edwin Ng and Ron Purser, "White Privilege and the Mindfulness Movement," *Buddhist Peace Fellowship*, October 2, 2015, http://www.buddhistpeacefellowship.org/white-privil ege-the-mindfulness-movement/, accessed May 12, 2021; James K. Rowe, "Zen and the Art of Social Movement Maintenance," *Waging Nonviolence*, March 21, 2015, https://waging nonviolence.org/2015/03/mindfulness-and-the-art-of-social-movement-maintenance/, accessed May 12, 2021. Perhaps in response to this, Kabat-Zinn eventually publicly ac- knowledged that he had remained relatively unaware of his privilege (racial and other- wise) until well into his seventies. See Jon Kabat-Zinn, "Foreword," in Rhonda Magee, *The Inner Work of Racial Justice: Healing Ourselves and Transforming Our Communities through Mindfulness* (New York: TarcherPerigee, 2019), p. x.

75. Sallie B. King, *Socially Engaged Buddhism* (Honolulu: University of Hawai'i Press, 2009), p. 1.

76. Jessica L. Main and Rongdao Lai, "Reformulating 'Socially Engaged Buddhism' as an Analytical Category," *The Eastern Buddhist* 44(2) 2013, p. 5.

77. Some claim that Buddhism has *always* been socially engaged from its very inception, because it has always been involved with reducing suffering. See King, *Socially Engaged Buddhism*; Main and Lai, "Reformulating 'Socially-Engaged Buddhism' "; Winston L. King, "Engaged Buddhism: Past, Present, Future," *The Eastern Buddhist* 27(2), 1994, pp. 14–29. But we need to be leery of this claim: We already saw that Buddhism was implicated in supporting unjust power structures in Asia, well before its migration to the West. Conversely, many scholars also insist that Buddhism has never been solely the purview of the oppressed, and that the purpose of meditative practice has never been to change an unjust world. See Gleig, *American Dharma*, pp. 67–68, 72. There appears to be no consensus then, that Buddhism has *always* been socially or politically engaged.

78. Duerr, "Toward a Socially Responsible Mindfulness."

79. Duerr, "Toward a Socially Responsible Mindfulness."

80. Eaton, "American Buddhism."

81. Geoff Nelson and Manuel Riemer, "Intervention," in Thomas Teo (ed.), *Encyclopedia of Critical Psychology* (New York: Springer, 2014).

82. Certainly, Gandhi's nonviolent activism is a notable exception: See Godrej, "Ascetics, Warriors, and a Gandhian Ecological Citizenship." And, even though Gandhi's advo- cacy of yogic principles was put in service of progressive causes—opposing both British

colonial rule and the caste system—contemporary yoga, as we have seen, has been employed by conservative forces in India intent on reinforcing Hindu supremacy.

83. Michelle Cassandra Johnson, "Dismantling Racism and White Supremacy," *Off the Mat into the World*, December 2019, https://otmtraining.offthematintotheworld.org/p/dism antling-racism-cr, accessed May 12, 2021, and Hala Khouri, Teo Drake, and Tessa Hicks Peterson, "Foundational Concepts in Social Justice," *Off the Mat into the World*, 2018, https://otmtraining.offthematintotheworld.org/p/foundational-concepts-social-justice-cr, accessed May 12, 2021.

84. Hala Khouri, "Trauma and Social Justice," *Off the Mat into the World*, 2018, https://otmt raining.offthematintotheworld.org/p/trauma-social-justice-course-recording, accessed May 12, 2021.

85. Ruth King, *Mindful of Race: Transforming Racism from the Inside Out* (Boulder, CO: Sounds True, 2018); Magee, "The Inner Work of Racial Justice;" Williams et al., *Radical Dharma*; hooks, "Buddhism and the Politics of Domination."

86. King et al., "Black and Buddhist in America," p. 42.

87. Beth Berila, *Integrating Mindfulness into Anti-Oppression Pedagogy: Social Justice in Higher Education* (New York and London: Routledge, 2016); Becky Thompson, *Teaching with Tenderness: Toward an Embodied Practice* (Champaign, IL: University of Illinois Press, 2017).

88. Bhikkhu Bodhi, "Let's Stand Up Together," *Lion's Roar*, February 11, 2017, https://www.lionsroar.com/lets-stand-up-together/, accessed May 12, 2021.

89. Bodhi, "Let's Stand Up Together."

90. Gleig, *American Dharma*, pp. 144, 155.

91. Gleig, *American Dharma*, pp. 151.

92. Zahra G. Ahmed, "Leading from the Inside Out: Contemplative Practice as Radical Self-Care for BIPOC Activists," *Journal of Women, Politics and Policy* 42(1) 2021, pp. 73–90; See also https://eastbaymeditation.org/programs/longprograms/#toggle-id-3, accessed June 3, 2021.

93. Gleig, *American Dharma*, pp. 250–254.

94. Eaton, "American Buddhism."

95. Mike Slott, "Engaged Buddhists Need Radical Social Theory," *Buddhist Peace Fellowship*, February 12, 2020, http://buddhistpeacefellowship.org/engaged-buddhists-need-radical-social-theory/. accessed May 12, 2021.

96. Nathan G. Thompson, "From Justice for George Floyd to Disbanding the Police: Minneapolis Sparks an International Movement," *Buddhist Peace Fellowship*, June 9, 2020, http://buddhistpeacefellowship.org/from-justice-for-george-floyd-to-disbanding-the-pol ice-minneapolis-sparks-an-international-movement/, accessed May 12, 2021.

97. Gleig, *American Dharma*, pp. 154.

98. Loretta Pyles, *Healing Justice: Holistic Self-Care for Change Makers* (New York: Oxford University Press, 2018).

99. Jessie Daniels, "This Holiday Season, Resist the Unbearable Whiteness of Wellness," *Huffington Post*, December 5, 2018, https://www.huffpost.com/entry/opinion-welln ess-holidays-trump-gwyneth-paltrow-goop_n_5c07e65de4b0fc23611249c6?guccoun ter=1&guce_referrer=aHR0cHM6Ly93d3cuZ29vZ2xlLmNvbS8&guce_referrer_sig= AQAAABPVRmU6Owtj9y0LJfcCzV4VR6iA9GhrTy0xEJ-9T10INIu1nriabFg35Axu

hp9O1HSlveVkbJCd8uSA2gbTEWCBsAxPwdEoDVeuclEj60OGFBOknDh0xnjK15
0SiMH0U_BXsFJ2z3i2yhppWOtbLFhnDsfxfY0QdDYMZEoJcdeR, accessed May 12,
2021; André Spicer, " 'Self-Care': How a Radical Feminist Idea Was Stripped of Politics
for the Mass Market," *The Guardian*, August 21, 2019, https://www.theguardian.com/
commentisfree/2019/aug/21/self-care-radical-feminist-idea-mass-market, accessed
May 12, 2021.

100. Sarah Van Gelder, "The Radical Work of Healing: Fania and Angela Davis on a New Kind
of Civil Rights Activism," *Yes!*, February 19, 2016, https://www.yesmagazine.org/issue/
life-after-oil/2016/02/19/the-radical-work-of-healing-fania-and-angela-davis-on-a-
new-kind-of-civil-rights-activism, accessed May 12, 2021.

101. Audre Lorde, *A Burst of Light: Essays* (Ithaca, NY: Firebrand Books, 1988); Sara Ahmed,
"Selfcare as Warfare," August 25, 2014, https://feministkilljoys.com/2014/08/25/selfc
are-as-warfare/, accessed December 10, 2021; Shanesha Brooks-Tatum, "Subversive
Self-Care: Centering Black Women's Wellness," November 9, 2012, https://thefemin
istwire.com/2012/11/subversive-self-care-centering-black-womens-wellness/, accessed
December 10, 2021.

102. Rowe, "Zen and the Art of Social Movement Maintenance."

103. Mushim Patricia Ikeda, "I Vow Not to Burn Out," *Lion's Roar*, December 28, 2020, https://
www.lionsroar.com/i-vow-not-to-burn-out/, accessed May 12, 2021.

104. Petrzela, "When Wellness Is a Dirty Word."

105. Shannon Mariotti, "Zen and the Art of Democracy: Contemplative Practice as Ordinary
Political Theory," *Political Theory* 48(4) 2020, pp. 469–495.

106. Horton, *Yoga Ph.D.*

107. Raymond Lam, "Conscientious Compassion," *Tricycle*, August 20, 2015, https://tricycle.
org/trikedaily/conscientious-compassion/, accessed May 12, 2021.

108. Magee, *The Inner Work of Racial Justice*, pp. 32–33.

109. Gross, "The Wisdom in the Anger," pp. 235–236.

110. Gross, "The Wisdom in the Anger," pp. 231–232. See also Sokthan Yeng, *Buddhist
Feminism: Transforming Anger Against Patriarchy* (New York: Palgrave Macmillan, 2020).

111. Horton, "Re-Imagining Yoga, Part 2."

112. Ahmed, "Leading from the Inside Out."

113. Godrej, "Nonviolence and Gandhi's Truth."

114. Purser, *McMindfulness*, p. 122.

115. Purser, *McMindfulness*, pp. 17–18.

116. Gleig, *American Dharma*, pp. 256.

117. All too often, people jump on the "activist yoga" bandwagon without really knowing much
in depth about the issues they are suddenly advocating for. The ease of social media–based
activism adds to this, turning "yoga activism" into yet another form of marketing and
branding. I owe this point to Carol Horton.

118. McMahan, "How Meditation Works," p. 42.

119. McMahan, "How Meditation Works," p. 43.

120. Jeff Wilson, *Mindful America: The Mutual Influence of Meditation and American Culture*
(New York: Oxford University Press, 2014).

121. Gleig, *American Dharma*, p. 13.

122. Alexander, *The New Jim Crow*, p. 215.

Chapter 4

1. Gottschalk, *Caught*, p. 2.
2. Michel Foucault, *Discipline and Punish: The Birth of the Prison* (New York: Vintage Books, 1995), p. 297.
3. Michelle Alexander argues that the post–civil rights backlash of racialized "law-and-order" rhetoric—by white politicians reacting to the end of white dominance—served to stoke moral panic, and formed the foundation of the carceral state. See *The New Jim Crow*, Chapter 1. The "aggressive intolerance" of disorder, Ruth Wilson Gilmore notes, paid "handsome political dividends." *Golden Gulag*, p. 20. Other scholars argue that the carceral state was built over decades by a consensus of liberals and conservatives, pushing punitive responses to urban disorder as a reaction to the civil rights movement. In fact, Naomi Murakawa argues that it was policies and rhetoric by liberal politicians—including "law-and-order" logic—that cemented the carceral state. Naomi Murakawa, *The First Civil Right: How Liberals Built Prison America* (New York: Oxford University Press, 2014). See also Elizabeth Hinton, *From the War on Poverty to the War on Crime: The Making of Mass Incarceration in America* (Cambridge, MA: Harvard University Press, 2016).
4. Gottschalk, "Conservatives against Incarceration?"
5. James Forman Jr., "Racial Critiques of Mass Incarceration: Beyond the New Jim Crow," *New York Law Review*, February 26, 2012.
6. Loïc Wacquant, "Class, Race and Hyperincarceration in Revanchist America," *Daedalus* 139(3) 2010, p. 80.
7. Dennis J. Stevens, "Caging Sex Offenders," in Mechthild E. Nagel and Anthony J. Nocella II (eds.), *The End of Prisons: Reflections from the Decarceration Movement* (Amsterdam and New York: Rodopi/Brill, 2013), p. 101.
8. Gilmore, *Golden Gulag*, pp. 26–28.
9. Gilmore discusses the "demographic continuities" between those who are caged in and employed by prisons. See *Golden Gulag*, p. 23.
10. Alexandra Natapoff, *Punishment without Crime: How Our Massive Misdemeanor System Traps the Innocent and Makes America More Unequal* (New York: Basic Books, 2018).
11. John Pfaff, *Locked In: The True Causes of Mass Incarceration—And How to Achieve Real Reform* (New York: Basic Books, 2017).
12. Gerard E Lynch, "Screening versus Plea Bargaining: Exactly What Are We Trading Off?" *Stanford Law Review* 55 (2003), 1399–1408.
13. Human Rights Watch, "An Offer You Can't Refuse: How U.S. Federal Prosecutors Force Drug Defendants to Plead Guilty," https://www.hrw.org/report/2013/12/05/offer-you-cant-refuse/how-us-federal-prosecutors-force-drug-defendants-plead#, accessed May 3, 2021.
14. Interview communication.
15. Erving Goffman, *Asylums: Essays on the Social Situation of Mental Patients and Other Inmates* (London: Penguin, 1963).
16. Gottschalk, "Yosarian Meets . . . ."
17. Victor Hassine, "Letter to Joanna," in Gaucher, *Writing as Resistance*, p. 61.
18. One author describes it as being "broken down or growing accustomed to prison life . . . prison life [is] the only kind of life that exists." Hames-Garcia, *Fugitive Thought*, p. 150.

19. Interview communication.
20. Alexa Koenig and Keramet Reiter, "Introduction," in Keramet Reiter and Alexa Koenig (eds.), *Extreme Punishment* (New York: Palgrave Macmillan, 2015), p. 12.
21. Koenig and Reiter, "Introduction," p. 3.
22. Kyle Lytle Hernández, Khalil Gibran Muhammad, and Heather Ann Thompson, "Introduction: Constructing the Carceral State," *Journal of American History* 102(1), 2015, p. 19.
23. See Wendy Sawyer, "New Government Report Points to Continuing Mental Health Crisis in Prisons and Jails," *Prison Policy Initiative*, June 22, 2017, https://www.prisonpolicy.org/blog/2017/06/22/mental_health/, accessed May 3, 2021; *Prison Policy Initiative*, "Mental Health: Policies and Practices Surrounding Mental Health," https://www.prisonpolicy.org/research/mental_health/, accessed May 3, 2021; Jennifer Bronson and Marcus Berzofsky, "Indicators of Mental Health Problems Reported by Prisoners and Jail Inmates," US Department of Justice, June 2017, https://www.bjs.gov/content/pub/pdf/imhprpji1112.pdf, accessed May 3, 2021.
24. Edward Lyon, "Imprisoning America's Mentally Ill," *Prison Legal News*, February 2019, https://www.prisonlegalnews.org/news/2019/feb/4/imprisoning-americas-mentally-ill/, accessed May 3, 2021.
25. Christine Montross, *Waiting for an Echo: The Madness of American Incarceration* (New York: Penguin, 2020).
26. Patrisse Cullors, "My Brother's Abuse in Jail Is a Reason I Co-Founded Black Lives Matter: We Need Reform in LA," *Los Angeles Times*, April 13, 2018, https://www.latimes.com/opinion/op-ed/la-oe-cullors-los-angeles-sheriff-jail-reform-20180413-story.html, accessed May 3, 2021.
27. Patrisse Khan-Cullors and Asha Bandele, *When They Call You a Terrorist: A Black Lives Matter Memoir* (New York: St. Martin's Press, 2018), p. 117.
28. Price, *Prison and Social Death*, p. 5.
29. Price, *Prison and Social Death*, p. 9.
30. Price, *Prison and Social Death*, p. 9. See also See Levi and Waldman, *Inside This Place, Not of It*, "Appendix II: Forms of Violence against Incarcerated Women, Part I—Sexual Abuse and Misconduct," "Appendix III: Forms of Violence against Incarcerated Women, Part II—Lack of Adequate Care," "Appendix IV: Pregnancy, Abortion, Sterilization and Shackling," "Appendix V: Access to Children, Loved Ones and Intimate Relations," "Appendix VIII: Barriers to Communication from Prisons," "Appendix IX: Rape in U.S. Prisons and How to Stop It."
31. Reiter, "Making Windows in Walls." One exception arises from various county- and state-level agencies known as Offices of Inspectors General, which employ teams of auditors, evaluators, investigators, and a variety of other specialists who monitor and report on conditions inside jails and prisons. These agencies regularly produce public reports that highlight a variety of institutional failures, such as staff misconduct, inmate grievances, and other forms of abuse. See, for instance, https://www.oig.ca.gov/publications/?search-string&institution&service&cycle&report&minDate&maxDate&mla_paginate_current=2 and https://oig.lacounty.gov/Reports, accessed March 18, 2021. Although prisons and jails are required to cooperate by offering institutional access to these investigators, relations between OIG staff and prison/jail employees tend to be strained at best, and OIG reports are largely nonbinding, with little mechanism for enforcement.

32. Reiter, "Making Windows in Walls"; Levi and Waldman, *Inside this Place, Not of It*, "Appendix I: The Legal Framework of Incarceration and Access to Remedies." Again, recent events have resulted in some exceptions, such as a federal court order requiring prison officials to install surveillance cameras and officers to wear body cameras in response to claims of targeted abuse of disabled persons inside California prisons. See https://www.courthousenews.com/judge-orders-cameras-at-five-state-prisons-as-abuses-persist/, accessed March 18, 2021.

33. Reiter, "Making Windows in Walls."

34. Braniger, *Critical Storytelling from behind Invisible Bars*; Levi and Waldman, *Inside This Place, Not of It*; Cristina Rathbone, *A World Apart: Women, Prison and Life behind Bars* (New York: Random House, 2006); Erin George, *A Woman Doing Life: Notes from a Prison for Women* (New York: Oxford University Press, 2014); Victor Hassine, *Life without Parole: Living and Dying in Prison Today* (New York: Oxford University Press, 2011); T. J. Parsell, *Fish: A Memoir of a Boy in a Man's Prison* (Cambridge, MA: Da Capo Press, 2009); Michael G. Santos, *Inside: Life behind Bars in America* (New York: St. Martin's Press, 2007); Kenneth E. Hartmann, *Mother California: A Story of Redemption behind Bars* (Lancaster, CA: The Steering Committee Press, 2009); K. C. Carceral, *Prison, Inc: A Convict Exposes Life inside a Private Prison* (New York: NYU Press, 2005); Wilber Rideau, *In the Place of Justice: A Story of Punishment and Deliverance* (New York: Vintage, 2010).

35. In her research, McCorkel describes a prison with "featureless, low-rise, green and gray buildings [rising] up from a grassy clearing . . . set apart from the landscape by perimeter fencing and razor wire . . . and heavy steel doors that greet visitors" along with "isolations cells, control booths and mechanized gates that regulate the movement of prisoners and staff." McCorkel, *Breaking*, pp. 27–28.

36. Patricia Leigh Brown, "The 'Hidden Punishment' of Prison Food," March 2, 2021, https://www.nytimes.com/2021/03/02/opinion/prison-food-farming-health.html?action=click&module=Opinion&pgtype=Homepage, accessed May 3, 2021. Leslie Soble, Kathryn Stroud, and Marika Weinstein, *Eating Behind Bars: Ending the Hidden Punishment of Food in Prison*, https://impactjustice.org/wp-content/uploads/IJ-Eating-Behind-Bars.pdf, accessed December 14, 2021. For nutritional analyses of prison meals, see Emma A. Cook, Yee Ming Lee, B. Douglas White and Sareen S. Gropper, "The Diet of Inmates: An Analysis of a 28-Day Cycle Menu Used in a Large County Jail in the State of Georgia," *Journal of Correctional Health Care* 21(4) 2015, pp. 390–399; Shayda A. Collins and Sharon H. Thompson, "What Are We Feeding Our Inmates?," *Journal of Correctional Health Care* 18(3) 2012, pp. 210–218.

37. In recent years, this distinction has started to become less clear, as more and more people end up serving their sentences in jails due to overcrowding in prisons, or functionally end up doing so due to delays that leave them waiting in jail for months and sometimes even years. For a detailed explanation of the difference between prisons and jails, see Dolovich, "Two Models of the Prison," pp. 968–969, fn 5.

38. In his undercover account of his time as a guard at Sing Sing, Ted Conover describes different cell blocks and housing units, some with yards containing running paths, benches, vegetable gardens, and views of the river; others with floors devoted to distinct groups, such as recent arrivals, mentally ill inmates or mess-hall workers; some with gyms, dining rooms, and barbershops. Common areas include the laundry, mess hall, and churchlike worship spaces, as well as a central outdoor area known as "Times Square." Conover, *Guarding Sing Sing*, pp. 63–69.

39. Dolovich, "Two Models of the Prison"; Robinson, "Masculinity as Prison;" Graeme Wood, "How Gangs Took over Prisons," *The Atlantic*, October 2014, https://www.theatlantic.com/magazine/archive/2014/10/how-gangs-took-over-prisons/379330/, accessed May 3, 2021.

40. Gilmore describes the further devastation wrought on families of incarcerated persons by the California Department of Corrections (CDC) policy of moving prisoners among facilities with little or no notice, routinely forcing family members to travel hundreds of miles to visit their loved ones (Gilmore, *Golden Gulag*, p. 153), amplifying the burdens of separation, and leaving the families of incarcerated persons to bear increasing costs—financial, logistical, and emotional—simply in order to see their loved ones. Family members are forced to petition prisons, often unsuccessfully, to have their loved ones moved closer (Gilmore, *Golden Gulag*, p. 228).

41. Foucault, *Discipline and Punish*.

42. Travis, Western, and Redburn, *Growth of Incarceration in the United States*, pp. 158–159.

43. Although it would be more accurate to say "female-identified" or "male-identified" prison populations, prison classification still follows traditional gender categories of "male" and "female." There is increasing flexibility for transgender and intersex prisoners to be incarcerated according to their gender identification rather than their biological sex. See, for instance, Dolovich, "Two Models of the Prison"; Robinson, "Masculinity as Prison."

44. These can include sex offenders and former police officers, groups often segregated from the general population for their own safety.

45. Rhodes, *Total Confinement*.

46. Rhodes, *Total Confinement*, pp. 3–4, 23–24, 28.

47. Keramet Reiter, *23/7: Pelican Bay Prison and the Rise of Long-Term Solitary Confinement* (New Haven, CT: Yale University Press, 2016), p. 10; Rhodes, *Total Confinement*, pp. 21–22.

48. Rhodes, *Total Confinement*, pp. 21–22.

49. Rhodes, *Total Confinement*, p. 29, Reiter, *23/7*, p. 11.

50. Rhodes, *Total Confinement*, 29–32. See also Terry Allen Kupers, *Solitary: The Inside Story of Supermax Isolation and How We Can Abolish It* (Oakland: University of California Press, 2017).

51. Reiter, *23/7*, pp. 2, 4.

52. Reiter, *23/7*, p. 2.

53. Gottschalk, "Yosarian Meets . . . ."

54. Reiter, *23/7*, p. 5.

55. In *Prison and Social Death*, Joshua Price, a scholar-activist who works with the NAACP to interview incarcerated persons and document the abusive conditions in jails, confirms that painful miscarriages and other potentially serious medical complications due to the lack of medical treatment for pregnant women are not uncommon. Price, *Prison and Social Death*, pp. 3–4.

56. Interview communication; Waldman and Levi, *Inside This Place, Not of It*, p. 34; Price, *Prison and Social Death*, p. 34.

57. Burton, *Becoming Ms. Burton*; Price, *Prison and Social Death*, pp. 34–35.

58. Price, *Prison and Social Death*, p. 42.

59. Price, *Prison and Social Death*, p. 44.

60. Price, *Prison and Social Death*, p. 45.

61. Interview communication.

62. Walker, "Race Making in a Penal Institution," p. 1072. See also Dolovich, "Two Models of the Prison."

63. McCorkel, *Breaking Women*, p. 124.

64. Interview communication. See also Price, *Prison and Social Death*; and Waldman and Levi, *Inside This Place, Not of It*.

65. Wood, "How Gangs Took over Prisons."

66. James Austen, Lauren-Brooke Eisen, James Cullen, and Jonathan Frank, "How Many Americans Are Unnecessarily Incarcerated?" (New York: Brennan Center for Justice, 2016), https://www.brennancenter.org/sites/default/files/2019-08/Report_Unnecessarily_Incarce rated_0.pdf, accessed May 4, 2021; Matt Ford, "A Blueprint to End Mass Incarceration," *The Atlantic*, December 6, 2016, https://www.theatlantic.com/politics/archive/2016/12/ mass-incarceration-brennan-center/510749/, accessed May 4, 2021; Jones, "Reforms without Results."

67. Ford, "A Blueprint to End Mass Incarceration"; Austen et al., "How Many Americans Are Unnecessarily Incarcerated?"

68. Studies show that between 60 to 94 percent of incarcerated women have a history of experiencing physical or sexual violence, and that their involvement in the criminal-legal system leaves them vulnerable to revictimization, as survivors are often criminalized for self-defense, and systematically punished for taking action to protect themselves. See ACLU, "Prison Rape Elimination Act of 2003 (PREA)," https://www.aclu.org/other/prison-rape-elimination-act-2003-prea?redirect=prisoners-rights-womens-rights/prison-rape-elimination-act-2003-prea, accessed December 14, 2012; Mariame Kaba, "Black Women Punished for Self-Defense Must Be Freed from Their Cages," *The Guardian*, January 3, 2019, accessed December 14, 2021; Beth Richie, *Compelled to Crime: The Gender Entrapment of Battered Black Women* (New York: Routledge, 1996); Kay Whitlock and Nancy A. Heitzeg, *Carceral Con: The Deceptive Terrain of Criminal Justice Reform* (Oakland, CA: University of California Press, 2021).

69. Jones, "Reforms without Results"; Dana Goldstein, "Too Old to Commit Crime?" *The Marshall Project*, March 20, 2015, https://www.themarshallproject.org/2015/03/20/ too-old-to-commit-crime, accessed May 4, 2021; Jamiles Lartey, "Can We Fix Mass Incarceration without Including Violent Offenders?" *The Marshall Project*, December 12, 2019, https://www.themarshallproject.org/2019/12/12/can-we-fix-mass-incarceration-without-including-violent-offenders, accessed May 4, 2021; Daniel Denvir, " 'Non-serious, non-violent, non-sexual': Fixing Our Mass Incarceration Problem Means Getting Past the Easy Steps," *Salon*, October 26, 2015, https://www.salon.com/2015/10/26/non_serious_ non_violent_non_sexual_fixing_our_mass_incarceration_problem_means_getting_past _the_easy_steps/, accessed May 4, 2021.

70. Jones, "Reforms without Results."

71. Eli Hager, "When 'Violent Offenders' Commit Nonviolent Crimes," *The Marshall Project*, April 3, 2019, https://www.themarshallproject.org/2019/04/03/when-violent-offenders-commit-nonviolent-crimes, accessed May 4, 2021.

72. Leon Neyfakh, "Ok, So Who Gets to Go Free?" *Slate*, March 4, 2015, https://slate.com/ news-and-politics/2015/03/prison-reform-releasing-only-nonviolent-offenders-wont-get-you-very-far.html, accessed May 4, 2021; Wendy Sawyer and Peter Wagner, "Mass Incarceration: The Whole Pie," *Prison Policy Initiative*, March 24, 2020, https://www.priso npolicy.org/reports/pie2020.html, accessed May 4, 2021.

73. Gottschalk, *Caught*, p. 197.

74. Allegra M. McLeod, "Prison Abolition and Grounded Justice," *UCLA Law Review* 1156 (2015), p. 1207.

75. McLeod, "Prison Abolition and Grounded Justice," p. 1205.

76. Dolovich, "Two Models of the Prison," p. 1100.

77. Dolovich, "Two Models of the Prison," p. 1101.

78. Dolovich, "Two Models of the Prison," p. 1113.

79. Rhodes, *Total Confinement*, p. 32.

80. Hames-Garcia, *Fugitive Thought*, p. 151.

81. Koenig and Reiter, *Extreme Punishment*, p. 12.

82. Lila Kazemian writes: "The aggregate data are clear: imprisonment is not effective in reducing criminal offending. . . . Prison may promote offending behavior by damaging the
'psychological and emotional well- being of inmates,'" *Positive Growth and Redemption*,
p. 66. See also Travis, Western, and Redburn, *Growth of Incarceration in the United States*;
Shadd Maruna and H. Toch, "The Impact of Imprisonment on the Desistance Process," in J.
Travis and C. Visher (eds.), *Prisoner Reentry and Crime in America* (New York: Cambridge
University Press, 2005), pp. 139–178; D. S. Nagin, F. T. Cullen, and C. L. Jonson,
"Imprisonment and Reoffending," *Crime and Justice* 38(1) 2009, pp. 115–200; W. D.
Bales and A. R. Piquero, "Assessing the Impact of Imprisonment on Recidivism," *Journal
of Experimental Criminology* 8(1) 2012, pp. 71–101; P. Gendreau, Claire Goggin, and
Francis T. Cullen, *The Effects of Prison Sentences on Recidivism* (User report; 1999–1993)
(Ottawa, Canada: Solicitor General, 1999); P. Villetaz, M. Killias, and I. Zoder, "The Effects
of Custodial vs. Non-Custodial Sentences on Re-Offending: A Systematic Review of the
State of Knowledge," 2006, http://dx.doi.org/10.15496/publikation-6058, accessed May 4,
2021; Don Weatherburn, "The Effect of Prison on Adult Re-Offending," *Crime and Justice
Bulletin* 143 (2010), pp. 1–11.

83. Bosworth et al., "Doing Prison Research," p. 261.

84. Hames-Garcia, *Fugitive Thought*, p. 156.

85. Hames-Garcia, *Fugitive Thought*, pp. 155–156.

86. Although I never had anything but the most cordial and polite relations with them, I generally grew to have more fear of the heavily armed correctional officers who, to the best of my
knowledge, appeared to have carte blanche to act with impunity.

87. Reiter, *23/7*, p. 35.

88. Price, *Prison and Social Death*, pp. 154–155.

89. See Dolovich, "Two Models of the Prison," and Robinson, "Masculinity as Prison."

90. Rhodes, *Total Confinement*, pp. 6, 12.

91. Sutton, "An Ethnographic Account of Doing Survey Research in Prison"; Waldram,
"Challenges of Prison Ethnography," and "Anthropology in Prison"; Crewe and Ievins,
"Closeness, Distance and Honesty in Prison Ethnography"; Liebling, "Whose Side Are We
On?" See also footnote 49 in Chapter 2.

92. Rachel Kushner, "Is Prison Necessary? Ruth Wilson Gilmore Might Change Your Mind,"
New York Times, April 17, 2019, https://www.nytimes.com/2019/04/17/magazine/prison-
abolition-ruth-wilson-gilmore.html, accessed May 4, 2021; See also Kazemian, *Positive
Growth and Redemption in Prison*, p. 55.

93. Kushner, "Is Prison Necessary?"

94. Bruce Western, *Homeward: Life in the Year after Prison* (New York: Russell Sage Foundation,
2018), p. 81; Kazemian, *Positive Growth and Redemption in Prison*, p. 5.

95. Angela Davis, *Are Prisons Obsolete?* (New York: Seven Stories: 2003), p. 20.

96. Pat Carlen and Jacqueline Tombs, "Reconfigurations of Penality," *Theoretical Criminology*
10(3) 2006, p. 344.

97. MacLeod, "Prison Abolition and Grounded Justice," p. 1179.

98. Macleod, "Prison Abolition and Grounded Justice," p. 1184.

99. Hames-Garcia, *Fugitive Thought*, p. 150.

100. McCorkel, *Breaking Women*; Schept, *Progressive Punishment*; Carlen and Tombs, "Reconfigurations of Penality"; Thomas Mathiesen, *Prison on Trial* (London: Sage,1990); Jesenia Pizarro, Vanja Stenius, and Travis Pratt, "Supermax Prisons: Myths, Realities, and the Politics of Punishment in American Society," *Criminal Justice Policy Review* 17(1) 2006, pp. 6–21; Mary Bosworth, "Creating the Responsible Prisoner: Federal Admission and Orientation Packs," *Punishment and Society* 9(1), pp. 67–85; Kelly Hannah-Moffat, "Moral Agent or Actuarial Subject: Risk and Canadian Women's Imprisonment," *Theoretical Criminology* 3(1) 1999, pp. 71–94; Kelly Hannah-Moffat, "Prisons That Empower: Neo-Liberal Governance in Canadian Women's Prisons," *British Journal of Criminology* 40 (2000), pp. 510–531; Kelly Hannah-Moffat, "Criminogenic Needs and the Transformative Risk Subject," *Punishment and Society* 7(1) 2005, pp. 29–51; James Kilgore, "Repackaging Mass Incarceration," *Counterpunch*, June 6, 2014, http://www.counterpunch.org/2014/06/06/repackaging-mass-incarceration, accessed May 4, 2021; Farah Godrej, "Yoga, Meditation and Neoliberal Penality: Compliance or Resistance?" *Political Research Quarterly* 2020, https://doi.org/10.1177/1065912920954537; Loïc Wacquant, *Punishing the Poor: The Neoliberal Government of Social Insecurity* (Durham, NC: Duke University Press, 2009), David Garland, *Culture of Control: Crime and Social Order in Contemporary Society* (Chicago, IL: University of Chicago Press, 2001).

101. Tiyo Attallah Salah-El, "A Call for the Abolition of Prisons," in Joy James (ed.), *The New Abolitionists: (Neo)Slave Narratives and Contemporary Prison Writings* (Albany: SUNY Press, 2005), pp. 69–74.

102. Carlen and Tombs, "Reconfigurations of Penality," p. 340.

103. Victor Hassine, "Monochromes from over a Prison's Edge," in Gaucher, *Writing as Resistance*, p. 275.

104. Hassine, "Monochromes from over a Prison's Edge," p. 286. See also Charles Baxter, Wayne Brown, Tony Chatman-Bey, H. B. Johnson Jr., Mark Medley, Donald Thompson, Selvyn Tillett, and John Woodland Jr. (with Drew Leder), "Live from the Panopticon: Architecture and Power Revisited," in James, *The New Abolitionists*, pp. 207–215.

105. Vicki Chartrand, "I'm Not Your Carceral Other," *Journal of Prisoners on Prisons* 25(1) 2016, p. 62; David Garland, "'Governmentality' and the Problem of Crime: Foucault, Criminology, Sociology," *Theoretical Criminology* 1(1997): 173–214.

106. Carlen and Tombs, "Reconfigurations of Penality"; Bosworth, "Creating the Responsible Prisoner"; Hannah-Moffat, "Prisons That Empower"; McCorkel, *Breaking Women*.

107. Lerman and Weaver, *Arresting Citizenship*, p. 160.

108. Bosworth, "Creating the Responsible Prisoner," p. 74.

109. Tara Perry and Colleen Hackett, "Justice in Gender-Responsiveness? Psychological Dominations and Internalized Oppressions at a Women's Prison in the U.S.," *Journal of Prisoners on Prisons* 25(1) 2016, p. 35.

110. Hannah-Moffat, "Moral Agent or Actuarial Subject," pp. 79, 84; "Criminogenic Needs," p. 43. See also Ronald Kramer, Valli Rajah, and Hung-En Sung, "Neoliberal Prisons and Cognitive Treatment: Calibrating the Subjectivity of Incarcerated Young Men to Economic Inequalities," *Theoretical Criminology* 17(4) 2013, pp. 535–556.

111. Perry and Hackett, "Justice in Gender-Responsiveness?" p. 19.

112. Bosworth, "Creating the Responsible Prisoner."

113. Hannah-Moffat, "Prisons That Empower," p. 523.
114. Carlen and Tombs, "Reconfigurations of Penality." See also Shoshanna Pollack, "'You Can't Have It Both Ways': Punishment and Treatment of Imprisoned Women," *Journal of Progressive Human Services* 20 (2009), pp. 112–128.
115. Perry and Hackett note that subjects are "coerced into accepting . . . the penal-therapeutic regime under threat of losing one's parole, or losing privileges, such as family visits." "Justice in Gender-Responsiveness?," p. 23.
116. Crewe, "Power, Adaptation and Resistance," p. 262. See also Anthony Grasso, "Broken Beyond Repair: Rehabilitative Penology and American Political Development," *Political Research Quarterly* 70(2) 2017, pp. 394–407.
117. McCorkel, *Breaking Women*, p. 11.
118. Hassine, "Monochromes from over a Prison's Edge," pp. 284, 285–286.
119. Little Rock Reed, "Rehabilitation: Contrasting Cultural Perspectives and the Imposition of Church and State," in Gaucher, *Writing as Resistance*, p. 236.
120. Reed, "Rehabilitation," p. 232.
121. Reed, "Rehabilitation," p. 236.
122. Reed, "Rehabilitation," pp. 234–236.
123. Reed, "Rehabilitation," pp. 232–233. On rehabilitative programming as a farce designed to ensure that incarcerated persons internalize the prison's view, see Crewe, "Power, Adaptation and Resistance," p. 264.
124. McCorkel, *Breaking Women*, p. 225.
125. Perry and Hackett, "Justice in Gender-Responsiveness?" p. 36.
126. Perry and Hackett, "Justice in Gender-Responsiveness?" p. 24; Crewe, "Power, Adaption and Resistance," p. 261.
127. Hames-Garcia, *Fugitive Thought*, p. 155.
128. McCorkel, *Breaking Women*, p. 110.
129. Bosworth, "Creating the Responsible Prisoner," p. 76.
130. McCorkel, *Breaking Women*, p. 179.
131. McCorkel, *Breaking Women*, 4–5. See also Crewe, "Power, Adaptation and Resistance," p. 263.
132. Rhodes, *Total Confinement*, p. 80.
133. McCorkel, *Breaking Women*, p. 3.
134. Lerman and Weaver, *Arresting Citizenship*, p. 182.
135. Lerman and Weaver, *Arresting Citizenship*, pp. 126–127.
136. Lerman and Weaver, *Arresting Citizenship*, p. 192.
137. Kazemian, *Positive Growth and Redemption in Prison*.
138. Newbold et al., "Prison Research from the Inside," p. 443.
139. Earle, "Insider and Out," p. 435.
140. Jewkes, "What Has Prison Ethnography to Offer in an Age of Mass Incarceration?" *Criminal Justice Matters* 91(1) 2013, p. 14.
141. Jewkes, "What Has Prison Ethnography to Offer?" p. 14. See also Jewkes, "Foreword," xi.
142. James Kilgore, "Let's Fight for Freedom from Electronic Monitors and E-carceration," *Truthout*, September 4, 2019, https://truthout.org/articles/lets-fight-for-freedom-from-electronic-monitors-and-e-carceration/, accessed May 4, 2021.
143. See Abrams et al., *The Voluntary Sector in Prisons*; Piche et al., "Facilitating Prisoner Ethnography"; Sutton, "An Ethnographic Account of Doing Survey Research in Prison"; Waldram, "Anthropology in Prison"; Waldram, "Challenges of Prison Ethnography."

144. Patrick Alexander, "'To Live and Remain outside of the Barb[ed] Wire and Fence': A Prison Classroom, African American Literature, and the Pedagogy of Freedom." *Reflections: A Journal of Public Rhetoric, Civic Writing, and Service Learning* 11(1) 2011, pp. 88–108.
145. Patrick Alexander, "Radical Togetherness: African-American Literature and Abolition Pedagogy at Parchman and Beyond," *Humanities* 9(2) 2020, pp. 1–14; Dylan Rodríguez, "The Disorientation of the Teaching Act: Abolition as Pedagogical Position," *Radical Teacher* 88 (2010), pp. 7–19; Joshua A. Miller, "Democracy and Education behind Bars," *Perspectives on Politics* 13(3) 2015, pp. 714–721.
146. Kushner, "Is Prison Necessary?"
147. Price, *Prison and Social Death*, p. 159.
148. Interview communication.
149. Alexander, *The New Jim Crow*, pp. 215, 248.
150. Lerman and Weaver, *Arresting Citizenship*, p. 198.
151. Lerman and Weaver, *Arresting Citizenship*, pp. 95, 140, 142.
152. Bosworth, "Creating the Responsible Prisoner," p. 74.

Chapter 5

1. David Sheff, *The Buddhist on Death Row: How One Man Found Light in the Darkest Place* (New York: Simon and Schuster, 2020) (hereafter *BDR*), p. 112.
2. Jarvis Jay Masters, *That Bird Has My Wings: The Autobiography of an Innocent Man on Death Row* (New York: HarperOne, 2010) (hereafter *BHMW*), p. 228.
3. Masters, *BHMW*, p. xii.
4. Masters, *BHMW*, pp. xiii–xiv.
5. Masters, *BHMW*, pp. 230, 233, 268.
6. Sheff, *BDR*, pp. xvi, 80.
7. Michael D. Huggins, *Going Om: A CEO's Self-Discovery Behind Bars* (Los Osos, CA: Hawkeye Publishers, 2019); Fleet Maull, *Dharma in Hell: The Prison Writings of Fleet Maull* (South Deerfield, MA: Prison Dharma Press, 2017).
8. Maull, *Dharma in Hell*, p. 80.
9. Calvin Malone, *Razor Wire Dharma: A Buddhist Life in Prison* (Boston: Wisdom Publications, 2008), pp. 59, 175.
10. Maull, *Dharma in Hell*, pp. 87, 89.
11. Sheff, *BDR*, p. 59; Malone, *Razor Wire Dharma*, p. 175.
12. Sheff, *BDR*, p. 192.
13. Lerman and Weaver, *Arresting Citizenship*, p. 168; John P. McKendy, "'I'm Very Careful about That': Narrative and Agency of Men in Prison," *Discourse and Society* 17(4) 2006, pp. 473–502.
14. Maull, *Dharma in Hell*, p. 113.
15. Sheff, *BDR*, p. 71.
16. Maull, *Dharma in Hell*, pp. 107, 110.
17. Huggins, *Going Om*, p. 221.
18. Maull, *Dharma in Hell*, p. 92.
19. Huggins, *Going Om*, p. 195.
20. Huggins, *Going Om*, pp. 190, 125–116.
21. Huggins, *Going Om*, pp. 221, 223. The prison researcher Ben Crewe notes that the relationship between accepting the legitimacy of one's own punishment and accepting the legitimacy of the prison system is not always straightforward. Crewe interviewed some

incarcerated research participants who accepted both the legitimacy of their punishment, as well as the legitimacy of the system that punished them, internalizing its objectives and values—Crewe calls this "committed compliance." Others, however, accepted the legitimacy of their punishment but rejected the goals and means of the prison system—Crewe calls this "detached compliance." Others, of course, rejected the legitimacy of their prison time and the prison system altogether. See Crewe, "Power, Adaptation and Resistance." The authors described thus far run the gamut: While they are all deeply critical of the prison system, they do not reject its legitimacy altogether. Some, such as Huggins, reject the legitimacy of their own punishment. Yet, they all arrive at a position that Crewe would characterize as "committed compliance": adopting the language of improvement and personal responsibility, in keeping with institutional objectives, aims, and values. Crewe, "Power, Adaptation and Resistance," pp. 265–267.

22. Maull, *Dharma in Hell*, p. 91.
23. Maull, *Dharma in Hell*, p. 86.
24. Huggins, *Going Om*, p. 105.
25. Sheff, *BDR*, p. 26.
26. Sheff, *BDR*, p. 26.
27. James, *The New Abolitionists*; Gaucher *Writing as Resistance*; Hames-Garcia, *Fugitive Thought*.
28. George Jackson, *Soledad Brother: The Prison Letters of George Jackson* (Atlanta: A Cappella Books, 1994); George Jackson, *Blood in My Eye* (Baltimore: Black Classic Press, 1990); Angela Y. Davis, *Angela Davis: An Autobiography* (Chicago, IL: Haymarket Books, 1974); Assata Shakur, *Assata: An Autobiography* (Chicago: Chicago Review Press, 1999); Dylan Rodríguez, *Forced Passages: Imprisoned Radical Intellectuals and the U.S. Prison Regime* (Minneapolis: University of Minnesota Press, 2006).
29. Eric Cummins, *The Rise and Fall of California's Radical Prison Movement* (Palo Alto: Stanford University Press, 1994); Emily Thuma, *All Our Trials: Prisons, Policing and the Feminist Fight to End Violence* (Champaign, IL: University of Illinois Press, 2019).
30. Jalil Muntaqim, "The Criminalization of Poverty in Capitalist America (Abridged)," in James, *The New Abolitionists*, p. 33.
31. Mumia Abu-Jamal, "A Life Lived, Deliberately," in James, *The New Abolitionists*, p. 198.
32. Viet Mike Ngo (with Dylan Rodríguez), "You Have to Be Intimate with Your Despair: A Conversation with Viet Mike Ngo," in James, *The New Abolitionists*, p. 253.
33. Kazemian, *Positive Growth and Redemption in Prison*, p. 132; A. T. Rubin, "Resistance as Agency? Incorporating the Structural Determinants of Prisoner Behaviour," *British Journal of Criminology* 57(3) 2017, pp. 644–663; Bosworth, *Engendering Resistance*; Ugelvik, *Power and Resistance in Prison*; Crewe, "Power, Adaptation and Resistance"; Mary Bosworth, and Eamonn Carrabine, "Reassessing Resistance: Race, Gender and Sexuality in Prison," *Punishment and Society* 3(4) 2001, pp. 501–515; McCorkel, *Breaking Women*.
34. In her examination of isolated mental health units in a maximum security prison, Lorna Rhodes writes about a particularly dramatic form of resistance in which incarcerated persons throw their own blood or excrement at prison staff, a last-resort act of agency and control via a refusal to submit, by those who are deprived of all other possibilities for resistance. See Rhodes, *Total Confinement*, chap. 1.
35. Lerman and Weaver, *Arresting Citizenship*, pp. 215–216.
36. Bosworth, *Engendering Resistance*; Ugelvik, *Power and Resistance in Prison*.
37. Ugelvik, *Power and Resistance in Prison*, pp. 4, 8.

38. James C. Scott, *Weapons of the Weak: Everyday Forms of Peasant Resistance* (New Haven CT: Yale University Press, 1985), p. xvi.
39. Bosworth, *Engendering Resistance*, p. 8.
40. McCorkel, *Breaking Women*.
41. Lerman and Weaver, *Arresting Citizenship*; Bosworth, *Engendering Resistance*.
42. Bosworth, *Engendering Resistance*, p. 116; Ugelvik, *Power and Resistance in Prison*, p. 14.
43. Bosworth *Engendering Resistance*, p. 120.
44. Ugelvik, *Power and Resistance in Prison*, p. 11.
45. Ugelvik, *Power and Resistance in Prison*, pp. 67, 11.
46. Hames-Garcia, *Fugitive Thought*, p. xvii.
47. Burton, *Becoming Ms. Burton*, p. 186.
48. Burton, *Becoming Ms. Burton*, p. 70.
49. Burton, *Becoming Ms. Burton*, p. 160.
50. Burton, *Becoming Ms. Burton*, pp. 165, 227.
51. While my respondents in this group were all deeply critical of the prison system, they did not reject its legitimacy altogether. Some vigorously contested the legitimacy of their own punishment, while others openly said, "I should have been sent to prison, that was the right thing." Yet, they all arrive at the position that Crewe calls "committed compliance." See Crewe, "Power, Adaptation and Resistance," pp. 265–267.
52. Lerman and Weaver, *Arresting Citizenship*, p. 198; Traci Burch, *Trading Democracy for Justice: Criminal Convictions and the Decline of Neighborhood Political Participation* (Chicago: University of Chicago Press, 2013).
53. Hannah L. Walker, *Mobilized by Injustice: Criminal Justice Contact, Political Participation, and Race* (New York: Oxford University Press, 2020).
54. Many prison researchers have created typologies of responses to incarceration that go well beyond binary categories. For instance, Candace Kruttschnitt and Rosemary Gartner offer a three-part typology of styles of "doing time": the "adapted" style, the "convict" style, and the "isolated" style, each of which entails a different set of attitudes toward the prison. See Candace Kruttschnitt and Rosemary Gartner, *Marking Time in the Golden State: Women's Imprisonment in California* (Cambridge: Cambridge University Press, 2004), pp. 134–135. In *Breaking Women*, Jill McCorkel offers three categories of ways in which incarcerated women respond to the prison's therapeutic mandates, which include surrender, defiance, and "faking" compliance. Similarly, Crewe's typology includes four versions or kinds of "compliance": committed, fatalistic, detached, and strategic. See Crewe, "Power, Adaptation and Resistance," pp. 265–272. Crucially, these scholars all conducted their research with incarcerated persons inside prisons, while my respondents were all formerly incarcerated, offering retrospective reconstructions of their prison experiences and responses.
55. Jackson, *Soledad Brother*, pp. 16, 154.
56. Sheff, *BDR*, p. 196.
57. Ugelvik, *Power and Resistance in Prison*, p. 7.
58. See Lerman and Weaver, *Arresting Citizenship*, chap. 7.
59. Ugelvik, *Power and Resistance in Prison*, pp. 9, 44.
60. Kazemian describes extensive research on how people adapt to and cope with life in the incarceration environment. See *Positive Growth and Redemption in Prison*, chap. 4.
61. For more on cases like Danny's and Lee's, see http://laist.com/2017/11/01/cambodian_ice.php, accessed December 11, 2021. Both Danny and Lee were rearrested by ICE after their

release but subsequently released under deportation stay orders. Later, Danny's case was resolved by a gubernatorial pardon, but Lee's is still pending.

62. Kazemian, *Positive Growth and Redemption in Prison*, p. 71.

63. The one notable exception to this was Elisa, who had strong structural critiques and critiques of the conditions she witnessed, yet spoke of her own incarceration as mostly "a positive experience," noting that she herself was treated extremely well by system officers and staff. Although we did not discuss this further, being the daughter of a police officer may have had something to do with this view.

64. Marshawn is one of four respondents who insisted on having his real name used.

65. Masters, *BHMW*, p. 255.

66. Sheff, *BDR*, p. 48.

67. Ugelvik, *Power and Resistance in Prison*, p. 11.

68. Sandra has also asked to be identified by her real name.

69. Desistance is not a criminal justice policy or program, but rather a "process that belongs to the desisters themselves." See Kazemian, *Positive Growth and Redemption in Prison*, p. 55; H. Graham and F. McNeill, "Desistance: Envisioning Futures," in P. Carlen and L. A. França (eds.), *Alternative Criminologies* (London: Routledge, 2017), pp. 433–451. Kazemian, *Positive Growth and Redemption in Prison*, p. 137: "If prisoners succeed in returning to the community as better, happier, and more resilient human beings, it is *despite* the prison environment and rather because of immense individual effort." Meanwhile, Ben Crewe found that "I'm doing this for me, not for them" was a common refrain among incarcerated persons who rejected the system yet adopted some of its goals. See Crewe, "Power, Adaptation and Resistance," p. 266.

70. One group of incarcerated scholars distinguishes between "certain [prison] values, like getting off drugs or not behaving violently, that you can internalize in a positive sense" and "other [prison] values that . . . are negative because they are turning humans into something machinelike." See Baxter et al., "Live from the Panopticon," in James, *The New Abolitionists*, p. 215.

71. Kazemian, *Positive Growth and Redemption in Prison*; Shadd Maruna, *Making Good: How Ex-Convicts Reform and Rebuild Their Lives* (Washington, DC: American Psychological Association, 2001).

72. Lerman and Weaver, *Arresting Citizenship*, p. 188.

73. Lerman and Weaver, *Arresting Citizenship*, pp. 185, 191.

74. Crewe, "Power, Adaptation and Resistance," p. 266.

75. James C. Scott, *Domination and the Arts of Resistance: Hidden Transcripts* (New Haven and London: Yale University Press, 1990), p. 199.

76. Crewe, "Power, Adaptation and Resistance," p. 257.

77. Anonymous survey response.

78. Lerman and Weaver, *Arresting Citizenship*, pp. 215–216.

79. Ugelvik, *Power and Resistance in Prison*, p. 6.

80. Ugelvik, *Power and Resistance in Prison*, p. 151.

81. Maruna discusses how incarcerated persons navigate their own identity and self-understanding. Positive self-belief in a "good core self"—separated from one's actions—was key to successful self-transformation. See Maruna, *Making Good*.

82. Bosworth and Carrabine, "Reassessing Resistance," p. 506. See also Crewe, "Power, Adaptation and Resistance," p. 257.

83. Crewe, "Power, Adaptation and Resistance," p. 257.

84. I owe this excellent formulation to Tiffany Willoughby-Herard.
85. See Bosworth and Carrabine, "Reassessing Resistance," p. 506.
86. Personal communication, interview respondent.
87. Bosworth and Carrabine, "Reassessing Resistance," p. 506.
88. B. Crewe, S. Hulley, and S. Wright, "Swimming with the Tide: Adapting to Long-Term Imprisonment," *Justice Quarterly* 34(3) 2017, pp. 517–541.
89. Margaret Leigey, *The Forgotten Men: Serving a Life without Parole Sentence* (New Brunswick, NJ: Rutgers University Press, 2015); Marguerite Schinkel, *Being Imprisoned: Punishment, Adaptation and Desistance* (Basingstoke: Palgrave, 2014); S. Vanhooren, M. Leijssen, and J. Dezutter, "Coping Strategies and Posttraumatic Growth in Prison," *The Prison Journal* 98(2) 2018, pp. 123–142; S. Vanhooren, M. Leijssen, and J. Dezutter, "Ten Prisoners on a Search for Meaning: A Qualitative Study of Loss and Growth during Incarceration," *Humanistic Psychologist* 45(2) 2017, pp. 162–178; Mar Griera, "Yoga in Penitentiary Settings: Transcendence, Spirituality, and Self-Improvement," *Human Studies* 40 (2017), pp. 77–100.
90. Lerman and Weaver, *Arresting Citizenship*, p.185.
91. Crewe, "Power, Adaptation and Resistance," pp. 256–257. See also Bosworth and Carrabine, "Reassessing Resistance," p. 506.
92. Scott, *Domination and the Arts of Resistance*, p. 17.
93. Tiffany Willoughby-Herard, personal communication.
94. Crewe, "Power, Adaptation and Resistance," p. 273. Scholars have shown how incarcerated persons must often outwardly "fake" compliance with the institution's objectives, while privately remaining committed to an oppositional perspective. See McCorkel, *Breaking Women*; Kruttschnitt and Gartner, *Marking Time in the Golden State*.
95. Another inevitable question concerns the split between the low-level nonviolent offender and the so-called dangerous criminal, a touchstone of debates about mass incarceration. Were those who caused the most violent harm most likely to internalize the prison's logic, and were those who considered themselves largely innocent more likely to develop a resistant consciousness? In fact, several of the respondents in group 1 caused no harm to anyone, yet fully internalized the logic of personal responsibility. Meanwhile, several of the respondents in group 2 did admit to causing some harm to others, yet held steadfastly to a critical view and refused to see the responsibility as theirs alone, continuing to emphasize structural factors and critique the system. As I have already noted, the point of these conversations was not to assess whether compliance or resistance was correlated with severity of one's harmful acts, but rather to learn something about the meanings that my respondents attributed to yogic and meditative practices while incarcerated.
96. Crewe, "Power, Adaptation and Resistance," p. 256.
97. Bosworth, *Engendering Resistance*, p. 8.

Chapter 6

1. Given the need for anonymizing the facility—a strict requirement of access—I sacrifice textural details to provide only its rough location, which is the same city in California where I conducted my volunteer work and interviews.

2. The arduous two-year-long process of obtaining such approval (now increasingly rare for researchers) is described at length in Chapter 2, as are the ethical issues surrounding the obtaining and giving of consent for participant-observation research by incarcerated people.

3. Crucially, we discovered that those housed in the educational dorms must be enrolled in a certain minimum number of accredited educational classes. Students who would otherwise have been interested in our non-accredited mindfulness class would be forced to leave the educational dorm if it caused them to drop below the minimum level of enrollment in accredited courses, making the cost of enrollment in our class artificially high for many, and reducing the pool of potential participants.

4. In this, as in most other things in jail or prison life, "inmate classification" dictates everything. A complex classification system assigns every individual a security level of 1 through 10, along with lettered codes that describe the class of crime for which the person is incarcerated, and/or the conditions of their incarceration. The security levels guide where someone will be housed based on their individual risk for misconduct. Lower-security housing areas offer more programming and privileges, while higher-security housing is more restricted and limited in programming offering. Different classes of incarcerated persons wear different-colored clothing, indicating their security status and their classification code. Even after over five years of serving various different populations in the same facility, the chaplain confesses that the question of which populations are allowed to go where, escorted or otherwise, and which populations remain segregated from others, remains an "eternal mystery."

5. Because the MoU contains a strict confidentiality clause that prohibits revealing the name of the facility, this limits the scope of detailed geographic and architectural revelations about the site. Most ethnography seeks to give the reader a fine-grained picture of the research site, including the internal layout of buildings, the location of various rooms or offices, colors, sights, sounds, and smells. While confidentiality considerations necessarily require me to sacrifice some of this texture, I attempt to provide some details to take the reader into the life of this facility, without compromising confidentiality.

6. Some of the notices address pension funds, maternity rights, or other workplace rights and duties. Others are more specific to law enforcement, eulogizing fallen colleagues, advertising funds in their names and posting thank-you letters from their families. Some notices, such as those pertaining to transgender rights or alcoholism and domestic violence among law enforcement officers, make the workplace seem relatively progressive. The notice on transgender rights includes an entire paragraph titled "What is a transgender person?" and carefully outlines the rights of transgender employees. Another one warns about rates of alcoholism, domestic violence, and suicide among law enforcement officers, offering tips for how to spot the signs in oneself or one's colleagues.

7. All non-escort volunteers and other personnel must pass an extensive security clearance process, including a four-hour orientation.

8. Chaplain Eric does not represent any particular group or organization, but rather offers his time as an individual volunteer. Prison chaplaincy has traditionally meant ministering to incarcerated persons by performing a wide variety of both religious and secular tasks, including counseling, coordinating religious programs, and offering religious services. In recent years, the roles and expectations of prison chaplaincy have changed. While the free exercise of religious faith in prisons was always protected by the First Amendment, in practice the only chaplaincy available in prisons was predominantly Christian or Jewish. Recent legal and policy interventions have ensured that minority faiths such as Islam, Buddhism,

Wicca, and Native American religions are now represented and accommodated by the chaplaincy provisions in many prisons. As in most other matters, there is also great variation in the status and role of chaplains in different incarceration systems: While some chaplains are employees of the prison, many jails and prisons now rely on "volunteer" chaplains, who sometimes represent local faith groups and need not have any formal qualifications or training. For more on prison chaplaincy, see John M. Scorsine, "Buddhist Practice: Within an Environment of Concrete and Steel," *Teaching Dhamma in New Lands: Academic Papers Presented at the 2nd IABU Conference Mahachulalongkornrajavidyalaya University, Ayutthaya, Thailand*, 2012, pp. 82–96; Jody L. Sundt and Francis T. Cullen, "The Role of the Contemporary Prison Chaplain," *The Prison Journal* 78(3) 1998, pp. 271–298; Andrew S. Denney, "Backgrounds and Motivations of Prison Chaplains," in Kent R. Kerley (ed.), *Finding Freedom in Confinement: The Role of Religion in Prison Life* (Santa Barbara, CA: Praeger 2018), pp. 214–243; Jody L. Sundt and Francis T. Cullen, "The Correctional Ideology of Prison Chaplains: A National Survey," *Journal of Criminal Justice* 30(5) 2002, pp. 369–385.

9. The category of nonviolent sex offender may of course be confusing, since sex offenses by nature may seem violent. However, as Marie Gottschalk has noted, a wide array of infractions can be classified as sex offenses, including ostensibly nonviolent ones such as public urination, possession of child pornography, making obscene phone calls, and so on. See Gottschalk, *Caught*, p. 197.

10. At one point, an older white gentleman with thick glasses pipes up: "I'm not into all this supernatural stuff, this is just not for me." Despite Chaplain Eric's attempts to clarify that there is nothing "supernatural" about the practice, he is escorted back to his dorm at his own insistence. This is the only open refusal we encounter.

11. An area where individuals are kept waiting for their court hearing until their case is called.

12. My fieldnotes referred to the lifting of weights, but the chaplain later corrected me on this, noting that the facility does not offer any movable weights or resistance strength-training equipment, and offering clarification on the stationary equipment.

13. Mark complains bitterly about of the lack of secular programming opportunities offered to those marked as sex offenders, despite participation in programming being the foremost criterion in determining leniency during trial or sentencing.

14. Here, it is the chaplain who gently interrupts Ed and Logan's complaining to note, "We have to remember that a lot of these people need mental health treatment that they're not getting."

15. Sara Rushing, "What's Left of 'Empowerment' after Neoliberalism?" *Theory and Event* 19(1) 2016.

16. Jami Attenberg, "Is Resilience Overrated?" *New York Times*, August 19, 2020, https://www.nytimes.com/2020/08/19/health/resilience-overrated.html?action=click&module=Top%20Stories&pgtype=Homepage&contentCollection=AtHome&package_index=2, accessed May 5, 2021.

17. Attenberg, "Is Resilience Overrated?"

18. However, this exhortation to productive action was immediately qualified with the warning that we can question and inquire, but cannot make someone into an enemy or blame them. Absent a deeper exploration of how meditative traditions may combine nonjudgmental acceptance with active critique of systemic suffering, it remains unclear how one could acknowledge systemic issues—which inherently requires placing responsibility beyond the individual self—without "blaming" or "making wrong."

Chapter 7

1. Dire warnings about the preponderance of an antibiotic-resistant staph infection (Methicillin-resistant *Staphylococcus aureus*, more commonly known as MRSA) in prisons, along with the generally unclean floors on which we lay down our yoga mats, means that I save a thorough shower for after my return.

2. Many preferred to teach alone, while others preferred to stay paired-up. I am unsure as to what explained the preference for teaching in pairs/groups: some volunteers carpooled long distances together to reach the prison; others who taught yoga enjoyed having someone to assist with both the class dynamics as well as the bureaucratic protocols; and some perhaps felt safer navigating the prison context in a "buddy" system.

3. Some staff tended to run through the training materials quickly, skipping over several sections in the interest of keeping things short, while others tended to take their time and make sure to run through all the material, with little regard for time.

4. The distinction between civilian and custodial staff in prisons is an important one. Custodial staff are typically uniformed, sworn law enforcement officers, who operate along a military-style chain of command, and are equipped with arms due to their responsibility for custody and control of incarcerated persons. Civilian staff, in contrast, are not sworn officers, and are not equipped with arms, nor authorized to restrain or control incarcerated persons. Civilian staff tend to be administrative, therapeutic, or medical personnel.

5. However, some volunteer interviewees from other states reported that there were no training requirements at the local prisons or jails where they volunteered.

6. A few volunteers did get a payment or stipend from their organization, and in some cases, nonprofit organizations are contracted by prisons to offer therapeutic services. But in my experience, this was the exception rather than the norm.

7. Sonja Sharp, "How the Women Who Visit Rikers Island Navigate the Complex Dress Code," *Vice*, September 22, 2015, https://www.vice.com/en_us/article/avyjpg/how-the-women-who-visit-rikers-island-navigate-the-stressful-complex-dress-code-923, accessed May 5, 2021.

8. In one rare case, volunteers teaching Buddhist philosophy were able to award academic certificates toward community-college credit.

9. Godrej, "The Neoliberal Yogi"; Mark Singleton and Ellen Goldberg, *Gurus of Modern Yoga* (New York: Oxford University Press, 2014).

10. Elliott Goldberg, *The Path of Modern Yoga: The History of an Embodied Spiritual Practice* (Rochester, VT: Inner Traditions, 2016), p. 382.

11. Jain, *Selling Yoga*.

12. Thomas Lyons and W. Dustin Cantrell, "Prison Meditation Movements and Mass Incarceration," *International Journal of Offender Therapy and Comparative Criminology* 60(12) 2015, p. 1370.

13. Some local organizations I joined exclusively taught yoga, others exclusively taught meditation. Most yoga volunteers taught short meditations only at the beginning and/or end of yoga classes, while the meditation volunteers taught formal sitting meditation on its own, typically for more prolonged periods of time. Because I volunteered with both kinds of organizations, I was exposed to a variety of different meditation offerings by volunteers in prisons.

14. Subsequently, in the years since I began doing prison work, the mainstream culture of yoga has shifted quite a bit, and sensitivity to touch has now become a far more common concern. Still, at least until the pandemic shut down most studio yoga classes, I found that many studio teachers assumed they could touch students without consent.

Chapter 8

1. Prison Yoga Project, https://prisonyoga.org/who-we-are/our-mission/, accessed August 15, 2016.
2. Amy Osborne, *A Year in Yoga* (Kearney, NE: Morris Publishing, 2016), pp. 79–80.
3. Osborne, *A Year in Yoga*, pp. 79–80.
4. Prison Yoga Project, https://prisonyoga.org/our-mission/, accessed February 29, 2020.
5. Prison Yoga Project, https://prisonyoga.org/our-mission/mission-and-impacts/, accessed February 29, 2020. For similar constructions of incarcerated persons by another prominent prison contemplative organization, see Phe Bach, Gus Koehler, and Jaana Elina, "Mindfulness Meditation: A Narrative Study of Training in Buddhist Meditation, Mindfulness and Ethics in B-Yard, California State Prison, Sacramento," *Journal of the International Association of Buddhist Universities* 8 (2016), pp. 55–69, where incarcerated persons are described as "killers, thieves, rapists, gang members, dope fiends" (pp. 58–59), who need "to improve impulsive and compulsive thoughts" and develop "behaviors less harmful to oneself and others" (p. 56).
6. Maull, "The Prison Meditation Movement," p. 8. See also pp. 1, 2, 3, 14, 15.
7. Maull, "The Prison Meditation Movement," pp. 8–9.
8. Maull, "The Prison Meditation Movement," p. 10.
9. Carol Horton (ed.), *Best Practices for Yoga in the Criminal Justice System* (Atlanta, GA: Yoga Service Council, 2017).
10. This manual is the third in YSC's Best Practices series, following *Best Practices for Yoga in Schools*, and *Best Practices for Yoga with Veterans*, with *Best Practices for Yoga with Survivors of Sexual Trauma* being next in the series. The focus of this series appears to be on yoga with disadvantaged populations lacking access.
11. Horton, *Best Practices*, p. 2.
12. Horton, *Best Practices*, p. 12.
13. Horton, *Best Practices*, p. 11.
14. Horton, *Best Practices*, 83.
15. Maull, "The Prison Meditation Movement," pp. 7–13; *Best Practices*, 22–30.
16. Dan Carlin, "The Mindful Justice Initiative Report 2016," Prison Mindfulness Institute, pp. 4, 6. See https://www.prisonmindfulness.org/mindful-justice-conference and https://afc724b7-5fdd-4ef2-92bf-6d2ad2de05d4.filesusr.com/ugd/8ea141_a04b4937d6594e80b435aaebc0dad895.pdf, accessed May 7, 2021.
17. Kate Crisp, *Prison Mindfulness Institute Volunteer Training Manual* (South Deerfield, MA: Prison Mindfulness Institute, 2002), p. 14. https://afc724b7-5fdd-4ef2-92bf-6d2ad2de05d4.filesusr.com/ugd/8ea141_2f9d5d29de8e41e0aae681cda977d31c.pdf, accessed May 7, 2021.
18. Although I focus more on the narratives than on offering detailed portraits of the individuals who disseminate them, a more in-depth look at the founder of this organization can be found in Maull, *Dharma in Hell*, and Maull, *Radical Responsibility: How to Move beyond*

Blame, Fearlessly Live Your Highest Purpose, and Become an Unstoppable Force for Good (Louisville, CO: Sounds True Publishing, 2019).

19. Kalliopeia Foundation, "Path of Freedom," http://www.beyondprison.us/chapter/path-of-freedom/, accessed May 7, 2021.

20. Kalliopeia Foundation, "Path of Freedom."

21. Bill Brown, "I'm Actually Thankful I Was Denied Parole," Prison Yoga Project, https://prisonyoga.org/im-actually-glad-i-was-denied-parole/?mc_cid=7e0e7de3cc&mc_eid=4f006f2e1b, accessed May 7, 2021.

22. "The LPY Unconditional Model," Liberation Prison Yoga, https://www.liberationprisonyoga.org/lpy-unconditionality-model/, accessed May 7, 2021.

23. Horton, *Best Practices*, pp. 65, 2, 80.

24. *Best Practices*, pp. 65, 74, 83.

25. Katherine M. Blee, *Understanding Racist Activism: Theory, Methods and Research* (London and New York: Routledge, 2018), pp. 1–2: Ideas "spelled out in . . . publications communicate what . . . groups want the public to know. They . . . don't reveal the backstage . . . : what members really believe . . . and what . . . groups want to accomplish."

26. Schept, *Progressive Punishment*, p. 124: Those with "proficiency in such discourses—consultants, local officials, criminal justice practicioners, civic leaders—can more readily engage in conversations. Official discourses marginalize other forms of knowledge."

27. Laura S. Abrams, Emma Hughes, Michelle Inderbitzin, and Rosie Meek, "Introduction: The Significance of Voluntary Sector Provision in Correctional Settings," in Abrams et al., *The Voluntary Sector in Prisons*, p. 5.

28. Abrams et al., "Introduction," pp. 5, 8, 23. R. Tewksbury and D. Dabney, "Prison Volunteers: Profiles, Motivations, Satisfaction," *Journal of Offender Rehabilitation* 40(1–2), 2004, pp. 173–183.

29. Michel Foucault would call them the "technicians of behavior." See Schept, *Progressive Punishment*, p. 136.

30. Subsequently, of course, the size and composition of these organizations has fluctuated, as volunteers have come and gone over time.

31. Schept, *Progressive Punishment*, p. 110.

32. Schept, *Progressive Punishment*, p. 78.

33. Schept, *Progressive Punishment*, p. 77.

34. Horton, *Best Practices*, p. 74.

35. See Jeffrey Berry, "Nonprofits and Civic Engagement," *Public Administration Review* 65(5) 2005, pp. 568–578; Jeffrey Berry and David Arons, *A Voice for Nonprofits* (Washington, DC: Brookings Institution Press, 2003); Samantha Majic, *Sex Work Politics: From Protest to Service Provision* (Philadelphia: University of Pennsylvania Press, 2014).

36. Schept, *Progressive Punishment*, p.110.

37. Schept, *Progressive Punishment*, p. 88.

38. Reuben Jonathan Miller, "Devolving the Carceral State: Race, Prisoner Reentry, and the Micro-Politics of Urban Poverty Management," *Punishment and Society* 16(3) 2014, pp. 305–335.

39. McCorkel, *Breaking Women*, p. 11.

40. Schept, *Progressive Punishment*, p. 73.

41. Fleet Maull, the founder of the Prison Mindfulness Institute, who served a fifteen-year sentence in a federal prison, is the striking exception. In his extensive writings, speeches, and online presence, Maull makes little reference to political issues such as the impacts of race

or poverty on incarceration. Although there is at least one person of color currently on the organization's Board of Advisors—and several other individuals of color are featured as expert advisors—one interviewee who served as an advisor in the past confirmed that there was a "disappointing" lack of attention paid to issues of race or inequity during her involvement with the organization.

42. Katherine Bell, "Raising Africa? Celebrity and the Rhetoric of the White Saviour," PORTAL: *Journal of Multidisciplinary International Studies* 10(1) 2013, pp. 1–24.

43. Abrams et al., "Introduction," p. 15.

44. Abrams et al., "Introduction," p. 6.

45. INCITE! Women of Color against Violence (eds.), *The Revolution Will Not Be Funded: Beyond the Non-Profit Industrial Complex* (Boston: South End Press, 2009).

Chapter 9

1. The coauthors of this chapter have chosen their own pseudonyms. For a variety of reasons discussed at length in Chapter 2, the coauthors have chosen to remain anonymous. We have therefore deliberately avoided providing further demographic information such as their age, race, education levels, and so on.

2. Such a "non-escort" card is usually issued at the discretion of prison staff, once a volunteer is determined to have spent enough time at the prison, and appropriately learned all procedures regarding security.

3. Like the prison researcher Mary Bosworth, one of the few scholars who has produced collaborative writing with incarcerated coauthors, I have wrestled with the challenges of such an undertaking, which "prevent complete egalitarianism," despite the collaborators having worked as a group to produce this chapter. "Although we have in some places identified which individual is speaking," Bosworth and her coauthors write, "we purposefully seek to present this account as a collective endeavor in which our differences intertwine to create a new voice for us all," Bosworth et al., "Doing Prison Research," p. 251. Bosworth details the many methodological challenges involved in ensuring that incarcerated coauthors feel as though their views and experiences are accurately heard and represented in such collaborative projects, so that the presumptive authority and knowledge of the researcher do not overwhelm the situated expertise of the incarcerated coauthors.

4. Phillip Moffitt, "Make Peace," *Yoga Journal*, May 2006, pp. 105–106.

5. The formal process to file internal grievances and complaints against prison personnel, policies, or practices within the California Department of Corrections and Rehabilitation. See Levi and Waldman, *Inside This Place, but Not of It*, p. 221.

Chapter 10

1. I owe this point to the generous and constructive reading of Tiffany Willoughby-Herard.

2. Price, *Prison and Social Death*, p. 163.

3. Crisp, *Prison Mindfulness Institute Volunteer Training Manual*, pp. 9–10.

4. Carrette and King, *Selling Spirituality*, p. 85.

5. Moore, "Mindfulness Is All about Self-Help."

6. See also Perry and Hackett, "Justice in Gender-Responsiveness?," pp. 33–34: "Some [incarcerated persons] use the strategy of accommodating themselves to the power structure ... [they] mold themselves into 'model' prisoners ... [who] conform to what they think administrators expect of 'good' prisoners ... [they] internalize [prison beliefs] ... and status quo ideologies ... in order to sustain a rapport with staff and to keep their privileges ... silence, or remaining subdued and docile, represents 'doing one's time well' ... [becoming] complicit in their own captivity."

7. Alexander, *The New Jim Crow*, p. 184.

8. Steven F. Hick and Charles R. Furlotte, "Mindfulness and Social Justice Approaches: Bridging the Mind and Society in Social Work Practice," *Canadian Social Work Review* 26(1) 2009, pp. 14–17.

9. Maull, *Radical Responsibility*.

10. Lerman and Weaver, *Arresting Citizenship*, p. 215.

11. Chartrand, "I'm Not Your Carceral Other," p. 64.

12. Price, *Prison and Social Death*, p. 70.

13. I owe this insightful point to the generous reading of Ben Fleenor.

14. McMahan, "How Meditation Works," p. 42.

15. I am indebted to Bronwyn Leebaw for clarification on this point.

16. Price, *Prison and Social Death*, p.154.

17. Price, *Prison and Social Death*, p. 149.

18. Price, *Prison and Social Death*, p. 161.

19. Alexander, *The New Jim Crow*, p. 215.

20. Steven Poole, "The Wellness Syndrome by Carl Cederström and André Spicer— Exploitation With a Smiley Face," *The Guardian*, January 22, 2015, https://www.theguard ian.com/books/2015/jan/22/the-wellness-syndrome-carl-cederstrom-andre-spicer-per suasive-diagnosis;, accessed June 2, 2021.

21. Petrzela, "When Wellness Is a Dirty Word."

22. Jessie Daniels, "This Holiday Season, Resist the Unbearable Whiteness of Wellness," Huffington Post, December 5, 2018, https://www.huffpost.com/entry/opinion-welln ess-holidays-trump-gwyneth-paltrow-goop_n_5c07e65de4b0fc23611249c6, accessed December 12, 2021.

23. Ahmed, "Selfcare as Warfare."

24. Gottschalk, "Conservatives against Incarceration?"

25. McLeod, "Prison Abolition and Grounded Justice," p. 1161.

26. Kazemian, *Positive Growth and Redemption in Prison*, p. 66; Ford, "A Blueprint to End Mass Incarceration"; David Roodman, "The Impacts of Incarceration on Crime," Open Philanthropy Project, September 2017, https://www.openphilanthropy.org/files/Focu s_Areas/Criminal_Justice_Reform/The_impacts_of_incarceration_on_crime_10.pdf, accessed June 2, 2021.

27. Lin, *Reform in the Making*, p. 4: "To the extent that ex-prisoners are to be at all prepared to return to society, therefore, that preparation must come in prison, at least for the foreseeable future."

28. Kushner, "Is Prison Necessary?"

29. Alexander, "Let Our People Go."

30. Kilgore, "Repackaging Mass Incarceration."

31. Davis, *Are Prisons Obsolete?*, chap. 3.

32. Kazemian, *Positive Growth and Redemption in Prison*, p. 26.

33. Gottschalk, "Yosarian Meets . . . ."
34. Rodríguez, *Forced Passages*; Cummins, *The Rise and Fall of California's Radical Prison Movement*.
35. Personal communication, Tiffany Willoughby-Herard.
36. Jonathan Simon and Malcolm Feeley, "True Crime: The New Penology and Public Discourse on Crime," in T. Blomberg and S. Cohen (eds.), *Punishment and Social Control: Essays in Honor of Sheldon L. Messinger* (Berlin: De Gruyter, 1995), pp. 170–174; Schept, *Progressive Punishment*, pp. 68–69.
37. Price, *Prison and Social Death*, p. 158.
38. Personal communication, Tiffany Willoughby-Herard.
39. Davis, *Are Prisons Obsolete?*, p. 113.
40. McLeod, "Abolition and Grounded Justice," p. 1238.
41. Davis, *Are Prisons Obsolete?*, p. 16.
42. Kushner, "Is Prison Necessary?"; Dan Berger, Mariame Kaba, and David Stein, "What Abolitionists Do," *Jacobin*, August 24, 2017, https://www.jacobinmag.com/2017/08/prison-abolition-reform-mass-incarceration, accessed June 2, 2021.
43. Berger, Kaba, and Stein, "What Abolitionists Do."

Methodological Appendix

1. Majic, *Sex Work Politics*, p. 147.
2. Fujii, *Interviewing in Social Science Research*, p. 3. In a few cases, if I had not met or co-taught with a particular volunteer (usually for scheduling or logistical reasons), or if I was introduced to someone over email, I was interviewing someone with whom I had no prior rapport.
3. James A. Holstein and Jaber F. Gubrium, *The Active Interview* (Thousand Oaks, CA: Sage Publications, 1995), p. 4.
4. Majic, *Sex Work Politics*, p. 152.
5. Majic, *Sex Work Politics*, p. 152.
6. Lerman and Weaver, *Arresting Citizenship*, p. 106.
7. In only one case did a person outright refuse to speak with me, and I received about four non-responses—people who either never responded at all, or stopped responding after an introductory conversation in which they initially seemed willing.
8. In *Punished: Policing the Lives of Black and Latino Boys* (New York: NYU Press, 2011), p. 171, Victor Rios argues that even when his research participants told him they did not care about the use of their real names, he determined it would be ethical for him to continue using pseudonyms. However, Rios worked with young men, many of whom were not yet of age. My respondents were all adults, and in these four cases, expressed strong views about the use of real names. I decided their autonomy trumped my paternalistic views on how best to "protect" them, if they had determined they were no longer at risk.
9. See Rios, *Punished*, p. 171.
10. Lerman and Weaver, *Arresting Citizenship*, p. 106.
11. Kazemian, *Positive Growth and Redemption in Prison*, p. 27.
12. See Brian Moeran, "From Participant Observation to Observant Participation," in Ybema, Yanow, Wels, and Kamsteeg, *Organizational Ethnography*, pp. 139–155.

13. Cheryl Mattingly, "Toward a Vulnerable Ethics of Research Practice," *Health: An Interdisciplinary Journal for the Social Study of Health, Illness and Medicine* 9(4) 2005, p. 455.

14. Alice Goffman, *On the Run: Fugitive Life in an American City* (Chicago and London: University of Chicago Press, 2014), p. 235.

15. Jennifer M. J. Yim and Peregrine Schwartz-Shea, "Composite Actors as Participant Protection: Methodological Opportunities for Ethnographers," *Journal of Organizational Ethnography* 2021, October 18, 2021, https://doi.org/10.1108/JOE-02-2021-0009, accessed December 14, 2021.

16. Fujii, "Research Ethics 101," p. 721; Martin Tolich, "Internal Confidentiality: When Confidentiality Assurances Fail Relational Informants," *Qualitative Sociology* 27(1) 2004, p. 104.

17. Fujii, "Research Ethics 101," p. 721. Martin Tolich calls this "internal confidentiality": the "ability for research subjects involved in the study to identify themselves or each other in the final publication of the research." Although internal confidentiality is not discussed in research ethics, it may require far more attention than researchers give it, taking time to learn what information might be potentially damaging if read by another insider from the same community of participants. See Tolich, "Internal Confidentiality," pp. 101, 103, 105. See also Will C. Van Den Hoonaard, "Is Anonymity an Artifact in Ethnographic Research?" *Journal of Academic Ethics* 1(2) 2003, pp. 141–151; and Arlene Stein, "Sex, Truths and Audiotape: Anonymity and the Ethics of Exposure in Public Ethnography," *Journal of Contemporary Ethnography* 39(5) 2010, pp. 554–568.

18. Van Den Hoonaard, "Is Anonymity an Artifact in Ethnographic Research?" p. 145. See also Stein, "Sex, Truths and Audiotape."

19. Karen Locke and S. Ramakrishna Velamuri, "The Design of Member Review: Showing What to Organization Members and Why," *Organizational Research Methods* 12(3) 2009, p. 493. See also Y. S. Lincoln and E. G. Guba, *Naturalistic Inquiry* (Beverly Hills, CA: Sage, 1985); G. Marcus and M. Fischer, *Anthropology as Cultural Critique: An Experimental Moment in the Human Sciences* (Chicago: University of Chicago Press, 1986); R. Rosaldo, *Culture and Truth: The Remaking of Social Analysis* (Boston: Beacon, 1989).

20. Locke and Velamuri, "The Design of Member Review," p. 498. M. Bloor, "Techniques of Validation in Qualitative Research: A Critical Commentary," in G. Miller and R. Dingwell (eds.), *Context and Method in Qualitative Research* (London: Sage, 1997), pp. 37–50. J. Maxwell, *Qualitative Research Design: An Interactive Approach* (Thousand Oaks, CA: Sage, 1996); A. Stewart, *The Ethnographer's Method* (Thousand Oaks, CA: Sage, 1998).

21. Locke and Velamuri, "The Design of Member Review," p. 499. See also Rosaldo, *Culture and Truth*; U. Kvale, "The Social Construction of Validity," *Qualitative Research* 1(1) 1995, pp. 19–40; M. L. Wax, "Research Reciprocity Rather Than Informed Consent in Fieldwork," in J. E. Sieber (ed.), *The Ethics of Social Research: Fieldwork, Regulation, and Publication* (New York: Springer, 1982), pp. 33–48.

22. Yanow and Schwartz-Shea, *Interpretive Research Design*, p. 106.

23. Dvora Yanow and Peregrine Schwartz-Shea, "Reading and Writing as Method: In Search of Trustworthy Texts," in Ybema et al., *Organizational Ethnography*, pp. 56–82.

24. Yanow and Schwartz-Shea, *Interpretive Research Design*, p. 106.

25. Matt Bradshaw, "Contracts and Member Checks in Qualitative Research in Human Geography: Reason for Caution," *Area* 33 (2001), pp. 202–211; David Mosse, *Cultivating Development: An Ethnography of Aid Policy and Practice* (London: Pluto Press, 2004).

26. The passage of time can affect the reactions of participants—many research participants can retrospectively alter their stances toward the research results, depending on the amount of time that has elapsed. See Locke and Velamuri, "The Design of Member Review," p. 492.

27. Locke and Velamuri describe this as the "comprehensive transparency" approach: "access to a comparatively complete narrative makes clear what kind of theoretical story researchers' reconstructions of research participants' life worlds will amount to," p. 497.

28. Locke and Velamuri call this "selective transparency": "sharing with participants segments of research writing in which their data are implicated," p. 496.

29. Tollich, "Internal Confidentiality," pp. 101–106; C. B. Brettell (ed.), *When They Read What We Write: The Politics of Ethnography* (Westport, CT: Bergin and Garvey, 1993).

30. G. R. Williamson and S. Prossner, "Action Research, Ethics and Participation," *Journal of Advanced Nursing* 40(5) 2002, 587–594.

31. Locke and Velamuri, "The Design of Member Review," p. 499. See also C. B. Brettell, *When They Read What We Write*.

32. Locke and Velamuri, "The Design of Member Review," p. 495.

33. Locke and Velamuri, "The Design of Member Review," pp. 499, 501.

34. Locke and Velamuri, "The Design of Member Review," p. 497.

35. Yanow and Schwartz-Shea, *Interpretive Research Design*, p. 107.

36. Locke and Velamuri, "The Design of Member Review," p. 495.

37. Locke and Velamuri, "The Design of Member Review," p. 491; see also R. E. Stake, *The Art of Case Study Research* (Thousand Oaks, CA: Sage, 1995).

Index

Figures are indicated by *f* following the page number

Chomsky, Noam, 107
citizenship
    non-US citizens, criminalization and
        incarceration of, 72, 108
    second-class, 6, 271
class inequity, addressing, 59–60
collaboration with research
        participants, 30–31, 249–265
comfort zone, traveling outside the, 158–160,
    158f
compassion. see also self-compassion, 62
    volunteers, 91, 161, 175, 205, 222, 230
    prison staff, 169
    incarcerated persons, nonreactive,
        258–260
confidentiality. See also anonymity, 151, 215,
    289–290
consciousness, resistant, 3-4, 11, 12, 14, 65,
    117–127, 227–236, 249–263
consent forms, 23–27, 150-154
control units, 77-79
Crewe, Ben, 88, 129
criminal justice system, failure of, 84
crimmigration, 72
Cullors, Patrice, 72

Davis, Angela, 57, 98, 229, 231, 248, 270, 282,
    283–284
debtors' prison, 5
degradation, 72, 73, 78–81, 85-86, 167–168,
    258–259, 263
dehumanization, routinized, 78-81, 85–86
discomfort, learning to be ok with, 158-160,
    259
discrimination
    by prison chaplains, 191
    racial disparities in incarceration, 5
    in law enforcement, 44
    legalized, against the formerly
        incarcerated, 6, 90, 97, 257, 277
Dolovich, Sharon, 83
dormitories, prison, 142, 161, 168–169, 172

economic inequity, 5, 6, 7, 60
empowerment
    critiques of, 175
    self-management as, 156
    taking ownership as, 161
    victim mindset, moving from, 163–165
    varying interpretations of, 219, 226-229,
        232, 234-235, 264, 269,

yoga and meditation for, 122, 226, 228–230,
    232
of internal freedom, 234–235, 270

felony murder, conviction for, 82
Floyd, George, 44
food, hidden punishment of, 74, 81, 167
Forman, James Jr., 70, 283
formerly incarcerated, the
    activism, 32, 133-134, 265
    imposition on time and energy, mitigating,
        38
    interviewing, sampling and access, 286–287
    legalized discrimination against, 6, 90, 97,
        257, 277
    social reintegration, 6, 84, 90, 97, 238
Fujii, Lee Ann, 38

Gandhi, M. K., 8–9, 51, 63, 256
Gilmore, Ruth Wilson, 70, 85, 281, 282, 283–284
Gleig, Anne, 59
Goffman, Erving, 72
Gottschalk, Marie, 72, 188
Gross, Rita, 62
Guevara, Che, 107

Hames-Garcia, Michael, 100
Hassine, Victor, 88
healthcare, prison, 73, 80–81, 161
high-security units, 76, 84, 140, 193
Hinduism
    ethical action to change the world,
        emphasis on, 50
    detachment and transcendence, 49
    inherent conservatism, 50-52
    schools of thought, 47
    yoga tradition, contemporary, 47
hooks, bell, 57
Huggins, Michael, 95–96, 97, 98, 102
humanity
    violation of, 12, 65, 84, 105, 288
    affirmation of, 91, 146, 149, 150, 267
humiliation
    basic, prisons use of, 73, 84, 88, 167-168
    pervasive and institutionalized, 80
    sexualized, 80, 263
    of visitors, 188

Ikeda, Mushim Patricia, 61
immigrants, criminalization and
    incarceration of, 72, 108

incarcerated, the. *See also* prison population
 author's treatment by, 84
 backgrounds of, 7–8
 collaboration with author, 29–31, 40,
  250-266
 classifying, 75–76
 institutionalization of, 72, 261
 justifying harsh treatment of, 81
 literacy rates, 25
 non-US citizens, 72, 108
 in pretrial detention, 5-6
 racial imbalances, 5-7, 70–71
 releasing the unnecessarily
  imprisoned, 82
 stereotyping, 222–223
 unconvicted, numbers of, 5–6
incarceration
 fear, disgrace, and stigma of, 39
 kinder, gentler, 85–86
 as opportunity, 261
 personal responsibility as an explanation
  for, 3, 7
 psychological damage of, 72-73, 81, 86
 retributive logic underlying, 262–263,
  282-283
 therapeutic (*see* rehabilitation)
incarceration, basic qualities of
 degradation and abuse, 72, 73, 78–81, 85-86,
  167–168, 258–259, 263
 generalized humiliation, 73
 institutionalized violence, 12, 73
 isolation and severance from families and
  communities of support, 73, 80
incarceration rates, United States, 5
inequity
 socioeconomic, 5, 6, 7, 44-46, 60
 normalizing, neoliberalism and, 54–57
institutionalization, 72, 261
Institutional Review Board (IRB), 22, 25–28,
 42, 150-151, 289
institutional violence, 12, 73
integrative practices, 49
interview analysis, methods of, 287
interviewees
 binary analysis, 11-14, 95–103, 210-214
 incarcerated, common themes, 104-106
 incarcerated, compliant, 106-117
 incarcerated, resistant, 117-127
 volunteers, common themes, 217-219
 volunteers, dissenting narrative,
  227-238

 volunteers, motivations, 216-217
 volunteers, predominant narrative, 219-226
Iyengar, B. K. S., 35, 47, 201, 204

Jackson, George, 83, 98, 102, 270, 282
jails, prisons vs., 74–75
Jewkes, Yvonne, 90
Jois, Pattabhi, 47, 201
juvenile facilities, 75, 76, 107, 193–194, 229.

Kabat-Zinn, Jon, 54, 57
karma-yoga, 62
Karpman, Mark, 163
Krishnamacharya, 47
Kushner, Rachel, 92

law enforcement, 44, 70-73
Lerman, Amy, 6, 90, 93, 132
Lorde, Audre, 61, 229, 248
loving-kindness toward self, 145–146

Magee, Rhonda, 62
Malcolm X, 107, 233, 282
Malone, Calvine, 96, 98, 102
mass incarceration, 5, 7, 70–72, 113, 117, 196,
 198, 199, 209, 212, 223–225, 232
Masters, Jarvis Jay, 95-98, 102, 115-116, 117,
 129, 278.
Maull, Fleet, 96-97, 98, 102, 296, 332
maximum security units, 75, 76, 77-79
McCorkel, Jill, 88, 90, 238
McLeod, Allegra, 83, 86
medical care, 73, 80–81, 161, 170
meditative practices. *See also* yoga and
  meditation practice
 inward-turning, 48-49
 purposes of, 48
 types of, 48–49
 social control through, 9, 45-46
medium security units, 75
member-checking, 178, 273–276, 290–292
mental illness, 72–73, 75, 81
Miller, Reuben, 238
mindfulness
 laissez-faire, 63–64
 medicalized versions of, 54–55
 neoliberalism and, 55–56
 neuroscience research on, 155–156, 156*f*
 and sociopolitical force, 63–64
 teaching in corporations and schools, 9
 wars, 54-55